THE ANNUAL
OF
PSYCHOANALYSIS

THE ANNUAL
OF
PSYCHOANALYSIS

A Publication of the
Chicago Institute for
Psychoanalysis

Volume VIII

International Universities Press, Inc.
New York

Library of Congress Catalog Number: 72-91376
ISBN: 0-8236-0369-5
Published annually and available in print:
    Vol. I, 1973; Vol. II, 1974; Vol. III, 1975; Vol. IV, 1976;
    Vol. V, 1977; Vol. VI, 1978; Vol. VII, 1979

Manufactured in the United States of America

The Editorial Committee of *The Annual of Psychoanalysis* wishes to express its great appreciation to Mr. Fred M. Hellman, whose continuing interest and generosity have made publication of this volume possible.

CONTENTS

I

PSYCHOANALYSIS AS SCIENCE

II

PSYCHOANALYTIC EDUCATION

III

CLINICAL THEORY

IV

CLINICAL PSYCHOANALYSIS

V

INTERDISCIPLINARY RESEARCH

VI

APPLICATIONS

CONTRIBUTORS

Calvin A. Colarusso, M.D.
> Training and Supervising Analyst, San Diego Psychoanalytic Institute; Director, Child Psychiatry Fellowship, University of California, San Diego, La Jolla.

Susanna Isaacs Elmhirst, M.D., F.R.C.P.
> Member of the British Psychoanalytical Society and Institute of Psychoanalysis; Teaching Consultant, Reiss Davis Child Study Center.

Otto Fenichel, M.D. (1898–1946)
> Originally of Vienna, last of Los Angeles, one of the leading psychoanalysts of his time. Best known for his encyclopedic work *The Psychoanalytic Theory of Neurosis* (1945).

Joan Fleming, M.D.
> Late Professor of Psychiatry, University of Colorado Health Sciences Center; Training and Supervising Analyst, Denver Institute for Psychoanalysis.

Robert M. Galatzer-Levy, M.D.
> Lecturer in Psychiatry, University of Chicago; Faculty, Child Therapy Program, Chicago Institute for Psychoanalysis.

Sanford Gifford, M.D.
> Associate Clinical Professor of Psychiatry, Harvard Medical School; Senior Associate in Medicine (Psychiatry), Peter Bent Brigham Hospital; Librarian, Boston Psychoanalytic Society and Institute

Merton M. Gill, M.D.
> Professor of Psychiatry, Abraham Lincoln School of Medicine, University of Illinois, Chicago; Faculty Member and Supervising Analyst, Chicago Institute for Psychoanalysis.

Jerome Kavka, M.D.
> Training and Supervising Analyst, Member of the Psychoanalytic Council, and of the Faculty, Chicago Institute for Psychoanalysis; Professorial Lecturer in Psychiatry, University of Chicago.

Waud H. Kracke, Ph.D.
> Associate Professor of Anthropology, University of Illinois, Chicago.

Frank M. Lachmann, Ph.D.
> Faculty, Senior Supervisor, and Training Analyst, Postgraduate Center for Mental Health, New York.

Fred M. Levin, M.D.

>   Faculty, Department of Psychiatry, Northwestern University School of Medicine; Attending Psychiatrist, Michael Reese Hospital and Medical Center, Institute for Psychosomatic and Psychiatric Research and Training.

J. Gordon Maguire, M.D.

>   Assistant Professor, Department of Psychiatry, Northwestern University Medical School; Attending Psychiatrist, Michael Reese Hospital and Medical Center, Institute for Psychosomatic and Psychiatric Research and Training; Training Analyst, Canadian Institute of Psychoanalysis.

Robert A. Nemiroff, M.D.

>   Training and Supervising Analyst, San Diego Psychoanalytic Institute; Director, Psychiatric Residency Training Program, University of California, San Diego, La Jolla.

Peter A. Olsson, M.D.

>   Associate Clinical Professor of Psychiatry, Baylor College of Medicine, Houston, Texas; Senior Faculty, Houston Group Psychotherapy Society; Psychodrama and Group Psychotherapy Consultant, Day Hospital, V.A. Medical Center, Houston.

Jerome D. Oremland, M.D.

>   Chief of Psychiatry, San Francisco Children's Hospital and Adult Medical Center; Faculty, San Francisco Psychoanalytic Institute; Vice-Chairman and Director of Continuing Education, Department of Psychiatry, University of California, San Francisco.

George H. Pollock, M.D., Ph.D.

>   Director, Chicago Institute for Psychoanalysis; President, Center for Psychosocial Studies, Chicago; Professor, Department of Psychiatry, Northwestern University Medical School.

John Rhoads, M.D.

>   Professor of Psychiatry, Duke University Medical Center; Training Analyst, University of North Carolina-Duke Psychoanalytic Training Program.

Roy Schafer, Ph.D.

>   Training and Supervising Analyst, Columbia University Center for Psychoanalytic Training and Research; Clinical Professor of Psychology in Psychiatry, Cornell University Medical College; Adjunct Professor of Psychology, New York University.

Alan J. Stern, Ph.D.

>   Associate Professor of Political Science, University of North Carolina at Chapel Hill; Research Candidate, University of North Carolina-Duke Psychoanalytic Training Program.

Robert D. Stolorow, Ph.D.
    Associate Professor of Psychology, Ferkauf Graduate School, Yeshiva University; Training and Supervising Analyst and Faculty Member, National Psychological Association for Psychoanalysis, New York.

Paul L. Wachtel, Ph.D.
    Professor of Psychology and Associate Director of the Clinical Psychology Ph.D. Program, City University of New York.

Stanley S. Weiss, M.D.
    Training and Supervising Analyst, Denver Institute for Psychoanalysis; Clinical Associate Professor of Psychiatry, University of Colorado Health Sciences Center.

James E. Wilson, M.D.
    Clinical Assistant Professor, Department of Psychiatry, Northwestern University School of Medicine; Attending Psychiatrist, Michael Reese Hospital and Medical Center, Institute for Psychosomatic and Psychiatric Research and Training.

Ernest S. Wolf, M.D.
    Training and Supervising Analyst, Chicago Institute for Psychoanalysis; Assistant Professor of Psychiatry, Northwestern University Medical School.

I

PSYCHOANALYSIS
AS SCIENCE

Freud as Scientist
and Psychoanalysis as Science

GEORGE H. POLLOCK, M.D., Ph.D.   (Chicago)

I

This is a historic meeting and one that will, I hope, initiate exchange of knowledge on a more regular basis. Developments in our field require such information sharing if we are to continue to make advances in an essential area of human functioning that involves all of us. When discussing the broad concept of the unconscious, we should consider related philosophical and historical perspectives, and I shall introduce elements of these considerations when they seem relevant. Our goal is to learn from each other, to appreciate the contributions made by dedicated scholars and researchers, to pinpoint questions that should be addressed, and to chart directions for future investigations. With these objectives in mind, I have focused upon several topics which reflect my own interest and work, but which also have applicability to our task at hand.

II

Psychoanalysis was born in the clinical setting. Sigmund Freud was the obstetrician, and in many areas he is also closely identified with the baby itself. There were elements that were present before conception. But the unique combination of these elements created a new science: a science that has grown, has developed, and is still in the process of evolving. I will shortly describe the ways in which this young science is becoming differentiated and is continuing to unfold. For many,

Presented to the First International Symposium of the Unconscious, Tbilisi, Georgia, U.S.S.R., October 1, 1979.

Supported in part by the Anne Pollock Lederer Research Fund of the Chicago Institute for Psychoanalysis.

psychoanalysis continues to be primarily a therapeutic venture. For others, the therapeutic situation reflects the application of aspects of the science of psychoanalysis. Clinical science is the study of man in health and disease. It is in the clinical setting that we formulate hypotheses that extend beyond the therapeutic. Although there still exists an antithesis between the clinician and the researcher, the conflict is beginning to diminish. As we gather data from diverse settings — e.g., infant and child observations, multicultural studies, experimental approaches, longitudinal investigations throughout the life course, cross-sectional researches — we find that the newer knowledge influences our clinical approaches and our theories. Debates will and should continue, for it is through such dialogues that clarifications, challenges, and newer vistas for further research and thought emerge.

The history of psychoanalysis is filled with controversies. Advocates of particular theoretical orientations, at times fervent in championing their ideas, have given rise to different schools. As further exchanges occur, newer ideas emerge, and syntheses take place. Barren theoretical controversies are counterproductive for a science erected on careful observation. We are dealing with complexities, and it is important to bear this is mind lest we become too dogmatic, simplistic, and reductionistic. Our models and metaphors help us in our understanding and in ascertaining new meaning. But great caution must be exercised. Analogies can become viewed as fact and reality. Freud himself was mindful of this danger and warned against it. As a scientist, Freud looked for evidence that could disprove his own hypotheses, and in the course of his scientific career he changed and modified his ideas — e.g., the singular importance of the seduction hypothesis in pathogenesis. What Freud emphasized was the spirit of inquiry and truth. This orientation is a cornerstone of the foundation that plays a critical role in the transformation of psychoanalysis from a clinical discipline into a science of man.

As more scholars become immersed in the study of psychoanalysis, some emphasize its philosophical and hermeneutic aspects. Others are more involved in empirical data, hypothesis formulation, and the testing in systematic fashion of various psychoanalytic propositions. Scientific method — or, put in psychoanalytic terms: reality testing — becomes increasingly possible as serious and careful consideration is given to the role of *prediction*.

After World War II psychoanalysis as a clinical discipline had a golden age in the United States. This has now passed, and in the clinical areas alternative methods of treatment have appeared. On the one hand, since psychoanalysis has been closely linked to psychiatry as psychiatry draws closer to medicine and biology, psychoanalysis is no longer the major therapy that it once was, although it still forms the basis for most dynamic psychotherapies. On the other hand, the behavioral and social sciences — i.e., psychology, anthropology, sociology, history, education, political science, and economics — have found psychoanalysis useful in expanding their research horizons. More currently, psychoanalysis is beginning to address new areas such as those of divorce and child custody in an attempt to understand what may be in the best interests of children and parents and what is required in addition to material support. As we find a widening utilization of psychoanalytic knowledge by many other fields, the opportunity for new horizons for research, scholarship, and practical applications presents itself. Prevention is a topic that is currently arousing a good deal of interest and excitement.

III

Sigmund Freud—scientist, pioneer, and refugee—died in London on September 23, 1939, after many, many personal tragedies, and after self-challenges as well as challenges from the academic and professional community as to the validity of his theories and their significance. One of his last papers, written in London and dated October 20, 1938, was entitled "Some Elementary Lessons in Psycho-Analysis." In this essay, as in many of his other writings, Freud continues to address scientific methodological issues. He invites his reader to consider from a different perspective what he knows, thinks he knows, or regards as self-evident. Then, by adding new facts, the reader will be able to extend his earlier judgments, consider new points of view, and contemplate new hypotheses. Freud describes how in this way fresh theoretical ideas are built and then can be carefully tested, a path he himself followed and one that has been pursued by those involved with his work. He refers to an alternative to this scientific developmental or "genetic" approach as the "dogmatic" method in which conclusions are presented without tracing how they are arrived at and how they are tested. In order to present his work most effectively, Freud does not rely on either of these two methods of presentation exclusively, but makes use of one or the other at different times.

Freud (1938) notes that "our science involves a number of hypotheses—it is hard to say whether they should be regarded as postulates or as products of our researches" (p. 282). He then asserts that "Psycho-analysis is a part of the mental science of psychology. It is also described as 'depth psychology' " (p. 282). Its psychical constituents consist of perceptions, ideas, memories, feelings, and acts of volition. Furthermore, psychology is a natural science, and "psychical phenomena are to a high degree dependent upon somatic influences" (p. 283). This has been a basic premise of the psychosomatic research of our Chicago group (Alexander, French, and Pollock, 1968). Freud rejects the parallel "body-mind" duality as unsatisfactory. He points out that "the psychical, whatever its nature may be, is in itself unconscious and probably similar in kind to all the other natural processes of which we have obtained knowledge" (p. 283); thus psychical processes can be investigated scientifically. Psychical phenomena can be described, the laws governing them can be discovered, and these can then be put to practical use, even though we may still be unaware of some of the fundamental aspects of the nature of the phenomena we are investigating. These may be discovered later, but proclaiming our ignorance is part of the ongoing process of research in science.

Freud illustrates his ideas about psychical phenomena by describing observations that can be confirmed by all. First, thoughts suddenly come into consciousness without an awareness of the steps that led up to their emergence. The sequence of steps leading to a thought are frequently unconscious, and in many instances remain so, unless intensively investigated. This observation requires no new theory. The second illustration is that of slips of the tongue. Instead of dismissing these as accidents, they can be observed in context, in the situation in which they occurred. When this is done carefully, an alternative explanation is suggested, namely, that the slip of the tongue — and one might add "mistakes" of the pen or of other means of communication — has meaning and significance. When one can observe many such slips and when one has data about the individual which goes beyond the superficial, one can learn that these unintended acts are psychical and that the steps leading to their expression were unconscious. The unconscious appears to be victorious over the conscious intentions. The person who makes the nonintended communication, then, can react in various ways that are quite familiar to us: e.g., he may be unaware of it, he can ignore it, he can notice it and become embarrassed or ashamed, or he can recognize that there may be a deeper meaning to the "error," even though he may be unable to find an immediate explanation for it. And even if one is suggested, it may be rejected. Freud simply illustrates the necessity and possibility of making simple observations of psychical phenomena and then asking questions about their meaning. This questioning attitude is the beginning of scientific inquiry, and it requires no extensive theories or technical vocabulary.

The third illustration that can easily be observed is that of posthypnotic suggestion. Here Freud notes that one can actually demonstrate the phenomenon experimentally and test the hypotheses that there are "such things as unconscious psychical acts and that consciousness is not an indispensable condition of [psychical] activity" (p. 285). In similar fashion, dreams and pathological symptoms can be shown to have meaning that is not consciously apparent to the subject or even to the observer without further data about context, relationship, and past events. With current research indicating that suggestion, hypnosis, and placebos are intimately linked to altered brain peptides, we are now approaching a more meaningful synthesis of the psychical and the biological — a goal Freud himself believed would be attained someday when it would be "possible to construct a comprehensive and coherent theory of mental life" (p. 286).

Although the focus of my presentation deals with the scientific method of psychoanalysis, Freud's clear, almost final statement about the unconscious illustrates the usefulness of this higher-order hypothesis. Freud explains how its manifestations can be observed and even tested experimentally, and how, by its researches, psychoanalysis has "led to a knowledge of characteristics of the unconscious psychical which have hitherto been unsuspected, and. . .has discovered some of the laws which govern it. . .none of this implies that the quality of being conscious has lost its importance for us. It remains the one light which illuminates our path and leads us through the darkness of mental life. In consequence of the special character of our discoveries, our scientific work in psychology will consist in translating unconscious processes into conscious ones, and thus filling in the gaps in conscious perception" (p. 286) and adding to our knowledge.

IV

Robert Waelder, an outstanding psychoanalyst, has long been interested in the validation of psychoanalytic theories and questions of universal demonstrability. In an essay on "Psychoanalysis, Scientific Method and Philosophy" (1962), he makes a significant contribution when he distinguishes the various *levels* of theories in psychoanalysis. This scheme can do much to give us an ordering framework for further scientific study, since much confusion arises when there is a mixing of levels, especially by critics whose skepticism might be reduced if one keeps in mind the difference between intralevel investigations (especially those closest to the data of observation and hence more testable) and interlevel comparisons (where one is dealing with condensed abstract conceptions far removed from the more easily consensually validated, empirical, observable data).

Waelder initially concerns himself with the data of observation derived from the psychoanalytic situation. These data include external observables such as behavior, language, verbal content, or somatic sensations, as well as reports of internal phenomena which appear in particular patterns and configurations and which seem to be linked to antecedent states. External observable data — e.g., action, behavior, language, and the observable reports of internal states (symbols, metaphors, dreams, fantasies, sensations), derived from both the analysand and the psychoanalyst — constitute the *level of clinical observation*. Clinical observation uses various methods for data gathering: from the analysand, for example, free association, recollection of memories and biographical information, accounts of dreams and fantasies, slips of all sorts, forgetting and remembering, language usage, descriptions of feelings, wishes, desires, fears, accounts of daily activities, thoughts, and fantasies — either directly about the analyst or derivative from others associated with him.

On his or her part, the analyst listens but, while doing so, has his or her own "hovering associated thoughts" in response to the analysand's productions, feelings, fantasies, memories, slips, comparisons. Using empathy, self awareness, knowledge, and theories, as well as paying careful attention to the context of analysand-analyst data, he may recognize which patterns may or may not require interventions of various kinds — e.g., interpretation, clarification, confrontation, bridging communications, and questions. Newer confirming memories and insights can appear, and change may be in evidence. But metapsychological constructs are not the facts of observation!

Waelder's second order, the *level of clinical interpretation*, is still close to the clinical data. Attempts here are in the direction of understanding interconnections and their relation to other behavior, present or past, with more direct conscious content and awareness. Countless illustrations of this clinical activity in which both analysand and analyst participate can be given. Unlike the earlier level of clinical observation where phenomena are described, here explanations come into being which, though very close to the data of observation, are still not theory.

The third level, that of *clinical generalization*, begins to include consideration of broader concepts and of lower-level explanatory theory. From the groups of clinical data and their interpretations, clinical generalizations are made. These may lead to more general categorical statements for which clinical variables begin to be considered — e.g., sex, age group, symptoms, character type, object loss, physical illness, intactness of family, socioeconomic status. Clinical generalizations are the beginnings of hypotheses. These can be stated so as to be testable — i.e., refutable — using different varieties of evidence.

When the clinical generalizations or hypotheses prove to have some validity, we reach the *level of clinical theory*. At this level we have higher-order abstractions which involve possibilities of prediction and subsequent intervention. This is an addition to the earlier levels of description and explanation. A more appropriate designation of this level, especially as it relates to psychoanalysis, is that of clinical theories, which will shortly be discussed further.

Waelder designates his next-higher level as that of *metapsychology*. It consists of highly abstract and condensed concepts — e.g., death instinct, libido, cathexis, psychic energy — which cannot be tested, proven, or disproven. They may function as metaphor or analogy and seek to facilitate understanding of complex phenomena. In a sense they are "above theory." They may be treated by some as if they were real entities that can be identified and demonstrated, but such is not the case. Recent psychoanalytic researchers and scholars have disagreed about the value of metapsychology. As a means of describing a process in metaphoric terms, some have found these concepts useful. For example, cathexis/de-cathexis/re-cathexis can facilitate our understanding of the mourning process. One can also use alternate terms such as "investment" with significance or meaning. The important goal of scientific theory — to describe, to explain, and to predict — should be kept in mind; we must be concerned with more than the means or terms used to illustrate the phases of the scientific reality-testing process.

My own addendum to the Waelderian scheme would be to add a *level of attempting to synthesize the various theories* into a *systematic body of knowledge* that constitutes a science. David Rapaport and Merton Gill (1959, 1960) have made such attempts for psychoanalysis. Psychoanalysis is more than one theory; it has several theories.

Waelder's most general level and one that obviously is not scientifically researchable is the *level of Freud's philosophy* or "world view." It includes how Freud looked at the world, his hopes and fears, his ideals and values. This level, though important, deals with broader, more general, more subjective, and more personal statements and testimonies. All of us have such world-view philosophies.

My purpose in presenting Waelder's scheme in detail is to demonstrate how he, with a few additions by the author, ordered levels in an ascending or descending fashion, beginning with the data of clinical observation and moving to more general and abstract nontestable concepts. I have also attempted to discuss some methods for obtaining data of clinical observation; other levels use other methods, e.g., deduction, induction. The importance of such clinical-theoretical concepts as transference and repetition compulsion, or the clinical use of reconstruction compared to observation in the present, as methods of ordering data of clinical observation has remained unemphasized despite their great importance in clinical psychoanalysis.

Unlike some psychoanalytic researchers, I believe that prediction before the outcome is known is possible for psychoanalytic theories. The emphasis should be on the type of prediction, the data used for the prediction, the evidence to be used in testing the prediction, and the distinction between inferring or assuming correlations of some features from the identification of others. Consequents and outcomes test predictions. When outcomes are predictable it is possible through intervention to change the postulated outcome from that which would normally and probably result to that which is expected as a result of the alteration of conditions. This latter consideration forms the basis for prevention. Preventive intervention does require some statistical considerations, but this, too, applies to all prediction. What is scientific is the ability to test and falsify hypotheses!

Once a science is established with a body of theory it proceeds more or less independently except for newer, border-level problems and questions of method. Psychoanalysis is a science. It has its observations, explanations, predictions, and interventions which can change expected outcome. It is based on empirical studies in field, clinic, and laboratory. It is the only science that addresses itself to depth psychology: its development, its operations, its logic, its deviations, and its possible alteration to facilitate ongoing, more optimal functioning through a unique therapeutic process. Like all sciences it has several basic, as well as some less encompassing and general, theories.

V

In the Preface to the volume Gedo and I edited on *Freud: The Fusion of Science and*

Humanism, we wrote:

> The first half century of the history of psychoanalysis is closely intertwined with the personal biography of Sigmund Freud. Analysis is unique as an intellectual discipline in having been entirely created by one man; critics who attack present-day psychoanalysis by alleging that Freud's inheritors have erected a cult with the founder as hero have simply ignored this unparalleled aspect of the origin of this field of science. As a matter of fact [since Freud's death], psychoanalysts have, by and large, lost sight of his vision of humanist introspection; the profession of psychoanalysis has become something like a medical specialty, emphasizing the therapeutic goals over Freud's primary aim of understanding man's inner life [Gedo and Pollock, 1976, p. 1].

Freud's goal was not only the relegation of psychoanalysis to clinical practice; he also had as an aim the establishment of a science which would, like all sciences, abide by the method of testing hypotheses in accordance with our traditional methods of scientific validation or refutation.

The use of the various findings and theories of psychoanalysis could be and are applied to the clinical-therapeutic situation. The distinction I seek to make is not as clear-cut as one might find in other sciences, especially the physical ones, but it can be approximated even with its relatively fluid boundary. The theories of psychoanalysis were derived primarily from work with patients and from self-explorations on the part of Freud and other analysts of their own psychological functioning. He and they attempted to formulate their ideas more objectively into testable hypotheses, ever mindful of the necessity of avoiding self-deception through self-fulfilling prophesies or succumbing to the hero role others wanted them to fill. Analytic researchers are concerned with evidence and understand that example is not in and of itself proof of an assertion or principle. Freud attempted to examine assumptions, such as the role of religion in man's life, even though this earned him wrath and scorn. His single most important value was love of truth, an ideal of all true scientists. He could challenge the outside and himself when indicated, and then change, modify, reject, or adopt new concepts. Schafer (1970) and Trosman (personal communication) have suggested that a characteristic of Freud's conceptualizations was to think in terms of dualities and dichotomies — e.g., unconscious and conscious, sexual and aggressive, latent and manifest, self and object. I am of the belief that Freud thought more in terms of process, with its ebb and flow, and of continuum — e.g., the complementary series.

Freud discovered a new terrain of man. He attempted to formulate descriptions of this heretofore unappreciated aspect of human functioning, and he used terms and concepts in order to convey his ideas, some of which initially evoked suspicion and confusion but today have become part of our everyday vocabulary: for example, the unconscious, intrapsychic conflict, transference, repetition compulsion, dream symbols, defense mechanisms. Lest there is concern that the attempt here is to present Freud once again as the hero, let me add that much has gone on in psychoanalysis since Freud's discoveries, and, as is true of all sciences, newer directions indicate that there will be further developments in the years to come. I might add parenthetically that some current findings already have resulted in modification of some of Freud's earlier ideas, such as some of his views on women, the efficacy of psychoanalytic treatment of individuals older than age forty, and his "timetable" of psychological development. Other Freudian concepts have stood the test of challenge and continue to have validity today, although, as with all scientific theory, newer findings necessitate revision and modification.

Ralph Waldo Emerson (1836), an eminent writer of the last century, wrote in the introduction to "An Essay on Nature":

> Our age is retrospective. It builds on the sepulchres of the fathers. It writes biographies, histories, and criticism. The foregoing generations beheld God and nature face to face; we, through their eyes. Why should not we also enjoy an original relation to the universe? Why should not we have a poetry and philosophy of insight and not of tradition?... why should we grope among the dry bones of the past, or put the living generation into masquerade out of its faded wardrobe? The sun shines today also. There is more wool and flax in the fields. There are new lands, new men, new thoughts [pp. 186–187].

As Freud broke with tradition, while maintaining a continuity with it, so today's psychoanalytic scientists, in similar fashion, identifying perhaps with his spirit of inquiry, seek new levels and new thoughts. Emerson was no brash scientist, nor was Freud. Each grew up in a humanistic tradition. Albeit on opposite sides of the Atlantic, both were scholars, and both were conservative — i.e., they wished to conserve that which was valuable, but were involved in thinking and exploring newer alternatives. Freud was a scientist, an empiricist, and a man of investigation. Josef Breuer's account of Anna O. caught his interest, motivated him to examine his own clinical experience. But he knew that this was not enough. On the one hand, explanatory notions that he and Breuer described had to be tested. If his tests were inconclusive, he could, "after surveying the overwhelmingly unfavorable evidence standing against the central thesis in his book [*Moses and Monotheism*]...say in effect, 'But one must not be misled by the evidence'" (Holton, 1964, p. 254). Some ideas could not be convincingly tested in accord with the scientific method. They still could be useful even if unproven or unrefuted. In his overall conception of science, Freud could encompass both positions; as I mentioned earlier he had the ability to see a continuum and not just a polarity.

In addition, I believe Freud could distinguish between the universal and the more limited specific or particular theory. When a science is young it deals with assumptions and themes which, as it matures, become elaborated into a complex hierarchical structure of connected hypotheses, each of which has some demonstrable phenomenal, explanatory, and predictive utility. The early psychoanalysts postulated general all-encompassing principles, some of which over time have been reduced to relatively simpler interrelated propositions.

Unlike Athena, who sprung from her father's head fully formed and mature, a scientific theory of discipline does not emerge fully formed from one person's mind or, for that matter, even from a single group's joint efforts. Observations are made, they are seen in patterns of reoccurrence wherever implicit ideas may have readied the observer's ability to perceive them, and then general explanatory possibilities suggest themselves. This is the beginning. The examination of propositions, reworkings, the appearance of new questions not explained by the initial formulations—all require new observations and/or modifications of the explanatory statements, testings, refutations, challenges, confirmations, and then again new questions. These are part of the ongoing and continuing process of science. Intuitions and inspirations and the recognition of new configurations contribute to this process, which Kris (1952) divided into inspirational and elaborational phases. I would add the confrontational as a necessary additional component. The scientific process is not linear, even though we may describe it as such. Inspiration, elaboration, and confrontation may occur in various ways, and at various times; the process is basically circular. The prepared mind makes use of all chances for the further refinement, elaboration, and refutation of more abstract theoretical explanations. Science deals with reality, be it internal or external, and is ever mindful that new and reliable observations can challenge and turn over existing theory. Art—dealing with aesthetics, form, shape, content that is not necessarily external or internally real—does not have to be in a constant state of questioning, with its production overturned or changed if new facts appear. It stands on its own and has no particular predictive reality-testing function.

Gould (1978) puts it succinctly when he notes that "science is an interplay of changing theories about the world and its structure. New theories are complex products of creative thinking, changing social circumstances, advances in other fields, daring analogies, and, to be sure, new facts. New facts may disturb old theories, but they do not, by themselves, specify new ones. Rather, they achieve their fullest meaning as exemplifications of theory. If changing theory is the stuff of science, then we cannot understand science by cataloguing new facts. And we cannot grasp the history and meaning of taxonomy by focusing only upon discovery" (p. 31).

VI

Several basic issues underlie any serious and scholarly examination of the topic we are discussing here. In particular they begin with a consideration of the philosophical dimensions of psychoanalysis—its *Weltanschauung* its humanitarian orientation, its major contribution to our study of man: that is, the discovery and understanding of the unconscious and how it operates. The universal language of the unconscious forms the basis of psychoanalysis and, by extension, of all forms of dynamic psychology. Having stated this, I shall now attempt to examine the premise from several points of view. Let me begin with Freud's *Weltanschauung*.

Freud came from a humanistic tradition. His was a classical education steeped in literature, the humanities, and the arts. Although never trained as a psychiatrist, his background in science, and particularly the neurosciences, made him a keen observer, a discerner of the regularity of patterns as they appeared, a courageous investigator daring to enter domains within himself and in others that few before had dared to study. In addition he was sensitive to and aware of the dignity of the individual.

In the last of his *New Introductory Lectures,* published in 1933 when Hitler was assuming his diabolical role on the world stage, Freud addressed the question of a *Weltanschauung*. He noted that "a *Weltanschauung* is an intellectual construction which solves all the problems of our existence uniformly on the basis of one over-riding hypothesis, which, accordingly, leaves no question unanswered and in which everything that interests us finds its fixed place. . . . The possession of a *Weltanschauung*. . . is among the ideal wishes of human beings. Believing in it, one can feel secure in life, one can know what to strive for, and how one can deal most expediently with one's emotions and interests" (p. 158). However, since psychoanalysis is "a specialist science, a branch of psychology—a depth-psychology or psychology of the unconscious—it is quite unfit to construct a *Weltanschauung* of its own: it must accept the scientific one" (p. 158). However, the scientific view overlooks "the claims of the human intellect and the needs of the human mind" (p. 159). Nonetheless, the intellect and the human mind can be studied scientifically and researched in the same way as many other questions. Psychoanalysis extended research to the mental field and to the products of the mind, e.g., art, religion, philosophy. To be sure, one must still look for truth. But "truth cannot be tolerant, . . . it admits of no compromises or limitations, [its] research regards every sphere of human activity as belonging to it and. . .it must be relentlessly critical if any other power tries to take over any part of it" (p. 160).

"Of the three powers which may dispute the basic position of science, religion alone is to be taken seriously as an enemy" (p. 160). Art and philosophy, the other two, are not harmful. Religion gives human beings "information about the origin and coming into existence of the universe, it assures them of its protection and of ultimate happiness in the ups and downs of life and it directs their thoughts and actions by precepts which it lays down with its whole authority. Thus it fulfills three functions" (p. 161). But, unlike science, "it soothes the fear that men feel of the dangers and vicissitudes of life, when it assures them of a happy ending and offers them comfort in unhappiness" (p. 161). Furthermore, unlike science, religious principles cannot be tested. They can be accepted or rejected, but they cannot be proven wrong. Religious principles are dogma that cannot be tested for falsifiability (Popper, 1972). Again, unlike science, religion consists of belief systems which provide consoling assurances, strict ethical demands, and a cosmology. Freud suggests that the religious *Weltanschauung* is a recapitulation of the situation of our childhood, when we are helpless and in need of strong paren-tal protection, guidance, and approval in order to attain the good life. In a beautiful, clear, and simple statement, Freud draws parallels between the infantile and childhood state and the religious *Weltanschauung.*

But he points out that the scientific spirit of inquiry, strengthened by the observation of natural processes, treats religion as a human activity which, like all other human activities, can be critically examined. When this occurs, religion cannot "stand up to this." Psychoanalysis has shown "how religion originated from the helplessness of children" and how it satisfies some wishes and needs of childhood, how it is a subject for scientific study, and how some of its premises cannot be disproven, i.e., are dogma.

Scientific thinking is characterized by certain features:

> It takes an interest in things even if they have no immediate, tangible use; it is concerned carefully to avoid individual factors and affective influences [in the observer]; it examines more strictly the trustworthiness of the sense-perceptions on which it bases its conclusions; it provides itself with new perceptions which cannot be obtained by everyday means and it isolates the determinants of these new experiences in experiments which are deliberately varied. Its endeavour is to arrive at correspondence with reality — that is to say, with what exists outside us and independently of us and, as experience has taught us, is decisive for the fulfillment or disappointment of our wishes. This correspondence with the real external world we call "truth." It remains the aim of scientific work even if we leave the practical value of that work out of account [Freud, 1933, p. 170].

Scientific method is reality seeking and testing.

Freud asserts that our best hope for the future is in intellect — the scientific spirit — in reason, in the pursuit of "truth." In other words, Freud's *Weltanschauung* is the scientific *Weltanschauung* — the discovery through observation, the study of uniformities, the postulation of testable-disprovable hypotheses. He asserts that

> the path of science is indeed slow, hesitating, laborious. . . . Progress in scientific work is just as it is in an analysis. We bring expectations with us into the work, but they must be forcibly held back. By observation, now at one point and now at another, we come upon something new; but to begin with the pieces do not fit together. We put forward conjectures, we construct hypotheses, which we withdraw if they are not confirmed, we need much patience and readiness for any eventuality, we renounce early convictions so as not to be led by them into overlooking unexpected factors, and in the end our whole expenditure of effort is rewarded, the scattered findings fit themselves together, we get insight into a whole section of mental events, we have completed our task and now we are free for the next one. In analysis, however, we have to do without the assistance afforded to research by experiment [p. 174].

Science is intimately related to the real external world. The criterion of truth is correspondence with the external world! This scientific *Weltanschauung* must be a fundamental basis for our professional education now and in the future.

Freud writes that "Strictly speaking there are only two sciences: psychology, pure and applied, and natural science" (p. 179). He concludes his lecture of almost fifty years ago by stating that "A *Weltanschauung* erected upon science has, apart from its emphasis on the real external world, mainly negative traits, such as submission to the truth and rejection of illusions" (p. 182).

In conclusion, let me turn briefly to a few issues which follow from the above. To speak of psychoanalysis as a single monolithic theory (the usual characterization) is a view with which I disagree. Psychoanalysis is a science encompassing several areas of knowledge. These areas, some closer to observations in the clinical or other situations than others, can be broken down into hypotheses which can or will be able to be tested in ways that will allow for falsifiability. In telegraphic fashion I shall now present some of these in brief outline form, mindful that this scaffolding can be fleshed out in greater detail.

Psychoanalysis is:

First, a core of ethical values in human interactions. The therapeutic situation calls directly for understanding, humane appreciation of the fears and hurts of the other, and prohibition against any activity that can be harmful to the patient. This humanitarian approach, which involves respectful communications and honesty, forms the basis for the therapist-patient relationship. Implicit and explicit are the values of the analyst.

Second, a theory of emotional and mental development based upon observation, reconstruction, and repetition in the clinical situation of prior developmental conflicts and resolutions which extend throughout the course of life.

Third, an appreciation that behavior, feelings, reactions have meaning at various levels and stem from the present as well as from all prior developmental periods, including the earliest days of life. In our efforts at understanding and deriving meaning we must be aware of the dangers of looking for meaning in everything and everywhere. This in itself can become a meaningless obsession. A reaction to this concern with meaning can be seen in those who avoid meaning and flee from it with the same energy on every occasion and wherever possible.

Fourth, an understanding of psychopathology based upon developmental conflicts, deficiencies, and distortions, which can be applied to the entire developmental span from neonate to geriatric situation.

Fifth, a technical-skills approach to the treatment situation, initially based upon the observation of the famous Bertha Pappenheim. There has been a steady increase in our knowledge of catharsis, directed association, suggestion, free association, freely hovering attention, and the importance of transference in the therapeutic process in psychoanalysis as well as in all dynamic psychotherapies.

Sixth, the application of psychoanalytic knowledge to other fields, e.g., law (especially adoption law), child abuse, divorce and child custody, art, literature, biography, history, anthropology, education, etc. Many of these applications are by-products and stem from clinical observation and clinical theory but now may and do add to clinical theories.

Seventh, an appreciation that therapeutic cure in the absolute sense is less likely to occur than improvement in life quality and functioning as an outcome of therapy. Furthermore, cure or improvement is not proof for or against theory.

Sterile theoretical confrontations, attempts at dethronement, and distorted "therapies" cause confusion, skepticism, and even cynicism or hostility. What is needed is more, careful research, the asking of new questions, the making of new observations, the formulating of new hypotheses, the devising of new tests of existing hypotheses, and the formulation of alternative explanations and interpretations. In short, we must emphasize the scientific *Weltanschauung* of Freud in our teaching, in our learning, in our therapy, and in our research. These tasks, though formidable, are not unrealistic or unattainable.

In closing, I wish to cite two long quotations from Freud the scientist about psychoanalysis the science. The first was written in 1915:

> The true beginning of scientific activity consists . . . in describing phenomena and then in proceeding to group, classify and correlate them. Even at the stage of description it is not possible to avoid applying certain abstract ideas to the material in hand, ideas derived from somewhere or other but certainly not from the new observations alone. Such ideas—which will later become the basic concepts of the science—are still more indispensable as the material is further worked over. They must at first necessarily possess some degree of indefiniteness; there can be no question of any clear delimitation of their content. So long as they remain in this condition, we come to an understanding about their meaning by making repeated references to the material of observation from which they appear to have been derived, but upon which, in fact, they have been imposed. . . . It is only after more thorough investigation of the field of observation that we are able to formulate its basic scientific concepts with increased precision, and progressively so to modify them that they become serviceable and consistent over a wide area. Then, indeed, the time may have come to confine them in definitions. The advance of knowledge, however, does not tolerate any rigidity even in definitions. Physics furnishes an excellent illustration of the way in which even "basic concepts" that have been established in the form of definitions are constantly being altered in their content [p. 117].

The second, written in 1938, addresses the same issue and demonstrates how almost twenty-five years later, at the end of his life, Freud still was writing about, developing, and concerned with the issue of research methodology. He notes:

> Every science is based on observations and experiences arrived at through the medium of our psychical apparatus. But since *our* science has as its subject that apparatus itself, the analogy ends here. We make our observations through the medium of the same perceptual apparatus, precisely with the help of the breaks in the sequence of "psychical events": we fill in what is omitted by making plausible inferences and translating it into conscious material. In this way we construct, as it were, a sequence of conscious events complementary to the un-

conscious psychical processes. The relative certainty of our psychical science is based on the binding force of these inferences [1938 (1940), p. 159].

Freud's enduring significance for man has been described as follows:

With Copernicus the earth moved from its position of centrality in the universe, with Darwin man moved from his position of centrality in the eye of the creator, with Marx the individual human subject moved from its position of centrality in history and with Freud consciousness moved from its position of centrality in the structure of the psyche [Taylor, 1977, p. 518].

Louis Althusser has acknowledged Freud's pioneering role in a new science in poetic fashion. Freud had "to be himself his own father, to construct with his craftsman's hands the theoretical space in which to situate his discovery, to weave with thread borrowed intuitively left and right the great net with which to catch in the depths of blind experience the teeming fish of the unconscious, which men call dumb because it speaks even while asleep" (cited in Taylor, 1977, p. 518). But there are more nets with which to catch more fish in more oceans. Only now, when it is less inextricably linked with clinical practice and yet soundly based on human observation, is the science of psychoanalysis coming into its own. Freud observed the workings of the unconscious. He did not invent it; he attempted only to describe it.

REFERENCES

Alexander, F., French, T., & Pollock, G. H. (1968), *Psychosomatic Specificity*. Chicago: University of Chicago Press.

Emerson, R. W. (1836), An essay on nature. In: *The Selected Writings of Ralph Waldo Emerson*, ed. W. H. Gilman. New York: New American Library, 1965, pp. 186–187.

Freud, S. (1915), Instincts and their vicissitudes. *Standard Edition*, 14:109–140. London: Hogarth Press, 1957.

———— (1933), New introductory lectures on psycho-analysis. *Standard Edition*, 22:158–182. London: Hogarth Press, 1961.

———— (1938), Some elementary lessons in psycho-analysis. *Standard Edition*, 23:279–286. London: Hogarth Press, 1964.

———— (1938 [1940]), An outline of psycho-analysis. *Standard Edition*, 23:138–207. London: Hogarth Press, 1964.

Gedo, J. E. & Pollock, G. H., eds. (1976), *Freud: The Fusion of Science and Humanism [Psychological Issues*, Monogr. 34/35]. New York: International Universities Press.

Gould, S. J. (1978), Heroes in nature. *New York Review*, September 28, p. 31.

Holton, G. (1964), Presupposition in the construction of theories. In: *Science and Literature: New Lenses for Criticism*, ed. E. Jennings. Garden City, N.Y.: Doubleday, 1970, pp. 237–262.

Kris, E. (1952), *Psychoanalytic Explorations in Art*. New York: International Universities Press.

Popper, K. R. (1972), *Objective Knowledge: An Evolutionary Approach*. New York: Oxford University Press.

Rapaport, D. & Gill, M. (1959), The points of view and assumptions of metapsychology. *Internat. J. Psycho-Anal.*, 40:153–162.

———— ———— (1960), *The Structure of Psychoanalytic Theory: A Systematizing Attempt [Psychological Issues*, Monogr. 6]. New York: International Universities Press.

Schafer, R. (1970), An overview of Heinz Hartmann's contribution to psychoanalysis. *Internat. J. Psycho-Anal.*, 51:425–455.

Taylor, L. (1977), Freud. *New Society*, December 8, pp. 515–518.

Waelder, R. (1962), Psychoanalysis, scientific method and philosophy. *J. Amer. Psychoanal. Assn.*, 10: 617–637.

February, 1980

II

PSYCHOANALYTIC EDUCATION

Theoretical Implications of the Didactic Analysis

OTTO FENICHEL, M.D.

with preambles by
MERTON M. GILL, M.D.   (Chicago)
and
JOAN FLEMING, M.D.

I came upon this paper in the material from her library which the late Dr. Hanna Fenichel, the widow of Otto Fenichel, generously left to me. The best information I have been able to get is that Fenichel presented the paper to a group of training analysts in 1938 and that the Topeka Psychoanalytic Institute mimeographed it in 1942 and distributed it to some other institutes. A copy in the archives of the San Francisco Institute is dated 1942.

Naturally, I have misgivings about the publication of a paper that the author had decided not to publish. Norman Reider tells me that Fenichel was concerned that candidates might use it as a source of resistance. In the paper itself Fenichel seems instead to be concerned about the general public having access to it: "Why are all these and related problems discussed so rarely?...I believe it is much more due to the fact that publications cannot be limited to a certain circle of readers, and that it would be unfortunate to inform the public of certain aspects of psychoanalytic training..." (p. 25). As the text continues the implication seems to be that the public should not know that the analyst can make "mistakes rooted in the analyst's unconscious." Fenichel's own emphasis on the analyst's "humanness" in his discussion of the analyst's smoking (p. 29) suggests a very different attitude. He could scarcely have intended that a patient should consider the analyst infallible. In any case resistance will always find some plausible justification. It cannot be prevented by censorship of analytic writings.

Actually, a major part of the paper is devoted to the psychology of the analyst and of analyzing, so although it does have implications for special attention to these issues in the conduct of a training analysis, it deals with matters of continuing importance to any analyst in his work. It has Fenichel's usual clarity, cogency, and conciseness. It contains gems like his illustration of identification in the

21

transference: the candidate who kissed a patient because he was behaving as he wanted his analyst to behave toward him (pp. 27–28).

I decided, therefore, with apologies to Fenichel's shade, to submit the paper for publication. It is too valuable to lie buried in archives.

M. G.

The section on psychoanalytic education in *The Annual of Psychoanalysis* is honored to be able to publish this paper by Otto Fenichel which was first distributed by the Topeka Institute in 1942. There is still active debate about the "didactic analysis" among the candidates and faculty of analytic institutes. This paper contains fomulations of significant issues by one of the pioneers of psychoanalysis.

Fenichel was one of the first analysts, other than Freud, who attempted to develop a theory of technique, especially with regard to the problems of interpretation. This paper includes some of his early ideas, and although much of the content is presented in his lectures on *Problems of Technique* (1938–1939), here it is made relevant to the problems confronting a training analyst. I believe the repetition is helpful since the technical principles Fenichel talks about emphasize that in the context of professional education the work of psychoanalysis is based in scientifically conceptualized knowledge which applies to all efforts to understand and modify all forms of behavior — that of "normal candidates" as well as patients with neuroses, psychoses, etc.

Fenichel's stress on the analyst's working instrument being his "unconscious" confronts us again with this didactic goal which a candidate should experience firsthand. Fenichel emphasizes this goal but does not neglect the other aspects of psychoanalytic education. He advocates integration of the three kinds of learning and a method of teaching which "objectifies the contributions of each to a perspective on psychoanalysis as a science and a technique of treatment."

Fenichel places the decisive influence of the training analyst on his candidate's career in a context of openness between analyst and candidate. He says: "The training character of the training analysis might show itself in the way in which the analyst, after certain pieces of analysis (certainly not while these pieces of analysis are still going on), may reflect on them and show the candidate what has been done; or in certain admonitions after emotional experiences of the candidate's, that he might not forget in his later analytic work how being analyzed feels 'from within'; but that does not pose any difficult problem" (p. 25).

The "problem" of the power of the training analyst and how to use it optimally is further discussed. This "problem" persists, and no satisfactory consensus with regard to it has been reached by analytic educators. The problem belongs to the syncretistic role of the analytic educator. The complex mixtures of transference and realities, the overlapping objectives of therapeutic and educational change in the training analysis, have not yet been solved.

In this paper Fenichel gives us a glimpse of the difficulties as he saw them in 1938. At that time, little had been written and even less had been published. I feel this paper has much of value and should be scrutinized and put together with what has evolved in our knowledge about the technique of analyzing and educating analysts today.

J. F.
November, 1978

I

I shall begin with factual and historical introductions.

The factual introduction:

Psychoanalytic training, developed in practice and discussed in "Training Committees," has slowly become standardized, without many written papers about the theoretical background of its problems. All psychoanalytic societies and institutes today are in agreement that four institutions of psychoanalytic training are necessary:

(a) Training analysis
(b) Theoretical lectures and seminars
(c) Supervised work on patients
(d) Case-history seminars

All four institutions may be conducted in very different ways by different teachers; but, taken as a whole, a pattern has been worked out which is handed down orally. I suppose that there is complete agreement that all four are necessary. A few objections which I have heard do not find many adherents any more; thus we mention and reject them briefly:

(a) Are case-history seminars, in addition to supervised work, essential? I think they are, because they give the candidates something which no supervised work can give them: a substitute for clinical demonstration. A decisive disadvantage of psychoanalysis as compared to other medical disciplines is the fact that the individual candidate (or analyst) sees a very limited number of cases only. There is no method except case-history seminars to make him acquainted with as many cases as possible. Besides, such seminars, especially if one whole case is discussed in one evening, provide the opportunity of teaching the candidate how to see the "forest" instead of merely the "trees," i.e., to perceive the "Gestalt" of the structure of a case, to distinguish essential (dynamic) relations from accidental ones, to differentiate between facts and hypotheses, etc., etc.

(b) But, then, the other way around, is individual supervised work necessary in addition to case-history groups? Yes. Here other things are taught which cannot be given there: the details of analytic procedure in individual analytic situations.

After having understood the principles of analytic interpretation and of handling the transference, the candidate has to learn to apply these principles *in concreto*, which makes the detailed discussion of individual analytic hours necessary. Such individual discussion would even be rather boring for a whole group, and the candidate also would not be frank in the presence of many people.

(c) The Budapest group, for a long time, advocated the idea that control analyst and training analyst should be identical. We are of the opinion that that would not be practical. It is true that criticism of the individual work of a candidate will sometimes make it necessary to discuss problems of the candidate's unconscious. But that does not mean analyzing him. It makes a difference whether certain attitudes of the candidate's are "analyzed," that means brought back to their unconscious origin, or criticized in the interest of his patients. The control analyst is not supposed to analyze the candidate; but he may sometimes be obliged to discuss the candidate's behavior with his training analyst, and call to the latter's attention certain peculiarities of the candidate's. This, by the way, is a decisive reason why I am of the opinion that the candidate should start his work with patients while he is still in training analysis. That makes it possible to work through analytically his reactions to "analyzing"—which is necessary.

Since the theoretical lectures and seminars do not offer any problems which are in principle different from the problems to be found in any other medical instruction, training analysis remains as the problematic analytic *specificum*.

Is a training analysis essentially the same thing as a therapeutic analysis; or does it have to be conducted in some other way?

I am of the opinion that it actually is to a high degree the same thing. There is but one analysis, and the candidate has to learn to face and to overcome his unconscious conflicts in the same way as any neurotic.

The specific situation of a training analysis may cause certain aspects of transference or practical procedure to come especially into the foreground; but there is no essential difference. As is well known, this opinion differs to a certain degree from that of Freud. Freud (1937) stated that a training analysis of a normal person should not be too deep; it would suffice if it proceeded to the point where the candidate has gained (a) an insight into the reality and effectiveness of the unconscious, and (b) an insight into the principles of the technique applied by the analyst. I think that in consideration of the circumstance that the analyst's unconscious is his working instrument, our understanding of the dynamics and effectiveness of "neurotic character traits" makes it necessary for analysts to have gone through an especially thorough and deep psychoanalysis, and I shall endeavor in the following to show why. For the present, I only want to mention a few points in which training analysis differs from the average therapeutic analysis:

The first point concerns indication. Whereas the principles of indication of psychoanalysis in neuroses are much discussed, we do not know much about the principles according to which future analysts should be chosen. It is generally accepted that a first sifting of the candidates should be performed before the training analysis starts, and in practice the training committees generally succeed in refusing unsuitable candidates — as for example persons with too severe a neurosis, or without any psychological disposition, or with very limited possibilities of empathy — but probably without being able to formulate clearly the criteria according to which they judge the abilities of the candidates. Here also lies a field of "Theoretical Implications of Training Analysis" still to be investigated.

The training character of the training analysis might show itself in the way in which the analyst, after certain pieces of analysis (certainly not while these pieces of analysis are still going on), may reflect on them and show the candidate what has been done; or in certain admonitions after emotional experiences of the candidate's, that the candidate in his later analytic work might remember how being analyzed feels "from within"; but that does not pose any difficult problem. But one more important difference between training analysis and therapeutic analysis remains:

Whereas Freud taught us that the handling of the transference makes it necessary that between analyst and analysand there exist no other relationship than the analytic one, it cannot be denied that *the training analyst is actually a decisive person in the life of the candidate.* The candidate knows that it will depend on his analyst's decision about him whether or not he will be permitted to actually take up the profession of his choice. This fact is very unfortunate, and actually, as I had occasion to see several times, seriously complicates the transference relationship. I see only two circumstances which might ease this difficulty:

(a) The point could and should be stressed that not the analyst personally, but a whole training committee will make the decision. This point, however, will be of little help, since the candidate certainly realizes that in this committee, too, the voice of his analyst will be the decisive one. Therefore I absolutely agree with the rule of the American Psychoanalytic Association that a candidate who has been refused by a training analyst should be given the opportunity to make a second attempt with another analyst.

(b) The complication, which really exists, has to be admitted frankly to the candidate. In my experience, when refusing a candidate, I usually succeed in convincing him about the reasons for my decision, and in gaining his agreement to giving up the wish to become an analyst. But I did not always succeed, and there remain cases in which the candidates violently disputed the negative decision.

Now, a short historical introduction:

Why are all these and related problems discussed so rarely? Certainly not because there would be no more to say about them. There are many complications which need consideration. I believe that it is much more due to the fact that publications cannot be limited to a certain circle of readers, and that it would be unfortunate to inform the public of certain aspects of psychoanalytic training.

The special task of the training analysis is: to undo the resistances of the analyst (that is, the difficulties rooted in the analyst's unconscious). There is no "theory of training analysis" which would not discuss the "mistakes rooted in the analyst's unconscious." After fourteen years of analytic training practice, I once, in 1938 — together with Annie Reich — made the attempt to summarize my experiences, and to make them accessible to other training analysts. I saw immediately that this material could not be published. But when the Training Committee of the San Francisco Psychoanalytic Society planned to discuss the same problems, I volunteered to repeat for them the paper of 1938. And then we thought that it might also be of interest to other analysts who are not members of the Training Committee. It is true — *for analysts only*.

I should like to stress once more that the following remarks were developed in cooperation with Dr. Annie Reich of New York City.

II

The analyst's unconscious is his working instrument. The training analysis has the aim of making this working instrument effective. Repressions and other unconscious defensive measures on the part of the analyst may either cause "blind spots" — that means making the analyst incapable of seeing in his patients things which he does not like to become aware of in himself — or "projections" — that means making him see "motes" in his patient's eye, where he does not like to see "beams" in his own; that is, he might see everywhere only his own "complexes" instead of reality. Another way in which the analyst's conflicts disturb his work lies in the circumstance that his conflicts may make him incapable of taking emotional transference actions of his patients as "material" only, without responding to them with his own emotions. As is well known, the "transference" character of a transference action can be better demonstrated to the patient the less precipitating reality is involved, for which reason the analyst is supposed to be only a "mirror" of the patient's emotions.

The danger that an analyst might react emotionally and respond to a patient's actions with "counteractions" instead of being a "mirror" increases if (a) the patient's action touches unconscious weak "complex" points of the analyst; (b) the analyst unconsciously connects other aims with his "analyzing" activity.

The training analysis aims at undoing the analyst's "complexes" and "unconscious aims." The practice of training analysis and control analysis gives ample material about both the analyst's complexes and his unconscious aims. "To analyze," to the analyst, may have as many various unconscious meanings as "being analyzed" may have for the patient, with the same — or even greater — dangers to the analysis. But while the patient's aims are discussed at length in the analytic literature about "transference," nothing is said about the aims of the analyst.

Nunberg (1926) once wrote a much-quoted paper, "The Will to Recovery," in which he explains that on the part of the patients the wish to recover may serve as rationalization for many a less rational unconscious wish. A similar paper should be written on the "Will to Make Recover." Everything which in general brings about "neurotic acting out," that is, the introduction of unconscious aims of the past into a misapprehended actuality, may also be effective in the analyst who uses his analytic activity as an opportunity of "neurotic acting out." A summary of the possibilities, therefore, would be no less than a repetition of the whole theory of neurotic mechanisms, seen from the special aspect: how are the neurotic mechanisms in question reflected, especially in analytic activity?

There are three possibilities for the analyst to use "analyzing" for some other purpose:

(1) Genuine instinctive object wishes toward the patient.

(2) "Countertransference" proper — that is, an unconscious resurrection of an infantile object relationship of the analyst's in his relationship to his patient.

(3) "Neurotic Acting Out" proper — that is, an impersonal use of the relationship to the patient for some unconscious purpose, such as the smoothing over of anxiety, satisfaction of narcissistic needs, easing of intrapsychic conflicts.

You know that many actual "interpersonal relationships" are of an impersonal nature, the other person being used as a kind of "witness" in some inner conflict, for example, for confirming or contradicting some guilt feeling. In the same way, an analyst might use his patient.

(1) The first possibility, a genuine object relationship, has to be considered in principle a greater danger on the part of the analyst than on the part of the patient. Since the patient does not know anything personal about his analyst, intense feelings toward him are likely to be transference. *But* the analyst knows every detail about the personality of his patient. He may actually intensely like or dislike his personality, and, I think, nothing can be said about this point except that any intense personal binding makes analysis impossible; therefore an analyst in such a case would have to send his patient to some colleague. I may add that I am skeptical about actual intense dislike. The normal analyst should have such a wealth of empathy that he is capable of finding enough sympathy to work with any type of patient. If patients actually are too "repulsive" to analysts, we may suspect that it is either a "countertransference" or "acting out" on the part of the analyst.

(2) *Countertransference*, according to my experience, is generally less important as an actual disturbing factor than "neurotic acting out." Wherever a positive "countertransference" disturbed the candidate's work, the erotic wishes toward the patient turned out to be of a "pseudo-sexual" character. Usually, that which was experienced with the patient was an expression of the relation toward a third person — for example, the training analyst. I remember, for example, a candidate who once gave in to the temptation to kiss a woman patient. It turned out that he

was not very much interested in that patient as a person, but was identified with her. He behaved toward her as he wished his analyst to behave toward him. Generally, it is frequent that analysts behave toward their patients in the same manner as they themselves unconsciously wish to be treated by others. Such intentions might be repressed and overcompensated — analysts may behave toward their patients exactly in the manner in which they *do not* want to be treated themselves. But it cannot be denied that there still remain enough possibilities of direct unconscious instinct satisfactions which might be hidden in "analytic" activity: scoptophilia (watching the patients might unconsciously mean a perpetuation of primal scenes; analysts of this kind have a fatal preference for dramatic scenes, emotional outbreaks, "ab-reaction," and do not understand or like a patient and slow "working through"), exhibitionism ("analyzing" might mean showing to the patient one's own potency; such analysts always fatally have to prove that they are in the right, and they cannot stand any "negative transference" on the part of their patients), sexualization of "giving" and "taking" (interpretations might be thought of as magic substances by the analyst as well as by the patient).

(3). Like everybody, every analyst has unconscious reasons for the choice of his profession. That does not necessarily mean that these unconscious reasons will hamper his work. The normal choice of profession is similar to the normal choice of love object: both always are rooted unconsciously in past experiences, but this root is not disadvantageous as long as no repressions and fixations make the necessary adaptations to reality impossible. A normal person might fall in love with somebody who reminds him of his mother in one or another respect, but the influence of his mother on this relationship is limited to this first choice, and the subject remains capable of being aware of the real character of his object, and of reacting to it. A neurotic person does not see the real object, but instead either misinterprets her as his mother, or is unhappy because of her not being his mother. The same things holds true for the choice of profession. The unconscious root of it is fatal as long as the analyst is neurotically fixated on it, and either misapprehends "analyzing" as what he unconsciously hopes for, or becomes unhappy and dissatisfied because of the discrepancy between reality and what he had hoped for.

The unconscious aims in "analyzing" are mostly either attempts at (a) direct smoothing of anxiety, or (b) indirect attempts at smoothing of anxiety by fulfilling "ideals," or by satisfaction of narcissistic needs.

(a) Direct smoothing of anxiety can be attempted through the attitude: I do not need to fear the unconscious, because, being an analyst, I control the unconscious. Such an attitude is dangerous in a double way: the special character of the anxiety which the analyst unconsciously has to smooth may influence the choice of analytic material which the analyst treats, in an unobjective way; and the attempt at smoothing anxiety may fail, and the anxiety reappear; most neurotic attempts at smoothing anxiety have a characteristic "double-edged" character: up to a certain intensity they may be successful and bring to the subject a kind of happiness, "I do not have to be afraid any more"; with a higher intensity the full anxiety (which, representing an infantile instinctive situation, is mostly not only feared but also simultaneously striven for) reappears.

Persons with the attitude of "I do not fear the unconscious any more" must necessarily strive to hold their patients and their patients' emotions at a distance from their own feelings. In extreme cases, we find in analysts an inability to understand the ego-dystonic character of the neuroses. In their attempt to "control" the unconscious, they eventually deny its existence, and consider neuroses to be mere adaptations or "arrangements," as Adler said. In their own behavior, such analysts have the habit of misusing the rule of being a mirror in order to behave toward their patients as inhuman registering apparatus. I know about one analyst—not a candidate, but the president of a psychoanalytic society—who prohibited his pupils from smoking while analyzing, because the patients would see in the analyst's smoking too human a trait. If the patients of such analysts have certain mechanisms to avoid anxieties, the analyst, instead of analyzing these mechanisms, may participate in them.

According to my own experience, patients' "isolations" especially may be shared by their analysts. The whole analysis may be conducted "at a distance," not only from the analyst's but also from the patient's feelings, and therefore remain ineffective. Or we may see a general lack of identification on the part of the analyst, who fears being infected by the patient's anxieties. The analyst sees his patient's neurosis only "from without," and not "from within." Such a lack of identification with the patients in general may — paradoxically — be combined with too much identification at certain points or under certain conditions. Instead of analyzing the patient's resistances, the analyst might identify himself with the patient in his resistant attitude, and participate in his resistance. He then becomes unable to fulfill the principal task of the analyst: to show the patient what the patient himself, because of resistances, cannot see. Patient and analyst together are then as limited as a patient alone who tries to analyze himself.

Accustomed to recognizing how near opposites are to each other in the unconscious, we shall understand that the analyst's resistance shown in remaining too distant from the patient is very closely related to the opposite resistance—that of not having the necessary distance. Instead of identifying with the patient where that is necessary for the understanding of the patient, the analyst identifies himself also with the patient's resistances, as described before. The consequence is a lack of feeling for "genuine-ness" and "falseness" in the patients' expressions. Frequently, we see a misunderstanding of defense attitudes as instinctive attitudes. The material is taken at its face value instead of being taken in its dynamic-economic evaluation as a part of the whole.

In general: There are two types of resistant patients: the type who has no understanding of the primary process and behaves in an exaggeratedly rationalistic way, and the opposite type, who completely gives himself up to the primary process and thus becomes incapable of gaining the necessary distance from it. The same two types of resistance we also find in analysts.

If the analyst tries to confirm his own repressions by the attitude: "I have no repressions any more, because I know about the theory of repression," he necessarily must tend to theorizing in his whole analytic work, and thus lose contact with the practical material.

Since all these analysts need their patients as "witnesses," they necessarily are interested in keeping their favor; this is one of the reasons for "too much identification." Such analysts do not see the signs of negative transference in their patients, or try to minimize them, or become angry at their patients when they develop negative attitudes—not because they, the analysts, love the patients unconsciously, but because they narcissistically need the supply of "admiration" from their patients. Under certain circumstances they might be overcompensated, and we see the opposite. The analysts provoke their patients to become angry at them, and they may rationalize that by stating that the "mobilization of the negative transference is necessary."

The tendency "I control the unconscious" brings about the wish always to handle very "unconscious" material. Deep interpretations are given too early, or without the necessary preparation, or under wrong economic circumstances. I once saw a candidate with a pronounced "compulsion of interpretation." In fear of his own unconscious, he was unable to stand a situation in which he did not "understand" his patients' material immediately; he was compelled to "interpret" everything his patients said right away, first to himself, then also to the patient. Other analysts have the opposite symptom of "fear of interpretation." Full of fear of the magical power of their words, they behave like a surgeon who stops operating when the wound bleeds. (Once again not a candidate but a training analyst gave the following advice: "It might occur that the transference reactions of certain patients become so stormy that it becomes necessary to interrupt the analysis for a while. After the stormy reactions have slowed down, the analysis might be resumed." I am of the opinion that such a suggestion really is identical with the advice given to surgeons to interrupt an operation if the wound bleeds more than had been anticipated.)

A third disturbance of the interpretative activity of the analyst, besides the possibilities of interpreting too much or too little, is the qualitatively wrong choice of what is interpreted. Here belong the scotomas and projections, which we have mentioned in our introduction. If an analyst again and again interprets to his patients things which are actually disturbing him in his own unconscious, that is not only a simple "projection" but simultaneously an "overcoming of passive experiences by acting them out actively."

Here the problem of the subjective determination of the fields of interest of individual analysts might be added. Frequently, such a subjective determination of specific scientific interests is very obvious. But that does not necessarily mean that the scientific work done on such a basis is of poor quality. What we have said about the choice of profession might also be said about the choice of scientific subjects. The question is whether only the *choice* of the subject is determined by the unconscious past (which is harmless), or whether the way in which the research work is conducted also has such roots (which would be harmful). Preference for or anxiety over emotional outbreaks of the patients shows the unconscious relation of the analyst to magic.

With considerations of this kind, we began already some time ago to discuss (b): the satisfaction of narcissistic needs in "analyzing" for the purpose of indirect smoothing of anxiety. There is one special temptation in the analytic situation for persons who are dependent on narcissistic supplies. The patient's longing for "magical help" (which is a resistance) might be met halfway by a fatal tendency on the part of the analyst to play the part of a "magical helper." You remember Freud's footnote in "The Ego and the Id" (1923), where he especially warns the analysts against this danger. The "hypnotic" submissiveness of certain patients is felt as an unconscious temptation by many analysts. The analyst then may either play the role of a prophet, or he may repress such a wish and not dare to do anything. Whatever the patients do or say is more or less seen by the analyst only insofar as it touches his person. As you know, the state of "transference" has the effect that actually many feelings and bonds on the part of the patients may refer to the analyst, without the patients being aware of it. But the patient's life does not consist in transference alone, and often the analyst's resistance is shown in his neglect of the patient's life outside the transference. The patient who responded to a transference interpretation with the words, "But, doctor, you are conceited — everything I say you refer to yourself only!" sometimes may be correct.

Related to this is the "pedagogical ideal," and many an analyst may come to his choice of profession from the same motives which cause other people to become pedagogues. About the "pedagogical ideal" there exists already much more literature than about the "analytic ideal." There may be the tendency: "My patient shall be better off than I was" or "my patient shall *not* be better off than I was." Very often that means, more specifically, "my patient should or should not experience the specific situations which I had to experience." Many analysts constantly try to convince their patients, "look, it doesn't hurt so much after all!" and it is clear that these analysts become unable or inhibited if it becomes necessary to hurt really (or they may even hurt really where it is not necessary, by the very means by which they try to avoid doing so).

The analyst's unconscious sadism may be decisive for much of his faulty behavior. The correct application of interpretations presupposes the ability to use aggressiveness adequately. Too much aggressiveness, as well as too little, on the part of the analyst is fatal, and often the same analysts show too much aggressiveness under certain circumstances, and too little under others. Here I may add that, in analyzing analysts, I also frequently met with the problem of analysts feeling bored during their analytic work. Very often it turns out that the pathological boredom is due to an unconscious aggressiveness, and comes about if the analyst unconsciously has motives for being angry at his patient.[1]

We mentioned above a special case of all these attempts at smoothing unconscious anxieties: the attempts might fail. The analyst's anxiety might become obvious and disturb his analytic work. We met such anxiety already in discussing possible fears or in interpreting fears of emotional outbreaks on the part of the patients. Often these anxieties are masked as the opposite by means of overcompensation. You know that there are very different means of hiding anxiety, and all these means may also be used by analysts. Important in practice is the case in which anxiety is masked as a more or less manifest aggressiveness against the patients, which may go from a mere slight irritation to open fury. An analyst who is unconsciously dependent on getting narcissistic satisfaction from his patients necessarily gets angry at patients who deny him the necessary supplies. We mentioned boredom as a possible consequence of unconscious hostility against the patients; another possibility is the development of guilt feelings toward the patients because of this unconscious hostility. Guilt feelings toward the patients, it is true, may also be rooted in other sources; it might, for example, be a simple "countertransference"; the guilt feeling may have originated in the analyst's childhood and now the analyst is unconsciously trying to fight it by means of his profession. If an analyst has guilt feelings toward his patients, he will need reassurances from them. If the patients deny him such reassurances, the analyst unconsciously will become hostile toward them. Such analysts become unable to tolerate reproaches or accusations from their patients, and if you want to find out whether or not a candidate suffers from unconscious guilt feelings, you simply have to watch how he re-

---

[1] Here perhaps is the place to mention that the feeling of being bored certainly is not the only possible form of disturbance of attention on the part of the analyst. Attentive disturbances of any kind are, as is to be expected, the most frequent neurotic difficulty of analysts, and the most frequent type of "counterresistance." They are a special type of the frequent neurotic disturbances of concentration or attention, which have not yet found the scientific investigation which they deserve. It is understandable that they are not specific in their unconscious content. Whenever the activity of "analyzing" has taken on unconscious significance for the analyst—and this unconscious significance might concern special analytic situations, special subjects, special types of patients, or "analyzing" in general—it may occur that the activity becomes inhibited because of this unconscious significance, and that this inhibition finds expression in a more or less plain withdrawal of attention. But also if the patient's material is reacted to by the analyst as a starting point for daydreams, or—more generally—as a mobilizer of material in the analyst's unconscious which asks for attention on the part of the analyst, this attention is then lacking in his analytic activity. All these disturbances of analytic attention may also be overcompensated: The analyst may be aware of them, develop guilt feelings, and try now to be especially attentive, with the result that the attention becomes cramped and rigid instead of mobile and "freely suspended," which is equally disturbing to the analytic work. I am under the impression that the tendency to take all the patients' utterances down in shorthand, which is to be observed in some analysts and even taught in certain institutes, necessarily involves a distraction of the analyst's attention of this type. However, this topic transgresses the subject of "training analysis," and its necessary discussion should be given at another occasion.

acts if he gets a patient of the orally demanding and accusing type. There are analysts who cannot handle such types because they feel that all their patients' reproaches are simply justified; they have the tendency to agree with all of their patients' oral demands. Sometimes, there are not only patients but also analytic teachers of such an oral-demanding type. I remember when I analyzed several colleagues who used to attend the same seminar directed by a colleague of this type. The next day brought the opportunity to analyze how they reacted toward their patients due to the mobilization of their guilt feeling which had taken place in the previous seminar.

The "pedagogic attitude," "I have to help my patients immediately," as well as a narcissistic desire to do better may create an "emotional therapeutic ambition" which makes the necessary analytic patience impossible. But an overcompensation of such an emotional therapeutic ambition, or an inferiority feeling of actually not being able to help, may be equally fatal. Certain analysts rationalize a pathological lack of therapeutic ambition by stating that they do "research," or by avoiding necessary self-criticism in the hope that the next year of analysis will bring the success which has failed to materialize through several years.

In general: There is the danger of the analyst's indifference, as a defense against too great a proximity to too much unconscious material. We see then that the analyst might misuse the rule "the patient determines the subject of the hour" by becoming passive, waiting until the patient brings the "subjects" (which for a long time already he actually has "brought" by his behavior), and by "floating around" instead of controlling the situation dynamically and economically—the most frequent and most fatal counterresistance on the part of the analyst.[2]

In a more general way, the analyst might be influenced by his own, unconsciously determined ideals. It seems to me that—unfortunately—there are analytic marriage disturbers as well as marriage savers, and even analysts who tend to analyze the unconscious determination of certain political points of view—but not that of the opposite ones. Just as a man with pseudo-debility protects himself against undesired experiences simply by not facing them, there may also be analysts who develop a lack of broadness in their capacity for empathy, for the purpose of avoiding certain experiences. They may then do well with certain types of patients, but will be unable to handle others. In extreme cases, they may totally misunderstand strange environments by interpreting them as denials of what is familiar to the analyst; the most extreme case of this type of mistake can be found in some anthropological papers of certain analysts.

We may summarize: There is only one kind of protection against all these mistakes on the part of the analyst: a deep and thorough training analysis. We saw that the foremost dangers are not rooted in neurotic symptoms on the part of the analyst, but in "neurotic character attitudes." How such trends are undone

[2] Cf. the discussions of these problems in Fenichel (1938-1939).

by thorough analysis of their origin cannot be shown here, and we have frequently discussed the special problems of "character analysis" in other places. But it is clear that "character analysis" is deeper and takes more time than "symptom analysis." So the training analysis has to be an especially good therapeutic analysis after all.[3] For while the average neurotic is content when his unconscious does not disturb his everyday life, so that he is happy when he does not feel anything of his unconscious at all, the analyst has to use his unconscious constantly as his working instrument. It is not easy to purify the unconscious for this purpose.

We did not discuss today the questions of "mental hygiene of the analyst" and the question of possible later renewals of the analyst's analysis, as Freud suggested them.

REFERENCES

Fenichel, O. (1938–1939), *Problems of Psychoanalytic Technique*. Albany, N.Y.: The Psychoanalytic Quarterly, Inc., 1941.
Freud, S. (1923), The ego and the id. *Standard Edition*, 19:3–66. London: Hogarth Press, 1961.
_____ (1937), Analysis terminable and interminable. *Standard Edition*, 23:216–253. London: Hogarth Press, 1964.
Nunberg, H. (1926), The will to recovery. In: *Practice and Theory of Psychoanalysis*. New York: International Universities Press, 1961, pp. 75–88.

[3] In the 1938 discussion, Ernst Simmel stressed the point that there remains one important difference between training analysis and the average therapeutic analysis: the outer situation itself determines a difference in the average aspect of the transference in the respective cases. The training candidate who intends to become an analyst "like his training analyst," and who is even supposed to learn the technique in his own training analysis by observing what his analyst says and does for the purpose of imitating it later, will necessarily develop tendencies to identify himself with his analyst. Also, in the usual analysis of neurotics we regularly find such identifications in the transference, but they may be hidden behind object strivings. The handling of this identification sets up several problems for the training analyst. Instead of a libidinous "transference" identification, a practical, mobile, and not rigid "real identification" has to be achieved. But that is done by the same principles of handling the transference which are valid in any transference analysis. Actually, I saw several times severe difficulties in training analyses originating in this "identification with the analyst." In the same way as it is necessary that the cured neurotic has to become independent of the person of his analyst and of "supplies" from him, so the candidate has to stop imitating his training analyst and become an independent personality in his work before he can be considered an analyst.

The following paper "On the Teaching and Learning of Termination in Psychoanalysis" by Stanley S. Weiss and myself is part of a series begun several years ago that focuses on educational questions. Like the paper published in the 1979 volume on how members of an admissions committee can learn more about the tasks of selecting candidates, this paper speaks more specifically to the teacher of a case conference on termination. We have tried to discuss the planning of such a course in relation to the whole curriculum on theory and to present a clinical report from which an assessment of a student's knowledge about termination and his clinical competence in this area can be made.

If anyone has comments on this paper or others in this section, we would be glad to receive them. Examples of experiences in other institutes will also be welcome; we will try to get going a dialogue on pertinent topics even if we may not be able to publish them all.

Joan Fleming, M.D.

On the Teaching and Learning
of Termination in Psychoanalysis

STANLEY S. WEISS, M.D.   (Denver)
and JOAN FLEMING, M.D.

Introduction

The teaching and learning of termination in psychoanalysis are most important and complex tasks. Yet only rather recently have most institutes given the study of the terminal phase of psychoanalysis the proper emphasis that it deserves in their curriculum planning and teaching.

Early in the history of psychoanalytic education it was taught that the analysis "just dies of exhaustion" (Ferenczi, 1927, p. 85). It was also assumed by many psychoanalytic educators that anybody who could conduct a proper analysis could surely terminate one. In fact, many institutes did not require a terminated case for graduation, and termination was not taught in specific courses or even given special attention in supervision. The American Psychoanalytic Association, however, was aware of the educational advantages of supervision during the termination phase of analysis and believed that an applicant for membership should demonstrate an ability to conduct at least one analysis to a reasonably successful termination. However, if the membership application was sufficiently strong in other areas, the requirement for a terminated case was often waived.

The uncertainty about the significance of the termination phase in psychoanalysis may be traced to Freud's 1937 paper, "Analysis Terminable and Interminable." Freud stated that "I am not intending to assert that analysis is altogether an endless business. Whatever one's theoretical attitude to the question [of termination] may be, the termination of an analysis is, I think, a practical matter. Every experienced analyst will be able to recall a number of cases in which he has bidden his patients a permanent farewell *rebus bene gestis* [things having gone well]. In cases of what is known as character analysis, there is a far smaller discrepancy between theory and practice. Here it is not easy to foresee a natural end, even if one avoids any exaggerated expectations and sets the analysis no excessive tasks" (pp. 249–250). It was in this same paper that Freud also suggested that "every analyst should periodically — at intervals of five years or so — submit himself to analysis once more, without feeling ashamed of taking this step. This would mean, then, that not only the therapeutic analysis of patients but his own analysis would change from a terminable into an interminable task" (p. 249). Today, of course, training analyses last significantly longer than in the early years of psychoanalytic training, but, in spite of that fact, even now, many analysts follow Freud's advice and return for further analysis. The lifetime practice of analysis requires the analyst to have a very deep grasp and mastery of his own unconscious as well as a significant ability to do self-analysis.

However, by 1950, Buxbaum reported that termination is an important phase of analysis. "It is like the finale in a musical movement which repeats the leading motives of the piece" (p. 190).

Glover, in his textbook, *The Technique of Psychoanalysis* (1955), was the first to stress that "unless a terminal phase has been passed through, it is very doubtful whether any case has been psycho-analyzed" (p. 140). He stated, "in all cases. . .our first concern must be to apply a *technical criterion* for termination, viz. the limits of psychoanalytic influence" (p. 154). Glover went on to say, "If we believe that this limit has been reached, it is our duty to terminate the analysis as soon as possible." Glover apparently did not appreciate at that time the full importance of setting a termination date or the significance of working through in the terminal phase as much as Buxbaum did with her musical analogy.

In Glover's questionnaire on technique of psychoanalysis, originally published in 1940 and included in his 1955 textbook, which he sent to those members of the British Psycho-Analytical Society who were engaged in active psychoanalytic practice, he asked about criteria for termination (1955, p. 327). It is significant that one-third of the contributors failed to answer this question and a majority admitted that their criteria were essentially intuitive. A few emphasized that they always tested these intuitions as intelligently and thoroughly as they were able. However, these few analysts did not spell out how they assessed a readiness for termination and what criteria they used.

In 1966, Fleming and Benedek, in their book on psychoanalytic supervision, presented a rather new view when they stated, "When the student has terminated a patient's analysis with a good resolution of the transference neurosis, he will have had the opportunity to learn how to differentiate progression from regression and psychological growth from resistance. This learning experience is a maturing one for him as well as the patient. For these reasons, we look upon the termination phase as crucial for the student-analyst" (p. 193).

Rangell, in an address on termination at the Pan-American Congress for Psychoanalysis in 1964, highlighted the post-termination period. He believed that it, too, was important enough to be considered a phase which also required further study (p. 158).

During this time there was a focus of attention on assessment of analyzability, ego structure, intrapsychic change, and prediction of outcome. This focus required follow-up studies which were pioneered by Pfeffer (1959, 1961, 1963) and confirmed and continued by Schlessinger and Robbins (1974), Oremland et al. (1975), and Norman et al. (1976). These studies involved patient, analyst, and external observer.

In 1978, the first textbook devoted entirely to termination in psychoanalysis appeared. The author, Firestein, reported the analyses of eight adults, four men and four women, conducted by candidates under supervision at the New York Psychoanalytic Treatment Center. Firestein reviewed the clinical records and interviewed the analysts, the supervisors, and the patients. He was interested primarily in a study of termination and outcome of analyses and did not attempt an evaluation of the ego organization or the analytic process of the cases and did not discuss the educational issues which we believe to be crucial. In our view it is most important for candidates to be able to link the criteria for analyzability, the criteria for termination, and evidence for structural changes to the clinical and observational data. This was not done by many of the candidates whose cases were reviewed by Firestein, nor, it appears, was it encouraged by their supervisors.

However, we believe that Firestein's research offers a fertile field for the investigation of many complex and important issues involved in psychoanalytic education and especially for an extension of a student's learning experience in the area of evaluating the results of analytic work.

As peer review, third-party payment, and continuing education for recertification and relicensure gain wider acceptance, it will be most important for analysts to be able to clearly document why analysis is indicated in contrast to other forms of therapy and to be able to describe clearly all phases of the analytic process, to record the evidence for intrapsychic changes, and to fully assess and evaluate the analytic experience.

In three previous papers we have discussed the importance of evaluation and assessment as an ongoing process in psychoanalytic education. In 1975, we (Weiss and Fleming) discussed the criteria for assessing progress in supervision and the problems involved in making an educational diagnosis of the candidate's learning difficulties which manifested themselves at the point of evaluation. In 1978, we (Fleming and Weiss) discussed the evaluation of the training analysis to determine a candidate's readiness to analyze a patient under supervision. We have also reviewed selection criteria and the teaching and learning of the process of assessment of the potential to become an analyst (Weiss and Fleming, 1979). In this paper we will review the criteria for evaluating a terminated analysis and discuss the teaching objectives for a seminar on termination.

In a terminated analysis we hope patients will have acquired insight with conviction leading to lasting personality changes; this implies, of course, much more than symptom relief. We wish our students to assess accurately if this has been done and to what degree, or, if it has not been accomplished, why not. Freud in 1937 emphasized that the conditions for failure of analysis should be studied more thoroughly. We fully agree with this and would add that the conditions for success should also be able to be clearly documented. The development of this skill should take place in a termination seminar.

In Section I of this paper we will highlight what we feel a candidate should have been taught during the theoretical phase of the tripartite educational program before he attends a course on termination. Successful curriculum planning and teaching during the theoretical phase of psychoanalytic education should lead to genuine mastery of psychoanalytic psychology and effective integration with clinical concepts and techniques.

In Section II we will review what we feel the candidate should be taught in a course on termination and how his diagnostic and interpretive skills have to be developed.

In Section III we will discuss criteria for determining that a termination phase has been reached and that the important date setting and working through to the final good-bye can now be successfully accomplished.

In Section IV we will emphasize that candidates in a termination seminar must gain experience in correlating and connecting termination criteria with the data of the analytic process. We will (1) present an advanced candidate's case summary of a successfully terminated case, and (2) show the process of assessing the candidate's report as it is judged by the teachers of the course.

Dewald (1973), after several years of studying the case reports submitted to the Membership Committee of the American Psychoanalytic Association, has stated that these write-ups are poorly executed. "Those case reports which indicate a good working concept of the process of psychoanalysis are indeed a rarity" (p. 266). This observation would indicate that the learning objectives of writing and summarizing analytic cases have not been given the proper attention they deserve by psychoanalytic faculties. We believe that this learning experience of summarizing a terminated case is an excellent way to learn about the analytic process. Such a report can be a useful instrument in assessing and evaluating clinical competence and analytic scholarship.

I. What Should A Candidate Know Prior to a Termination Seminar?

By the time a candidate is ready to proceed in his psychoanalytic education to a seminar on termination, it seems logical to expect that he should (1) possess a strong foundation in the basic concepts of psychoanalytic psychology and the basic theory of psychoanalytic therapy (COPER, 1974, pp. 32-33);

(2) understand, recognize, and be able to assess the process nature of the analytic experience; and (3) have achieved a growing appreciation of evidence and criteria for structural changes derived from a well-conducted analysis and be able to describe the intrapsychic reorganization in dynamic, economic, genetic, and adaptive terms.

From the very beginning of their training, candidates should appreciate the essential relation between clinical and theoretical thinking. The teaching and learning of analytic process should begin in the first year of training with a course on analytic technique and a clinical conference. We are aware that certain institutes do not have a clinical conference or a course on technique in the first year. However, we believe it is important throughout training to link theoretical concepts to clinical data, and this can be done most effectively in clinical-conference teaching. Teachers and supervisors need to integrate the "how to" approach, which is technical, with the "why" approach, which is conceptual.

The teacher of the termination seminar can logically expect that the candidate should have learned about the establishment of the analytic situation, the development of the working alliance, the evolving of the transference neurosis, and the process of interpretation. Learning about the process nature of the analytic experience is not easily conceptualized. To treat this topic adequately requires further elaboration which would take us beyond the scope of this paper. However, we will refer to a few learning experiences that touch on this learning objective.

A first step in teaching about the analytic process can be accomplished by presenting to beginning candidates the long-term perspective of a successfully completed case. Such a perspective begins to lay the groundwork for an understanding of the process nature of the analytic experience. This perspective on process helps a candidate at the beginning of training to build an "analytic cognitive map" (Tyler, 1974, p. 91) and serves as a useful prerequisite for his advanced learning in a termination seminar. This learning continues and deepens with the first case and the first supervisor. It continues throughout the theoretical and clinical phases of the educational process as basic and advanced courses are mastered and clinical experience is acquired.

The beginning courses should include the theory of development in early years and throughout the life cycle. The candidate begins to master the important task of making a structural diagnosis and acquires an ability to know where his patient is on a developmental line. This leads into the important area of criteria for analyzability and an appreciation of the importance of ego structure, which are important prerequisites for a course on termination.

As training proceeds, the candidate begins to learn more about interpreting, regression in the analytic situation, appreciation of the transference neurosis, and signs that the patient is changing. The candidate should appreciate the patient's growing ability to associate, to listen to his associations, and to begin to make some interpretations himself; i.e., as the analysis proceeds the candidate should recognize the development of the patient's self-analytic skill. As the analytic process moves forward—with less acting out, improved synthetic functioning, increased insight, and uncovering of more childhood memories with accompanying ego strengthening—the candidate should be able to document crucial changes in the patient's self representation, object relations, and reality testing.

The candidate must also be able to recognize by the time he reaches a termination seminar when an analytic process is not moving or when it has gone awry. Of course, chaotic situations are easily identified; but many stalemates are not so easily recognized, and the candidate has to know how to identify them and how to intervene. In a Panel (1969) on "Problems of Termination in the Analysis of Adults," Wiedeman noted that some patients tend to assume an analytic "way of life" (p. 229) in which they engage in what is regarded as psychoanalysis but which, in fact, represents only a replacement of the early dependency on the parents.

In summary, by the time a candidate enters a course on termination, he should have a fairly sophisticated understanding that the aim of analysis is the lasting insight that comes from the ongoing exploration of the patient's unconscious, and that significant changes and growth are essentially the result of the science and art of interpreting defenses, resistances, content, and transference. The integrative function that is facilitated in a properly conducted analysis gives the ego better command of id, superego, and outer reality.

II. Given the Prerequisite Learning, What Additional Objectives Belong in a Course on Termination?

In a well-taught seminar on termination, the candidate has the opportunity to integrate all that he has learned about the theory and practice of analysis in previous courses, clinical conferences, supervision, and in his own training analysis. Analytic educators are aware that although synthesis must be individually accomplished by each candidate, it can be assisted by good teaching efforts.

The learning objectives of a termination seminar include not only a review of what the candidate has already learned but the advanced objectives of mastering the theory and technique of the termination process. At the beginning of a termination seminar, it is important for the teacher to present to the candidates the signs that a termination phase has been reached and the indications for recognizing structural change which has occurred as the result of the process of analysis. Throughout the course the significant literature about termination also needs to be read and discussed.

It is also important at the beginning of a termination seminar to discuss with candidates the educational value of the task of reviewing and writing a case report of a completed analysis which has been conducted without the introduction of parameters or manipulations and has been successfully terminated.

Another important objective of the termination seminar is the actual experience of writing and presenting a case report that is evaluated by colleagues and teachers for evidence of structural change, the ongoing process of the analysis, and the progress and learning of the candidate. In addition to a termination report, the candidate should also be given the opportunity to write up a completed case summary in about four or five pages. The candidate needs to learn how to condense significant analytic events and how to document the process of change during the beginning, middle, and end phases of the analysis. In the termination summary, the candidate must map the entire course of the analysis in language both cognitive and experiential and be able to trace the beginning, development, and resolution of the transference neurosis. The summary should demonstrate the inner dynamics of the patient and the bringing to light of their origins. The report should also show the development of the candidate as he brings his growing knowledge, capacity for empathy, understanding, self-awareness, and self-analysis to the analytic situation.

The analytic termination of the patient should be the result of effective analysis and effective working through. The issue of termination should, of course, have been the subject of analytic work, and the decision to terminate should have been mutually agreeable to both patient and analyst. Countertransference problems and resolution, and details as to what the candidate learned from supervision and the analytic experience should be reported. The termination summary should include the candidate's assessment of the effectiveness of the analytic work, and follow-up data, if available, should, of course, be noted.

Initially, many candidates are somewhat anxious and awed by this assignment of having to condense an analysis that took place over many years and to describe its uniqueness, subtleties, and movement from initial interview through termination in a relatively few pages. However, the candidate should have achieved some experience in this important skill before reaching a termination seminar, through having written six-month and yearly summaries of his cases and having had them evaluated and discussed by his supervisors.

III. What Are the Criteria That A Termination Has Been Reached?

As we have noted, the learning about criteria that a termination phase has been reached and the manner in which it should be conducted are the special objectives of this advanced seminar. The movement of a properly conducted analysis leads to more conflict-free functioning, to autonomous functioning with more self-reliance and self-confidence, to secondary-process thinking with improved reality testing and improved sublimations, to an individuated sense of self and objects with improved object relations, and to a growing appreciation of the difference between analyst as analyst and analyst as transference imago.

If the analytic process has shown this progressive development over time and the working through of the middle phase has proceeded well, there comes a time in the analysis when the patient himself begins to recognize these changes and movements. The patient can now observe and comment on his improved ego functioning, especially his defenses and impulses. Insight has replaced acting out. The patient's unconscious has become more conscious, accessible, and controllable. During this time, the patient's associations deal more with present and future and less with past, and the patient usually begins to associate about wishes to complete the analysis, to separate from the analyst, and to go on to new experiences on his own. These associations about character changes, future plans, separations, etc., initiate the end phase of the analysis (Fleming and Benedek, 1966). The duration of the onset of termination varies, and the analyst is usually aware of the changes long before the patient is. The transforming of insight from an intellectual into a total experience takes time and is one of the essential parts of "working through" (Kris, 1956a, p. 337). The analyst, at this time, might begin to have a different feeling about the patient, i.e., a feeling of more equality (Weigert, 1952).

Evidence of this change or growth can be missed or not given proper attention by patient and/or analyst, since resistances regarding final separation may now come into play. However, if countertransference problems are not present in the analyst, and understanding and interpretation continue, both patient and analyst will soon be aware of important changes in the patient's total integrated psychic functioning.

When termination is approaching and when the termination phase is under way, "good analytic hours" become more frequent. They lead to new insights, new connections, new memories; the integrative function and the self-analytic function of the patient's ego are observable by both patient and analyst; and both are aware of the relation of these changes to the analytic material (Kris, 1956b).

The candidate, of course, has to know if associations about change and termination represent a true beginning of the end stage of analysis or a resistance against further significant analytic work and a wish for premature closure. In this vein, Kris (1956b) speaks of a need to differentiate the "good analytic hour" from the "deceptively good hour" which is due to resistance. Freud (1923), in discussing the theory and practice of dream interpretation, mentioned that associations "converge" when the analytic work is going well (p. 110). When the pressure of resistance is high, associations broaden instead of deepen, and, of course, at a time of high resistance the patient is not ready for termination.

If the analytic process reveals that structural changes in ego, superego, and drive organization do not parallel the patient's report of his improved external life, or if the analyst's observations indicate structural changes without corresponding improvement in the patient's real life, there is doubt that termination is really at hand. Greenson (1964, p. 265) has also noted that if talk of termination takes either the analyst or the patient by surprise something is amiss.

By the time the termination phase is reached, the transference neurosis should be resolving and diminishing, the infantile amnesia should have been lifted, and the Oedipus uncovered, reworked, and resolved. Good analytic work should have prepared the patient for the final synthesis that will take place during termination (Nunberg, 1931).

In the end phase of the analysis, a specific time is set for termination, and the working through of the final separation takes place. Painful feelings of separation, estrangement, and mourning are usually part of the final work. Narcissistic rage, perfectionistic expectations, and infantile wishes might, once again, reappear and be reworked and mastered. In a panel on termination, Kanzer (Panel, 1974, p. 173) noted that besides anxiety, anger, and depression, there is also relief, joy, and hunger for new experiences for which time, money, and psychological preparedness are now available. In a good termination, separation from the analyst can be differentiated by the patient from a sense of being deprived or rejected. It is hoped that any analytic patient will have achieved enough insight and security to recognize a need for further analysis if it should arise and to be able to seek it.

IV. How Can the Achievement of the Learning Objectives on Termination Be Evaluated?

The exercise of condensing significant analytic events and writing a summary of a completed case is a most important learning experience for candidates. It is from such a summary that an experienced analytic clinician and educator can assess a candidate's development as an analyst and his readiness to graduate. In our experience the writing of such a summary as an assigned task in a termination seminar offers a view of the candidate's comprehension of the analytic process.

We will now present a case report written by an advanced candidate in a termination seminar, followed by the thinking of the teacher as he assesses the candidate's write-up and clinical data.

The learning-teaching material which we are presenting has been disguised and altered somewhat to protect and insure the confidentiality of the patient, candidate, and supervisor. The first person pronoun in the following report refers to the candidate.

Termination Report—Mr. A. F.

Length of analysis—four years, nine months.

Frequency of analysis—five times a week.

Frequency of supervision—once a week for two years; once every two weeks for two years; once a month for six months; once a week for final three months.

The patient, a 29-year-old married high school teacher, had three evaluation sessions before starting on the couch.

The patient appeared friendly and pleasant looking and was dressed in a casual, sporty manner. He was neat and well-groomed and looked several years younger than his stated age. He related in an open, relaxed, and comfortable manner during the evaluation. This was in contrast to the start of the analytic work on the couch when anxiety was evident in the rapid rush of associations.

In the first sitting-up session, the patient described regressive behavior at home and stated clearly and somewhat firmly that he wished and needed analysis because of "turmoil in the marriage" which he did not understand and could not control and many severe arguments with his wife over the question of having or not having children.

The patient's wife wanted to raise a family, and she believed the patient's wish to wait for "just the right time" was an emotional problem for her husband and that if he did not receive analytic help the right time would never appear. The patient stated that he knew his wife was right about his "fear of becoming a father," but only recently could he admit this to her and also actively seek analysis. However, in the first session he told me that not until his wife seriously threatened divorce did the patient call the analytic clinic for an appointment.

During the evaluation, I became impressed with this man's honesty, his ability to introspect, and his psychological-mindedness. This initial impression about his ego functions which pointed toward analyzability was confirmed during the beginning phase of the analysis. I thought it was an especially good sign for analyzability that he was so curious about his inner life and anxieties, and so unhappy and concerned about his regressive functioning in the marriage.

I did wonder about the meaning of his not applying for analysis until the wife threatened divorce, and I thought, is my impression about healthy motivation for analysis wrong? Might he be seeking analysis to placate his angry wife because of the threat of object loss? However, my overall impression was that this was not a passive, infantile man, and I thought that the marriage was basically solid and that both he and his wife understood that some "emotional block" (his term) was holding him back from continuing to grow. In fact, he seemed to be one of those sophisticated patients who even initially has some awareness that with insight he could change and improve his life and functioning. I was not surprised to learn that he had always been interested in psychology, had been a good student, and had even read some Freud in college.

The following history was obtained during the evaluation sessions and in the beginning phase of the analysis.

The patient was born and raised in a large eastern city and moved west "to get away from the family and from all old friends." He wanted to make a new start in life in a part of the country where no one knew him.

The patient's father, an accountant, died suddenly of a coronary when the patient was sixteen years of age. The patient had always been very close to his mother, "especially around tax time" when the father spent many extra hours at the office. On the way home from work during the busy time of the year, the father "suddenly fell over and died immediately."

After the father's death, a change took place in the closeness between mother and son. The patient began to withdraw more and more from his mother and from the home. He began to get very busy in school, indulged in sports and in many other extracurricular activities, but also continued to do well in classes. He was eager to go to college and insisted that the college be quite a distance from home. He began dating a girl in his high school class, and soon after graduation they married. His wife had a Catholic background but did not consider herself religious and did not attend church regularly. The patient came from a nonreligious Jewish family. Both families knew each other. In fact, the patient's father thought the patient's future wife was "extremely pretty and very bright." Two and one-half years after the father's death, the patient married.

Prior to the marriage, the patient experienced no sexual problems. However, once married, the turmoil began, and the patient also developed episodes of premature ejaculation and marked anxiety when he contemplated approaching his wife sexually. The arguments over raising a family also soon began.

My supervisor agreed with my diagnostic impression that the patient suffered from an anxiety neurosis tied to unresolved oedipal issues. The healthy resolution of the Oedipus was interfered with by the sudden death of the father when the patient was sixteen years of age. It seems that following the father's death the patient's oedipal conflict intensified. He attempted to solve the problem by turning away from the mother to a non-Jewish girl friend who must have represented the yearned-for and feared incestuous object. I speculated that he also handled his traumatic object loss by identifying with the busy and hard-working father who had suddenly died. I also thought that he was feeling guilty for what he unconsciously perceived was an oedipal victory which had been reinforced by the actual death of the father. His wish to leave home and start a new life elsewhere sounded like he felt himself to be a criminal who wanted to move where people would not know of his crime. The child he fears having could be the oedipal baby who he feels will kill him and with whom he is also unconsciously identified.

The patient appeared to be analyzable, and my supervisor and I thought he surely deserved a trial of analysis.

Once he was on the couch, I gave him the basic rule about free association. He talked rapidly, seemed anxious, and stated that he "didn't expect to miss any sessions, never gets sick, never misses time at work, and plans to live for a long, long, time." The initial associations about his excellent health sounded to me like a need to reassure himself, and I felt that he must need to defend against a fear of death. As the analysis progressed, this conjecture proved to be true. I had been taught in class about the importance of the initial associations and that seemed to be clearly borne out in this case.

The patient focused early in the analysis on his father's death, and he was surprised that he had never really been overtly upset. The family had also commented on this. He was busy, working hard in school, soon dating and making plans for the future. He had thought that possibly he just had no time to indulge in mourning. It seemed to me that he had repressed all depressive affects at the time of the loss, and my supervisor suspected that at some time in the analysis this patient was going to experience much pain. He had obviously warded off the depression with activity.

Early in the analysis he joked often about "enjoying analysis" since he can "rest for an hour each day," and "I am in no rush to ever finish." He associated that my office "looked and felt" somewhat like his father's office and he had always enjoyed going regularly to visit his father. It became clear that in the transference I was becoming the replacement for the lost father and he did not wish to ever have to relinquish me.

Following the first summer vacation, he said that he missed me and that he had experienced "some pain in the chest." He felt, at times, like he was going to faint but didn't want to worry his wife and didn't tell her about the frightening and painful symptoms. He also thought of trying to get in touch with me but rapidly rejected this thought. Instead, he went to his doctor for a checkup and to get some medication. The physical proved to be completely normal, and he wasn't given any medication, to his "disappointment and relief." I understood this important episode as an identification with his sick father, triggered by the anxiety, rage, and depression at our vacation interruption.

I interpreted to him his identification with his father. He confirmed this by bringing up new material: that his mother would get angry at his father since the father had the need to hide his symptoms and doctor's appointments from her, and she would become angry and hurt when she learned later about his symptoms. He could see that during the vacation break he had tried to hide his symptoms from me and could say, "I must have treated you like my father treated my mother." New material was brought forth. The father had angina for a "year or so" before his massive coronary, and he took "medication for the pain."

The patient "confessed" with embarrassment that he does worry "at times" that he will die at an early age like his father. I was able to connect for him, at this point, that his initial associations about never being sick and living for a long time were a defense against this fear of an early death. He was surprised and obviously pleased that I had remembered his first associations and stated that maybe he is not "fated and programmed" to die at the same time his father did. Actually, the physician had said that the patient was in very good health.

The summer vacation had brought out in bold relief his identification with his ill father and his fear of an early death. I wondered to myself how the termination work would eventually proceed since this first long interruption had been so intense, yet so fruitful for the analysis.

After another vacation, he spoke of developing anxiety in the classroom as his students returned. He was upset when a fellow teacher commented that all these youngsters will be running the world before long. The teacher pessimistically stated that they probably will not do any better than their parents. He told his colleague that the new generation will surely be smarter, kinder, and less angry and destructive than the present generation. He made an interesting slip. He meant to say children help man to become "immortal." Instead, he said children help man become "impotent."

The analytic work on this slip led to my being able to show him that he became anxious at what the teacher said because it triggered a fantasy that these students want to kill the parents. I interpreted to him that he is frightened of parenthood because he fears his child would kill him, and he magically attempts to stay alive and avoid father's fate by not having children.

He responded to this interpretation in an interesting way. He ignored the interpretation, which I understood as his wish to destroy my interpretation. He also became anxious and associated that I was planning to raise his fee since he had just bought a used sports car and had not discussed it with me.

The "confession" about buying the sports car also brought up some other associations that he had not brought into the analysis because "they seemed too unimportant." These "unimportant thoughts" were verbalized when I asked him if he had ignored any other thoughts, such as the one about the sports car. He stated that he had wondered about my house, my car, and had attempted to figure out my income. He wondered how many hours a day I work and how much each patient pays me. He said these associations "*usually* did not appear during the analytic sessions but at other times." He also said that he spent one recent Sunday morning riding around my neighborhood attempting to view my house.

My supervisor was very helpful in discussing with me transference acting out since I became anxious when I learned that the patient was driving over to see my house. I had anxiously wondered how far the patient would act out instead of initially correctly evaluating this opportunity to impart insight with conviction through interpretation. I was able to identify my anxiety as being tied to a fear of closeness that I had successfully worked out in my own analysis. I enjoyed working with this patient, liked him, and became anxious when the transference acting out began.

The patient, however, began to feel that I somehow did not like him and wanted to get rid of him for a higher paying patient. He thought I must resent clinic patients.

Following analytic work on the "unimportant" associations and the acting out, I was able to interpret to him that he thought I should get rid of him since he wished to get rid of me and take over my home, wife, and children. I pointed out that he was the child who wanted to make the parent "impotent" instead of "immortal."

He laughed nervously and made an important genetic connection himself. "*Maybe* that's why I wanted to leave home after my father's death. I must have been very frightened and pushed by my guilt." I agreed with his interpretation and asked him about the *maybe*. He said that the impulse is so frightening that "I wanted to give myself an out but I know it's true. I knew my wife was right that I was frightened of becoming a father but I could not admit that to her for a long time. It was like admitting that I killed my father and that our child would kill me."

Well into the working through of the middle phase the patient reported that while having intercourse with his wife he thought, "I must be a better lover than my analyst." This thought caused much guilt and shame and led to recall of an adolescent fantasy in which an older woman appreciates him much more than her sick husband and both he and the woman force the man to leave. This theme of being loved by the older woman and together sending the sickly husband away was the theme of his masturbation fantasies of adolescence. He associated his father to Van Gogh's picture of a depressed old man which had touched him deeply since he first saw it in a book when he was five years of age.

I was able to effectively connect the guilt over his masturbation fantasy with his premature ejaculation and marital problems. He also mentioned a family story from childhood that at age six he once told his father "in a very grown-up and cute way" that his father should not come home from the office since he was capable of taking care of his mother. As working through took place, I learned that his wife and mother had the same birth date. "Hadn't I told you that before? I thought I had." It turned out that both wife and mother were very similar women — bright, strong, maternal women — and I was able to show him that in the unconscious his wife and mother were felt to be the same. I interpreted to him that his fear of my retaliating had interfered with his telling me this important piece of data that linked wife and mother. He obviously viewed me not only as the depressed and weak father but as the angry and revengeful father.

Several years into the analysis he had a dream in which I appeared as a Nazi hunting out Jews to kill. The day residue was a newspaper story in which a fight broke out between two men following a traffic accident and one man killed the other.

This led to associations about the Holocaust and that my name sounded German. He felt horror and yet some "strange fascination" with that period of history. He had always been frightened of crowds and felt that aggression could suddenly erupt, inflicting death and suffering.

Following analytic work on this dream, I interpreted that he had felt he was responsible for the death of his father like the Nazis in the dream. In the dream, he had projected his own Nazi feelings onto me. He reported that at one time in the past he had a "peculiar thought" that the Nazis had killed his father, even though the family had no direct contact with the Holocaust. He associated that he had been very interested in the story of SS Colonel Adolf Eichmann's capture by the Israelis, and he could never understand some feeling of compassion that he had for Eichmann. He now understood that he had made some "weird" kind of identification with Eichmann.

In an hour following an extra-analytic contact in the elevator, the patient associated to how surprised he was to notice that we were about the same size. His father was quite tall and he had always felt that I was taller than he was. I felt that this was a good example of the power of transference. He had always felt like a young boy in an adult's body and was not sure of the exact height or age of this young boy self-image. Much work was done on this interesting phenomenon, which seemed to have become more conscious since his father's death. At this particular point in the analysis, he bought a new watch and started wearing it regularly instead of the inexpensive watches that he "could afford to lose or break." His sense of time seemed to have taken on a more realistic view. I remembered from my reading on patients with "parent loss" that they have problems with time and seem to be "stuck" at the point of the loss. This was confirmed in this patient, and it was an important step for him when time was viewed more realistically.

The patient had improved in his sexual life. His self-object representations were more realistic. He had gained insight into his Oedipus. His life experiences had taken on new meaning and integration. He was for the first time very interested in his family history and also in his wife's history. Thoughts of termination began to cross my mind but had not yet been verbalized by the patient.

One day he came into the office elated. He thought his wife was pregnant and he was very pleased. He now knew that he had solved the riddle of why he had been so scared of having children, since a few years back he would have been "anxious and agitated" at the thought of becoming a father. His wife became pregnant four-and-one-half years after the analysis began. For the first time he spoke of terminating "before very long." Since I had also been thinking of termination, his associations had not surprised me, but I wondered if the talk of termination was tied in some way to the pregnancy and was possibly a resistance to further work.

Initially, I did not pursue the topic, and he dropped it for another three weeks. Then he brought it up again with humor, "Since I am becoming a real father in the real world, I should give up the luxury and pleasure of being a child five times a week."

He stated that he can now really accept the fact that his father is dead, that the cause of death was heart disease, not a result of his son's wish to murder his father and take over his mother. The associations and the movement of the analytic process did not point to resistance, and several months after his wife had become pregnant we set a definite termination date.

Once the exact date was set, which was to be in four months, the patient became very tense and anxious, cried, and wondered if he could go on alone. The intensity of his affect surprised me, even though I knew from my reading that such phenomena could occur. My supervisor reminded me that we had discussed in the beginning that termination would be quite painful for this man. With the help of supervision, I was meaningfully able to tie this quite intense and vivid mourning reaction to the death of his father at age sixteen when the patient could not experience any overt grief.

The patient could understand what was happening but also wanted me to know that at least some of the tears were meant for his sense of loss in the present. He went on to say that this analysis had been so helpful and that he will always remain very grateful.

Many of his associations dealt with future plans and with wishes to give his child the security of good parents and a loving home. I told him that I enjoyed our work together. I received a card following the birth of his daughter, thanking me again for my help. I sent a note congratulating him.

I believe he learned about himself and profited from the analysis. I, too, gained from the analytic work and the supervision.

Teachers' Assessment of this Report

The assignment of good analytic cases by psychoanalytic educators is an important task, and we feel this was successfully accomplished here. The candidate had a good case from which to learn the art and science of analysis.

The report is well written, and there is evidence throughout the report that the candidate was familiar with many important analytic concepts and that he has learned from previous cases and seminars. What is very positive in this report is that the candidate communicates his experience with patient and with supervisor. This was the candidate's third supervised case, and the candidate has shown that he can learn from supervision and use it well (pp. 49, 51). Obviously, a good supervisory alliance had been present. In our experience it is rare for the average candidate to bring into the write-up and presentation of a case report the experience of supervisory learning. There is a tendency in psychoanalytic education for candidates to isolate apsects of the tripartite educational experience. This was not the case with this candidate.

The candidate appears to have an appreciation and understanding of analyzability as judged by his early assessment of the patient's ego functions and his motivation for change (p. 46). He showed throughout the report that he can interpret content, resistance, and transference, and that he understands the importance of connecting analytic data. The candidate also made conjectures about the psychoanalytic data, conjectures that would be confirmed or discarded at a later time (pp. 47, 48). In a poor report we usually do not see evidence of retrospective evaluation by the candidate.

We were impressed with the candidate's sensitivity to transference (p. 50) and his ability to identify the early manifestations of the transference (p. 48). The candidate has an appreciation of the developmental point of view in his understanding of the importance of the trauma of the father's death on concretizing unconscious fantasy and wishes and giving the transference a strong stamp of reality (p. 47). The report also demonstrates that the candidate appreciated the importance of the unresolved Oedipus complex in the formation of the patient's neurosis and a need to recover and rework this important constellation.

However, in this report practically nothing is reported from the infantile period, except for a significant memory about Van Gogh's "old man" from age five and a family story about the patient at age six (p. 50). The focus of the analysis, as reported, appears to be mainly adolescence, the death of his father when the patient was sixteen years of age, his marriage soon after, his reaction to death, and present difficulties. In the termination seminar this significant omission would be checked to see whether the infantile neurosis was not explored, recovered, or reconstructed adequately, or just does not appear in the write-up. In writing a report on the course of the analysis, analytic material from the infantile period is very relevant to evaluation of the analysis as well as to the analytic skill of the analyst. In this report, since there is no mention of siblings, it has to be assumed that the patient is an only child.

There is evidence in the report of the candidate's ability to use self-analysis successfully, which points toward a positive personal analytic experience for the candidate (p. 49). The candidate also briefly alludes to relevant literature (p. 51). Connecting the patient's material and analysis to appropriate literature is one sign of a good candidate. In our experience it is rather rare for a candidate to note the significant literature in a completed case write-up or presentation.

The patient through the analysis gained insight with conviction and made significant changes (p. 51). In this report, the candidate does not classify the changes brought about by the analysis specifically as structural changes, and we would discuss this omission in the termination seminar. However, the candidate did seem to recognize that a more realistic appreciation of time, a more realistic view of self and object representations, and the gaining of insight are evidences of important structural changes.

The candidate has learned that during termination old defenses may come back into play, such as regression and repetition of old patterns (p. 51). He also correctly wondered if the initial associations to termination were due to resistance (p. 51), and he did not set a definite date for stopping until he was sure that termination was an adaptive step toward growth and development and not a resistance against further analytic work (p. 51).

We believe that this candidate has shown a good appreciation of the analytic situation and the analytic process, and has a good grasp of the theory and technique of analysis for someone at his level of training, in spite of some partial negatives and omissions in the write-up. His sensitivity to the unconscious and his interpretive skill are developing well, and we would consider him from this report a candidate with high aptitude and potential.

Conclusion

We have discussed in the Introduction how, in the early period of psychoanalytic theory and practice, the concept of termination as providing evidence of intrapsychic reorganization was much less in the foreground of analytic study than was the focus on the practical ending of the formal analytic work. Later, as structural and developmental theory became more sharply formulated and integrated with the theory of therapy, the significance of a terminal phase came into better focus (Hurn, 1971), and the importance of studying termination in supervision and in the classroom became more evident. We would like to emphasize that termination is much more than a study of the formal ending of the analytic situation, since the analytic process is an ongoing and even endless task, as Freud already noted in 1937. Today, termination encompasses a cross section of the theory of development and takes in the full sweep of our present knowledge of psychoanalytic theory.

At the present time many psychoanalytic educators have begun to concentrate on a study of analyzability, analytic process, and outcome of analysis involving assessment of structural development as well as evidence for structural change produced by the analytic experience. The concept of structural change as an outcome of psychoanalytic process has become an essential element in every phase of the tripartite educational program, including the training analysis. In this paper we have focused on the learning objectives and the learning experiences offered by a course on termination dealing with this essential concept.

REFERENCES

Buxbaum, E. (1950), Technique of terminating analysis. *Internat. J. Psycho-Anal.*, 31:184–190.

COPER (Conference on Psychoanalytic Education and Research) (1974), Commission I: The tripartite system of psychoanalytic education. The American Psychoanalytic Association (unpublished).

Dewald, P. A. (1973), The clinical conference in teaching and learning the psychoanalytic process. *This Annual*, 1:265–279. New York: Quadrangle/New York Times.

Ferenczi, S. (1927), The problem of the termination of analysis. In: *Final Contribution to the Problems and Methods of Psychoanalysis*, ed. M. Balint. New York: Basic Books, 1955, pp. 77–86.

Firestein, S. K. (1978), *Termination in Psychoanalysis*. New York: International Universities Press.

Fleming, J. & Benedek, T. (1966), *Psychoanalytic Supervision*. New York: Grune & Stratton.

—————— & Weiss, S. S. (1978), Assessment of progress in a training analysis. *Internat. Rev. Psycho-Anal.*, 5:33–43.

Freud, S. (1923), Remarks on the theory and practice of dream-interpretation. *Standard Edition*, 19:109–121. London: Hogarth Press, 1961.

—————— (1937), Analysis terminable and interminable. *Standard Edition*, 23:209–254. London: Hogarth Press, 1964.

Glover, E. (1955), *The Technique of Psycho-Analysis*. New York: International Universities Press.

Greenson, R. R. (1964), Discussion. In: *Psychoanalysis in the Americas*, ed. R. E. Litman. New York: International Universities Press, 1966, pp. 263–266.

Hurn, H. T. (1971), Toward a paradigm of the terminal phase: The current status of the terminal phase. *J. Amer. Psychoanal. Assn.*, 19:332–348.

Kris, E. (1956a), The recovery of childhood memories in psychoanalysis. In: *The Selected Papers of Ernst Kris*. New Haven, Conn.: Yale University Press, 1975, pp. 301–340.

—————— (1956b), On some vicissitudes of insight in psychoanalysis. *Internat. J. Psycho-Anal.*, 37:445–455.

Norman, H. F., Blacker, K. H., Oremland, J. D., & Barrett, W. G. (1976), The fate of the transference neurosis after termination of a satisfactory analysis. *J. Amer. Psychoanal. Assn.*, 24:471–498.

Nunberg, H. (1931), The synthetic function of the ego. *Internat. J. Psycho-Anal.*, 12:123–140.

Oremland, J. D., Blacker, K. H., & Norman, H. F. (1975), Incompleteness in "successful" psychoanalysis. *J. Amer. Psychoanal. Assn.*, 23:819–844.

Panel (1969), Problems of termination in the analysis of adults, S. K. Firestein, reporter. *J. Amer. Psychoanal. Assn.*, 17:222–237.

Panel (1974), Termination: Problems and technique, W. S. Robbins, reporter. *J. Amer. Psychoanal. Assn.*, 23:166–176.

Pfeffer, A. (1959), A procedure for evaluating the results of psychoanalysis: A preliminary report. *J. Amer. Psychoanal. Assn.*, 7:418–444.

—————— (1961), Follow-up study of a satisfactory analysis. *J. Amer. Psychoanal. Assn.*, 9:698–718.

_____ (1963), The meaning of the analyst after analysis. *J. Amer. Psychoanal. Assn.*, 11:229–244.

Rangell, L. (1964), An overview of the ending of an analysis. In: *Psychoanalysis in the Americas*, ed. R. E. Litman. New York: International Universities Press, 1966, pp. 141–165.

Schlessinger, N. & Robbins, F. (1974), Assessment and follow-up in psychoanalysis. *J. Amer. Psychoanal. Assn.*, 22:542–567.

Tyler, R. W. (1974), Teaching and learning. COPER, Appendix, Report I, pp. 88–101 (unpublished).

Weigert, E. (1952), Contribution to the problem of terminating psychoanalysis. *Psychoanal. Quart.*, 21:465–480.

Weiss, S. S. & Fleming, J. (1975), Evaluation of progress in supervision. *Psychoanal. Quart.*, 44: 191–205.

_____ _____ (1979), The teaching and learning of the selection process: One aspect of faculty development. *This Annual*, 7:87–109. New York: International Universities Press.

January, 1980

III

CLINICAL THEORY

Transference, Schema, and Assimilation: The Relevance of Piaget to the Psychoanalytic Theory of Transference

PAUL L. WACHTEL, Ph.D.   (New York)

I

The Freudian concept of transference originated in observations of disturbed adults, obtained in the context of therapy, and was an attempt to account for certain distortions in their perception of reality. The Piagetian concept of schema derived from observations of healthy children, obtained in the context of research, and was an attempt to account for their increasingly accurate perception of reality. Two more disparate origins would be hard to find. Yet, I will argue, the Piagetian concept can provide a very useful and clarifying perspective on the phenomena to which Freud directed our attention.

Freud's first reports of transference phenomena were published in the "Studies on Hysteria" (Breuer and Freud, 1893-1895). There he referred to the patient establishing a *"false connection"* (p. 302) between the doctor and a figure from the past. Transference reactions were "a compulsion and an *illusion*, which melted away with the conclusion of the analysis" (p. 304; italics added).

In his discussion of the Dora case Freud (1905) elaborated somewhat on the concept and introduced an interesting complexity, related to the major theme of the present paper. Though transferences were generally to be regarded as "facsimiles" which "replace some earlier person by the person of the physician," some were found to be "more ingeniously constructed" and "may even become conscious, by cleverly taking advantage of some real peculiarity in the physician's person or circumstances and attaching themselves to that" (p. 116).

In "The Dynamics of Transference" (1912) Freud states that, "The peculiarities of the transference to the doctor, thanks to which it *exceeds, both in amount and nature, anything that could be justified on sensible or rational grounds* [italics added], are made intelligible if we bear in mind that this transference has precisely been set up not only by the *conscious* anticipatory ideas but also by those that have been held back or are unconscious" (p. 100).

Three years later, in further considering the idea that transference reactions should not be understood as real reactions to what is going on, Freud (1915) discusses as an "argument against the genuineness of this love . . . the fact that it exhibits not a single new feature arising from the present situation, but is entirely composed of repetitions and copies of earlier reactions, including infantile ones. We undertake to prove this by a detailed analysis of the patient's behavior in love" (p. 167).

He then goes on to indicate, however, that in thus proceeding "we have told the patient the truth, but not the whole truth" (p. 168). The argument that transference love is not genuine because it is a repetition is weak, Freud says, because "this is the essential character of every state of being in love. There is no such state which does not reproduce infantile prototypes" (p. 168). Of particular relevance to the arguments to be advanced in the present paper, Freud notes that the difference between transference love and what we call normal love is one of degree, and further adds, "it displays its dependence on the infantile pattern more clearly and is less adaptable and capable of modification; *but that is all and not what is essential*" (p. 168; italics added). Thus Freud indicates here that the processes responsible for the emotional and perceptual phenomena we label as transference are essentially the same as those in all relationships between two people, differing only in degree.

Yet only a year later, in his "Introductory Lectures" Freud (1916) repeats the kinds of statements which were the basis for the prevalent tendency (discussed below) to treat transference reactions as something quite distinct from "realistic" reactions to others. There, discussing transferences, Freud wrote that "we do not believe that the situation in the treatment could justify the development of such feelings. We suspect, on the contrary, that the whole readiness for these feelings is derived from elsewhere, that they were already prepared in the patient, and, upon the opportunity offered by the analytic treatment, are transferred on to the person of the doctor" (p. 442). He goes on to say, discussing negative transferences, that there can be "no doubt that the hostile feelings towards the doctor deserve to be called a 'transference,' since the situation in the treatment quite clearly offers no adequate grounds for their origin" (p. 443). And in discussing how to deal with transferences in treatment, he says, "We overcome the transference by pointing out to the patient that his feelings do not arise from the present situation and do not apply to the person of the doctor, but that they are repeating something that has happened to him earlier" (pp. 443–444).

Increasingly, this latter emphasis became the standard and predominant psychoanalytic view. Transference reactions were regarded as inappropriate and unrealistic. They were not to be viewed as responses to the current reality of the analyst or the relationship he had established with the patient, but had to do with something in the patient's past which was being erroneously transferred to the present context. Despite developments in ego psychology, which have alerted us to the complex interaction between long-established psychic structures and current environmental input, contemporary formulations and definitions continue to treat transferences strictly as unfounded departures from reality. Greenson (1967), for example, states unequivocally that "transference reactions are always inappropriate" (p. 152). And Langs (1973a) says that "to identify a fantasy about, or reaction to, the therapist as primarily transference... we must be able to refute with certainty *any* appropriate level of truth to the patient's unconscious or conscious claim that she correctly perceives the therapist in the manner spelled out through her associations" (p. 415; italics added).

At the same time, however, it has been increasingly recognized that the actual behaviors and attributes of the analyst do play some role in evoking transference reactions. Informally, it is frequently pointed out that transference distortions often have a reality "hook" or "peg" on which they are hung; and, more formally, Langs (1973b) has referred to "reality precipitates" of patients' transference fantasies. Macalpine (1950) has pointed to the particular features of the psychoanalytic situation which foster and call forth regressive transference phenomena. Gill[1] has even suggested — correctly, I think — that unless the analyst acknowledges the role of his own behavior in evoking the patient's reaction, the patient's ability to accept and make use of the analyst's interpretation will be severely limited.

But the continuing emphasis on viewing transference as a distorted or inappropriate reaction, a displacement of something from the past, has required the introduction of a number of other concepts to account for the patient's ability to react to the realities of the treatment situation — to accept, for example, that the analyst's silence is a technical part of the procedure rather than a deprivation aimed specifically at the patient and designed to hurt or punish him, or to recognize after a while that the analyst does value him even if he does not give overt reassurances.[2] Such concepts as the "therapeutic alliance," the "working alliance," and the "real relationship" are designed to address these aspects of what occurs during the course of an analysis (Greenson, 1965, 1971; Greenson and Wexler, 1969; Zetzel, 1956).

Since the same patient who is able to continue to cooperate in the analysis because he recognizes the technical nature of the analyst's silence may also fantasize that the silence is really a sadistic act or a retribution for sins, it is usually

---

[1] Gill makes this point in a monograph in preparation on the analysis of transference. See also Muslin and Gill, 1978.

[2] It is not simply a matter of having more "realistic" reactions. Also relevant is the capacity to react — even if excessively — in coordination with the actual events of the analysis. For example, patients are more likely to have memories and associations regarding fears of abandonment stirred when the analyst's vacation is imminent than at other times.

suggested that the transference and the working alliance may exist, as it were, side by side, proceeding apace as two different features of the therapeutic process. Such a way of conceptualizing does acknowledge the complexity of the patient's manifold levels of reactivity to what is happening, but it also creates serious dangers of reification, in which the transference, the working alliance, and the real relationship are separate and discrete "things."

Schafer (1977), from a slightly different perspective, has also addressed the at once realistic and unrealistic aspects of the patient's reactions to the analyst. He suggests that Freud had not quite reconciled two varying views of transference. "On the one hand, transference love is sheerly repetitive, merely a new edition of the old, artificial and regressive. . .and to be dealt with chiefly by translating it back into its infantile terms. . . .On the other hand, transference is a piece of real life that is adapted to the analytic purpose, a transitional state of a provisional character that is a means to a rational end and as genuine as normal love" (p. 340). He notes that integrating the two perspectives is an important theoretical problem, and suggests that one major obstacle to such integration is the tendency to draw too sharply such distinctions as "past and present, old and new, genuine and artificial, repetition and creation, the subjective world and the objective world" (p. 360), etc. As we shall shortly see, applying the perspective of Piaget's theory to these questions helps to transcend these dichotomies and to foster the integration of the different views of transference.

II

Piaget's concept of schemas, characterized by the two basic functions of assimilation and accommodation, seems particularly useful for understanding the diverse phenomena of transference and other more or less closely related relationship phenomena. Piaget's work in general highlights the active role of the developing individual in shaping and defining his experiential world. Neither as children nor as adults do we respond directly to stimuli per se. We are always *constructing* reality every bit as much as we are perceiving it. This emphasis on the importance of evolving structures which mediate the individual's experience and behavior is quite compatible with the psychoanalytic view. Both theories suggest that man is not stimulus bound, that he does not just reflexly respond to external stimuli but rather selectively organizes and makes sense of new input in terms of the experiences and structures which define who he is.

The concept of transference was an attempt to come to terms with an extreme version of this tendency to experience events in terms of structures and expectations based on earlier experiences. The observations which generated the concept seemed to suggest such an unusually strong role for internal mediating structures that the reality of who the analyst was or what he was doing was virtually ignored by the patient. The tendency to perceive the present in terms of the past became, in certain affectively laden areas of experience, so acute that it seemed to override all evidence of the analyst's actual neutral, investigative role.[3]

The difficulty with the concept of transference as it is usually formulated is that it is so *exclusively* focused on distortion, on the lack of perception of the real characteristics of the analyst. It is for this reason that the observation that the patient does also recognize the analyst as a real person in a professional helping relationship to him must be represented by a completely different concept than that of transference (e.g., therapeutic or working alliance, or real relationship). It is difficult, therefore, to know quite where or how to fit the observations that transference reactions do seem to have a "reality peg." The difficulty, discussed above, in integrating the varying perspectives on transference phenomena is a result of this dichotomous theorizing.

From a Piagetian perspective, one can readily see a continuity between those phenomena usually described as transference and those designated by terms such as therapeutic alliance or real relationship (or indeed, more generally, between transference phenomena and the accurate gauging of other people's motives and characteristics which facilitates effective adaptation). Transference reactions, in Piaget's terms, may be seen simply as reflecting schemas which are characterized by a strong predominance of assimilation over accommodation. The experience with the analyst is assimilated to schemas shaped by earlier experiences, and there is very little accommodation to the actualities of the present situation which make it different from the former experience.

In part, of course, such a way of talking about transference phenomena is simply a translation from one language system to another. But it is a translation that has some important implications, both in terms of pointing inquiry in somewhat different directions and of facilitating the integration of varying views of the phenomena of interest. Perhaps most importantly, once one views these phenomena in terms of schemas, one is confronted with the idea that schemas can never be characterized *only* by assimilation. Assimilation may at times predominate over accommodation, but there can be no such thing "pure" assimilation — or, for that matter, as "pure" accommodation (Piaget, 1952, 1954).

However necessary it may be to describe assimilation and accommodation separately and sequentially, they should be thought of as simultaneous and indissociable as they operate in living cognition. Adaptation is a unitary event, and assimilation and accommodation are merely abstractions from this unitary reality. As in the case of food ingestion, the cognitive incorporation of reality always implies both an assimilation *to* structure and an accommodation *of* structure. To assimilate an event it is necessary at the same time to accommodate to it and vice versa. . . . the balance between the two invariants can and does vary, both from stage to stage and within a given stage. Some cognitive

---

[3] I shall later suggest that this neutrality has probably been exaggerated (see also Wachtel, 1977).

acts show a relative preponderance of the assimilative component; others seem heavily weighted toward accommodation. However, "pure" assimilation and "pure" accommodation nowhere obtain in mental life [Flavell, 1963, pp. 48-49].

Transference, seen in this light, can be understood as the result of a state of affairs in which assimilation is strongly predominant, but is nonetheless not inexorable. Some accommodation to the actual details of what is being experienced, and to how they differ from those of previous experiences assimilated to that schema, must also occur. Since assimilation is strongly predominant, it does not take a particularly close fit to activate the transference schema. So two very different analysts may, in separate analyses with the same patient, be subjectively experienced in very similar fashion by the patient. The schema is easy to activate, and it does not change very readily despite the lack of fit. But since "pure" assimilation cannot occur, it is not completely arbitrary. The range of activating events is wide but nonetheless does have some bounds. The occurrence of transference reactions can seem at times to be almost completely the playing out of an internal dynamic, so striking and deviant can it be from the reality of what is going on between patient and analyst; but it is never completely unrelated to what is transpiring. This is what Gill is calling our attention to in his emphasis on the importance of acknowledging the analyst's role in eliciting such reactions, and this is why a perceptive observer can often find a "reality peg" or "hook" in even the most extreme transference reaction.

This perspective also shows us why Gill's emphasis on the finding of a reality peg in no way undermines the important clinical core of the concept of transference; nor does it ignore Freud's insights about how the continuing effect of the patient's childhood way of experiencing reality is revealed in the transference. If anything, it provides a basis for making the traditional psychoanalytic formulation even more powerful by making it more precise: It points us to ask in all instances of transference precisely what aspect of the analytic situation or of the analyst's behavior or characteristics led to the occurrence of this particular transference reaction at this particular time. Since the predominance of assimilation is emphasized, no loss of the role of intrapsychic factors or the patient's unique individuality is entailed by this particular kind of effort to relate the patient's behavior to events currently going on about him. The schema notion implies responsiveness to environmental cues without positing stimulus-bound, slavish reactivity to environmental events. Thus, one can avoid the pitfall of the false and limiting dichotomy between understanding in terms of intrapsychic factors or "psychical reality" and understanding in terms of the "actual" situation, and appreciation of reality factors can enhance rather than compete with a psychodynamic perspective. An understanding of what particular features of the situation bring forth the transference reaction can in this way be seen as a legitimate part of what is pointed to by psychoanalytic understanding, rather than as the undermining or watering down of that understanding. A broader and firmer base is thus provided for the psychoanalytic view, which also gains increased power and utility.

Further clarity is also provided by this perspective regarding the question, both substantive and definitional, as to whether transference reactions are manifested only in the analytic situation or go on in the patient's daily life as well. From the present vantage point, one can readily see that *all* perceptions and behaviors are mediated by schemas which are the product of past experiences and which attempt to assimilate new input to them — as well as to accommodate to their novel features. Understanding just which aspects of the analytic situation make assimilation more likely or help to highlight the way in which it occurs in the patient's mental functioning (cf. Gill, 1954; Macalpine, 1950; Stone, 1961) has important clinical utility. Such understanding can also shed light on the question of how best to generalize from the data of the analytic session and integrate the formulations such data suggest with those deriving from other sources.

III

Much of the confusion which arises from the traditional way of talking about transference phenomena is a result of the cognitive and perceptual theory which underlay Freud's theorizing. As Schimek (1975) has recently clarified, Freud's view of cognition was at odds with the essential thrust of the rest of his theorizing, which was obviously strongly dynamic, motivational, and developmental in its emphasis. In contrast, his ideas about cognition, Schimek shows, were based on the simple associationism that one finds among many S-R learning theorists who have been particularly opposed to psychoanalysis. This simple associational psychology has been sharply criticized by Piaget (1952), by critics of behavior therapy sympathetic to psychoanalysis (Breger and McGaugh, 1965), and recently even by a number of prominent behavior therapists who have seen the necessity of taking into account man's active role in defining what the effective stimulus is and how it will be experienced (Bandura, 1974; Mahoney, 1974). It would be unfortunate if psychoanalysis, to which such a view is really most alien, were to retain it.

Precisely because psychoanalysis is in its other aspects so strongly a dynamic, motivational psychology, this aspect of its conceptual underpinning went unnoticed for a long time. The stagnant, nonpersonalistic conception of perception and cognition was obscured because dynamic and personal factors were so strongly brought into the theory at the point *after* the percept or cognition was formed. As Schimek points out clearly, Freud assumed a simple, cameralike registration of reality and formation of memory traces which, again, stored "accurate" images of reality that were somewhere retained in their true and original form — but then he concentrated, in the more important and original aspects of his work, on how these images and representations were transformed or distorted under the pressure of drives and defenses. It was *here* that the dynamic features of the theory were evident. So powerful and original were Freud's ideas in this regard, that it was little noticed that the perceptual building blocks for these dynamic processes were conceptualized by him in a far less dynamic fashion than they were by many academic psychologists in the developing area of cognitive psychology.

In conceptualizing transference phenomena, this cameralike view of perception and memory traces led to the formulation that a fully formed, pre-existing set of reactions is plucked from their original context and *displaced* from an early figure to the analyst. As Greenson (1967) puts it, "Transference is the experience of feelings, drives, attitudes, fantasies and defenses toward a person in the present which do not befit that person but are a repetition of reactions originating in regard to significant persons of early childhood, unconsciously displaced onto figures in the present" (p. 155).

Such a formulation leaves little room for any accommodation to the reality of the analyst and the interaction. Something static and pre-existing is simply "displaced," moved from one object to another. The postulation of a somewhat malleable and responsive structure, built up on the basis of prior experience, but shaped as well by new experiences that do not quite fit it, would permit a reconciliation and synthesis of observations of "distortion" in the transference and observations of accurate perceptions and of realistic, cooperative engagement in the analytic process. But a "displacement" formulation, which implicitly requires a fully formed representation to be displaced, ends up leading to the proliferation of separate and discrete postulated quasi-entities — the transference, the therapeutic alliance, the real relationship, etc.

Rather than dichotomizing between perceptions that are accurate and those that are "distorted," the schema notion helps us to see that *all* perception is a selective construction, in some respects a creative act. It is not arbitrary, but it never lacks the personal element. Even the supposedly "objective" observations that underlie scientific theory-building are richly suffused with the idiosyncratic and personal, as modern philosophers of science — Polanyi (e.g., 1958, 1966) in particular — have strongly emphasized. In the perception of other persons, and especially in the perception of their intentions and affective states and qualities, the variability from observer to observer is so great that it is extraordinary that a sharp distinction between "accurate" and "distorted" perceptions could have been retained for so long. To be sure, each patient's experience of the analyst is highly individual and shaped by personal needs and fantasies. But consider the enormous variation in perception of the analyst by those other than his patients — the differences in how he is experienced by his spouse, his children, his teachers, his students, his friends, his rivals. Which is the "undistorted" standard from which the transference distortion varies?

Discussing the phenomena traditionally designated as transference in terms of schemas, assimilation, and accommodation does not present us with such conundrums. It avoids the sharp dichotomizing implicit in most discussions of transference, yet retains the clinical core. To recognize a unity in the modes of apprehending reality that encompasses both the transference perceptions of the analysand and the observations of the physicist or chemist is not to ignore the differences between the two, or to blunt the problematic features of the former. Indeed, it enables us to incorporate the role of the analyst's real properties and behavior not as something which somehow limits, reduces, or "excuses" the patient's highly personal interpretation, but as a way of amplifying it and gaining a finer sense of its determinants.

IV

Ideally, one might expect to see a fairly even balance between assimilation and accommodation, with neither predominating to any great extent. In that case the individual would be able to be responsive to variations in environmental stimulation while maintaining a certain consistency and managing to make sense out of new events on the basis of previous experience. The phenomena discussed in psychoanalytic writings under the rubric of transference suggest an imbalance in this ideal relationship, an excessive degree of assimilation that impedes efforts to adaptively gauge and deal with the events of the present. In attempting to account for how this imbalance comes about, two main lines of explanation seem to have developed.

The traditional psychoanalytic explanation stresses the role of repression and other defenses in creating a structural differentiation which, in effect, prevents accommodation. Accommodation per se is, of course, not referred to in most psychoanalytic accounts. Rather, what is stressed is that defenses relegate certain contents and processes to the id, preventing them from becoming part of the ego. Since it is the ego which is the part of the personality which is in touch with the perceptual world and which has well-developed properties of organization and coherence (Freud, 1923), the result of repressing something is to prevent it from being modified by new perceptual input—i.e., to prevent accommodation. This is why the contents of the id are described as "timeless" and why, for change to occur, they must be integrated into the ego, where they are brought into contact with perceptual input and with the demands for logic and consistency. Freud's famous phrase "Where id was let ego be" reflects the view that only when id contents are integrated into the ego can they be modified to conform to current reality demands. If one employs (and extends) the conceptual scheme of Piaget in this context, it can be seen that one effect of defensive processses is to interfere with the accommodation of certain schemas to new input. When manifested as transference phenomena, these schemas are revealed in their original structure as they are applied inappropriately to stimulus objects which would be more appropriately assimilated by schemas which have undergone a developmental evolution.[4]

When viewed in the light of the Piagetian notions of schema, assimilation, and accommodation, some questions are raised about this traditional account of how transference reactions persist in unchanging form. Such an account seems to contradict Piaget's view that accommodation and assimilation must *both* be present. Now, of course, one need not postulate that transference schemas show *no* accommodation whatever. Even changes in the particular cues which serve to elicit the transference reaction reflect *some* degree of accommodation; and the postulation of at least a certain degree of evolution and change in transferential schemas (even apart from whatever change can be brought about by analysis) is not really inconsistent with the traditional psychoanalytic view. Moreover, transference schemas are ones in which affective and defensive processes — which Piaget did not address — are centrally implicated. It is certainly possible that in this realm Piaget's observations regarding the dual role of accommodation and assimilation might have to be modified. The question of precisely *how* defenses can impede accommodation would seem from this perspective a particularly important one.

A different way of accounting for the apparent lack of accommodation in transferential schemas relies less on structural differentiation and a conception of the id as a zone of nonaccommodation. Instead, one might assume that transference schemas, like any others, will show accommodation in response to clear, disconfirming feedback. In that case a lack of change would imply that the actual feedback is either unclear or not really disconfirming. To understand how this might happen, it is useful to examine some contrasts between our interactions with the physical world and those with other persons.

The schemas which come to represent the physical world to the child, and which form the basis for much of our commerce with the world, do change a great deal as feedback requires accommodation of extant schemas. (At the same time, of course, this input is also assimilated to those evolving schemas.) Whether one is observing an infant learning to grasp an object, a child learning about conservation of various quantities, or an adult learning to drive or ski, one sees a process, varying in speed and efficiency, in which feedback shapes and changes the existing schema. Why then do the schemas associated with transference seem

---

[4] It should be noted that although perception is clearly in the province of the ego in Freud's theorizing, id processes are not completely cut off from perceptual input. Were the separation total, there would be no way to account for the stimulation or stirring of repressed drives, even if such stirring occurred out of awareness. Moreover, the observations referred to earlier regarding the reality hooks or pegs for transference reactions would be difficult, if not impossible, to explain. Rather, what seems implied in the traditional psychoanalytic view is that current perceptual input may serve as a *trigger* for that which is repressed, releasing it to be played out in another repetition, but not serving to shape or modify it (see Wachtel, 1977, pp. 42 ff.).

to change so little despite their apparently poor match to the input with which they are coordinated?

One thing becomes clear if one pursues this line of thought: for the schemas that represent the physical world, disconfirmation is relatively clear and dramatic. The skier or driver who organizes input incorrectly falls or goes off the road; the infant fails to grasp the object he seeks; etc. In the realm of interpersonal and affective events, it is much harder to know one has been in error. Such events are highly ambiguous, and consensus is much harder to obtain. Almost everyone would agree when you have gone off the road. That is not the case as to whether you have incorrectly construed anger in another (or *failed* to construe anger). The ambiguity of affectively laden events and the consequent difficulty in determining when feedback requires accommodation make accommodation far less efficient in this realm and the persistence of old schemas in early form more likely.

It must further be noted that the nature of the affective and interpersonal stimuli which we encounter (and which we must assimilate and accommodate to) is substantially a function of our own actions. This is, of course, true to some extent in the physical realm as well. Driving presents us with different stimuli — and a different adaptive task — if we turn the wheel to the left or to the right. But with physical stimuli the process is not nearly as complex, and the potential input is more predictable and varies over a narrower range. Moreover, it is much easier to know when a change in input is due to our own actions and when it is an independent event — the difference, say, between the variation in direction of a hit tennis ball as a function of one's stroke or as a function of a sudden strong gust of wind.[5]

With affective and interpersonal events, however, the sorting-out process is particularly difficult. It is very easy to be convinced one has experienced what someone "is like" without realizing how much the experienced property (even if accurately gauged in this or other particulars) is a function of one's own actions when with him. Each of us tends to consistently elicit particular aspects of others' personalities, and must of necessity experience the sum of these elicitations as "the way people are." For relatively healthy personalities, the range of elicitations is fairly wide, and variable enough to be roughly representative and in agreement with the experience of others. But it is important to recognize that none of us really lives in an "average expectable environment." We all experience some particular idiosyncratic skewing of the possible kinds of encounters with others. And this skewing is not just accidental but is a function of who we are. One of the ways

[5] The comparison between physical and interpersonal events is, to be sure, not a completely dichotomous one. In the former realm, too, difficulty in sorting out what is due to our own actions and what is fortuitous can be difficult (and indeed can make the difference between a good and a poor tennis player). In earlier times a good deal of confusion existed as to what physical events were a result of our own actions. (What did I do to make the volcano erupt?) Complementarily, there are wide variations in how accurately people can gauge not only what someone is feeling but whether that feeling is primarily a reaction to one's own behavior.

in which consistency in personality is maintained is by the selective choice of
situations and interactants and the elicitation of a particular side of those we do
interact with. Given who we are, we select and create a particular kind of interpersonal world; and given that world, we experience the need to go on as we
have—and thus elicit that same kind of personal world again.[6]

The persistence of transferential schemas, then, with little change over the
years despite what one might expect to be considerable pressure for accommodation, can be seen as due both to the ambiguity of interpersonal-affective feedback
(making it easy not to notice that disconfirmation or lack of fit has occurred) and
to the tendency for events to in fact confirm the seemingly inaccurate perception.
If the world were, in effect, to "hold still" for the developing child rather than to
change with his conceptions of it, *he* would change to accommodate to it. In learning about the physical world, this is in fact what happens, and it happens enough
in the interpersonal world for most of us not to be grossly out of touch. But to a
substantial degree, the world of affective and interpersonal events does not hold
still. *It* accommodates to our initial conceptions and expectations (as they are
translated into actions toward others) and short-circuits our accommodative activities in this realm. Our suspicions, and the actions they motivate, lead others
to in fact be hostile; our expectations of seductive behavior lead to eroticized interactions with others; our submissive behavior, based on past experiences as well
as defensive needs, induces others to expect more compliance from us than they
do from others.

By the time the patient comes to see an analyst, he has probably had hundreds
of such quasi-confirmatory experiences. I call them *quasi*-confirmatory because
the patient's perceptions *are* in one sense anachronistic, even if they may turn out
to be confirmed. For what happens is that the person encounters another who is initially quite ready to relate to him differently than the patient expects, but who
over time responds to the patient's pattern of interaction with an all-too-familiar
complementary pattern. What to the patient feels like an accurate *perception* may
be inaccurate as that but fairly reliable as an implicit *prediction*: this is how the other
will act toward him after some time in his interactive field (cf. Wachtel, 1977).[7]

---

[6] In the academic psychology of personality, the question of consistency of personality across situations is currently a hotly debated topic, and the data of recent research have been construed by some
as casting doubt on psychoanalytic assumptions. The conception of cyclically reconfirming events
described here enables one to reconcile psychoanalytic conceptions with the findings of the
academics, and points to areas in which their research strategy has been insufficient—though also to
ways in which certain psychoanalytic assumptions may perhaps best be modified (cf. Endler and
Magnusson, 1976; Magnusson and Endler, 1977; Mischel, 1968; Wachtel, 1973a, 1973b).

[7] Such patterns are, of course, not inexorable. The *other*, too, has an independent contribution and
is not just putty in the hands of the patient's transferentially motivated actions. But, given the factor
of ambiguity noted, it takes only a very rough approximation to confirmation to permit assimilation.
Also, those people who have had the good fortune to have a sustained disconfirmatory experience
with an important other are not likely to show up as analytic patients.

V

The experience with the analyst is, one hopes, a major and dramatic disconfirmation that can permit accommodation to occur. The analyst facilitates accommodation in at least two ways. First, by interpreting unconscious fantasies (and by establishing the analytic situation, in which such fantasies are likely to become more intense and vivid) he helps the patient to be more aware of both the schemas that guide his transactions with others and the kinds of events that constitute confirmation or disconfirmation of his expectations. Thus he helps reduce the ambiguity which makes for easy assimilation and impedes accommodation. Second, he avoids falling into the complementary behavior pattern which the patient's style of relating has so frequently brought out in others. As I have described in more detail elsewhere (Wachtel, 1977), every neurosis requires "accomplices" to maintain itself, and a good deal of the analyst's effectiveness may be seen as residing in his ability not to become one more accomplice. Both his neutral, analyzing stance and his skill in spotting and interpreting the patient's subtle and unconscious maneuvers enable him to accomplish this task.[8]

It is not necessary, however — nor do I think it is possible — for the analyst to *completely* avoid falling into complementary behavior patterns. Wolf (1966) has described particularly well how such unwitting participation in the neurotic pattern can occur. For therapeutic purposes, it is sufficient that (1) the analyst *for the most part* avoid becoming an accomplice to the neurotic process (in other words, that he do a better job at this than most of the people the patient encounters, even if he is not perfect); and (2) he be able to acknowledge when and how he has acted in a way consistent with the patient's transference expectations and to help the patient understand how such patterns come to be repetitive features of his life.[9] Thus, I would agree with Langs (1973a) that when the therapist's behavior "has been correctly and unconsciously perceived by the patient, his interventions will begin, as a rule, with an acknowledgment of the veracity of the perception and refer to the way it served as a stimulus for the patient's responsive fantasies and conflicts." I would further agree that "once the therapist has acknowledged his contribution to the situation . . . the patient's responsibility for his reactions must be recognized and subsequently analyzed" (p. 430). As a result of the considerations put forth in this paper, however, I would strongly disagree with Langs's contention that this is appropriate only when the therapist's or analyst's behavior has been "erroneous" or that all such occurrences are in fact errors in any useful sense of that term.

[8] The advantages of "neutrality," however, may not outweigh the disadvantages (see Wachtel, 1977).

[9] I do not mean to imply here that this is all there is to the process of therapeutic change. Rather, the sufficiency I am referring to is with regard to the analyst's avoidance of the typical complementary pattern of behavior encountered by the patient. In *this* connection, the considerations described seem to me sufficient.

VI

Transferences can at times seem quite fantastic. All analysts have seen patients express feelings and ideas about them that seem grossly off the mark and appear to have much more to do with their experiences and fantasies with regard to other — usually earlier — figures. In order to understand this common sort of observation from the present point of view, several points must be considered. To begin with, one can recognize that transference reactions are indeed very often grossly inappropriate without drawing a theoretically problematic dichotomy between transferences and realistic perceptions. If one starts from the assumption that all perceptions and actions are mediated by schemas characterized by both assimilation and accommodation, then it would appear that we *label* as transference that portion of the continuum in which assimilation is predominant. Even in this range, however, assimilation is not inexorable, and a particular schema will be called into play only if there is something in the analytic situation that bears some resemblance to the stimuli which have nourished the schema in the past. Since, however, the dimension of similarity can be a highly personal one, there need not be much of an "objective" similarity. Hence the transference reaction may seem completely arbitrary and brought about by "internal" factors. Examination of what in the analytic interaction elicited it at this point, however, is likely to be richly rewarded, for it affords an understanding not only of the kinds of fantasies the patient is capable of, but also of the conditions for their arousal and the particular difficulties to which they may be related.

In considering just how unrealistic transferences really are, it is important to recognize that the transference reactions of most interest and concern to the analyst are those involving substantial anxiety and conflict. In such circumstances the patient is highly motivated not to see clearly what he is experiencing. Rather than communicating directly what his experience is with the analyst, he is likely to express it indirectly and symbolically. For defensive reasons, his statement about some aspect of his experience of the analyst may be so oblique it is unrecognizable. It simply sounds like an outlandish and incorrect perception that must really be about someone else. If the analyst is not prepared to translate the symbolism not only into childhood references but also into references to what is currently transpiring, he can easily be persuaded that the patient's reaction is simply a "displacement" from somewhere else and has little or nothing to do with actual occurrences in the analysis.

Thus, if the patient has the fantasy that the male analyst is a woman in disguise or has no penis, or that he is much older than he really is, or is a notorious and immoral seducer, the analyst, feeling secure that the fantasy as stated is not true, may not recognize how it symbolically reflects the patient's reaction *to some particular action or pattern of acions by the analyst.*[10] Depending on the specific meaning of "woman" to the patient in that context, for example, his fantasy that the analyst is a woman might mean he viewed something about the analyst as weak, or soft, or emotional, or nurturing, or smart, or whatever.

It is, of course, important for the analyst to determine the *meaning* of "woman" to the patient in order to understand fully the transference reaction. But, having done so, it is also important to know *just what he did* that seemed weak, nurturing or whatever to the patient; and this not primarily for the purpose of discovering his "error" and attempting to weed it out in the future by more self-analysis (though either of these aims is certainly at times appropriate), but rather for the purpose of understanding just what kind of input the patient's schemas assimilate in just what way (for not just *any* behavior on the analyst's part would get registered as "weak" or as "woman"). Such understanding enables the analyst to apprehend much more precisely how and when the patient's psychic processes create problems for him, and importantly, the range of situations in which problems and misperceptions are *not* likely to occur. All too often, lack of specificity and failure to understand intrapsychic organizing processes in their situational context interfere with an appreciation of the patient's *strengths*, of where and how intact functioning is manifested (see Wachtel, 1973a, 1980).

In addition, understanding what behavior of the analyst elicited the patient's transference reaction can enable analyst and patient to explore whether other people in the patient's life have tended to behave as the analyst did, and what meaning the patient has given to their behavior. The analytic work can then examine both the kinds of behavior the patient elicits from others and the impact of such behavior as filtered by the patient's complexly motivated perceptual processes, as well as the way in which this in turn leads to behavior on the patient's part which is likely to again elicit similar behavior from others — thus starting the cycle all over again. One then gets a picture of transference reactions as not just the residue of some early experience which is being displaced or replayed, but as part of a *continuous* process that has characterized the patient's life for years yet has only become fully explicated in the experience with the analyst. Such a perspective, I would contend, provides both a more complete understanding of transference reactions and improved possibilities for facilitating therapeutic change (see Wachtel, 1977).

---

[10] It is worth noting, regarding fantasies of this sort and even many others that are less extreme, that frequently the patient, too, recognizes that his thought or feeling is not "realistic." Not all transference reactions imply a loss of distance. Many are *experienced* by the patient as fantasies rather than perceptions (i.e., they are categorized by him as products of his imagination). The distinction between transference perceptions which are registered by the patient as "real" and those registered as "fantasy" (and the range of phenomenological experiences in between) is itself a topic worthy of a whole paper. It is related to the common distinction between transference and the therapeutic alliance but not reducible to it.

VII

The considerations presented here do not pose a challenge to the basic observations of psychoanalysis regarding transference phenomena. I regard as soundly based on clinical observation such central psychoanalytic tenets as that patients regularly show rather substantial distortions in their perceptions of the analyst; that such distortions are personally meaningful and related to the person's history; and that they are in important ways the product of unconscious conflicts and fantasies.

The present perspective does suggest, however, certain modifications in how we *think about* our observations, and points toward the inclusion of a *wider range* of observations than has been typical in psychoanalytic practice. It also suggests that the path between early experiences and later transference reactions may be more *continuous* than has been typically portrayed; that interactions with many figures throughout the person's life tend to occur in such a way as to confirm and perpetuate the modes of perception and reaction that eventually appear as transferences in the patient's analysis; that transference reactions, even when seemingly unrelated to the reality of the analyst or the analysis, are often symbolic expressions of conflicted perceptions of what has actually transpired, or at least of the personal meanings which actual events and characteristics have had for the patient; that accommodation occurs to such a slight degree in some interpersonal and affective schemas both because of the ambiguity in this realm, which makes it harder to know when disconfirmations have occurred, and because of the reactivity of events in this realm to our own actions: what we expect to occur is likely to happen even if it would not have been likely to occur if it were *not* expected (and if we did not act accordingly).

The potential value of conceptualizing transference phenomena as reflecting schemas in which assimilation predominates over accommodation has not been exhausted by the considerations put forth here. It is to be hoped that future efforts will carry this work forward.

Summary

Transference phenomena have traditionally been viewed as reactions which are inappropriate and based on the distorting effect of the patient's past. At the same time, they convey an important reality about the patient's life (or at least his subjective life) and — it has been increasingly recognized — an important reality about the therapeutic interaction as well. Integrating these varying perspectives on transference has created some (not always clearly understood) theoretical difficulties. The present paper has suggested that Piaget's notion of schema, with its stress on the simultaneous processes of assimilation and accommodation, can help to clarify these theoretical issues. By regarding transferences as schemas in which assimilation predominates over accommodation to an inordinate degree, one can incorporate both the traditional clinical knowledge about the distorting effects of transference and an emerging recognition of the importance of what actually transpires between patient and analyst. Such a way of looking at transference both points to and is aided by an understanding of the differences between the ways in which we learn about the physical world and the world of people and emotions. It also leads to a number of other important new questions for psychoanalytic inquiry and new perspectives on psychoanalytic practice.

REFERENCES

Bandura, A. (1974), Behavior theory and the models of man. *Amer. Psychol.*, 29:859–869.

Breger, L. & McGaugh, L. (1965), A critique and reformulation of "learning theory" approaches to psychotherapy and neurosis. *Psychol. Bull.*, 63:338–358.

Breuer, J. & Freud, S. (1893–1895), Studies on hysteria. *Standard Edition*, 2. London: Hogarth Press, 1955.

Endler, N. & Magnusson, D. (1976), *Interactional Psychology and Personality*. New York: Halsted.

Flavell, J. (1963), *The Developmental Psychology of Jean Piaget*. Princeton, N.J.: Van Nostrand.

Freud, S. (1905), Fragments of an analysis of a case of hysteria. *Standard Edition*, 7:3–122. London: Hogarth Press, 1953.

———— (1912), The dynamics of transference. *Standard Edition*, 12:97–108. London: Hogarth Press, 1958.

———— (1915), Observations on transference-love. Further recommendations on the technique of psycho-analysis. *Standard Edition*, 12:157–171. London: Hogarth Press, 1958.

———— (1916), Introductory lectures on psycho-analysis. *Standard Edition*, 16. London: Hogarth Press, 1963.

———— (1923), The ego and the id. *Standard Edition*, 19:3–66. London: Hogarth Press, 1961.

Gill, M. (1954), Psychoanalysis and exploratory psychotherapy. *J. Amer. Psychoanal. Assn.*, 2:771–797.

Greenson, R. (1965), The working alliance and the transference neurosis. *Psychoanal. Quart.*, 34: 155–181.

———— (1967), *The Technique and Practice of Psychoanalysis*. New York: International Universities Press.

———— (1971), The "real" relationship between the patient and the psychoanalyst. In: *The Unconscious Today*, ed. M. Kanzer. New York: International Universities Press, pp. 213–232.

———— & Wexler, M. (1969), The non-transference relationship in the psychoanalytic situation. *Internat. J. Psycho-Anal.*, 50:27–40.

Langs, R. (1973a), The patient's view of the therapist: Reality or fantasy? *Internat. J. Psychoanal. Psychother.*, 2:411–431.

———— (1973b), *The Technique of Psychoanalytic Psychotherapy*. New York: Aronson.

Macalpine, I. (1950), The development of the transference. *Psychoanal. Quart.*, 19:501–539.

Magnusson, D. & Endler, N. (1977), *Personality at the Crossroads: Current Issues in Interactional Psychology*. Hillsdale, N.J.: Erlbaum.

Mahoney, M. (1974), *Cognition and Behavior Modification*. Cambridge, Mass.: Ballinger.

Mischel, W. (1968), *Personality and Assessment*. New York: Wiley.

Muslin, H. & Gill, M. (1978), Transference in the Dora case. *J. Amer. Psychoanal. Assn.*, 26:311–328.

Piaget, J. (1952), *The Origins of Intelligence in Children*. New York: International Universities Press.

———— (1954), *The Construction of Reality in the Child*. New York: Basic Books.

Polanyi, M. (1958), *Personal Knowledge: Towards a Post-Critical Philosophy*. Chicago: University of Chicago Press.

———— (1966), *The Tacit Dimension*. Garden City, N.Y.: Doubleday.

Schafer, R. (1977), The interpretation of transference and the conditions for loving. *J. Amer. Psychoanal. Assn.*, 25:335–362.

Schimek, J. (1975), A critical re-examination of Freud's concept of unconscious mental representation.

Internat. Rev. Psycho-Anal., 2:171–187.

Stone, L. (1961), *The Psychoanalytic Situation*. New York: International Universities Press.

Wachtel, P. (1973a), Psychodynamics, behavior therapy, and the implacable experimenter: An inquiry into the consistency of personality. *J. Abnormal Psychol.*, 82:324–334.

_____ (1973b), On fact, hunch, and stereotype: A reply to Mischel. *J. Abnormal Psychol.*, 82:537–540.

_____ (1977), *Psychoanalysis and Behavior Therapy: Toward an Integration*. New York: Basic Books.

_____ (1980), What should we say to our patients? On the wording of therapists' comments to patients. *Psychotherapy: Theory, Research and Practice*, 17:183–188.

Wolf, E. (1966), Learning theory and psychoanalysis. *Brit. J. Med. Psychol.*, 39:1–10.

Zetzel, E. (1956), Current concepts of transference. *Internat. J. Psycho-Anal.*, 37:369–376.

November, 1979

Characterizing Our Ignorance

ROBERT M. GALATZER-LEVY, M.D.   (Chicago)

Much of the progress of science consists in a recognition of what we do not know, what we cannot know, and the nature of our ignorance.

Major developments in science reflect the recognition of various kinds of ignorance. The development of empiricism implies that there are aspects of reality unknowable through sheer cogitation (e.g., Hume, 1739). Error and imprecision in empirical investigation were seen first as correctable human failings but later understood to be aspects of the empirical method itself (Fisher, 1951). Nevertheless, the term "experimental error" is used to this day for that branch of statistics which studies these phenomena, as a tribute to the hope that these "errors" may be "corrected" (e.g., Topping, 1955). Inherently statistical phenomena (e.g., genetics and entropy) suggest the idea of the inevitable limits of our knowledge; however, the situation seems to be saved by positing that a deeper knowledge of the same phenomenon would restore our potential to predict and understand fully (Bohm, 1957). The idea of what it is possible to know shifts with the development of the special theory of relativity (Einstein, 1931) and the related emergence of positivistic philosophy. Now the idea of an absolute reality whose nature we seek to discover disappears. It is replaced with a reality whose nature lies in the process of observation. However, our "ignorance" or rather recognition of the absence of an absolute reality still permits prediction and a world view in which nature can be known precisely. The new quantum mechanics, as exemplified by the Heisenberg uncertainty principle, takes away even this comfort and demonstrates that real experiments, by their very nature, may have unpredictable outcomes (Heisenberg, 1930). Ignorance of the physical world is an inevitable re-

I would like to express my gratitude to my analytic supervisor, Dr. Leo Sadow, whose remarks on the effects of the analyst's activity on analytic material and the importance of attention to such effects for both clinical and scientific purposes stimulated many of the thoughts discussed here. I would also like to thank Drs. Michael Basch, Jarl Dyrud, John Gedo, Merton Gill, Arnold Goldberg, J. Gordon Maguire, George Pollock, Donald Swanson, David Terman, Marian Tolpin, and Ms. Susan Galatzer-Levy for their comments on various drafts of this paper.

sult of the process of observation and is not neat and orderly. Our inevitable ignorance extends even to mathematics where Gödel (1931) demonstrated that
there are true statements which cannot be proven. Cohen (1966) showed that
these "undecidable propositions" include matters of substantial mathematical interest. An additional class of problems is forever insoluble because it can be proven that the computations necessary are too complex ever to be performed
(Stockmeyer and Chandra, 1979).

This bleak picture has another side. As the fact of our ignorance has been demonstrated, the nature of our ignorance has been elucidated. Empirical methods
were developed; the statistical distribution governing errors of observation
became known; the laws of probabilistic phenomena were elucidated; the special
theory of relativity specified interrelation of observations from differing inertial
frames; Heisenberg discovered the relation of the imprecisions in measured position and momentum; and the unprovable true statements of mathematics were
partially characterized as were the practically uncomputable problems. The
discoveries cited above initiated research into what we could not know. Each of
these contributions has added to a new sort of knowledge which I will call the
characterization of ignorance. Such knowledge has two virtues: it is itself a surprising
piece of information about the world, and it saves us from futile efforts to discover
what is unknowable or meaningless.

Most psychoanalysts have maintained an optimistic view that ignorance
always reflects failings in observational methods. This leads to a fruitful,
meticulous attention to correctable sources of misperception. Countertransference distortion in observation and theory (Stolorow and Atwood, 1979) is closely
scrutinized. Analysts are preoccupied with basic methodological issues to an extent that is unique among scientists. Errors arising from these two sources,
however, are not the object of this paper. (Yet it is pertinent to the idea of the
characterization of ignorance that the recognition and delineation of countertransference phenomena, which were originally seen as interferences in analysis,
lead to powerful ways of knowing about patients [e.g., Racker, 1957; Tower,
1956].)

Freud (1920) believed that the ignorance demonstrated by the analyst's inability to predict reflects a potentially rectifiable lack of knowledge of quantities whose
interactions are manifest in human behavior. Following Waelder's (1963) observation that such ineptitude at prediction occurs only in unusual circumstances, I
have suggested that the failure of prediction does not result from the absence of
knowledge of underlying quantities, but rather from the inherent erratic quality
of behavior in the vicinity of sudden shifts and changes (Galatzer-Levy, 1978).
This unpredictability results from the very structure of such phenomena and has
been extensively studied mathematically under the rubric of "catastrophe theory."
When psychological phenomena are usefully modeled by the methods of
catastrophe theory, we are not only inevitably ignorant (in the sense of being un-

able to predict behavior), but we also have an intimate knowledge of our ignorance. For example, though we are unable to predict the manifest behavior of a highly ambivalent person, we can state that it is subject to sudden shifts between two states with minimal stimuli. It can be demonstrated that there are only seven types of catastrophe in a nonchaotic system. Our pragmatic focus shifts with this realization from a search for more detailed knowledge of quantity to an examination of phenomena to discover which sort of catastrophe is in effect. This is a relatively benign kind of ignorance. It leaves us with a surprising but quite knowable world.

A more disturbing sort of ignorance results from the analyst's inevitable effect on the patient. Such effects have long been familiar in that the analyst provides a preconscious focus for transference and thereby functions in a way that is analogous to day residues in the dream formation. The nature of the patient's unconscious is elucidated by the recognition that transference manifestations are the result of the day residue and the transference from the unconscious. If the analyst can identify both the day residue and the transference manifestation, he is able to determine the remaining term — the patient's unconscious fantasy. The model is roughly that of a beam of light shining through an object — knowing the nature of the initial light and the light that emerges we are able to determine things about the nature of the object through which the light passed.

We know this model does not adequately describe psychoanalysis; analysis affects the patient, it is therapeutic. Even though basic structures may remain relatively unaltered or at least retain their form, the fact of therapeutic change indicates that analytic procedures alter the observed substrate. Even this is not altogether unsatisfactory. Processes which alter what is observed may at least tell us what was there originally (as chemical analysis often does). The most distressing and most likely effect, however, is that the observed is altered by the process of observation in a way that is only partially knowable. This would be analogous to the Heisenberg uncertainty principle in which it is recognized that the process of observation itself changes the observed so that its preobservational states can never be precisely known. In psychoanalysis the situation is further complicated because the analyst himself is changed by the experience of analyzing.

The severity of this situation is somewhat relieved if we attempt to characterize our ignorance. We quickly observe what is essentially tautological but also a matter of clinical experience — stable configurations are relatively unaffected by a variety of things the analyst does, and unstable or absent configurations are grossly affected.[1] The analyst's capacity to affect psychic configurations is a measure of the instability of that configuration. As an illustration, consider again

---

[1] Configurations refer to a set of elements *and* the relations among these elements. The elements may be "psychic structures," "actions," "functions," "thoughts," "fantasies," etc. In particular, this discussion does not depend on a reified notion of psychic structure, nor, for that matter, is it incompatible with such a notion.

a beam of light passing through an object. If this object is extremely stable in its chemical and physical structure, the passage of the beam of light will not affect it in any significant way. In contrast, if this is not the case, the very method of observation will lead to alterations in the structure—say, through bleaching or melting. Further, the nature of these alterations will be determined by properties of the light itself, e.g., wave length and intensity.

The alteration and creation of psychic configuration through observation may be illustrated by depressive affect which many people lack the language to verbalize. If in the course of treatment the analyst provides words for previously unverbalized and unverbalizable experiences, entirely new processes are initiated by this step. However, the analyst's action is necessary for the observation to take place (Anthony, 1975). The process of putting ideas, fantasy, and emotion into words is generally recognized as shaping the experience itself (e.g., Whorf, 1956; Wittgenstein, 1968).

"Inexact interpretation" may also produce new configurations as "the patient seizes upon the inexact interpretation and converts it into a displacement substitute" (Glover, 1931, p. 356). These may be like religious conversion experiences. For example, a borderline patient came across a book on sadism and "recognized" that he was a sadist. He then took on many of the characteristics described in the book.

Observing that a new process is initiated is in itself a datum of the greatest importance. The degree to which the analyst's activity shapes what emerges becomes not merely a warning to avoid the delusional notion that what is thereby discovered existed prior to its discovery, but also provides us with the information of the instability (or absence) of pre-existing structure.

Patients for whom the analytic material is relatively uninfluenced by the analyst's activity have highly stable psychological configurations. Their analysis, modeled on the analyst as day residue, will be slightly influenced by the nature of the analyst and his activity. The difference between compliance and instability may be illustrated by highly stable character defenses. The obsessional patient who complies with the analyst's demand that he be more affective will carefully mimic affective experience in an obsessional way. The analyst quickly realizes that nothing basic has changed and further appreciates the stability of the character defenses.

In contrast, there are groups of patients whose analyses are profoundly influenced by the analyst's activity. It is customary to see the differences in the findings of these analyses as a reflection of the inadequacy of the analyst's theory and technique. The "true" underlying configurations are then debated as if they were independent of the analytic process. From the point of view of this paper we may assume instead that these variations are indications of the instability or absence of these configurations prior to analysis. It is interesting that both major theories attempting to explain middle-range pathology (borderline and narcissistic conditions) (Kernberg, 1975; Kohut, 1971, 1977), though radically divergent on other points, concur in the notion of absent or unstable structure. I hold that skillfully conducted analysis of patients who demonstrate such divergent results indicates that the original structure was unstable or absent but nothing else. Kernberg and Kohut each hold that certain findings of the other are iatrogenic. From the point of view of this paper both authors' statements are correct and in fact this is the most important datum about the patients. The fact that the stable configurations which are ultimately demonstrated depend strongly on the analyst's technique suggests that the configurations are products of the analysis. They did not antedate the analysis. We can conclude that there was a relative absence of stable configurations before the analysis.

Pine (1974) has come to a similar conclusion from his observation that it is difficult to specify the nature of borderline pathology. In his clinical exploration of borderline conditions in childhood he says, "Much of the general use of the concept 'borderline' is somewhat fuzzy, it seems to me, because the phenomena are fuzzy...A geologist may describe the shape of a stone with precision; but not so a meteorologist a cloud. Some of the children who have been described as borderline have the quality of changing shape, a fluidity, which is far less characteristic of the neurotic child. The apparent imprecision in description may itself be a reflection of the imprecision, i.e., the absence of clear structure in some of these children" (p. 350). (Incidentally, this is a beautiful example of using the fact of one's ignorance to gain insight into the situation being studied.)

The viewpoint of this paper implies that there is a spectrum of instability in psychic structure, the details of which are knowable through the study of our ignorance. M. Tolpin (1978, 1979) has demonstrated the crucial ignorance of diagnostic assessment of the degree of structure formation. It is to be hoped that we will not feel obliged to pay undue attention to the search for nonexistent, preexisting configurations in our patients but rather will wonder whether our ignorance reflects the absence or instability of what we are attempting to know.

Summary

Like other sciences, psychoanalysis can benefit by both recognizing and eliminating areas of ignorance. However, the very unknowability of a structure indicates the most important fact about it—its instability.

REFERENCES

Anthony, E. J. (1975), Childhood depression. In: *Depression and Human Existence*, ed. E. J. Anthony & T. Benedek. Boston: Little, Brown, pp. 231–277.
Bohm, O. (1957), *Causality and Chance in Modern Physics*. New York: Van Nostrand.

Cohen, P. (1966), *Set Theory and the Continuum Hypothesis*. New York: W. A. Benjamin.

Einstein, A. (1931), *Relativity: The Special and General Theory*. New York: Crown.

Fisher, R. A. (1951), *The Design of Experiments*. Edinburgh: Oliver & Boyd.

Freud, S. (1920), The psychogenesis of a case of homosexuality in a woman. *Standard Edition*, 18: 145–172. London: Hogarth Press, 1955.

Galatzer-Levy, R. (1978), Qualitative change from quantitative change: Mathematical catastrophe theory in relation to psychoanalysis. *J. Amer. Psychoanal. Assn.*, 26:921–935.

Glover, E. (1931), The therapeutic effects of inexact interpretation. In: *Techniques of Psychoanalysis*. New York: International Universities Press, 1955, pp. 353–366.

Gödel, K. (1931), Über formal unentscheidbare Sätze der Principia Mathematica und verwandte Systeme I. *Math. u. Phys.*, 38:173–198.

Heisenberg, W. (1930), *The Physical Principles of the Quantum Theory*. New York: Dover.

Hume, D. (1739), *A Treatise on the Nature of Human Understanding*, ed. L. A. Selby-Bigge. Oxford: Oxford University Press.

Kernberg, O. (1975), *Borderline Conditions and Pathological Narcissism*. New York: Jason Aronson.

Kohut, H. (1971), *The Analysis of the Self*. New York: International Universities Press.

———— (1977), *The Restoration of the Self*. New York: International Universities Press.

Pine, F. (1974), On the concept "borderline" in children: A clinical essay. *The Psychoanalytic Study of the Child*, 29:341–368. New Haven: Yale University Press.

Racker, H. (1957), The meaning and uses of countertransference. *Psychoanal. Quart.*, 26:303–357.

Stockmeyer, L. & Chandra, A. K. (1979), Intrinsically difficult problems. *Sci. Amer.*, 240:5, 140–154.

Stolorow, R. & Atwood, G. E. (1979), *Faces in a Cloud*. New York: Jason Aronson.

Tolpin, M. (1978), Selfobjects and oedipal objects: A crucial developmental distinction. *The Psychoanalytic Study of the Child*, 33:167–184. New Haven: Yale University Press.

———— (1979), Discussion of "The sustaining object relationship," *This Annual*, 7:219–225. New York: International Universities Press.

Topping, J. (1955), *Errors of Observation*. London: Institute of Physics.

Tower, L. (1956), Countertransference. *J. Amer. Psychoanal. Assn.*, 4:224–255.

Waelder, R. (1963), Psychic determinism and the possibility of prediction. In: *Psychoanalysis: Observation, Theory, Application*. New York: International Universities Press, 1976, pp. 287–306.

Whorf, B. L. (1956), *Language, Thought and Reality*. New York: Wiley; and Cambridge, Mass.: MIT Press.

Wittgenstein, L. (1968), *Philosophical Investigations*. New York: Macmillan.

November, 1979

Action Language and the Psychology of the Self

ROY SCHAFER, Ph.D.   (New York)

I undertook to prepare this short paper on the relation between action language and Heinz Kohut's psychology of the self because I regard his work as perhaps the most significant effort in recent years to introduce a systematic and fresh clinical-theoretical viewpoint in psychoanalysis. I have been very much concerned with problems of theory construction; a large part of my own efforts to develop action language may be understood in the light of that concern (Schafer, 1976, 1978).

I share with Dr. Kohut the interrelated assumptions that guide his effort: that psychoanalysis is an investigation of meaning; that once psychoanalysis is viewed as an empathic-introspective method the place of determinism in psychoanalysis is uncertain at best; that there must be a constant and close relation between theory, technique, and the phenomena of the psychoanalytic situation; and that psychoanalysis is a unique discipline which creates a reality of its own in which things can only appear in a certain way and not in others. These assumptions are at variance with the traditional metapsychological assumptions according to which a natural-science model is accepted as a precommitment and an objectivist stand toward data is accepted without question. According to the objectivist (or empiricist) stand, the data are out there in the world waiting to be encountered; data are discovered rather than constituted within a framework of assumptions and methods.

My interest in problems of theory construction might also be described as an interest in the as-yet-underdeveloped discipline or method of comparative psychoanalysis. In this connection I want to mention that in my own teaching of Freud and Freudian psychoanalysis, I have found it very useful to bring in Kohut's ideas as a way of indicating that theory construction is always a matter of choosing options and then trying as systematically as one can to abide by the rules or conventions inherent in the option chosen. I have also found, both in my

An edited version of a talk presented to members of the Chicago Institute for Psychoanalysis on October 24, 1979.

own analytic case load and in the cases I hear presented by others, a substantial if not predominant incidence of severe narcissistic disorders. All the more reason to study Kohut closely.

Despite my high regard for the theory Kohut presents, I think it can be better than it is, and, owing to its very great interest and clinical relevance, it ought to be better than it is. I know that Kohut has said that his guiding consideration in setting forth his ideas is that clinical utility should be given priority over theoretical elegance. But on his own terms — that is, his argument concerning the essential connectedness of theory and technique and clinical phenomena — one cannot separate elegance and utility so easily. Moreover, his theoretical efforts *are* elegant even in those respects that one would want to reject or modify. I realize, too, that Kohut has presented his ideas as being incompletely developed and has argued for a gradualist approach to the development of psychoanalytic ideas. Still, I think my effort at a critique is not presumptuous. I think of Wittgenstein's conception of philosophy as a therapy, and I think a critique of an unfinished, attempted psychoanalytic theory can be a therapy, too. Such at least is the spirit of the remarks to follow.

I am not going to undertake a complete summary and discussion of all aspects of the ideas Kohut has presented. Nor can I hope to reflect adequately the complexity of his thinking on many issues. Inaccuracy is always a risk of undertaking a critique of a rather large and forceful body of work. I shall merely be offering some general observations and questions; and my principal reference work will be *The Restoration of the Self* (Kohut, 1977).

Although I shall be introducing into my critique certain points of view connected with action language, I shall not be, in a strict sense, engaging in an exercise of comparative psychoanalysis, for action language is not the same kind of theoretical enterprise as Kohut's psychology of the self. Even though the two approaches overlap, action language is more metatheoretical than clinical-theoretical: it has to do with how to formulate theoretical psychoanalytic propositions nonmechanistically far more than it has to do with the content of specific propositions. Further, not every one of the ideas I have set forth in my discussions of action language is necessarily tied to that language, which should be viewed as an attempt to solve some problems of theory construction. In the same way, not every one of Kohut's general ideas is necessarily part of the psychology of the self.

The main idea in action language is to speak of the person rather than the mental apparatus and to formulate propositions in which the person figures as a unitary agent in the sense that there is one person who is the doer of the actions that are being described or interpreted along psychoanalytic lines. Action language represents an effort to avoid the fragmentation of the person into independently acting subagencies, which occurs in Freud's metapsychology (often in extraordinarily anthropomorphic or animistic forms) and which also occurs in the psychology of the self (see below). Consequently, the emphasis in action language is on verbs and adverbs as against the kinds of nouns that set up independent agencies in the mind, whether they be the divisions of the tripartite mental structure, unconscious drives or forces, mechanisms of defense, separate selves, or other such concepts. Action is not simply overt behavior; it takes in thinking and feeling in their various forms.

That people perform many of their most significant and conflictual actions unconsciously and that they resist emphatically or subtly—but in any case persistently—any interpretive efforts to bring to their attention the meaning, significance, or intentionality of what they do unconsciously—these and other psychoanalytic observations are in no way denied or minimized by an action-language approach. Nor is there denial or minimization of chance or necessity or happening as opposed to action. The effort is to capture that distinguishing aspect of psychoanalytic interpretation in which the disclaimed agency of the analysand is brought home to him or her in the course of the work, even when this is done through metaphoric language that is loaded with mechanistic, anthropomorphic, or other nonaction forms of discourse. The way analysands change as they benefit from psychoanalysis seems to me clearly to be in the direction of increased experience of personal agency and of the responsibility of that agency. Here is a point of contact between action language and Kohut's "cohesive self" as a center of initiative, a conception on which much of his theory depends.

Metapsychological Residues in the Psychology of the Self

With this brief account of action language, let us turn to some of the questions I would like to raise and the observations I would like to offer concerning the ideas of Heinz Kohut. The first large question is this: How free from metapsychology is the psychology of the self in its broad sense? That is to say, how experience-close (to use Kohut's term) is the psychology of the self? Action language would say that it should be entirely free from metapsychology in order to be optimally close to personal experience. My impression is that mechanism lingers on. For · example, one finds in Kohut's discussions remnants of psychoeconomic formulations: formulations in terms of forces such as libido or drives; references to discharge patterns; quantitative concepts, as in the "enfeebled self." One also finds the concept of structure being used very much in the metapsychological sense. The drive theory and psychoeconomic formulations of metapsychology are connected with a philosophical a priori which holds that, in order for a person to do anything, there must be some push that makes him or her do it; similarly, the structural concepts are necessary to metapsychology because it is assumed a priori that there has to be something there to guarantee stability and constancy in the face of the fluid and mobile psychic energies and forces with which the mental apparatus has to deal. If one gives up this kind of metapsychological formulation, as

Kohut rightly does in his psychology of the self, we must ask whether he still requires the traditional concept of structure and what sense we can attribute to his use of this concept. Can "structure" now mean anything more than this: that certain kinds of experiences and activity pertaining to self and selfobjects can be characterized as relatively stable and organized over time and in a variety of situations?

Another way in which metapsychology persists in the psychology of the self is in the emphasis on the principle of complementarity. According to this principle, metapsychological concepts do have a necessary place in psychoanalytic theory: they come into their own once a cohesive self has been adequately established so that it figures on both or all sides of conflict. The point is that two incompatible theories may be accepted in order to do two different explanatory jobs. It is, however, not at all clear that complementarity is needed. I say this again on Kohut's own terms: for example, his discussion in *The Restoration of the Self* of the severe or psychopathological Oedipus complex seems to me to show that the psychology of the self in its broad sense is well on its way to becoming a general psychoanalytic theory that requires no complementarity at all. The uses of Freud's structural theory become increasingly trivial in psychoanalytic work when it is organized in terms of the psychology of the self. Recourse to the principle of complementarity is perhaps an expression of the gradualism of theory modification favored by Kohut.

A third respect in which the psychology of the self preserves metapsychology — and this is more subtle — is in the way the self is presented and discussed very much as though it were a drive. Many formulations of the self are cast in the same teleological form as Freud's drive psychology. The self is portrayed as trying to protect itself, develop itself, actualize itself, etc. From the standpoint of action language, it would seem adequate to say that people are characterized by, among other things, their insistent efforts to organize an idea and an experience of a self that is not excessively restricted, inauthentic, contradictory, fragmented, empty, inert, and the like. In action language, the self is an item of experience, and like all experience, it is a construction made by a person. The construction of self experience is, of course, of considerable importance to each person, as it is in each analysis. But it is not necessary to portray the self as dictating its own evolution and fulfillment. Even Kohut cannot do without a distinction between the person and the self, but the person collapses into the self when the self is given drivelike qualities.

I will mention only in passing that some of Kohut's critiques of metapsychology are not a strong as they should be, and thus his argument is less impressive than it could be. I refer especially to his presentation of ego psychology and the technical developments with which it is associated. His presentation — as in his first analysis of Mr. Z (1979) — is quite undeveloped; it does not convey very much of the experiential subtlety of the analysis of intrasystemic relations and of working through that are well-established aspects of the analysis of the ego in the more contemporary version of the traditional Freudian approach.

But there are other shortcomings in this respect. It should also be pointed out that, contrary to Kohut's proposition that the principle of complementarity allows for structural propositions after the formation of a cohesive self, the traditional Freudian metapsychology is concerned with the presence of structural factors and phenomena from the very first: for example, in the differentiation of the id and ego from a primary undifferentiated matrix; and in an extensive history of the ego prior to the time of the resolution of the Oedipus complex. In this view the history of ego functions and their primary or secondary autonomy from drives is always a matter of theoretical and observational concern. Kohut essentially puts the development of ego functions in brackets, apparently taking the position that, as long as the development of the self proceeds normally, the maturation of skills and talents will take place appropriately. This is the same option that Kleinian psychoanalysts have adopted. Now, there is no point in saying that in this respect one approach is theoretically superior to another. Every theory puts certain issues in brackets in order to deal more effectively with other issues. My point is that the distance between sophisticated modern Freudian ego psychology and the psychology of the self is not so great as Kohut's weak account of modern ego psychology would make it appear. By exaggerating this distance, Kohut diminishes the force of his argument. I know, however, how hard it is to develop a new point of view without exaggerating differences.

Residues of Positivism in the Psychology of the Self

I come next to a major problem of consistency in Kohut's formulations. Kohut bases his approach to psychoanalytic theory on a forceful critique of the simple positivism that has traditionally prevailed in psychoanalytic discourse. Yet, he handles this critique inconsistently. First, he presents many of his empirical propositions in an either/or fashion, as though he has forgotten his guiding principle of the inevitably close relation between theory, method, and observation. Thereby he suggests, positivistically, that he has found *the* truth or *the* ultimate reality. This is the same sophisticated thinker who has argued that the "same" phenomena may be looked at in different ways and may of course even be defined or constituted differently according to the general framework within which one is working. These lapses are, however, easily remediable; one would have to argue for the explanatory and technical advantages of one view over the other — and this Kohut does, too, in many places.

The next residue of positivism is more difficult, though still not impossible, to remedy. Kohut seems to suppose that some kind of direct introspection and empathy is possible, whereas on his terms and on the terms of action language intro-

spection and empathy are themselves to be viewed as constructions, as ways of
defining mental activity, and as methods that themselves cannot be theory-free.
The notion of introspection itself implies a certain model of mind in which one
stands outside the mind and observes it; and the model of empathy, as I have
tried to show in a recent paper (Schafer, 1980) on the subject, also requires a notion of the analyst as constructing in the analytic situation both an empathic
analyst and a person to be empathized with, as against engaging in some kind of
direct and theory-free contact and observation. Kohut's ideas are, however,
adaptable to a constructivist view of the matter, in which more would be said
about introspection and empathy as being themselves further analyzable as to
their assumptions, modes, and meanings.

A third form in which the positivist or empiricist assumptions persist in
Kohut's work is in the ideas of separate lines of development and separate sectors
of the personality. It is unclear to what extent Kohut is presenting these as empirical findings, methodologically fruitful assumptions, or, as I would suggest
must be the case, both. My suggestion would follow from Kohut's own basic
assumptions: what is empirically "found" cannot be separated from the methodology that constitutes it. Yet Kohut does seem to argue in places that one just
simply observes separate lines of development and separate sectors, that one just
finds that they do exist. It is not necessary for him to make this unqualified empiricist claim.

Another problem connected with the idea of separate lines of development
deserves more attention than it has been given. It is Kohut's departure from the
guiding assumption in Freud's theory that the mind, however fragmented, is
always developing and functioning as a totality; it is a system of necessarily interrelated parts. In action language this idea is preserved in the concept of the
unitary though conflicted agent. Kohut's claim that different parts of the self show
relative independence of development and functioning reinstates some of the
mechanistic features of metapsychology, which are not essential to psychoanalytic thinking, whereas it seems to discard the notion of the unitary "dynamic"
field, which I would suggest Freud was right in taking as a basic methodological
principle.

A fourth respect in which the positivist or empiricist problem comes up is that of
the possible charge of adultomorphism in Kohut's interpretations of the early
development of the self. Much of his discussion of the development of the self in
early years suggests a degree of capacity for abstract thinking and reflectiveness
on the part of the child that would not be supported by evidence gathered through
direct approaches in developmental psychology. Customarily, adultomorphism
has been presented as a danger to be avoided. And yet it is the case, as is recognized by Kohut along with other analysts who have discussed this issue, that the
model situation of psychoanalysis is the analysis of an adult person who never
does become wholly a child again and who is therefore always mediating in some

adult form the apparent re-experiencing or recovering of childhood experience. I suggest that it is not consistent with the assumed integral relation of theory, method, and phenomena to think that adultomorphism can be altogether avoided. So long as one adheres to the idea that psychoanalysis is a unique method that constructs a unique reality, adultomorphism is part of the order of things. In this respect, adultomorphism, far from being an evil or even a necessary evil, is to be expected in analytic reconstructions. Freud's theory of drives is in its own way adultomorphic, too: on his description, the drives are full of adult cunning and opportunism.

At the same time, however, I would suggest that in Kohut's presentation of the early self there is an underrepresentation of what Freud (1923) called the "bodily ego" (p. 26). Kohut describes this early self as exhibitionistic and grandiose, but he does not seem to give as much prominence to the body-centeredness of this exhibitionism and grandiosity as would seem to be warranted in any type of psychoanalytic framework. His leaving the self relatively empty or abstract in his formal propositions is a legitimate theoretical move, but, perhaps in order to sharpen the differences between his ideas and those attached to drive theory, he does play down the explanatory potential of infantile bodily theories and experience. Consequently, he gives the impression of childhood development and the organization of the self as being slanted more than they need to be in the direction of subjective experience that is self-reflexive in a most sophisticated existential way. Although in one place Kohut says that the picture of infancy held by the analyst shapes his or her view of the analytic process, one might justifiably say that in his playing down of the "bodily ego," the shaping seems to go in the opposite direction instead or as well. That is to say, adult analysands adultomorphically describe early experience in sophisticated terms of the self and the need for a cohesive self, and these descriptions shape Kohut's views of infancy. For psychoanalytic theory, this is not inappropriate; but it does seem unnecessarily narrow.

A fifth issue, closely connected with the one just discussed, centers on the notion of "disintegration products." From the standpoint of action language, one would want to ask to what degree these disintegration products should be viewed as actions—that is, as manifestations of the agency of the analysand, however primitivized. To what extent, in other words, should these disintegration products be identified and discussed as to their meanings? Although Freud approached these phenomena in terms of his theory of drives and the infantile ego, he made the analysis of the meanings of these products central to the psychoanalytic undertaking. In his view, here is where one discovers what each person is made of.

In contrast, Kohut plays down this approach partly on technical grounds. He asserts that it is dangerous to analysands, particularly those with severe narcissistic problems, to try to analyze the disintegration products. But more is involved than technical caution. In his clinical theory, Kohut emphasizes that it is necessary to interpret the disintegration products from the standpoint of what they are reactions to (particularly failures in empathy) rather than from the standpoint of the origin and functions (hence, the meanings) of the reactions themselves. From a theoretical standpoint, this move of Kohut's is legitimate though somewhat confining. It is important to take up this point here, under the heading of the lingering positivism in Kohut's approach, in order to bring out once again the following point: what is known or discoverable or assertable about these disintegration products is very much a function of the methods and presuppositions with which Kohut is approaching the phenomena in question. They are disintegration products within his approach; they are not disintegration products within the more traditional Freudian approach. And from the standpoint of action language, they seem to be analytically describable to varying degrees as actions; that is, they are analyzable to varying degrees, and not always dangerously so. Danger itself is a function of the method being used, though to what extent this is so is not easy to determine. Kohut himself sometimes explains the meaning of one or another of these perverse or otherwise disrupted modes of action that he calls disintegration products; yet he mostly draws the line against doing so on allegedly purely empirical grounds.

The Problem of Multiple Selves

Multiple selves (e.g., the grandiose self as a distinct entity) occupy a prominent place in Kohut's psychology of the self. When multiple selves appear explicitly in a theory, one does, as I mentioned earlier, inevitably end up with mechanistic formulations. Now, instead of forces or psychic structures autonomously having it out with one another, subselves do the same. The problem here is that of importing subjective reports of experience directly into the theory. It seems to be forgotten that these reports of experience are what have to be explained, and that they are not explained by importing them into the theory. Certainly, analysands of all sorts spend a good deal of time describing how their minds or their selves have different parts that are at war with one another or cannot be pulled together or are in different states of repair, etc. But when this (changeable) mode of giving an account of experience is brought into the theory explicitly, one is not far from talking about drives and mechanisms of which the analysand, as reporter or narrator, is a passive witness and for which he or she has no responsibility. There is no way around this problem unless one invokes some central agency: in action language this is called the unitary person, and in metapsychology, especially in Hartmann's work, the agency is referred to as the very high-level organizing functions of the ego (Hartmann, 1947).

The multiple-self theory appears implicitly in discussions of the central concept of self-esteem. In considering the psychology of the self, one wants to know who or what esteems or does not esteem the self. It seems that some sort of superself or superordinate self is implied, in which case one does implicitly get back to some central and unitary agency as a point of reference. The same multiple- or superordinate-self theory is subtly implied when the self is said to work on itself, to try to make up for its deficits, to fill its voids, etc. The problem is also contained in the twofold presentation of the self in the broad sense as both that which initiates action and that which is experienced (itself an action in the scheme of action language). Here Kohut seems to be theoretically at about the point that Freud was in his paper "On Narcissism" (1914), when he was still working with the idea of the ego as both the experienced self and an active agency. Later, in "The Ego and the Id" (1923), Freud tried to deal with this difficulty by introducing his structural psychology. But, from what I have been able to gather, Kohut has not yet faced this issue.

In the terms of action language, all experience is a construction of the person, and the methods as well as the contents of these constructions change in the course of analysis. The self, then, is not what one *has* but what one *does*; and it is what one tells about what one does. It is always a matter of one person giving or implying more or less varying accounts of a self or a number of selves that have varying degrees of contradiction or discoordination. (A self may also be ascribed to one person by another.) Like Freud and other Freudians, Kohut often falls back on speaking of the child or the patient or some other equivalent of the person in order to deal with his, at least implicit, recognition that self experience and self narration are constructions. I do not think his doing so is fundamentally a matter of casual exposition or stylistic variation. Rather, when he does so, Kohut is up against the limits imposed by his use of the self in this dual aspect of initiator of action and content of experience. He needs something outside the self to give a full account of his self psychology. The same problem can be traced throughout the Freudian literature, even in its most highly developed structural forms, as in the superordinate ego functions of Hartmann which I just mentioned.

But Kohut need not be in this difficult position. The kind of psychology of the self that he has attempted to present could retain its various multiple-self features so long as Kohut remained consistently and explicitly aware that this is the way things appear, that these are the kinds of phenomena that one encounters within an approach such as his, based on the assumptions he has adopted. His specific clinical generalizations could still be cast very much in terms of self experience, but the person as agent constructing this experience would have to be consistently implied and would have to be explicitly emphasized in key theoretical propositions.

In conclusion, let me repeat that my "therapy" of Kohut's psychology of the self, which I have undertaken with the help of action language, has not been presented as a complete appreciation or critical review of Kohut's work. I have merely tried to indicate some of the major lines along which inprovements might be made in the theory, especially in those areas where it has been presented in what appears to me an incomplete, inconsistent, confining, or unnecessarily problematic fashion.

REFERENCES

Freud, S. (1914), On narcissism: An introduction. *Standard Edition*, 14:67–102. London: Hogarth Press, 1957.

_____ (1923), The ego and the id. *Standard Edition*, 19:3–66. London: Hogarth Press, 1961.

Hartmann, H. (1947), On rational and irrational action. In: *Psychoanalysis and the Social Sciences*, Vol. 1. New York: International Universities Press, pp. 359–392.

Kohut, H. (1977), *The Restoration of the Self.* New York: International Universities Press.

_____ (1979), The two analyses of Mr. Z. *Internat. J. Psycho-Anal.*, 60:3–27.

Schafer, R. (1976), *A New Language for Psychoanalysis.* New Haven and London: Yale University Press.

_____ (1978), *Language and Insight: The Sigmund Freud Memorial Lectures, 1975–1976, University College, London.* New Haven and London: Yale University Press.

_____ (1980), The psychoanalyst's empathy. Unpublished.

December, 1979

Empiricism, the Transference Neurosis, and the Function of the Selfobject: A Re-examination of the Dynamic Point of View

J. GORDON MAGUIRE, M.D.   (Chicago)

> *This alone would make the use of the analytic method in the analytic situation the via regia to the psychology of personality. In this setting, data do appear which are not, or not easily, accessible to other methods. This asset as to fact finding has, of course, a disadvantage in another respect: an observation an analyst makes may seem entirely credible to another analyst who possesses the necessary experience, an interpretation quite convincing, while the same observation may hardly appear credible, the same interpretation highly improbable or artificial, to one who approaches the field with a different method and in a different setting. For the analyst, one constant angle of his work is the observation of data and of sequences of data, the tentative interpretations (in search of the common element in such sequences), and the checking of his interpretations against the subsequent (and past) material. It is safe to say that the greater part of evidence for the psychoanalytic propositions still lies with this work.*
>
> *Heinz Hartmann (1959)*

As a theoretician noted for his precision and clarity of thought, Hartmann is generally and justifiably acclaimed; he is accorded a position of pre-eminence in the classical literature that is perhaps without peer. It is with this thought that I have selected a passage from his 1959 paper on "Psychoanalysis as a Scientific Theory" to introduce this essentially, though not exclusively, epistemological essay. The quotation, with its specific reference to the primacy of the empirical observational stance in psychoanalysis, also casts in sharp relief a specific epistemological issue devolving from empiricism. Such an issue necessarily involves the reciprocity between operation and conceptualization which must obtain in order to ensure the requisite rigor which characterizes all serious scientific enterprise. Thus, while endorsing the proposition that there is a unitary quality to

93

empiricism — i.e., a single observational stance, as defined in general terms — I would be inclined to suggest that, given the mode of observation, be it instrumentally derived and defined[1] or, as in the case of psychoanalysis, empathically determined, there will be data of one kind or another which, within a given scientific discipline, may prove to be complementary. This was the case in physics, as developments such as Planck's quantum hypothesis, Einstein's theory of relativity, and finally, Bohr's principle of complementarity have shown. It is not surprising, then, given our tradition in psychoanalysis initiated by Freud himself, which draws our metaphors, analogies, and systems of symbolic notation from the physical sciences, to find that our science has a parallel theoretical exercise to contemplate as we consider the relation between our classical metapsychology and the more recently developed psychology of the self.[2]

Such reflections must inevitably take into account the fundamental postulate of self psychology which affirms a separate line of development for narcissism, i.e., the transformation of archaic forms of narcissism into its higher and more mature analogues (e.g., humor, wisdom, empathy, and creativity), rather than into object love (Kohut, 1966, 1968, 1971, 1972, 1977, 1978a). Accordingly, it is the principal thesis of this paper that, given a separate line of development for narcissism, and the positing of a supraordinated position of the self as a practical and theoretical consequence of such a view, a re-examination of the transference neurosis is required, established as it was on the basis of a dynamic, conflict psychology (Freud, 1900, 1912). Thus, assuming a familiarity, if not agreement, with some basic tenets of self psychology on the part of the reader, I am advancing the proposition that the transference neurosis, in addition to its classical status, should be accorded a supraordinated quality and dimension congruent with that of the self. Such a perspective, while neither negating nor depreciating the classical view and derivation of the transference neurosis, would consider it in the same complementary fashion as Kohut (1977) has advanced the concept of the self — i.e., as a content of the psychic apparatus or one of its constituents in a narrower, more limited, and dynamic frame of reference, on the one hand, and as a supraordinated psychic and experiential configuration which includes the dimension of conflict, on the other. It is to this latter perspective that my contribution addresses itself, offering the Oedipus complex quite appropriately as a paradigm of the epistemological issue before us. In the exposition of such a

[1] Though I do not consider a discussion of those philosophies which are of legitimate interest for science (e.g., the Kantian *a priori* categories) as necessarily irrelevant here, I should like to leave to one side the role of cognition and mentation in both the use of instrumentation and the ordering and interpretation of the findings derived from its use. The same argument holds true for empathically derived data.

[2] Other aspects of complementarity in psychoanalysis have been proposed (Edelheit, 1976; Gillaumin, 1976) but appear to concern themselves with issues of psychophysical parallelism rather than with psychoanalytic theory formation per se. In this paper, I propose to restrict myself to those conceptual models that have been derived from "the intellectual working-over of carefully scrutinized observations" (Freud, 1933, p. 159) obtained from the psychoanalytic situation.

theme, I will ascribe particular importance to the selfobject function of the analyst as a recapitulated selfobject parental imago within the transference neurosis. The developmental aspects of this question will be mentioned but not considered in any detail at this time.

However, before I approach such basic questions, I must take up some subsidiary propositions which are not only relevant but must be regarded as essential constituents of my thesis. To begin, I should like to pursue my discussion of empiricism and its relation to "a guiding theory," neither an unfamiliar nor a novel topic in psychoanalysis. Although my comments may enjoy a wider currency than psychoanalysis, their delimited applicability to our science is preferred in spite of my repeated references and analogies to correlative and evolutionary events in other disciplines, most notably physics.

It is, indeed, illusory to speak of empiricism in pure culture, without antecedents which influence methodology and without determinants and referents for the act of observation itself. My earlier allusion to the resonating reciprocity which has always existed in our discipline between guiding theory and discovery was offered in order to highlight this well-known and acknowledged fact. It has been and will continue to be an integral aspect of our psychoanalytic scientific heritage. Consequently, although I believe the empirical observational stance characterizes science generally and psychoanalysis particularly (since we, too, observe in order to explain), our tradition and history both strongly suggest the appropriateness of the concept of "empirical attitude" rather than empiricism per se. Thus, depending upon "empirical attitude," the yield from observation will decidedly differ, and accordingly my quotation from Hartmann which served to introduce the paper is quite germane. Equally pertinent in this context is the metaphor of "bridging the gap," which stresses the heuristic value of that resonance which should obtain between existing bodies of hypotheses and the phenomena constituting that yield from observation. As an example of this epistemological problem, I should like to utilize the question of causality and its relevance to empiricism and conceptualization in psychoanalysis.

Our notion of causality in classical psychoanalysis has been essentially that propounded by Freud. Although a reference to Freud's philosophical, sociocultural, and scientific heritage and its determining influence on his empiricism or "empirical attitude" is appropriate at this juncture, a detailed exposition of such data is unnecessary, familiar as they are to analysts and so well documented as they are by others (Jones, 1953; Gedo and Pollock, 1976). Suffice it to say that Freud's dynamic psychology was a derivative of an empirical attitude consonant with the *Zeitgeist*, scientific and otherwise, of his day, which in turn had many determinants. To the extent that, in his investigation of the inner world, Freud tended to see the same mechanistic, causal relations between forces, events, and even psychological structures at work which presumably existed in the external, physical world — the Cartesian *res extensa* — it may be logically stated that his "mode of observation" or "empirical attitude," not empiricism per se, determined or "caused"[3] what he saw. In a somewhat similar vein, I should like to cite an insight offered by Schafer (1976) in which he suggested that there is a specificity to the transference neurosis insofar as the dyad which is formed in one psychoanalytic situation cannot be replicated in any other since it necessarily involves a confluence of both the analyst's personality in all its dimensions—i.e., the analyst's needs, conflicts, defensive organization, selectivity of response, etc.— with that of the analysand's in all its similar dimensions. The resultant amalgam is specific for that analysis, not to be replicated in any other. Restated analogously and topographically, we might consider the familiar use of Preconscious contents by Unconscious ideas in the formation of dreams.

This aspect of the psychoanalytic dyad was not unknown to Freud, and very early in his work he had occasion to comment on it. Indeed, as my quotations from Freud should demonstrate, it was one of the great inconsistencies in his practical and theoretical approaches to psychology that he could construct a dynamic, conflict psychology existing virtually in isolation, all the while recognizing the importance of the effect of the observer or even the act of simple (analytic) observation in both the observed and the results obtained. Though he never settled the issue, Freud did comment on this phenomenon several times. As Macalpine (1950) observed, Freud first raised the question on the occasion of translating Bernheim's work into German in 1886 when he considered the factor of suggestibility in hypnosis. The same consideration arose in his chapter on psychotherapy in the "Studies on Hysteria" (Breuer and Freud, 1893-1895) and much later in his reference to the interchangeability and interrelationship between analyzability and suggestibility (Freud, 1917).

But it is to his technical papers that I particularly wish to turn in advancing my thesis. In his paper "The Dynamics of Transference," Freud (1912) states:

> if we now follow a pathogenic complex from its representation in the conscious (whether this is an obvious one in the form of a symptom or something quite inconspicuous) to its root in the unconscious, *we shall soon enter a region in which the resistance makes itself felt so clearly that the next association must take account of it and appear as a compromise between its demands and those of the work of investigation. It is at this point, on the evidence of our experience, that transference enters on the scene* [p. 103; italics mine].

Thus, we have here a "deceptively simple" statement indicating that the act of

---

[3] Though it has a pejorative implication in the history of medicine, I should like to propose the concept of iatrogenicity as we consider the epistemological relation between empiricism and causality. Divorced from its deleterious connotation and having undergone an etymological "change of function," the iatrogenic aspect of observation could be considered here in an evocative sense. Such a characterization would appropriately fall within the tradition of psychoanalysis; witness the use and definition of transference neurosis (Freud, 1912) as the central technical and conceptual vehicle which distinguishes psychoanalysis as a therapy (Wallerstein, 1967).

psychoanalytic observation initiates the transference neurosis. The same view is expressed in his paper, "On Beginning the Treatment" (Freud, 1913), where he says:

> It remains the first aim of the treatment to attach him [the patient] to it and to the person of the doctor. To ensure this, nothing need be done but to give him time. If one exhibits a serious interest in him, carefully clears away the resistances that crop up at the beginning and avoids making certain mistakes, he will of himself form such an attachment and link the doctor up with one of the imagos of the people by whom he was accustomed to be treated with affection [pp. 139–140].

This comment, taken with Freud's admonishment on the next page (p. 140) regarding "wild analysis" and premature interventions, implies quite clearly that it is the analyst's specific way of listening which induces the transference. In his paper on "Transference-Love," Freud (1915) casually makes the point that the doctor

> must recognize that the patient's falling in love is induced by the analytic situation and is not to be attributed to the charms of his own person. . . For the patient, however, there are two alternatives: either she must relinquish psychoanalytic treatment or she must accept falling in love with her doctor *as an inescapable fate* [pp. 160–161; italics mine].

On a more theoretical note, Freud, in his insightful footnote (p. 220) of his paper "Two Principles of Mental Functioning" (1911), stated:

> It will rightly be objected that an organization which was a slave to the pleasure principle and neglected the reality of the external world could not maintain itself alive for the shortest time, so that it could not have come into existence at all. The employment of a fiction like this is, however, justified when one considers that the infant—*provided one includes with it the care it receives from its mother*—does almost realize a psychical system of this kind [italics mine].

By extension, we might say that an instinct cannot be considered operationally except in relation to an object, and furthermore in the same vein, within the transference neurosis, the influence of the act of psychoanalytic observation on the induction of that fundamental process within the dyad must be similarly considered. Even in his own analysis, as every analyst has routinely come to know and accept, Freud's investigation of his inner psychological life precipitated a requirement for a transference object in the form of Wilhelm Fliess, without which and without whom, the process of discovery would have been unable to proceed.

The inconsistency to which I alluded earlier, and which I have just cast in sharp relief with my references to Freud's technical and epistemological reflections, should be considered from the perspective of his guiding theory with its analogous determinants and systems of symbolic notation drawn from the physical sciences. Thus, it is not surprising that his empirical attitude led not only to the creation of our dynamic, conflict psychology, as I have previously stated, but also to his derivation and conceptualization of the transference neurosis, especially with its built-in dynamic, conflictual, adversary feature.

As a corollary, it may be added that a different empirical attitude may well have "caused" different findings, produced a different observational yield, and resulted in different explanatory constructs with conflict no longer occupying a position of centrality.[4] One determinant, however, may he isolated and highlighted since it has occupied such a prominent place in Freud's theoretical constructs and analogies: Newtonian mechanics and its implications for the classical view of psychic causality. Force, vectors, and energy concepts, to cite but a few familiar notions, are central, based as they are on classical physics. Consequently, it was possible to omit the key ingredient of the effect of the observer and the act of observation on the observed and the observational yield. The obverse of such an issue is central to quantum theory and the new tradition in physics (Heisenberg, 1958).[5] Correspondingly, it may be said that such an empirical and indeed even conceptual attitude is central to psychoanalysis today; it is forced upon us by an increasing awareness of new psychopathological configurations, or at least by their discovery. Such configurations naturally constitute the constituency of the "widened scope" and legitimately demand our empathic and therapeutic response. In other words, from the study of psychopathology and human psychological suffering come once again the realization of the insufficiencies and limitations of previous discoveries and the explanatory constructs and technical operation devolving from such perspectives.

It would be within this context of empirical attitudes, differing notions regarding causality, and consequently the implication of quite divergent guiding theories that I would like to continue my discussion of observational yield. Though my initial comments focused on the dynamic point of view in psychoanalysis, congruent as it is with the concepts of Newtonian mechanics, it would be equally correct to apply them to a different empirical attitude, one which would be consonant with quantum theory and to which I have so far but briefly referred, but upon which I intend to elaborate. But before I attempt such an exercise—i.e, an elaboration of the empirical attitude in self psychology—some preliminary discussion is in order which might offer an indication that in these two attitudes in psychoanalysis there exists a theme of continuity, evolution, and particularly complementarity. Accordingly, following the view enunciated by

---

[4] The interrelationship between guiding theory and discovery, the transience of theory yet the necessity of it, as well as the hazard of reification of theory, have been commented upon by numerous authors—e.g., Hartmann (1959), Kohut and Seitz (1963), and Goldberg (1976).

[5] In an as-yet-unpublished essay entitled "Physics and Psychoanalysis—An Epistemological Study," Levin (1976) has offered a unique elucidation of the parallels existing in the evolution of physics and its theoretical constructs and that of psychoanalysis with its conceptual models and systems of symbolic notation.

Heisenberg (1958, p. 144) regarding the utilization of the language of classical physics to articulate both the findings and conceptualizations belonging to the quantum sphere, the same principle may obtain in psychoanalysis, as Levin (1976) has suggested. However, due allowance must be made for, as well as attention paid to, the question of differing levels of abstraction and theorizing (Waelder, 1962) which necessarily occur in the "two psychologies" in our discipline. Thus, we have a psychology of conflict standing in complementary relation to a psychology of deficits. In the utilization of the language of conflict psychology, together with its tendency to draw on physics for its system of symbolic notation, we have continuity, evolution, and synthesis.

Although the transference neurosis was derived from and based upon the dynamic point of view, its significance, importance, and position of operational centrality in psychoanalysis are by no means altered by the introduction of this different empirical attitude predicated on principles more closely allied with quantum theory. In other words, that specific dyad which arises in and is created by the psychoanalytic situation — the transference neurosis — is not invalidated and rendered meaningless by such a shift in empirical attitude. When considered in the light of broader psychological and experiential units that both transcend and include the dimension of conflict, the transference neurosis can be regarded as but a breakdown product of that larger unit. Such a view accords the transference neurosis the same supraordinated status which the self in its broader aspect demands (Kohut, 1977). Such a view must include the entire spectrum of the psychosexual scale so that the Oedipus complex, observed in isolation or through its disordered manifestations in the transference neuroses (classical hysterics, obsessionality, etc.), must be considered as much a breakdown product[6] of this larger experiential and conceptual unit known as the self as isolated drive derivatives at the lower end of the scale (manifesting themselves, for example, as perversions, addictions, or other more severe psychopathological configurations). Although such a thesis may evoke some reflection, it can be supported by a further consideration of the transference neurosis from the perspective of the supraordinated position of the self.

In order to achieve such a "quantum jump," I must pick up the thread of my previous discussion regarding that inevitable consequence of positing a separate line of development for narcissism, i.e., the supraordinated position of the self.

---

[6] Although I have stated here that the pathological manifestations of the Oedipus complex and its vicissitudes are clearly to be viewed as breakdown products in much the same fashion as the expression of isolated, pregenital drives or their derivatives, I wish to emphasize as well that I do not consider the Oedipus complex or the drives as being necessarily of and by themselves pathogenic. This opinion, I believe, is in keeping with Kohut's views regarding the positive, enhancing, and self-firming experience which healthy, integrated drive expression offers to a cohesive self and the consolidating quality provided by the oedipal experience. But upon this topic of the growth-promoting aspect of the Oedipus complex as viewed from the perspective of self psychology, I intend to elaborate further at a later point in my paper.

In the process, I must distinguish such a proposition from the dynamic point of view and its consequences—i.e., a drive-defense, tripartite mental-apparatus psychology—and elaborate upon its implications for the transference neurosis in both its conceptual and technical dimensions. Such a task also requires an evolutionary perspective in which the two psychologies of psychoanalysis, classical theory and self psychology, stand in complementary and appositional relation to each other. As a corollary, it is implied that classical theory, together with its system of symbolic notation, must be retained.

I should like to begin with a consideration of what has hitherto been regarded as an important, indeed in the treatment of certain patients essential, but non-transferential feature of the psychoanalytic process. Such an aspect of the analytic situation has been variously described in the literature, with the most common designation until recently being "the therapeutic alliance" or some similar rubric. However, I will cite two examples, although there are many others, where this particular phenomenon has been more precisely studied and where an attempt to conceptualize it has been made. I am referring to Winnicott's (1965) phrase "holding environment" and Modell's (1976) utilization and elaboration of it. Although Winnicott did not regard that particular aspect of the clinical situation as being part of the transference neurosis per se, it would appear that Modell, in detailing his experience with narcissistically damaged or vulnerable patients, edges closer to a de facto recognition of the transference implications of the phenomenon, though admittedly delineating and differentiating it from the classical view of the transference neurosis.

Such inevitable attempts at description and even conceptualization of certain aspects of the psychoanalytic process derive in no small way from our empirical tradition in psychoanalysis which embodies the familiar and reciprocal dimensions of therapy and research. These more recent developments have been spawned directly by the clinical situation and represent an acquisition through work with patients having primarily narcissistic difficulties, whom Freud (1914) considered unanalyzable by virtue of their inability to form a transference neurosis as he had defined and conceptualized it. Nevertheless, "the widened scope" of our discipline has permitted the application and utilization of our classical technical protocol, with or without parameters. Indeed, in some crucial instances, it was "strict adherence" to our protocol and stance of neutrality which yielded new findings (Kohut, 1977, p. 250).

Though such clinical facts could be offered as preliminary evidence in favor of the retention of our classical protocol and particularly the theoretical framework with which it resonates and to a considerable extent upon which it is based, I doubt that such an argument would gain much currency, particularly if offered to those who favor repeal of our classical metapsychology. The debate which swirls about our theory, its underlying assumptions, and its analogous propositions would demand further argumentation than the simple operational and heuristic opinion which I advanced as a nodal point for further elaboration. In other words, an appeal solely to our traditional commitment to empiricism would be adjudged insufficient, as would the implied view that it was precisely the application of our classical technical protocol and its underlying theoretical constructs which permitted the discovery of new depth-psychological configurations, unless such an appeal were offered on the basis of our subscription to a general scientific *Weltanschauung* (Freud, 1933). It was with such a view in mind that I referred earlier to the formulations of Levin (1976) and Kohut (1977) regarding psychological complementarity and the task analogous to that of physics which now confronts psychoanalysis.

Although it is with reluctance that I enter the debate regarding metapsychology in this paper, certain aspects of it are both relevant and unavoidable, given the nature of my subject matter and thesis. Accordingly, I should make passing reference to the now familiar and frequently expressed dissatisfaction in the literature with our classical theory and concurrently suggest that I do not subscribe to the view that the issue has to do with cognitive finesse, an outmoded psychological theory predicated on an equally outmoded physical and physiological theory of a previous century, or with technological advances, particularly in data systems, which might offer better conceptual models. Instead, I wish to put forward the view that the search for new theoretical constructs, new models, or new conceptualizations of the analytic process has less to do with the alleged inadequacies of classical theory to conceptualize adequately the findings or yield from the analytic process obtained within the delimited framework of Freud's empiricism than with our expanded clinical perspective necessitated by the treatment and study of the constituency of the "widened scope" of psychoanalysis — i.e., the narcissistic dimension in both health and pathology. Coincidentally, I wish to propose again that our classical theory must not be abandoned any more than Newtonian mechanics had to be relinquished with the coming of age of quantum theory, and that it should be incorporated into a broader depth-psychological theory, the technical derivative of which should prove more responsive to our equally broadened therapeutic commitments.

In order to explicate such a thesis, I must return to my consideration of an expanded perspective of the transference neurosis, a perspective which is congruent with the supraordinated position of the self, a perspective which places drive psychology in an alternately complementary and alternately subordinate position, and which requires a specific empirical attitude of the analyst quite different from that of the traditional classical posture. It is, nonetheless, consistent with what has been put forward thus far to consider the transference neurosis also from a perspective of psychological complementarity. Viewed from an object-instinctual perspective, one may define and conceptualize the transference neurosis in classical oedipal terms, and viewed from the larger experiential unit of the self, one may define and conceptualize the transference neurosis in such a manner as to include not only the "narcissistic transferences" (or in Kohut's [1977] terms, selfobject transferences) within the framework of the transference neurosis, but also the classical transference neurosis as a constituent or crystallization point of such an expanded configuration. Such a point of view, while requiring further development (cf. below), would posit a complementary and interdependent relation between object-instinctual and narcissistic lines of development. It would also require a re-examination of our notions of resistance and defense as we consider the relation between a conflict psychology (the classical view) and a deficit psychology (the self psychology view). This reconsideration of the dynamic point of view would have particular significance in the handling of so-called narcissistic defenses, for example.[7]

Just as Freud's guiding theories, which were discussed earlier, led him to his great discoveries from which he constructed his dynamic, mental-apparatus psychology, so too our guiding theory and its operational correlate—i.e., Freud's classical theory and its accompanying technical protocol—allowed for the discovery of new evidence and configurations, which now fit neither easily nor comfortably into classical theory. Thus, we have a variety of terms to describe aspects of the psychoanalytic situation and process which more properly deserve precise conceptualization. This view is not reductionistic but is rather an attempt at clarification of those phenomena with which analysts—both serendipitously and empirically—have been familiar for some time. It is for such a reason, accordingly, that I suggested an approach to this conceptual and ultimately epistemological question through the transference neurosis. In other words, the exclusive application of our classical notion of the transference neurosis has limited operational significance and usefulness; indeed, it proves quite cumbersome and unwieldy in the context of conceptualizing these "other" phenomena of the psychoanalytic situation.

At this juncture, as part of my discussion of the relation of the supraordinated position of the self to the transference neurosis (and particularly my thesis advancing an expanded view of the transference neurosis), I must take up the question of the selfobject transference as a global transference-neurotic configuration, of which the classical transference neurosis is but a fragment (or in Kohut's [1977] terminology, a breakdown or disintegration product) of a larger experiential unit, in much the same way as the "transference neuroses" and the Oedipus complex itself when seen in isolation are fragments of a supraordinated self. In so doing, I shall assume once again a familiarity on the part of the reader with the argumentation contained in Kohut's work which describes a separate line of de-

---

[7] Resistance and defense also must have complementary features. In various places in this paper, it would be appropriate to speak of defenses not as being associated with concepts referring to forces in conflict or their adaptational and secondarily autonomous resolution, but rather as psychological needs related to microstructural deficits which compromise or embarrass cohesion. (Cf. Kohut [1977] for a discussion of defensive and compensatory structures.)

velopment for narcissism and leads inevitably to the construct of the supraordinated position of the self. In the same vein, I will not pursue the line of thought well-documented elsewhere (Kohut, 1978a) wherein the parts—i.e., isolated body-mind experiences and functions—are built into the independently established cohesive self, with both then forming an amalgam in which each, while undergoing its own respective transformations and development, reciprocally interacts with the other, can either facilitate or hinder the line of development of the other, and demonstrates considerable interdependence with the other. Thus, a healthy cohesive self facilitates the integration, transformation, and neutralization of the drives within and with itself, whereas a defective self may employ isolated drive derivatives in the interest of maintaining its cohesion through enhanced sensual experience but at the expense of its development and the appropriate transformation and neutralization of the drive itself. Stated in the obverse, which is more likely to be the less frequent finding nowadays, conflicts over drives, at whatever level of libidinal organization, can interfere with the appropriate development, maturation, and evolution of a self in its totality. These statements, however, are only comprehensible if appreciated within the narrower context of a psychology of the self, i.e., a context in which one can say that a cohesive self enhances ego functioning, one aspect of which would be drive neutralization and integration; a context in which one appreciates the self as a content of the mind or psychic apparatus.

But within an expanded context of the self—its supraordinated aspect—the dynamic or conflictual dimension of psychology loses its position of centrality. Although I shall return to this theme shortly when I discuss some of the vicissitudes of the oedipal situation as seen from the perspective of self psychology, I believe it is in keeping with the views recently expressed by Kohut (1977, 1978b) regarding the facilitation or the hindrance of normal conflict situations depending on the response of parental selfobjects. Thus, I am advocating the hegemony of the selfobject function of the parental imagos, which both reflects and is congruent with the supraordinated position of the self in the developing child and later adult. It refers to the primacy of the totality of one's experience, even if at given moments the self—be it in childhood, in epigenetically determined developmental tasks, or in adult activity—may be absorbed in the function and experience of a part. In Kohut's (1977) terms, it refers to the centrality of the self in the psychological universe (p. xv).

A more detailed consideration of the concept of the selfobject is warranted at this juncture in order to explicate further the views which I have just advanced. Traditionally, in psychoanalysis from Freud (1914) on, we have been accustomed to think of a mutual exclusivity existing between libidinal object relations and narcissism. This view has prevailed in psychoanalytic circles in spite of some evidence which tends to contradict this familiar U-tube theory—e.g., the state of being in love, far from depleting the lover, usually enhances his esteem and confidence. Hartmann (1950), while drawing attention in his "deceptively simple" statement that narcissism is the libidinal cathexis of the self and not the ego, nevertheless reaffirmed the antithesis obtaining between self cathexis and object cathexis.

Kohut (1971) conversely emphasized that some of our most intense narcissistic experiences relate to objects: to other people who are either experienced as part of the self or who subtend functions of the self, including the maintenance of its own narcissistic investment. In other words, as viewed by an independent, external observer, one "sees" two people; as experienced within oneself, one experiences but one person, i.e., oneself. To designate such a phenomenon in both its idealizing and mirroring aspects, Kohut (1971) created the term selfobject. The most dramatic aspects of the function of selfobject were found by Kohut (1978a) to occur in patients with narcissistic personality disorders where "the cohesion of the self is [so] insecure, that it depends on a relationship to a selfobject, that it reacts to the faulty empathy of the selfobject (or to analogous disturbances) by breaking up. . . ."

Though the discovery of important psychological configurations has always taken place in the clinical situation through the study of psychopathological constellations, the extrapolation of such discoveries to a more general psychoanalytic psychology has also enjoyed a time-honored tradition. Thus, the developmental function of the selfobject can be considered in terms of its "bridging action" in the evolution and completion of developmental tasks. One must posit, of course, a usual or average expectable environment, i.e., an average expectable behavior and response on the part of the selfobject toward the child. When viewed from the perspective of self psychology and the concept of the selfobject, the conceptualization of the function of behavior and response by the parental imago—not only to narcissistic needs but to object-instinctual drives as well—differs considerably and probably fundamentally from that of the classical position. The issue in a nutshell is "taming" versus "transmuting internalization" (Kohut, 1971). I will elaborate upon this point by way of illustration through a paradigm in which I utilize the Oedipus complex to highlight the developmental and transferential implications.

It would seem that, when Kohut (1977) refers to selfobject transferences as compared to his former designation of narcissistic transferences (Kohut, 1968, 1971), he has not only made more precise the nature of the narcissistic transferences and indicated their genetic roots, but has implied that the transference itself, to be congruent, must have a supraordinated quality and status commensurate with that of the self. Hence, my earlier statement to this effect is appropriately reiterated here. Devolving logically from the foregoing would be both the conceptualization of the therapeutic process in general and that of the focus of all psychoanalytic intervention in particular. Thus, intervention in the psychoanalytic situation, be it interpretative or reconstructive, would be targeted in on the totality of the patient's experience — his self, in other words — and not on isolated parts, drive manifestations, conflict situations, or defensive maneuvers per se. Though, to be sure, an analysis may be conducted with good results in some, if not many, instances on such a restricted basis, the analyst must reognize that in so doing he has addressed himself to a much smaller portion of the patient's psychological experience and has limited the field of observation, as Freud did with the transference neuroses. In keeping with this line of thought would be the technical issue of how one handles, for example, the patient's object-instinctual cathexes directed at the analyst in the transference neurosis. In the classical tradition, the field is limited to those cathexes and/or their defensive superficies and resistances, whereas in a broadened configuration and perspective, the supraordinated aspect of the analyst's selfobject function would predominate with a consequent quite different orientation of his interventions. Most definitely, this proposition does not exclude the dynamic point of view, but rather requires a re-examination of its position of operational primacy. To explicate further this position which I have taken, I will offer the complementary appreciation of the Oedipus complex as a paradigm.

It is unnecessary to offer a restatement of Freud's schema of the oedipal configuration, which has dominated our theory and technique, except to note that in such a dynamic framework with its emphasis on conflict, pathology is seen as the unsuccessful or maladaptive resolution of forces or agencies in conflict within the psychic apparatus as they pertained to energic dispositions directed toward mental representations of objects. Nor is it necessary to review the operational, as opposed to the metapsychological, definition of the transference neurosis (Freud, 1900, 1912) at this time. Within the classical framework, the Oedipus complex is viewed as the great fateful tragedy of mankind, pathogenic in and of itself. Correlated with this notion of its pathogenicity is that of its destruction to ensure psychological growth, developmental completion, and maturity.

A challenge to this pessimistic attitude towards the Oedipus complex has been offered recently by Kohut (1977, 1978b). Suggesting that the failure of empathic resonance to the oedipal child on the part of the parental imagos renders the oedipal drama and its passions pathological, Kohut sees the Oedipus complex as a normal, even joyous,[8] developmental milestone which contributes to psychological consolidation and the self-firming process and experience.

Certainly, it is possible to speak of the growth-promoting aspects of the oedipal situation as conceptualized and managed from the classical perspective. However, fundamental differences exist between the classical and self psychology perspectives, differences which concern not only these growth factors and the pro-

---

[8] The affect and experience of joy, again in keeping with Kohut's views, are "beyond the pleasure principle." Thus, in this context, one can speak of a joyous experience being associated with a sad or painful the event, provided that both the person and event are an integral part of a normal, evolving, and quite fulfilling total life experience!

cesses involved, but even the outcome of development and treatment, respectively. To reiterate, in the classical tradition growth and structure building occur as a consequence of the destruction of the Oedipus complex, whereas in self psychology the growth-promoting factors revolve around the integration, the assimilation, and particularly the transmutation of the experience, not its destruction. Taking the Oedipus complex in its most elementary form, may we not say, following Kohut (1977, p. 250), that the intensification of oedipal guilt, castration anxiety, penis envy, narcissistic mortification over oedipal defeat, etc., though present in both transference neuroses and narcissistic disorders, is indeed a legacy not only of the parental response to a normal psychological developmental milestone and its passions, but more importantly of the failure of the parental imago to participate adequately and appropriately in the child's oedipal experience, thereby giving rise to a pathological constellation rather than a self-firming one?

In the same way, one can speak of the pathological intensification of the oedipal drama in narcissistic disorders as a maladaptive attempt to find a crystallization point, albeit a transference-neurotic type, in order to support cohesion. Further evidence can be evinced for such a view from our experience with narcissistic patients, who very often, after prolonged analysis, begin to discover the oedipal drama, with both its pleasures and its pains, and to regard it as a joyful occasion enhancing self experience rather than instigating illness.

So, too, in the transference neurosis, if the patient's oedipal conflicts, strivings, and passions (projected as they are either directly or defensively onto the analyst) are handled not from the perspective of a narrower, dynamic and conflictual psychological configuration, but rather from one in which the analyst's attitude and response are quite different—i.e., from the perspective of the patient's total self experience. In that case the very nature of the analyst's interventions and the psychological configurations which he will "see" will be quite different from those grasped in the former dynamic framework. It may be argued, then, that the supraordinated position of the self, its corresponding technical protocol and ultimately empirical attitude must prevail. Operationally, this would mean inevitably that the analyst, in approaching the oedipal passions mobilized in the analyses of the transference neuroses, would not respond to the dynamic aspect of the patient's psychological experience but would stress its crucial, vital link to the totality of self experience.

As an example of what I mean, I might offer the analyst's interpretative and reconstructive acknowledgment of the patient's inhibiting oedipal guilt, not from the narrow dynamic, psychopathological dimension which has heretofore characterized our therapeutic attitudes, but rather from the perspective of a selfobject which helps the patient to discover that his oedipal struggles and their affective legacies are not to be eliminated or tamed. As a consequence, the analyst assists the patient in his assessment of his oedipal passions and their unsuccessful resolution, facilitating his gradual awareness that such experience resulted from parental selfobject empathic failure, which in turn led to their inappropriate intensification and neurotic resolution. Lest anyone engage in a *reductio ad absurdum* argument with regard to such a proposition, let me restate it in terms of the selfobject functions of both the parent in development and the analyst in the transference neurosis: these functions are to be found in a direct response, not to such oedipal passions, but rather to their indirect, nonstimulating (in a pathological, seductive sense, if it were stated in the obverse), growth-promoting features. Such a response would allow for the appropriate maturational and transformational process of the oedipal strivings to occur, as would be the case with any drive undergoing the vicissitudes of neutralization and sublimations (cf. lines of development, A. Freud, 1965). I am also suggesting that the area of transferences (Freud, 1933; Kohut and Seitz, 1963) which we know to be inevitable reaches pathological proportions in all patients as a consequence of selfobject failure. Such an assertion would be in keeping with the views Kohut has recently articulated regarding the Oedipus complex and would therefore allow for the statement that the Oedipus complex viewed in isolation must be regarded as a disintegration product, be it within the context of developmental psychology or within the transference neurosis. Oedipal guilt in the analytic situation, to cite an example, is iatrogenic and artifactual, though no less real, if the Oedipus complex is responded to within a narrow dynamic perspective.

Summary

In this paper I have attempted to show that, epistemologically, a significant and decisive implication devolves from the postulation of a supraordinated position of the self when considered from the perspective of the analyst's empirical attitude. I have also suggested that such an attitude will introduce an important bias into both the conceptualization of the transference neurosis and its operational dimension. Proceeding from a consideration of causality as it is conceptualized in psychoanalysis, I have also attempted to indicate the complementary aspects which obtain in our discipline by virtue of there being "two psychologies" for which one must account both theoretically and technically. The parallel with the physical sciences, most notably physics, was offered. The role of the concept of the selfobject was explicated in both its developmental and its transferential aspects.

REFERENCES

Breuer, J. & Freud, S. (1893-1895), Studies on hysteria. *Standard Edition*, 2. London: Hogarth Press, 1955.
Edelheit, H. (1976), Complementarity as a rule in psychological research: Jackson, Freud and the body/mind problem. *Internat J. Psycho-Anal.*, 57:23–30.

Freud, A. (1965), *Normality and Pathology in Childhood. The Writings of Anna Freud*, Vol. 6. New York: International Universities Press, pp. 62–92.

Freud, S. (1900), The interpretation of dreams. *Standard Edition,* 5:509–621. London: Hogarth Press, 1953.

_____ (1911), Formulations on the two principles of mental functioning. *Standard Edition,* 12:213–226. London: Hogarth Press, 1958.

_____ (1912), The dynamics of transference. *Standard Edition,* 12:97–108. London: Hogarth Press, 1958.

_____ (1913), On beginning the treatment. *Standard Edition,* 12:121–144. London: Hogarth Press, 1958.

_____ (1914), On narcissism: An introduction. *Standard Edition,* 14:67–102. London: Hogarth Press, 1957.

_____ (1915), Observations on transference-love. *Standard Edition,* 12:157–171. London: Hogarth Press, 1958.

_____ (1917), Introductory lectures on psycho-analysis. *Standard Edition,* 16:431–447. London: Hogarth Press, 1963.

_____ (1923), The ego and the id. *Standard Edition,* 19:12–66. London: Hogarth Press, 1961.

_____ (1933), New introductory lectures on psycho-analysis. *Standard Edition,* 22:5–182. London: Hogarth Press, 1964.

_____ (1937), Analysis terminable and interminable. *Standard Edition,* 23:209–253. London: Hogarth Press, 1964.

Gedo, J. & Pollock, G., eds. (1976), *Freud: The Fusion of Science and Humanism* [*Psychological Issues*, Monogr. 34/35]. New York: International Universities Press.

Gillaumin, J. (1976), Discussion of the paper by Henry Edelheit. *Internat. J, Psycho-Anal.*, 57:31–36.

Goldberg, A. (1976), Discussion of the paper by C. Hanly and J. Masson. *Internat. J. Psycho-Anal.*, 57:67–70.

Hartmann, H. (1950), The theory of the ego. In: *Essays on Ego Psychology.* New York: International Universities Press, 1964, pp. 113–141.

_____ (1959), Psychoanalysis as a scientific theory. In: *Essays on Ego Psychology.* New York: International Universities Press, 1964, pp. 318–350.

_____, Kris, E., & Loewenstein, R. M. (1953), The function of theory in psychoanalysis. In: *Drives, Affects, Behavior*, ed. R. M. Loewenstein. New York: International Universities Press, pp. 13–37.

Heisenberg, W. (1958), *Physics and Philosophy.* New York: Harper & Row.

Jones, E. (1953), *The Life and Work of Sigmund Freud*, Vol. 1. New York: Basic Books.

Kohut, H. (1959), Introspection, empathy and psychoanalysis. *J. Amer. Psychoanal. Assn.*, 7:459–483.

_____ (1966), Forms and transformations of narcissism. *J. Amer. Psychoanal. Assn.*, 14:243–272.

_____ (1968), The psychoanalytic treatment of narcissistic personality disorders. *The Psychoanalytic Study of the Child*, 23:86–113. New York: International Universities Press.

_____ (1971), *The Analysis of the Self.* New York: International Universities Press.

_____ (1972), Thoughts on narcissism and narcissistic rage. *The Psychoanalytic Study of the Child*, 27:360–400. New York: Quadrangle.

_____ (1973), Psychoanalysis in a troubled world. *This Annual*, 1:3–25. New York: New York Times/Quadrangle.

_____ (1977), *The Restoration of the Self.* New York: International Universities Press.

_____ (1978a), Remarks about the formation of the self. Presented at meeting at the Chicago Institute for Psychoanalysis. Also in: *The Search for the Self: Selected Essays of Heinz Kohut*, ed. P. Ornstein. New York: International Universities Press, 1978, pp. 737–770.

_____ (1978b), Untitled essay. Presented at meeting of the Psychology of the Self Study Group, January 13, 1978.

_____ & Seitz, P. (1963), Concepts and theories of psychoanalysis. In: *Concepts of Personality*, ed. J. M. Wepman & R. Heine. Chicago: Aldine, pp. 113–141.

Levin, D. (1976), Physics and psychoanalysis: An epistemological study (unpublished).

Macalpine, I. (1950), The development of the transference. *Psychoanal. Quart.*, 19:501–539.

Modell, A. (1976), "The holding environment" and the therapeutic action of psychoanalysis. *J. Amer. Psychoanal. Assn.*, 24:285–308.

Schafer, R. (1976), *A New Language for Psychoanalysis.* New Haven and London: Yale University Press.

Waelder, R. (1962), Psychoanalysis, scientific method, and philosophy. *J. Amer. Psychoanal. Assn.*, 10:617–637.
Wallerstein, R. (1967), Reconstruction and mastery in the transference psychosis. *J. Amer. Psychoanal. Assn,*, 15:551–583.
Winnicott, D. W. (1965), *The Maturational Processes and the Facilitating Environment.* New York: International Universities Press.

February, 1979

Authenticity and Narcissism
in the Adult Development of the Self

ROBERT A. NEMIROFF, M.D.   (La Jolla, Calif.)
and CALVIN A. COLARUSSO, M.D.   (La Jolla, Calif.)

A comprehensive psychoanalytic theory of adult development has yet to be formulated. In this paper, which builds on the work of Kernberg (1977), Kohut (1977), Loewald (1960), Saperstein and Gaines (1973), and other authors, we explore the nature of the adult self, concentrating on a description of its emergence and characteristics, and the narcissistic issues that underlie its development. Our ideas follow from an earlier paper entitled "Some Observations and Hypotheses About the Psychoanalytic Theory of Adult Development" (Colarusso and Nemiroff, 1979), in which we defined seven hypotheses about adult development. They are as follows:

1. The nature of the developmental process is basically the same in the adult as in the child.

2. Development in adulthood is an ongoing, dynamic process.

3. Whereas childhood development is focused primarily on the formation of psychic structure, adult development is concerned with the continued evolution of existing psychic structure and with its use.

4. The fundamental developmental issues of childhood continue as central aspects of adult life, but in altered form.

5. The developmental processes in adulthood are influenced by the adult past as well as the childhood past.

6. Development in adulthood, as in childhood, is deeply influenced by the body and by physical change.

7. A central, phase-specific theme of adult development is the normative crisis precipitated by the recognition and acceptance of the finiteness of time and the inevitability of personal death.

In essence, we conceptualized the developmental process as lifelong and as an integral part of the psychology of adulthood, describing the normal adult as being in a state of constant dynamic change and flux, subject to the influences of the external and internal environment, reactive to previous life experiences from the infantile and young-adult past, and engaged in such new phase-specific developmental tasks as response to complex bodily changes and heightened awareness of time limitation and personal death.

Review of Literature Relevant to the Concept of the Self

Kohut (1977), in describing the development of psychoanalysis from an id to an ego psychology, urges the addition of a concept of the self to the concepts of drive and ego. Similarly, Lichtenberg (1975) argues that the complexity of mental life requires full appreciation of *both* its experiential aspects (the psychology of the self) and its structural aspects.

However, the self as a specific concept has been difficult to integrate with existing psychoanalytic theory. Rosenblatt and Thickstun (1977) write:

> The self, which currently occupies a position within standard structural theory somewhere between the ego and limbo, can be conceptualized as the superordinate system, or the organism itself, encompassing *all* of the systems operating within the organism. This concept of the self in the sense of the person must, however, be distinguished from the experiential concept of *self as agent*, which involves awareness of choice, decision, and reflective awareness of oneself as the agent of such choice or decision [p. 300].

Edith Jacobson (1964) was one of the first authors to write systematically about the self concept. In a statement that has considerable descriptive value, she integrates theoretical aspects of structure and self.

> By a realistic image of the self, we mean first of all, one that correctly mirrors the state and the characteristics, the potentialities and abilities, the assets and the limits of our bodily and mental self: on the one hand, of our appearance, our anatomy, and our physiology; on the other hand, of our ego, our conscious and preconscious feelings and thoughts, wishes, impulses, and attitudes toward our physical and mental functions and behavior. Since ego ideal and superego are parts of our mental self, such an image must also correctly depict our preconscious and conscious ideals and scales of value, and the effectiveness — or ineffectiveness — of our self-critical functions. To the extent to which, at any level, the id communicates with the ego or finds access to it, the id, too, is naturally represented in the image of the self [p. 22].

Jacobson quotes Kramer (1955), who states that all of the above will have corresponding psychic representations: i.e., a concept of their sum total will develop "an awareness of the self as a differentiated but organized entity which is separate and distinct from one's environment" (p. 47). Jacobson also finds Lichtenstein's (1961) description of self useful: i.e., "the self has the capacity to remain the same in the midst of change" (p. 193).

Schafer (1973) further differentiates self into: the self-as-agent (the "I"), the self-as-object (the "me"), and the self-as-place (for which no pronoun is specific). He points to the danger of reifying the concept of self with that of the id, the ego, and the superego, as has been done at times in psychoanalytic literature.

Sutherland (1978) integrates the developing psychology of the self with structural theory through the following statement: "It requires no great upheaval to adopt the notion of a supraordinate self-system within the phenomena associated with what we have termed ego, id, superego.... It does offer the great advantage of bringing theory close to practice, and it may well help with our clinical understanding" (p. 116).

Saperstein and Gaines (1973) describe the confusion in the literature over the use of the term "ego" to refer to the personal self. They believe that it is important to use the term "personal self" to refer to those aspects of psychoanalytic psychology that relate to the individual's sense of self as agent, or as "I" — the experiential awareness of his uniqueness, as a creator of meanings..." (p. 415). This concept of self refers to the sense of the person's "I" as a free agent in the creation of what is meaningful to him. They refer the final determination of action to the self and suggest the usefulness of conceiving an overall integrative self system that mediates the interaction of the person as a whole with his environment. We are in essential agreement with Saperstein and Gaines's concepts and will utilize them in our description of the self in adulthood.

NARCISSISM AND THE ADULT SELF

Relatively little has been written about the vicissitudes of narcissism throughout the life cycle. Lichtenberg (1975), in decribing the sense of self in childhood, has organized three lines of development relating narcissistic issues to the sense of self: (1) self images based on body experiences associated with instinctual need satisfactions; (2) self images which emerge as entities having discrete differentiation from objects; (3) self images which by virtue of idealization retain a sense of grandiosity and omnipotence shared with an idealized object. In describing how the self becomes cohesive, Lichtenberg writes of a lifelong "blending and balancing" (p. 470) of the above three clusters of self images.

Eissler (1975) describes a shifting with aging of narcissistic investment in the superego and ego ideal, whereas Kernberg (1977) suggests that normal narcissistic gratifications in adulthood increase self-esteem. Insofar as such gratification is closely linked with object ties, it strengthens them and their inner representations, and in the process shapes the adult self. The self is further modified by narcissistic gratifications that come from work, creativity, and "an internal build-up of the non-personal world of nature and things" (p. 7).

In our effort to describe in detail the relation between the adult self and narcissism the following basic concepts will serve as an introduction. Each individual must engage the narcissistic issues involved in the major developmental tasks of adulthood which are central to the development of the adult self. It is not enough to resolve the narcissistic issues of early life, since adult life brings new ones into play. In adulthood, forces that modify the adult self are fueled by narcissistic gratifications and disappointments. We include in our use of the term "gratifications" the self-nurturing-fantasy process which in the integrated person is closely related to reality and which (like Kohut's "healthy narcissism") often leads to realistic action. We call this process in adulthood *healthy self-aggrandizement*. Narcissistic disappointments affect the evolution of self as differences between idealizations and realities become clear — differences, for example, between one's idealized infant and the real child who emerges with increasing clarity over time.

Narcissistic issues from earlier developmental phases obviously have a major effect on the evolution of the adult self. Just as the adolescent relied upon the accomplishments of latency to bolster him against the regressive and narcissistic injuries of adolescence, so the adult gains sustenance from the accomplishments of young adulthood and from gratifications of that period, such as the attainment of heterosexual intimacy and the definition of career goals.

The Authentic Self

From the Greek *authentikos, authentes,* which refers to "one who does things himself," "genuine," "real" (*Webster's,* 1975) we have chosen the word "authentic" to describe the mature adult self. It is a term that conveys a sense of intrapsychic recognition that one is singular, separated from infantile objects (yet interdependent with new ones), and capable of making and accepting a realistic appraisal of life, including suffering, limitation, and personal death. Authenticity, therefore, includes the capacity to assess and accept what is real in both the external and inner world, regardless of the narcissistic injury involved.

We see the attainment of authenticity as a central dynamic task of adulthood; because of the nature of the adult developmental process only then can it be achieved in its full sense. In the healthy adult, normative intrapsychic conflict involving opposing tendencies to inflate or deflate the self unrealistically is included. Gradually, the narcissistic position of childhood in which the self is characterized as special, unique, and qualitatively superior to all others (Kohut's grandiose self) must be abandoned and replaced by an acceptance of the self as special but not unique, a part of the mosaic of humanity. With the muting of the quest for perfection in the self, in others, and in the external world — a concept rooted in the vicissitudes of the early mother-child dyad — comes gradual acceptance of the self as imperfect.

Authenticity includes the capacity to resist the sometimes powerful middle-age impulse to search regressively for more complete gratification (infantile perfection) as a defense against the loosening of intrapsychic ties to aging or dead infantile objects and to operate alone (psychologically separated from the infantile objects) within the limits imposed by an imperfect, partially gratifying, and sometimes hostile world. Initially a source of narcissistic injury, the recognition of these external and internal limitations gradually becomes a source of pleasure and strength as the self accepts and develops the capacity to act independently within the limitations imposed by the human condition.

Implicit in this process is the *normal mourning* (Pollock, 1961) which accompanies the awareness of the loss of such earlier forms of gratification as the assertive independence and intense sexuality characteristic of adolescence or the opportunities that occur in young adulthood to make basic decisions about the future, such as the choice of spouse, career, or number of children. Mourning for the adolescent and young-adult past (as well as for the early-infantile past) leads to a gradual restructuring of the self with new awareness. "This is what I am." "These are the gratifications available to me."

This process of loss, mourning, working through, and restructuring of the self stimulates an active search for new, age-appropriate mechanisms for obtaining gratification as opposed to pathological forms of mourning, incomplete grief, and depression, which impede further development. We call the psychic process involved in these changes the shedding of naïveté or the *shearing from the self* of the fantasized, idealized, or negatively distorted conceptions of life prevailing in childhood and young adulthood.

An example of authenticity is contained in the following statement from a middle-aged man at the end of his analysis. "I'm not young anymore, but I'm getting old gracefully. I've come to know what's meaningful in life — people. Nothing else matters much. I have my wife, my friends, and my work. None of those things will last forever; neither will I, for that matter — my parents didn't; but for the first time in my life, I see how it all fits together, and I've accepted my lot."

Basic Influences in the Development of the Adult Self

Thus, the evolution of the self in adulthood is a dynamic process, part of the lifelong shaping of identity. We believe that a number of factors, some unique to adult experience, build on the self constructed from earlier phases of life and develop it further. Some of the most important are: (1) the body; (2) object ties; (3) time and death; (4) work, creativity, and mentorship.

THE BODY AND THE ADULT SELF

Freud (1915) placed great emphasis on the influence of the body in mental development. For example, the libido theory and the concept of erogenous zones are cornerstones of psychoanalytic thought. We refer to oral, anal, and phallic zones, circumscribed areas of heightened bodily sensations which are partially responsible for mental development in childhood.

The clearest integration of mind and body is described in the theory of adolescence. The profound biological upheaval at puberty renders much existing mental organization inadequate and requires a reworking of psychic structure with basic alterations in the ego and superego and the formation of new structure as in the ego ideal. A number of years are required to integrate these changes and again achieve a balanced relation between mind and body.

For the adult years we have no defined theory of mind-body relation until the obvious occurrence of the climacteric; then biological variables are again considered (Benedek and Maranon, 1954). Even Erikson (1952), who refers to bodily zones and modes through adolescence, speaks of adulthood only in abstract terms such as intimacy, generativity, and stagnation.

Recent studies on normal biological processes in the mature body and brain may have important implications for psychoanalytic theory because they describe mechanisms that characterize the adult body as being in a state of dynamic flux and change. Although the retrogressive process becomes increasingly powerful with age, it is not the only one at work. Progressive forces, including the possibility of new growth in the mature brain, stimulated in part by mental activity, have been described (Pribram, 1971).

Although there has been some recognition that the aging body can be a source of narcissistic injury (Cath, 1962) and that in some narcissistic patients it can result in regression, we would like to emphasize that the response to aging is a normative experience as well.

Developmentally, we suggest a *normative conflict* between wishes to deny the aging process and acceptance of the loss of a youthful body. The resolution of this conflict leads to a reshaping of the body image and a more realistic appraisal of the middle-aged body, which results in a heightened sense of appreciation of the pleasures the body can continue to provide if cared for properly through appropriate activities.

The narcissistic injury caused by aging seems to stimulate a regressive search for the idealized infantile object and a reawakening of aspects of the grandiose self. In mid-life this may emerge in a search for a new body. Some of our patients, in the grips of this regression, feel an urgent "need" for inappropriate forms of plastic surgery whereas others leave spouses and search out the young who have the "hard body feel." In these individuals the normal mourning for their young adult bodies seems to be short-circuited, and instead of the resolution of a normative developmental conflict they attempt a *magical repair of their body image* through surgery or by attempting to fuse with or borrow the younger body of another person. The re-emergence of aspects of the grandiose self is related to other mid-life developmental issues as well and will be further described.

Another, more pathological form of regression stimulated by changes in the adult body can be the sudden emergence, for the first time, of perversions. To be sure, these may be related to earlier fixations, but we believe that specifically adult factors, i.e., change in mid-life bodily appearance and sexual functioning, can act as powerful traumata to trigger regression and perverse behavior.

For example, for the first time in his life, a professional man in his forties found himself drawn to public bathrooms where he tried to catch sight of other men's penises. This progressed to a homosexual entrapment situation and arrest by the police. When he came to treatment, it emerged that he had been devastated by the loss of his youthful appearance and several episodes of impotence. His behavior was felt to be an attempt to deny normal aging and achieve a magical repair of the sense of inadequacy he felt in his body as a whole and his penis in particular.

In another instance, a middle-aged woman came to treatment because of a strong urge to have a number of sexual partners other than her husband. She said it was "like being in an ice-cream store; if you can have five flavors, why only one?" She verbalized a sense of urgency and a feeling that time was running out on her. Among a number of issues, a definite theme about bodily changes emerged. She had decided to have a hysterectomy but was terrified that loss of the capacity to have children would leave her "dried up, empty, and old." In a fusion of pregenital and genital imagery via a penis-breast equation, she expressed the wish that through her affairs the vital, nurturing penises of young men would arrest her aging process and be her fountain of youth.

These responses to the narcissistic injury involved in bodily changes during adulthood can be summarized as follows:

1. *Repairing the body* — actual attempts, including plastic surgery, dyeing hair, makeup, exercise, and diet.

2. *Finding a new body* — the search for a new body or parts of a new body through new hetero- or homosexual object choices.

3. *Substituting for the body* — the re-emergence of the need for transitional-like objects; adult toys and hobbies such as bigger and better boats, houses, horses, cars, and art collections used symbolically to compensate for and repair the changes in the body.

With the resolution and working through of the crises involved in adult bodily change comes a sense of narcissistic pleasure that includes a more conflict-free sexuality. This continued developmental enhancement of sexual pleasure and intimacy becomes an important expression of the integrated, authentic adult self.

It is also clear that the aging process causes a loosening of ties to infantile and childhood objects. By the thirties this becomes a significant influence on the normative adult separation-individuation process.

Self and Object in Adult Development

In a recent series of panels (Panel, 1973a, 1973b, 1973c) the theme of the separation-individuation processes was extended beyond childhood and adolescence through maturity and senescence. Margaret Mahler (Panel, 1973c) concluded that

> the entire life cycle constitutes a more or less successful process of distancing from and introjection of the lost symbiotic mother, an external longing for the actual or fantasied "ideal state of self," with the latter standing for a symbiotic fusion with the "all-good" symbiotic mother who was at one time part of the self in a blissful state of well-being [p. 138].

Thus the quest for a clearer self-object differentiation ends only with biologic death. In addition to the major separation-individuation phases that occur in childhood and in adolescence, we observe significant *new* separation-individuation phenomena in the young-adult period (the third separation-individuation phase). As Erikson (1952) has stated, each adult phase can be understood to have its intrinsic tasks and goals, leading to sharper self-object differentiation and new aspects of identity. What follows is our description of the effect of object relations in adulthood on the emerging adult self.

Shifting Object Ties

The healthy adult recognizes, as part of his authentic appraisal of reality, the central position of change in his life. A basic aspect of that change is the shifting nature of object ties as early-adult involvement with love objects, children, parents, colleagues, and friends is in constant realignment. These ties continue to shift in middle age — when healthy marriages deepen in significance (while others break up on the shoals of middle-age developmental issues); parents die or become dependent; children grow and leave; and friends increase in importance and in some instances leave or die themselves. As opposed to the priorities of old age, and in some respects of childhood as well, the task of middle age is to sort out, categorize, set priorities among one's object ties and achieve a balance between internal pressures and external demands.

We feel that these shifting object ties are major stimuli which influence change in the self through an increasing process of psychological individuation. A major function of the authentic self is the continual reassessment of who one *is* in relationships with objects as compared with who one *was*. The shearing from the self of preoccupations with objects from the distant or recent past and the forging of an identity based on current object ties (some gratifying and some painful) are the essential ways the self is altered by changing object relations. For example, one *was* a child, an adolescent, a new spouse, an apprentice in work, whereas one *is* the supporter of aging parents, a parent/grandparent, and an accomplished worker.

THE RECOGNITION OF INTERDEPENDENCE

As a direct result of such adult individuation, individuals attain more significant appreciation of a basic characteristic of all human relations—interdependence.

Examples are the parents' need of the child as a confirmation of their sexuality and as a vehicle for generativity, the reliance of spouses on each other in the sharing of joy and inevitable illness and suffering, and the reversal of roles between adult child and aging parent. Deeper understanding of this dimension of human need leads to a developing capacity for nonambivalent gratitude. In the authentic adult—unlike the child who takes, uses, controls, and dominates—further muting of the grandiose position of infancy propels the self toward deeper, more meaningful object ties. To illustrate we will focus on some of the most important ties—to parents, spouse, and children.

Parents and Grandparents

The separation-individuation process is enhanced in adult life by relationships to aging parents and grandparents. The increasing dependence and eventual death of parents undermines the naïve, infantile internal representations of the parent as omnipotent and increases recognition of the vulnerability and impermanence of the self as well as the parents. In other words, the part of the self that was narcissistically linked with internalized infantile representations is partially shed, and a less protected, more authentic self emerges. *Infantile narcissism loses its power to defend against the awareness of death and the passage of time.* We agree with Kernberg (1977) who describes changes in attitudes toward death as occurring throughout the life cycle. Jacques (1965) has specifically described death awareness and anxiety during mid-life crises, but that narrow time frame must be extended to cover the entirety of the process.

Narcissistic issues also play a part in grandparent-parent-child interactions. Grandparental idealization of grandchildren serves several defensive purposes: (a) a denial of the passage of time and of old age; (b) a chance for magical repair of one's own life through the grandchild; (c) a denial of the imperfection of the self by selective identification with particular qualities in the grandchild. The healthy grandparent sees the falseness of this idealization but still enjoys the continuity that multigenerational object ties bring. The recognition that death is final enhances appreciation of the limited ways in which the self lives on through one's creations and offspring.

The aging and death of parents, as well as adult experiences such as sexual intimacy, parenthood, and the achievement of a work identity, also change the self by producing basic alterations in the internal configuration of fundamental developmental issues of childhood which, in our opinion, continue as central aspects of adult life in altered form.

As an illustration, consider the changes that occur in adult oedipal representations of the parents. As an adult one has actually become a parent, and in a sense "won" the oedipal victory by obtaining (in altered form) many of the prerogatives wished for in childhood. The victory is hollow, however, since infantile gratifications cannot be enjoyed by an adult in relation to aging or dead parents.

A normal developmental task of middle-age, then, is to deal with this oedipal "victory" as the infantile wishes to dominate and replace the parents are realized. It is our contention that the aging and death of parents force a reworking of oedipal constructions just as surely as the biological upheaval of puberty. The alteration in the adult self is profound; the infantile oedipal construction is inappropriate to the *present*, and changes in internal representations of the parent further shear from the self the image of parent as competitor or lover and lead to a heightened sense of individuation and authenticity.

The Spouse

The adult separation-individuation process is centered in the marital relationship. A developmental task of late adolescence related to adult separation-individuation is the psychic configuration of an *idealized, fantasized mate*. Rooted in the original preoedipal and oedipal objects and the adolescent's experience with sexuality, this construction develops within the late adolescent self as the result of the loosening of ties to the infantile objects during the second individuation. With its formation, much of the narcissistic investment in the infantile objects is transferred to the idealized-mate representation.

After marriage a continuous shearing process goes on within the self as the idealized-spouse representation is replaced by the real-spouse representation. As the real spouse is reacted to and internalized, a second narcissistic transfer takes place from the idealized-spouse representation, which is diminished in importance but never completely abandoned, to the real-spouse representation. We suggest that this process occurs in every healthy marriage and is conflictual because the abandonment of the aggrandized infantile images is painful and the real-spouse representation never approximates the idealized state. This gradual narcissistic transfer is a prerequisite for the emergence of mature love. Table 1 presents the above issues schematically.

With the approach of middle age, the aging of the spouse and the self becomes the major narcissistic issue in marriage. The narcissistic injury felt in the aging process, particularly in relation to sexual activity, is compensated by the intimacy of the now long-standing, gratifying object tie. Normative conflict is experienced between the pull toward youthful bodies and sexual reassurance, and the realistic

TABLE 1
NARCISSISTIC TRANSFERS IN MARRIAGE

Early to middle	1. Separation from infantile objects	3. Conflict between idealized-spouse and real-spouse representations
Later	2. Narcissistic transfer and construction of idealized-spouse representation	4. Gradual abandonment of idealized spouse — more acceptance of real-spouse representation

acceptance of the adult body and internal body image. The development of the real-spouse representation greatly facilitates this process by enhancing real intimacy, thus diminishing the narcissistic sting of aging.

In summary, there are two major narcissistic developmental aspects of normal marriage: in early marriage, the gradual acceptance of the real spouse over the idealized fantasied spouse; and in middle age, the acceptance of aging in the spouse. Both of these tasks are gradual, painful processes which, if mastered, facilitate the continued growth of the marriage and of the self.

We suggest that the appreciation and valuing of long-standing object ties in contrast to the more youthful gratifications of the body and nonrelationship sex are characteristic of the adult self and a major mid-life developmental step.

Children

Child-rearing is another potential source of adult narcissistic gratification and disappointment. The vicissitudes of raising children powerfully affect feelings of self-worth and competence.

Parental gratifications and disappointments exist at each stage of a child's development, but probably peak in his or her adolescence. The healthy parent is gratified by the push toward independence of the adolescent instead of experiencing the loss of the child exclusively as a drain or injury. Through identification the parents attempt to re-experience and work through the disappointments and ambitions of their own youth, though they never quite realize either aim.

Clinical illustration: A patient in analysis ruminated about his adolescent son's continual victories over him in sports. Finally, he expressed it this way. "Actually, when I think about it, I feel some pleasure, too. In some ways he's like an extension of me, and even though I can't do it anymore the way I used to, he can, and he is my son."

Narcissistic experiences are a major influence on the quality of interaction with the child. The healthy parent, for the most part, quietly accepts the child's emerging identity and does not excessively "puff up or put down" his offspring. Rather, there is a steering toward a realistic self which is part of the parenting process. Basically, via parental empathy, self and object are continually clarified and differentiated. However, when children are related to as extensions of the self, the tendency to inflate unrealistically (puff up) or deflate (put down) the child can be more pronounced.

Clinical illustrations: (1) An analytic patient remembered her mother's excessive praise when she swept off the porch of her grandparents' house as a child. The patient in adult life expressed resentment over the mother's overblown and unrealistic praise: "I now see that she didn't do me any favor by puffing me up like that; nobody else thought I was so great." This patient is now putting a grandiose or overvalued self in perspective.

(2) Deflation of self by a parent was experienced by another analytic patient who remembered days of adolescent glory on the football field. This patient's mother continually responded to athletic triumphs with statements like, "Don't let it go to your head," "It's really not that important," or "The important thing is you didn't get hurt." For the adolescent the athletic victories were a once-in-a-lifetime experience, and their devaluation led to puzzling and confusing feelings.

There is an analogy between the parent's tendencies to overvalue or deflate as opposed to quiet, even acceptance of the child's emerging self, and the narcissistic interaction between analyst and analysand, for this relationship is essentially similar to the healthy parenting situation—with a quiet, even acceptance of the changing analysand self as the analysis proceeds. Interpretations and silence can be experienced as critical deflations (putting down), whereas excessive verbalizations and supportive praise can be felt as overvaluations (puffing up).

Further Acceptance of Sexual Differences

The adult experiences with objects affect not only separation-individuation but other aspects of development as well. One example which also illustrates the elaboration of infantile sexual themes in adulthood is the further acceptance of the female as different, not castrated.

The attempt to understand and accept the sexual differences between male and female is a lifelong process beginning in the preoedipal years and continuing throughout childhood. However, full acceptance and integration are only possible in adulthood when major adult experiences add new elements to the understanding of sexuality. Among them are:

1. Repeated experiences with sexuality and intimacy, which lead to a thorough understanding of the *complementary differences* of the male and female genitalia through repeated sexual exploration of one's body and the genitals of the opposite sex. We have analyzed several neurotic men and women, most married and sexually active, in whom the capacity to look at, touch, and think about the partner's

genitals was markedly inhibited. The gradual resolution of infantile and adult sexual problems allowed us to observe the developmental working through and integration of the complementary nature of the male and female genitals in subsequent sexual experience.

2. The experience of parenthood, which sharpens the sexual identity of a man and woman by underscoring their interdependence for procreation, thus validating the necessity for male and female genitalia. The experience of having produced an offspring with genitalia of either sex is another stimulus to this reworking and integration because of the powerful narcissistic investment of the parents in their child.

3. The experience of parenthood, which forces a reworking of earlier sexual attitudes as infantile sexuality is again engaged at each developmental phase but from the vantage point of adult experience.

4. The changing relations to aging and dying parents, which produce a further resolution of the oedipal aspects of sexuality.

5. The change in the nature of sexual capacity produced by physical aging (such as menopause), which produces a normative crisis that forces the subject of sexuality upon the self. The healthy adult who shares this experience with a loving sexual partner has the opportunity to integrate further aspects of sexual identity from a new perspective.

Time, Narcissism, and Authenticity

The normal middle-aged person is keenly aware of the limited amount of time in the future compared to that in the past. In our opinion, this recognition of time limitation and the inevitability of personal death are major psychic organizers in adulthood. The forces that produce this dynamic focus are many (for the most part fairly obvious) — the aging of the body, the death of parents and friends, the growth of children into adolescence and adulthood, and the intrapsychic lengthening of the personal past and loosening of ties to the infantile introjects.

We are not talking of a psychopathological preoccupation with aging and death, but of the internal and external temporal stimuli that constantly impinge on the healthy adult self, directing attention to thoughts of time. The engagement of this developmental task of assessing one's past, present, and future is, we feel, a little-understood, *positive* developmental stimulus which has a profound effect on the adult self.

Time sense in childhood and adolescence brings gratification because time seems to exist in unlimited quantity. But by mid-life, with the recognition that there is not enough time left to gratify all wishes or redo unhappy aspects of the past, time sense becomes a source of pain.

For the healthy person this realization is cushioned by what we call the "gratifying past"—those memories of childhood and young adulthood that are pleasurable and give the sense that one's life has been "good enough." This *middle-age nostalgia* is clearly a defense against the growing awareness of time limitation, the narcissistic aspect of which is suggested by the warm feelings of timelessness, continuity, fusion, and gratification which accompany the nostalgia. Here is the repository (within the adult self) of the relationship with the good-enough mother, added to by positive experiences beyond childhood.

By contrast, Kernberg (1977) writes about the narcissistic patient's reaction to the past: "In short, the narcissistic patient has no gratitude for what he has received in the past, experiences the past as lost, wishes he had it now, and is painfully resentful that it is no longer available to him. At the bottom, the narcissistic patient is painfully envious of himself in the past, having had what he no longer has now" (p. 9).

A hallmark of the mature, authentic self is the ability to appraise the personal past with a minimum of denial and distortion. For example, one analytic patient in his forties recognized with clarity for the first time that he grew up in a relatively poor area with limited cultural advantages. This recognition had been hidden because it caused narcissistic injury to the childhood self. But from the vantage point of mid-life, this aspect of his past was a relatively unimportant observation which could be more easily accepted.

Life in the *present* strongly influences attitudes toward the past and future. Mid-life is that phase in which a long sequence of development and maturation has either produced considerable internal integrity and external achievement—both bringing narcissistic gratification—or fragmentation and frustration—bringing pain. There is a strong sense of the present in mid-life, an urgency to live life fully *now*.

If the present is sufficiently gratifying, one is more likely to experience nostalgia about the past; if not, there is envy of the past, as Kernberg describes. For the healthy person the past may be viewed as follows: "Yes, I could have done it differently, even better; but things are pretty good now." The narcissistic sting (envy) is minimized.

There is a normative urge to retain aspects of the youthful self well into mid-life. The 50-year-old says, "I *feel* the same as I always did." This is both a denial of the aging process, a reflection of the regressive pull to the time of youthful fusion with infantile objects; and a reflection of the integrity of the adult self resulting from the lifelong process of separation-individuation and the continual reworking of narcissistic issues.

The *future* is also viewed in a new way and gains a special connection with the present and the past through the experience of *continuity*. Relationships and activities that have existed over a period of time connect the personal past with the present and future. Continuity becomes an organizing factor by connecting memories from different ages.

In the normal situation the authentic sense of the past and present allows the healthy individual to view the *future* with a sense of anticipation and a minimal amount of fear, for it holds the prospect of even greater gratification as well as the inevitable end of all gratification through death. Among the anticipated pleasures are genuine intimacy, increased wisdom and understanding, and continued involvement in the world in new and productive ways.

Creativity, Mentorship, and Authenticity

Work, which has been studied only superficially, is a central, definitive activity of adulthood and an important component of the self. To illustrate the effect of work on the development of the self, we have chosen to focus on creativity and mentor relationships.

Mentors are objects from whom young adults develop *new* aspects of identity. For many individuals, a close relationship with a mentor is a crucial factor in the choice of a career — be it as scientist, housewife, waiter, factory worker, or analyst. Although in part based on infantile identifications, this adult process is not a replication of the parent-child relationship. Whereas early identifications help build psychic structure, later identifications such as the mentor relationship add *specificity* to the adult personality, in this instance through the establishment of a work identity. The process seems to involve three phases: (1) an initial fusion with the mentor; (2) a middle phase in which through partial identifications aspects of the mentor are internalized within the self; and finally (3) a separation leading to further individuation.

As far as we know, the role of narcissistic issues in mentor relationships has not been described. In the initial phase the mentor is idealized, as the internal representation of the mentor is invested with narcissism displaced from the self. The sense of fusion during the middle phase brings great pleasure but leaves the self vulnerable since the mentor's approval is necessary for a sense of well-being. The self is dramatically changed as the desired attributes of the mentor are incorporated, usually with intense pleasure. During the separation process considerable pain is experienced, but after a period of working through, the self emerges stronger, enhanced by the greater sense of individuation and capability.

Becoming a mentor is an important task of mid-life which involves the painful realization of eventual replacement by another. Aggression toward the usurper must be sublimated into a facilitating, teaching role. Conflictual feelings extend not only to the younger person but to his work as well. The capacity to facilitate what is new and valuable *independent of its creator* must be developed. In the maturing person, particularly the mentor, this does not occur easily because of the wish to devalue that which was not created by the self, particularly when time or other limitations reduce the capacity of the self to create.

The Return of the Grandiose Self

In response to the basic issues of mid-life discussed in this paper, we hypothesize a re-emergence of aspects of infantile narcissism which we will describe by utilizing Kohut's concept of the grandiose self. These phenomena seem normative to us, as we have seen manifestations in well-integrated patients, friends, and colleagues. The return of the grandiose self reflects a futile but understandable search for reunion with the omnipotent preoedipal mother who magically controls all aspects of life.

We observe four steps in this process:

Step 1: The return of the aspects of the grandiose self as a narcissistic defense against the aging process, including the growing awareness of time limitation and personal death.

Step 2: A conflict between the regressive wish to accept the return of the grandiose self and the mature urges to reject or reintegrate it within the adult self. Narcissistic injury is involved as aspects of the grandiose self are tempered.

Step 3: Mourning for the loss of the narcissistic gratification promised by the return of the grandiose self.

Step 4: Alteration of the adult self with enhanced individuation and identity formation.

There are a number of possible responses to the return of the grandiose self. Some individuals react to the realization of impermanence by attempting to increase their control over current life situations. Although accompanied by increased reflectiveness and a clearer appraisal of the relation between the self and the environment, the need to maintain the status quo may stifle creativity and positive change. In others the conflict may stimulate growth and creativity. The tempering of infantile grandiosity causes a reappraisal of the value of object ties and the importance of current activities and may lead to major reorganizations in marriage and friendships as well as career and living environment.

When grandiose tendencies are pronounced, the conflict may result in pathological activity such as stagnation, regression, and self-limitation. Persons of either sex may abandon adult responsibilities and long-standing object ties. This behavior is in conflict with the awareness on the part of the authentic self of its interdependence with significant objects such as family, parents, friends, and colleagues. The very depth of these object ties may precipitate the inappropriate flight since the self cannot avoid the growing awareness of the passage of time demonstrated by changes such as the death of parents, the aging of spouse and friends, and the maturation and growth of children. The ability to remain invested in important objects in the face of the narcissistic injury involved in their change is a central developmental task of mid-life.

Clinical illustration: A woman in the midst of a mid-life crisis that was precipitated by the possibility of a malignancy and sterilization expressed strong feelings to have an open marriage, i.e., free and ready accessibility to multiple sexual partners before it was too late. "I don't think I'm going to live past 45." She wished to move into a small apartment separate from her husband and children. There, in splendid isolation, her needs would be paramount. For example, she imagined sitting alone in restaurants, having the exclusive attention of waiters.

In this woman the potential threat to her sexuality and increased fear of dying caused the strong emergence of preoedipal wishes, and a desire to fuse with the preoedipal mother (in the guise of splendid self-sufficiency and penis-breast lovers). However, another set of factors also played a part; she expressed fears of turning into the angry, bitchy menopausal mother of her adolescence, "the old woman." In this, the patient clearly illustrates Greenson's (1950) useful clinical concept of a struggle against identification since, in response to aging, she felt she was becoming the parent of her adolescence. The defense against becoming like "that bitchy menopausal woman" was to have affairs in a symbolic attempt to deny the aging process. Of course, this is a multiply determined situation with oedipal meanings as well. This patient not only illustrates a regressive response to the return of the grandiose self but a failure to integrate adult oedipal phenomena. A full understanding of the relation between these adult themes and the genetic antecedents of childhood provided the patient and analyst with meaningful insight.

We have constructed a schematic model of these mid-life processes.

TABLE 2

MID-LIFE MODEL OF REWORKING OF ADULT SELF

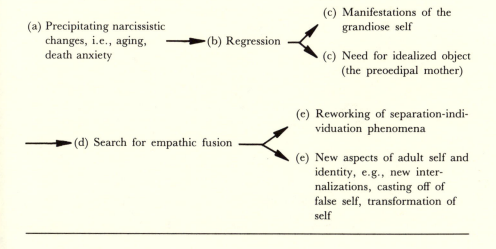

Summary

The purpose of this paper is to define characteristics of the self in adulthood and to describe the factors which shape it, with a particular focus on the role of narcissism in that process. These concepts are based on the hypothesis that the self in adulthood is not a static finished product but is in a state of dynamic flux and change within the developmental continuum.

We chose the term "authentic" to characterize the mature adult self because it describes the capacity to accept what is genuine within the self and the outer world regardless of the narcissistic injury involved. The capacity for authenticity emerges out of the developmental experiences of childhood and adulthood. Among the most important influences in adulthood are narcissistic issues related to (1) the aging body; (2) object ties, particularly to spouse, children, and parents; (3) middle-age time sense; and (4) the vicissitudes of work and creativity.

We conceptualized a normal narcissistic regression precipitated by the confrontation with these developmental tasks of mid-life leading to a re-emergence of aspects of infantile narcissism, which we characterized by using Kohut's concept of the grandiose self. The reworking and eventual integration of aspects of the infantile grandiosity are seen by us as an integral part of normal development in mid-life.

The study of the adult and elaboration of a psychoanalytic theory of normality for the adult years brings with it the exciting prospect of increasing the value of psychoanalysis as a general theory of human behavior for the entire life cycle.

REFERENCES

Benedek, T. & Maranon, G. (1954), The climacteric. In: *Men: The Variety and Meaning of the Sexual Experience*, ed. A. M. Karch. New York: Dell.

Blos, P. (1967), The second individuation process of adolescence. *The Psychoanalytic Study of the Child*, 22:162–186. New York: International Universities Press.

Cath, S. (1962), Grief, loss and emotional disorders in the aging process in geriatric psychiatry. In: *Geriatric Psychiatry*, ed. M. A. Berezin & S. H. Cath. New York: International Universities Press, pp. 21–72.

Colarusso, C. & Nemiroff, R. (1979), Some observations and hypotheses about the psychoanalytic theory of adult development. *Internat. J. Psycho-Anal.*, 60:59–71.

Eissler, K. (1975), On possible effects of aging on the practice of psychoanalysis: An essay. *J. Phila. Assn. for Psychoanal.*, 2:138–152.

Erikson, E. (1952), Eight ages of man. In: *Childhood and Society*. New York: Norton, 1963, pp. 247–274.

Freud, S. (1915), Instincts and their vicissitudes. *Standard Edition*, 14:109–140. London: Hogarth Press, 1957.

Greenson, R. R. (1950), The struggle against identification. *J. Amer. Psychoanal. Assn.*, 2:200–217.

Jacques, E. (1965), Death and the mid-life crisis. *Internat. J. Psycho-Anal.*, 46:602–614.

Jacobson, E. (1964), *The Self and the Object World*. New York: International Universities Press.

Kernberg, O. (1977), Pathological narcissism in middle age. Paper read at the Annual Meeting of the American Psychoanalytic Association, Quebec, Canada, May, 1977.

Kohut, H. (1977), *The Restoration of the Self*. New York: International Universities Press.

Kramer, P. (1955), On discovering one's identity: A case report. *The Psychoanalytic Study of the Child*, 10:47–74. New York: International Universities Press.

Lichtenberg, J. D. (1975), The development of the sense of self. *J. Amer. Psychoanal. Assn.*, 23:453–484.

Lichtenstein, H. (1961), Identity and sexuality: A study of their interrelationships. *J. Amer. Psycho-anal. Assn.*, 9:179–260.

Loewald, H. (1960), On the nature of therapeutic action of psychoanalysis. *Internat. J. Psycho-Anal.*, 41:54–79.

Panel (1973a), The experience of separation-individuation through the course of life: Adolescence and maturity, reported by J. Marcus. *J. Amer. Psychoanal. Assn.*, 21:155–167.

Panel (1973b), The experience of separation-individuation through the course of life: Maturity, senescence, and sociological complications, reported by I. Steinschein. *J. Amer. Psychoanal. Assn.*, 21:633–645.

Panel (1973c), The experience of separation-individuation in infancy and its reverberations through the course of life: Infancy and childhood, reported by M. Winestine. *J. Amer. Psychoanal. Assn.*, 21:135–154.

Pollock, G. H. (1961), Mourning and adaptation. *Internat. J. Psycho-Anal.*, 42:341–361.

Pribram, K. (1971), Neural modifiability and memory mechanisms. In: *Languages of the Brain: Experimental Paradoxes and Principles in Neuropsychology*. Englewood Cliffs, N.J.: Prentice-Hall, pp. 26–47.

Rosenblatt, A. & Thickstun, J. (1977), *Modern Psychoanalytic Concepts in a General Psychology* [*Psychological Issues*, Monogr. 42/43]. New York: International Universities Press.

Saperstein, J. L. & Gaines, J. (1973), Metapsychological considerations of the self. *Internat. J. Psycho-Anal.*, 54:415–424.

Schafer, R. (1973), Concepts of self and identity, and of separation-individuation in adolescence. *Psychoanal. Quart.*, 42:42–59.

Sutherland, J. (1978), The self and personal object relations (unpublished).

Webster's New World Dictionary of the American Language (1975), Cleveland and New York: Collins World.

February, 1979

"The Prisoner of Time": Some Developmental Aspects of Time Perception in Infancy, Sensory Isolation, and Old Age

SANFORD GIFFORD, M.D. (Boston)

In a previous presentation (Gifford, 1971) I attempted to connect: (1) the origins of time perception in the newborn infant's adaptation to the biological rhythms of the 24-hour solar day; (2) experiences from everyday life in which the subjective duration of time is altered, including both the periodic need for escape from the 24-hour cycle (in weekends, vacations, drug states, and religious ecstasies) and reactions to imposed changes in temporal landmarks (jet lag, solitary confinement, and experimental sensory deprivation); and (3) the familiar phenomenon of time passing more quickly with advancing age, which is usually associated with a gradual reduction in the variety and intensity of sensory stimulation. The apparent acceleration in the passage of time in old age was interpreted as a possible adaptation to the involutional phase of life. Changes in time perception with aging were discussed in terms of Freud's theory of the life and death instincts, in which both a predetermined life span and the aging process itself were considered innate tendencies of the biological organism.

For various reasons my efforts to connect these phenomena were not successful, and the manuscript remained an incomplete and unpublished torso. As a collection of raw data from widely scattered fields, uneven in quality and reliability, it represented little attempt at assimilation and synthesis. I came to see that the theoretical connections between infancy and old age were encumbered by two areas of investigation that are not necessarily related to the subjective duration of time. The experimental studies on the perception of short time intervals may well be unrelated to the sense of time over longer periods (days, years, even decades). The possible metabolic, hormonal, and physiologic substrates for time

---

This paper was originally presented at the Annual Meeting of the American Psychiatric Association, Atlanta, Ga., May 12, 1978.

perception are in fact controversial, difficult to interpret, and not really necessary for the formulation of an overall theory. Finally, the metapsychological implications of Freud's developmental concepts, two theories from different periods of his life, have not been clearly worked out. One theory comprises Freud's concepts of early ego development, which Hartmann and Rapaport drew out of references to "congenital ego-variations" in Freud's (1937) very last papers. These were synthesized by Rapaport (1960) in a fully developmental theory of epigenesis, in which innate maturational tendencies present at birth predetermine the unfolding of later phases of personality development. The other theory is Freud's earlier biological concept of the life and death instincts, which had been rejected or ignored by most analysts. The dual-instinct theory of sex and aggression was integrated into an overall developmental theory of personality, but the death instinct was overlooked (Gifford, 1969). Yet Freud's death instinct was in itself a developmental concept, postulating a predetermined life span with a predetermined end point in death, mediated by an innate lifelong tendency to reduce stimulation to its lowest possible level.

My present aim is to clarify this formulation of time perception early and late in life, by eliminating a consideration of short time intervals and most speculations about biochemical substrates of time experience. I have not reviewed a substantial analytic literature on clinical aspects of time perception, as in the work of Hartocollis (1972) and others, although Pollock (1971) deals with more general aspects of time. Metapsychological considerations will depend on the usefulness of an all-encompassing epigenetic concept of growth and development, including both the ascending and the declining slope of the life cycle. Most present-day biologists and psychoanalysts have little difficulty in accepting the ascending "progressive" slope, from birth to maturity, as a predetermined sequence of developmental phases. They accept its stages, marked by increasing degrees of differentiation and complexity, as orderly phenomena serving some adaptive purpose or possessing some evolutionary survival value. But in considering the downward slope, from the postreproductive years to death, many biological gerontologists, like Comfort (1964) and Strehler (1962), regard senescence as biologically meaningless, without adaptive or survival value. Comfort, for example, calls tissue aging a mere "running out of program" in the chromosomes, as successive cell divisions become less accurate, and he questions the "crypto-vitalistic" undertones in "the idea of senescence as the 'fated' or 'destined' end of the organism" (1964, p. 269). And among analysts, even Erikson (1959), who has virtually created a life-cycle theory by extending Freud's developmental concepts, has carried his maturational phases only to the brink of old age, with its issues of "ego-integration vs. despair."

During the past ten to fifteen years many analysts and social scientists have observed adaptation to vicissitudes of aging, terminal illness, and death. But few have emphasized the orderliness and possible biological purpose in the vicissitudes themselves, which they tend to regard as a succession of almost accidental physical impairments and emotional losses, inevitable but without adaptive purpose or meaning in themselves. Among the exceptions are Grete Bibring (1966), and Erikson in his comments on her paper, who suggested that the gradual decathexis of affects and emotional attachments in old age might have some adaptive value in relinquishing object ties. Cumming and Henry's (1961) theory of "disengagement," as a *mutual* withdrawal of involvement between the aging person and his social ties, also implies some adaptive value in a process that is partly imposed by society but partly "sought" by the individual "for internal reasons." Neugarten et al. (1964) and Gutmann (1966) have also described these phenomena and have given them a more fully developmental interpretation.

These topics will be examined in more or less chronological order, but perhaps a theoretical question will be helpful at the start: if we can agree that every living organism is endowed with an innate schedule of developmental stages, from birth to maturity, can we assume a preprogrammed schedule of devolutional stages from the postreproductive years till a death which comes at the end of a predetermined life span?[1] In earlier times, when the average life span was 40 years, this question may have been academic, but today — as many have pointed out — the downward slope may occupy one-third to one-half of our lives.

Freud's Contributions

Some of Freud's concepts of time experience, such as the timelessness of the unconscious and the "oceanic feeling" of eternity, are well known, whereas others are implicit in his most fundamental notions about the origins of the ego and the earliest awareness of separation between the self and the outside world. References to timelessness as one of the basic characteristics of primary-process thinking occur throughout Freud's writings, from as early as 1897, and were restated explicitly in his essay "The Unconscious" (1915): "The processes of the system *Ucs.* are *timeless*; i.e. they are not ordered temporally, are not altered by the passage of time; they have no reference to time at all. Reference to time is bound up, once again, with the work of the system *Cs.*" (p. 187). This property of the unconscious, as oblivious to time, is consistent with its other characteristics, as a realm of pure wish-fulfillment, in which reality testing, negation, mortality, and mutual contradictions do not exist. Freud also implied, throughout his metapsychological writings, that timelessness occurs during sleep, in dreams, and in

---

[1] The view of Comfort and others that senescence and death have no evolutionary "meaning" is based on several factors, too complex to discuss here. Among them are (1) a concept of tissue aging as an accumulation of chromosomal errors in cell division; and (2) the fact that events affecting the individual beyond his reproductive years are, according to Strehler (1962), "theoretically outside the reach of selection" (p. 222). For a discussion of these questions, see Gifford (1969, pp. 661–663).

certain "unusual states," like being in love, which resemble the newborn infant's blissful union with its mother. In opposition to the unconscious as the locus of total gratification, Freud placed the awareness of time, reality, the ego as its agent, the superego, and "that strict sergeant, Death" as the enemies of pleasure.

In "Beyond the Pleasure Principle" (1920), which introduced the structural concept, Freud elaborated this opposition between the drives and reality in discussing the origins of the ego, as well as the origins of life from inorganic matter. Using his favorite metaphor of a one-celled organism on a primordial ocean, Freud suggested that the stimulus barrier is the *Anlage* of the ego, in mediating between the self and external reality. "This little fragment of living substance is suspended in the middle of an external world charged with the most powerful energies; and it would be killed if it were not provided with a protective shield against stimuli" (p. 27). Later he added that "what has left its mark on the development of organisms must be the history of the earth we live in and of its relation to the sun" (p. 38). Since this includes the alternating periodicities of day and night, we may interpret this speculative passage as foreshadowing more recent interest in biological rhythms, suggesting that the developing ego is imprinted, as it were, with the alternating pattern of rest and activity during the 24-hour solar day.

In Freud's later paper (1930), where he commented on his friend Romain Rolland's "oceanic feeling," Freud's concept of the early ego had evolved along more familiar lines — the behavior of the infant at his mother's breast. He interpreted Rolland's sensation of "eternity," timelessness, and "oneness with the universe" as a distant echo of the infant's sensations after being fed, the infant who "does not as yet distinguish his ego from the external world as the source of the sensations flowing in upon him" (pp. 66–67). The infant learns to do so, through experiences of hunger, awakening, and "screaming for help," which causes his mother to reappear, feed him, and restore the blissful state of narcissistic union with the loved object. Thus the infant "comes to learn a procedure by which, through a deliberate direction of one's sensory activities and through suitable muscular action, one can differentiate between what is internal — what belongs to the ego — and what is external — what emanates from the outer world. In this way one makes the first step toward the introduction of the reality principle which is to dominate future development" (p. 67).

Origins of Time Perception as an Early Ego Function

The relation between time perception and early ego development was implicit in Freud's metapsychological papers, although time was not discussed as a specific ego function. Nevertheless, awareness of time was clearly equated with early differentiation of the self from external reality, with frustration, instinctual need, and awakening, whereas timelessness occurred in states of gratification and sleep. Hanns Sachs (quoted in Bergler and Roheim, 1946) may have been the first analyst to suggest that "the infant probably first learns appreciation of time during intervals between nursing" (p. 190). Long before this, a French sociologist, Guyau (1890), had arrived independently at a similar notion, that awareness of time had its origins in instinctual frustration: "when the infant is hungry, he cries and stretches out his arms toward his nurse: there is the germ of the idea of *future*. . . .In the beginning, the passage of time is only the distinction between the desired and the possessed. . . the distance between 'the cup and the lip' " (p. 32). After Freud and Sachs, direct observation of infant behavior by Anna Freud, Spitz, and others extended Freud's concepts of early ego development, when id, ego, and the external world were undifferentiated. Hartmann (1950) and his associates suggested that the infant's first acquisition of the capacity to postpone the need for immediate gratification — in conformity with the reality principle and the expectation of future feeding — represented the first awareness of time.

With this theoretical background, the publication of Kleitman and Engelmann's (1953) detailed observations on sleep patterns and self-demand feeding schedules in newborn infants provided an opportunity for testing the hypothesis that the earliest indications of time perception and ego functioning can be detected in the adaptation of sleep and wakefulness to the 24-hour rhythms of night and day. Kleitman's data were obtained from nineteen healthy infants, observed from the 3rd to the 26th week, whose mothers were dedicated to feeding them upon demand, with as little regard for the actual time of day or night as possible. Even at three weeks, however, the amount of nighttime sleep was significantly greater than daytime sleep (8.5 to 6.36 mean total hours), with an average of over 7 feedings per 24 hours. From 3 to 13 weeks there was a progressive reduction in the number of nighttime feedings, associated with a decrease in total feedings (and awakenings) per 24 hours, almost entirely due to the reduction in night feedings from 3.5 to 1. From the 13th to the 26th week, a more differentiated sleep-wakefulness pattern evolved, adapted to the daylight hours, with clear-cut morning and afternoon naps and night sleep broken by only one feeding. Kleitman called this change in sleep-wakefulness pattern, at 10 to 14 weeks after birth, "one of the first *learned* performances," to sleep through the night with only one feeding, a shift from "wakefulness of necessity" to "wakefulness of choice" (see Fig. 1).

Kleitman and Engelmann's detailed observations, as I have suggested (Gifford, 1960), could be interpreted as evidence of early ego functioning and time perception, as the infant's polycyclic, non-24-hour rhythms of waking and feeding made a progressive, two-stage adaptation to the 24-hour cycle of day and night. In the first phase, from 3 to 13 weeks, the infant was already reacting to differences between day and night. These differences were transmitted by diurnal variations in his mother's ability to fulfill his needs, because she herself, however

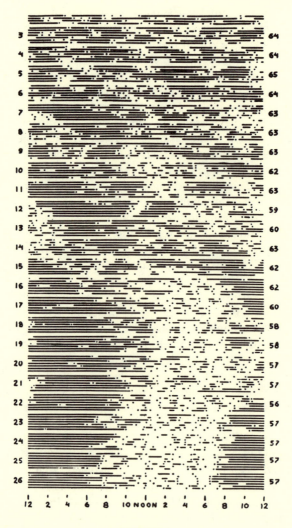

FIGURE 1

Sleep-waking patterns from the 3rd to the 26th week in an infant on a self-demand feeding schedule. The pattern is random until the 4th week, when a 25-hour rhythm appears, with a wakeful period at 4–6 A.M. This cycle overlaps the 24-hour cycle and displaces the waking interval later each day, until the 18th week, when 2 ½ laps have occurred and the wakeful interval falls between noon and 8 P.M. The 25-hour rhythm becomes a nearly 24-hour cycle and remains stationary until the 21st week, when the cycle is shortened to 23.86. A 24-hour rhythm is finally established at the 25th week, with the period of maximum wakefulness between 8 A.M. and 6 P.M. (From Kleitman and Engelman, 1953. Reprinted with permission of the *Journal of Applied Physiology*.)

devoted to feeding upon demand, could not escape the influences of her own 24-hour cycle. Precursors of the ego, emerging from an undifferentiated phase, enabled the infant to postpone immediate hunger, in anticipation of future gratification, and to begin his adaptation to the external reality of the 24-hour cycle. The second phase, associated with the appearance of the smiling response and the maturation of distance receptors, marked the beginning of more mature object relations. A more precise, well-differentiated adaptation to daytime wakefulness evolved, as the mother was first perceived as a person rather than as a need-gratifying object.

Time Perception in Everyday Life

Thus our earliest awareness of external reality is experienced as a function of time, which gradually enforces our adaptation to the 24-hour rhythms of night and day. We assume that the quality of these early experiences, how often we awakened and how quickly or pleasurably we were fed, comforted, and returned to sleep, influences our later lives. The individual variations in our reactions to the protective custody of the 24-hour cycle, which leaves its imprint on us in infancy, are reflected in our later attitudes toward sleep, punctuality, working schedules, and vacations. The experience of time in everyday life, as it is perceived over hours, weeks, and years, is a familiar subject in literature, anecdote, and commonsense observations. The subjective sense of how quickly time passes cannot be measured over long intervals, because the very act of measuring interrupts its flow, and the extensive psychological data on the estimation of short intervals may be measuring quite different mental functions. There is general agreement that states of discomfort or instinctual need, like cold and hunger, give a sense of the prolonged duration of time, and that states of gratification, drowsiness, or sleep accelerate or obliterate the passage of time. This corresponds roughly to the commonplace observation that time passes slowly in childhood and youth, when our appetites are keenest, when sense perceptions are most intense, and when novel experiences occur frequently. Later, time passes more and more quickly with advancing years, as our instinctual life gradually loses its intensity and our daily experiences fall into familiar routines. Attitudes toward the tyranny of the 24-hour cycle, which we both cling to and periodically seek to escape, are usually brought out by unusual experiences and changes of routine. These may be thrust upon us by sensory isolation, sleep-loss or changes in time-zones, induced by changing our routines on weekends and vacations, or sought by drug-experiences and states of religious ecstasy.

The range of individual variation, in our needs for adhering to or escaping the 24-hour cycle, is extreme, from the "prisoner of time," whose life is so well-regulated that he develops a "Sunday neurosis" on holiday, to certain poets, mystics and drug-addicts, for whom Rimbaud's "systematic de-regulation of the senses" is a life-long pursuit. For the majority, both needs coexist in various periodicities and equilibria, and they have been institutionalized in customs and practices so commonplace that we take them for granted. Our universal need to control time, which means placing ourselves under its domination, is attested by the history of time-measurement. Increasingly ingenious clocks, calendars and astronomical predictions have created our highest forms of science out of magical procedures for regulating the forces of nature, as in the intricacies of Mayan astronomy (Thompson, 1970).

The evolution of various calendrical systems has been richly documented, in which their usefulness in controlling crops was accepted as sufficient impetus for making these discoveries. Very little has been written about the historical origins of the week, or rather the Sabbath, and its various equivalents in different cultural traditions, which reflects an emotional rather than a practical need for a day of rest. R. H. Colson (1926) describes, in fascinating detail, "the silent and unofficial diffusion of a new time-cycle through a vast empire," in which our seven-day week, by the 2nd century A.D., emerged from a fusion of the Jewish Sabbath and the 7-day planetary week, replacing the Roman *nundinae*, or market day every 8th day. M. P. Nilsson (1920) describes five, six, and other non-seven-day market weeks in Africa, Indonesia, and South America, and ascribes the origins of the Jewish Sabbath to a primitive market day.

We are accustomed to the 7-day rhythm of the Mesopotamian Judeo-Christian tradition, which possibly evolved as a submultiple of the 28-day lunar month, whereas the Egyptians divided the year into 36 decans, or 10-day weeks, and the Chinese (Kates, 1952) evolved the "24 Spells," with seasonal names, making fortnightly intervals. The Maya (Leach, 1954), who were obsessed by time and "clearly pursued complexity because they enjoyed it," created an elaborate system of interlocking 20- and 13-day cycles, based on their mathematical preference for multiples of 20. Most cultures also observed periodic holidays and feast days of religious significance, which fulfilled the same need to interrupt the daily sequence of human activities with a periodic day of rest. The history of still longer rhythms of rest and activity, now institutionalized in annual, or even biannual, vacations, has not been studied, but the need for such intervals of rest seems to increase in highly developed civilizations.

Although we take these longer periodicities of rest and activity for granted, Sundays, holidays, and vacations have a common element in the temporary, partial suspension of obedience to the quotidian rule of the 24-hour workday. We sleep later, take meals at different hours, and modify other routines of daily life, in order to alter our subjective experience of the passage of time. For some, a single day or a weekend in New York makes time pass more quickly or slowly, and for others a prolonged vacation without our customary temporal landmarks induces a sense of relative "timelessness." Such experiences are so familiar that we wonder whether changes in the apparent duration of time have some physical basis, and whether there are physiological or biochemical substrates for these psychological changes that can be measured. Of various hypotheses suggested, only Hoagland's (1943) correlation between body temperature and time perception has endured. He observed that time passes more slowly during fevers, and that the subjective duration of elapsed time is systematically accelerated with each degree that body temperature is reduced.

Since the diurnal body-temperature cycle is closely interrelated with sleep-wakefulness patterns, this hypothesis is plausible, and one unpublished experiment of our own (see Fig. 2) lends some tentative support. In a comparison of diurnal temperature patterns for workdays and vacation days (each plotted on a single 24-hour grid), the tight workday pattern was visibly disorganized, was displaced by longer hours of sleep, and contained lower temperature readings during vacation days. Weekdays compared to weekends showed a similar scatter, but the determinations were too few to be statistically significant. Assuming that lower body temperature reflects lower rates of metabolic interchange and adrenocortical activity, Mason's (1959) observations on laboratory monkeys, whose blood-cortisol levels were reduced on weekends, when the usual hubbub of weekday activity was absent, provide another bit of evidence.

Drug States and Religious Ecstasies

Alteration in time perception induced by drugs and mystical experiences, self-imposed or deliberately sought after, occupy an intermediate position between everyday life and extreme situations. Freud (1930) doubted the "universal need" to experience "oceanic feelings" of timelessness that had been expressed in his discussion with Romain Rolland and found no such need in himself. Freud's own life, nevertheless, followed the well-established European tradition of the long summer vacation, usually devoted to the exalted admiration of Nature in its wilder aspects. These quasi-transcendental aesthetic experiences contained elements of escape from the quotidian 24-hour cycle, and a partial identification with the impersonal forces of Nature. Admiration for wild rather than cultivated Nature has been idealized in Western Europe since the mid-eighteenth century, when a taste for the primitive and the awe-inspiring, as in the cult of the "sublime and terrible," coincided with a decline in universal religious beliefs.

Historians and anthropologists have pointed out the nearly universal predilection of diverse human societies to discover intoxicating substances, to endow them with special significance, originally for magical or ritual purposes, and to set them apart from the activities of everyday working life. The literature on the psychopharmacologic properties of these various substances has rapidly increased

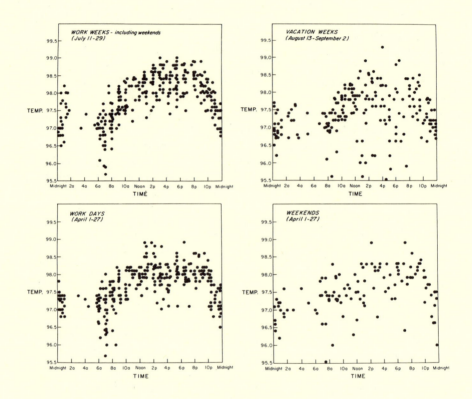

FIGURE 2

One subject under varying conditions of work and leisure; there is a significant difference in range and scatter between workweeks following a regular schedule and vacation weeks, while the difference between workdays and weekends is not statistically significant.

in recent years, and the effects of these substances include extreme changes in the subjective duration of time. Though I shall not attempt to review this vast literature, two contrasting effects may be mentioned. Nineteenth-century travelers and physicians give vivid accounts of the hashish experience, in which the passage of time seemed infinitely prolonged. From an elaborate description by an inveterate traveler, Bayard Taylor (1856) sums up the effects of hashish on time duration: "Though the whole vision was probably not more than five minutes in passing through my mind, years seemed to have elapsed" (p. 140). A physician (Wood, 1880) describes a house call under the influence of *cannabis Americana*: "Seconds seemed hours; minutes seemed days; hours seemed infinite. . . I would look at my watch, and then after an hour or two, as I thought, would look again and find that scarcely five minutes had elapsed" (p. 237). Heroin, in contrast, seems to speed up the passage of time. Zinberg (1972), in interviewing Vietnam veterans who lacked the usual psychopathology of the addict, was impressed by "healthy, all-around American boys" who consciously chose heroin for this effect, because it "makes time go away" and helped them get through a "thoroughly unpleasant year." Previous reports on addicts have also noted that their withdrawn state, called "on the nod," is not one of elation but suggests an attempt to abolish the awareness of time when all external stimuli were experienced as unpleasant.

Besides these extreme states induced by drugs, there is reason to believe that the everyday use of common substances like alcohol and tobacco has lesser but similar effects on time perception. Periodic drinking bouts clearly represent attempts to escape the time schedules as well as work routines of everyday life. The reduction of perceptual acuity and temporal disorientation can create "lost weekends" and even, in moderate amounts, miniature "deaths in the afternoon." Tobacco, in the addicted smoker, has even more familiar effects, in speeding time under conditions of boredom and in prolonging the duration of any experience in a state of withdrawal.

Many writers have noted similarities between drug states and the mystical experiences of religious votaries, induced without the use of drugs. The literature on the subject is too extensive to review here (Underhill, 1964; Spencer, 1963; Laski, 1961), but some physical conditions commonly used to facilitate mystical experiences are worth mentioning: (1) long-term states of instinctual privation, traditionally sexual abstinence and fasting; (2) sleep deprivation or periodic interruption of sleep; (3) various amounts of self-inflicted pain, from scourging to simple physical hardship; and (4) a narrowing of the range and/or a reduction in the intensity of external sense perceptions. From the extreme isolation of the hermit to prescriptions for meditation, methods of cultivating perceptual monotony are emphasized. Throughout this literature, from the austerities of the Desert Fathers to the spiritual exercises of modern Zen philosophers, there are examples of altered time sense. In the "timeless moment," an instant stretches into eternity, and in states of oblivious self-absorption hours or days pass in the twinkling of an eye. These seemingly contradictory phenomena suggest that the apparent duration of time is prolonged in states of instinctual need, and shortened, or even obliterated, by gratification, sleep, and mental states that re-create the experience of the satisfied infant, asleep in blissful union with his mother. The extreme variations and contradictory effects on time experience, drastically lengthening or cutting short its apparent duration, can be interpreted as the result of varied or shifting equilibria between relative instinctual deprivation and the supreme gratification of the religious devotee, the *unio mystica* of becoming one with the godhead.

Solitary Confinement

Changes in time experience may also be thrust upon us rather than sought out, for example, when we are forcibly dislodged, as it were, from our secure captivity in the comforting 24-hour rhythms of everyday life. Our examples come from two bodies of evidence, a large experimental literature on isolation, and a surprisingly small number of first-person prison memoirs that describe solitary confinement. Modern experimental studies go back to the work of Hebb and his followers in the late 1940s (Bexton, Heron, and Scott, 1954), and many excellent reviews of this literature can be found in Vernon (1963), Zubek (1969), and Rasmussen (1973). Among prison memoirs, many well-known accounts such as E. E. Cumming's *The Enormous Room*, Gramsci's *Letters from Prison*, and Dostoevsky's *The House of the Dead* describe what are primarily group experiences. The extensive concentration-camp literature deals with such extreme conditions of pain and physical cruelty, that time experience itself is rarely mentioned. But true conditions of solitary confinement, abnormal and extreme as some may be, are closer to everyday experience and also include features of real danger and prolonged duration that cannot be reproduced by the most rigorous experimental methods.

Prison routines, like the rigid schedules of monastic life, are infinitely more monotonous and unvarying than the daily activities of the world outside. But a common theme in memoirs of solitary confinement is the preoccupation with efforts to control time even more rigidly, down to the minutest detail. Burney's (1952) account of two years in solitary, in a French prison during the second World War, conveys the pleasure he took in minutiae, in maintaining the regularity and uniformity of his awakening and breakfast rituals. He began a series of walks, carefully measured and counted, to assure himself that after a certain number of miles his noonday meal would arrive. He dreaded counting faster than usual, lest he "finish" early and have to wait, enduring an uncontrolled, indeterminate interval before his meal. He was delighted by a shadow moving across his skylight, which he used to measure the "distance" till noon.

Various methods of controlling the passage of time are described by Kropotkin (1899), Vera Figner (1927), and Alexander Berkman (1912), who later indicate how, after various periods of confinement, they had become attached to their rituals and fearful of any novelty or change that interrupted their monotonous routines. Figner emphasized the "deathly stillness" that "little by little overpowers you, envelops you, penetrates into all the pores of your body. . . In this stillness the real becomes vague and unreal, and the imaginary seems real. The long grey day, wearying in its idleness, resembles a sleep without dreams; and at night you have such bright and glowing dreams. . ." (p. 185). At first horrified to discover that her voice had become weak and quavering from disuse, she gradually realized that she *wanted* to be silent, to avoid the monthly visit from her mother: "why change the tempo of life, the natural order of the day?" (p. 152). She also recognized her fear of returning to "ordinary life" when she was released from the Schlüsselburg after eighteen years' confinement, and she was told that this was a common experience among long-term prisoners.

Burney (1952) gives a more detailed account of this phenomenon. He mentions first his growing dislike of innovations, the unaccustomed stimulation of church services, the new prisoners attempting to communicate with him by tapping: "I was selfish and prized my silence, especially the silence of night. . . when your surroundings disappear and you may go where you will, and even the deadliest fear is tamed" (p. 29). Finally, when his impending release was announced, he wrote: "The idea of leaving still filled me with horror, but I knew that it was time to leave. . . The cell door was a kind of battlement behind which I practiced habits, and however futile they were, they had become familiar from long and unvarying usage and represented an element of stability which was more desireable than any hopeful hazard" (pp. 169–171). Another account by Edith Bone (1957), imprisoned in Budapest by Stalinist officials from 1949 to 1956, also conveys the "defensive wall of indifference" she maintained, and how reluctant she was to relinquish it. "I had read that time dragged in prison [but] I did not find it so, on the contrary it flew too fast. The guards often looked at me wonderingly when I got the evening meal mixed up with the mid-day one and thought supper was lunch" (p. 157).

Present-day political prisoners describe similar experiences, although accounts of pure solitary confinement, without physical torture or group methods of "thought reform," are difficult to obtain. The recollections of Richard Fecteau (personal communication) are the most nearly comparable to the experiences of eighteenth-century czarist prisoners. Fecteau tells of his confinement in a North Chinese prison for nineteen years, the first three and the last six of them in solitary. When he was released and returned home in 1971, he discovered that his voice had become very faint and his speech seemed inarticulate; he preferred to be alone and avoid conversation, especially in crowds and large groups of people. His "difficulty communicating," as he called it, affected both his ability to articulate his thoughts and put them into words ("I was so used to thinking everything over and over to myself"), and his ability to comprehend conversations, especially with more than one person at a time. All sounds were exaggerated and seemed much too loud, "like everyone was shouting," and there was also an increased intensity in his perception of colors. The greenness of the landscape seemed exceptionally vivid on his homecoming train journey via Hong Kong, and on his arrival in the United States he was "stunned" by the bright red shorts of a woman journalist. The heightened intensity of colors lasted for a few weeks, and his hypersensitivity to sounds for about six months. His difficulty in communicating persisted for almost two years, until finally he was comfortable listening to conversations and taking part in them.

During his captivity, like other prisoners before him, Fecteau attempted to control the passage of time by periods of physical exercise, in which, as a former athletic coach, he had some expertise. He also found, like Figner, that daydreams were the most effective means of abolishing time. He could lose himself in reveries and recollections of his past life until he forgot whether he had had lunch or whether he was walking to or from the toilet in a room outside his cell. He describes this as a semi-controlled activity, which he "learned" to make use of after about two years. He also learned how to "turn them off" before bedtime when they interfered with sleep, and to interrupt with periods of exercise. The reveries themselves included detailed reconstructions of past scenes, in which he recalled the names of grade-school classmates he had long forgotten or drives to and from familiar places near his hometown north of Boston. He looked forward to his spontaneous night dreams, which were vivid and often contained pleasurable experiences of eating and drinking. He became expert at measuring short intervals of time by changes in the sunlight that came through cracks in his boarded-up window, and during his early years of captivity he devised methods of keeping track of what day it was. Gradually, he lost interest in the exact day and measured time mainly by changes in the seasons. He was uncomfortably cold in winter (in his unheated stone prison cell, water sometimes froze in his drinking cup overnight), summer was hot and humid, and he looked forward to spring. Apparently, he had great patience in pursuing long-term projects: two years making a peephole in his cell door with a bent nail, which seemed "very fascinating to me," and four years establishing contact with his fellow prisoner who had been shot down with him.

Answers to direct questions about the subjective passage of time are always difficult to interpret, but Fecteau clearly indicates that his last six years in solitary passed more quickly than the first three. His first two pretrial years, in a dimly lighted cell where he was instructed to sit on the floor and gaze at a black spot painted on the wall, were the most difficult to endure. His ten years with three successive cellmates, during which he learned Chinese and taught one of his cellmates English, passed "ten times as quickly" as the periods in solitary. Nevertheless, he was actually glad to be returned to solitary, where his last six years were not as difficult as he expected, because of his ability to lose time by controlled reveries. In looking back on his total prison experience, he thinks he could endure the last six years again, but he would dread repeating the first two years.

The experiences of more recent political prisoners are complicated by physical torture and modified by group contacts and communication with others. Nevertheless, two Argentine college girls, Marta and Susana Panero (personal communication), who were imprisoned for one-and-a-half and two-and-a-half years respectively, under varying conditions that included some solitary confinement, said independently: "When you have a routine and every day is the same as the other, time passes very quickly. You don't remember time, except for your family's visits." The sister who was imprisoned longer said, "Time passes very quickly, I couldn't believe I was there two years."

Solitary confinement is a complex, highly individual experience that merits further study, but several phenomena have been described by prisoners of different personalities under widely varying conditions. One is the use of uniform daily routines to control the passage of time, with certain temporary fears, upon release, of resuming social interactions, engaging in ordinary conversation, and dealing with novel situations. Another postrelease phenomenon is a transient hyperacuity of perception, especially to sounds and colors, perhaps partly resulting from habituation to prolonged reduction of sensory stimulation. A third phenomenon that prisoners describe is experiencing the duration of solitary confinement as shorter than they had expected, even confusing the evening with the midday meal; in other words, a tendency to underestimate elapsed time. In contrast, according to a patient in an intensive-care unit, subjected to intensely painful stimuli, lack of time cues, and uniform reduced illumination, there was an overestimation of elapsed time, as if noon were already evening, or a restless afternoon had been a night of fitful sleep. Nevertheless, he, too, experienced a transient visual hyperacuity on leaving the hospital, as if he were seeing the monochrome urban scene in brilliant colors for the first time.

Experimental Isolation and "Time Deprivation"

Most of the experimental studies that bear on time perception begin with the first scientific reference to the subject, the observations of Ferrari (1909) during the Messina earthquake. He described three brothers who were imprisoned under the ruins for eighteen days and who estimated the time elapsed as four or five days. "This impression of the shortness of time during the most acute sufferings was mentioned by many survivors, and it is difficult to interpret because. . . it seems paradoxical." He also mentioned a professor, "a calm, well-balanced person," who could not believe that his watch was still running during the day of the earthquake; he became convinced, at nightfall, "that the laws of astronomy had also been overthrown."[2]

Among the small number of experimental studies concerned with the estimation of long time intervals, MacLeod and Roff (1935-1936) observed two subjects, each alone in a soundproof room, for periods of 86 and 48 hours without external time cues. Both subjects revealed a consistent underestimation of elapsed time, for intervals of 17 minutes to several hours, with mean errors of 21.6 percent and 22.3 percent respectively. Vernon and McGill (1963) repeated the experiment with two groups of subjects for 54 hours and 6 subjects for 96 hours. They found a mean underestimation of 4.25 hours for the first group and about 18 hours for the second, or about 20 percent.

This tendency to underestimate elapsed time under conditions of sensory isolation, in other words to experience time as passing more rapidly, impressed van Wulfften Palthe (1958), who had observed it in his own experiments. Under various conditions, from vibration-proof caissons to simulated cockpit situations, and for periods from 12 to 93 hours, his subjects underestimated elapsed time by a mean error of 56 percent, with a range of 24–75 percent. The tendency to underestimate was smallest during sleep, with a mean error of 25 percent, and greatest during waking periods. Palthe (1968) also analyzed the data from four other major experiments, obtained by observers who isolated themselves in caves without timepieces: Siffre for 58 days (1965), Senni for 125 days, Laurès for 88, and Lafferty for 127. All four experienced the passage of time as drastically shortened, the first three by a mean error very close to Palthe's mean error of 56 percent (57 percent, 54 percent, and 58 percent, respectively). The fourth observer, Lafferty, underestimated by a substantially smaller amount (about 22 percent). Palthe attributed this to his unusually long hours of sleep, over 11 hours per "cave day," compared to an average of 7 hours among the other three.

All four studies followed the same procedure: no clocks or external clues to the time of day and only one-way communication with the outside world, by which the observer reported his spontaneous hours of awakening, eating, and going to sleep. Thus each observer was following a free-running biological rhythm, according to his own "natural" physiological cycle. For this individual "cave day," Palthe used the conventional Dutch term "een etmaal," which means the circadian interval between one "morning's" awakening and the next. Siffre's "personal rhythm," for example, as calculated afterward from the recorded data, was based on a periodicity of 24 hours, 31 minutes (see Fig. 3). Thus he progressively displaced his "night," or hours asleep, later and later within the actual 24-hour interval of clock time, overlapping his cycle 1½ times during his 59 days underground, as in the sleep patterns of Kleitman's infants.

Siffre's subjective experience of these intervals was quite different, however.

---

[2] A similar experience was reported by a man in Joplin, Missouri. After being trapped and immobilized for three and a half days in a collapsing building, he commented, "It was a long Saturday . . . It seemed like about two days" (*Boston Globe*, November 16, 1978).

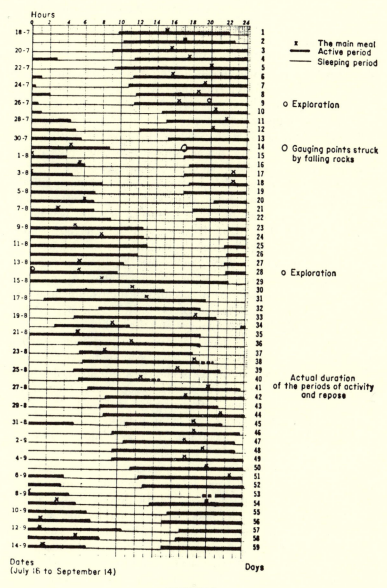

FIGURE 3

Sleep-waking patterns of a healthy young man in a cave without time cues. A 24.5-hour cycle is maintained throughout, but the waking interval is displaced later each day, overlapping the 24-hour cycle 1½ times in 8 weeks. (From Siffre, 1965. Reprinted with permission of McGraw-Hill.)

He felt the time was passing very rapidly, in spite of increasing physical and mental distress toward the end of the experiment. As he attempted to estimate the duration of intervals between sleep and activity, he became convinced that he was living according to a "natural" cycle of 12 to 14 hours, and found himself omitting one or two of his three customary meals. In communicating with the surface, he denied the evidence of several accidental clues, which indicated that his estimated dates were grossly incorrect. When the day of his release was announced, a day or two before the end of the two-month period they had agreed upon in advance, he refused to believe the news. He had entered the cave on July 16, and the experiment ended on September 14, but he estimated the date of release as August 20, representing 25 "missing days" out of the 58-day period.

Siffre repeated the experiment 10 years later, when he spent 205 days in a Texas cave. This time his spontaneous sleep-waking cycle averaged between 25 to 28 hours, with an occasional isolated cycle of 45 to 50 hours, which he failed to recognize as an unusually long "day." This is the only reported observation on the lengthening of a free-running circadian rhythm with advancing age. Siffre was now 33 instead of 23 (*New York Times*, September 20, 1972).

During the original experiment, Siffre described other reactions to the experience that are consistent with many accounts of imprisonment as well as accounts of isolation given by polar explorers (Scott, 1923; Byrd, 1938). Progressive impairment of short-term memory and the ability to concentrate on an intellectual task were reflected in trivial acts of absentmindedness and in occasional gross errors of judgment that could have been life-threatening. Siffre also experienced increasingly frequent waves of anxiety and despair, first strenuously denied but intermittently surrendered to. He wrote in his journal, two days before his release, "I'm still not sure of coming out of this alive" (1965, p. 184). Siffre had frightening confrontations with physical changes in his face and body; he was shocked by his emaciation, as Burney had been frightened by his dependent edema and Prince Kropotkin had become anxious about his muscular weakness. Siffre noted a deterioration in personal habits of cleanliness and neatness, with waist-high garbarge heaps accumulating around his living quarters with which he felt unable to cope. He also described some alterations in sense perceptions: blue and green colors lost their intensity and became difficult to distinguish, whereas the yellow of his tent lining became more intense and very irritating. Music ceased to be enjoyable, as if its individual notes had become desynthesized and disagreeable. His reaction brings to mind Richard II's reaction in his prison cell: "This music mads me; let it sound no more" (V.v.61).

Time Perception and the Aging Process

Siffre, like other prisoners and explorers before him, compared the mental and physical changes he noted during his confinement to an accelerated process of aging. In a previous paper (Gifford, 1971), I saw this as a powerful allegory, linking the accounts of explorers in deserts and Arctic wastes with my observations on the last years of an elderly colleague. He had withdrawn into his rubbish-filled "cave" and created, with the help of a devoted housekeeper, his own idiosyncratic sleep-wakefulness rhythm. He arose sometime in the early afternoon, had a moderate breakfast, and an hour or two later (just before his housekeeper left for the day) ate his principal meal. Then he was awake until some unknown time late at night, filling the rest of his "etmaal" with irregular periods of napping and fitful, rather disorganized, intellectual activity.

After further experiences with the elderly, with relatives and friends, and as a consultant to a hospital home-care service, I have come to feel that the analogy between aging and the hardships of prisoners and explorers is more than a metaphor. Apparently, psychophysiological changes can be induced in young, vigorous men under extreme conditions of sensory isolation which occur very gradually in old age. The relation between reduced sensory stimulation and a reduction in the apparent duration of long time intervals suggested an explanation for our commonplace observation that time passes more quickly with advancing years. If this association between the two phenomena has some biological sources, both the aging process and the abridgment of subjective time experience that accompanies it could be considered manifestations of the death instinct. The changes in time perception can then be understood as serving some homeostatic purpose, in speeding us more painlessly toward our appointed end.

Many of the clinical details that would support such an interpretation have become familiar to us over the past twenty years, when new and valuable observations on aging have been made by biologists, physicians, analysts, and social scientists. The fact that the elderly tend to adhere to familiar routines, gradually restrict their activities, and avoid innovations is well known. We also know their vulnerability to abrupt changes in surroundings, as in the transient psychoses and confusional states that occur when an elderly person is hospitalized or moved to an unfamiliar situation. The role of perceptual and emotional isolation in accelerating these tendencies toward restriction of their activities and social contacts has been increasingly recognized.

Many programs for improving the quality of life among the aged are quite rightly based on increasing sensory stimulation, maintaining emotional contact, and introducing suitable new activities. Many geriatric enthusiasts are exhilarated by finding intact ego functions among the old, the poor, and the wretched of the earth, like archeologists finding treasures in the dust heaps of history. Naturally, they tend to regard these prevailing trends in the aging process as mainly detrimental, to be counteracted at all costs. Often these young and middle-aged workers with an interest in aging are impressed by the brilliant exceptions, the gerontocracy of notables, like Sophocles and Bertrand Russell, who maintained their creative powers into advanced old age.

Among our friends, patients, and clients, we respond most positively to those who show remarkable resilience in maintaining their physical activities, intellectual interests, and emotional relationships. These examples of "successful aging" come to seem like the ideal norm, rather than like exceptions such as Verdi and G. B. Shaw, whose special endowments and favorable life situations enabled them to remain productive beyond the usual age. We can acknowledge a vast majority of aging persons whose adjustment is neither exceptionally good nor bad, and who show a characteristic resistance to change, as in their reluctance to make new friends, to accept corrective surgery or hearing-aids and recorded books. But we project our own ideals upon the elderly, our favorite examples of inspiring longevity, and hesitate to consider this increasing inertia as a biological trend, as a normal—or even advantageous—phase of the aging process. In spite of our own fears of aging, however, the older person's fatalism about physical and emotional losses, as well as his need to restrict the range of his social activities, can be seen as a homeostatic tendency to re-establish a new equilibrium on a more limited but safer level of functioning.

Relatively few writers on aging have regarded this tendency toward psychophysiological inertia as a normal part of the aging process. Grete Bibring (1966), and Erikson in his discussion of her paper, acknowledged both the assets and the liabilities of aging, suggesting that the reduction in the intensity of instinctual conflicts permits more tranquil and contemplative activities. She emphasized the rediscovery of intellectual interests from childhood and youth, and the enjoyment of the simpler pleasures of food and physical comfort, with a waning of sexual desire. She also suggested that the attenuation of intense emotional attachments, and the reduced capacity for making new ones, may serve some homeostatic purpose; that this trend makes it easier to accept the increasing losses of family and friends and eventually to relinquish all object ties in one's own death. Felix Deutsch (1936) and Eissler (1955) have made similar observations on patients with terminal illnesses, and their remarks can be equally applied to the aging process, as a terminal illness from which no one is spared.

Cumming and Henry's (1961) theory of disengagement tends to support this concept: that some degree of emotional withdrawal, some reduction in the number and intensity of object ties, is a normal part of the aging process. Approaching the phenomenon from a sociological viewpoint, they define "disengagement" as a mutual process taking place between the individual and society, initiated by one or the other through the usual vicissitudes of retirement, bereavement, and geographical separation from children. There are wide variations, caused by differences in personality, timing of the separations, and many accidental circumstances, but the result is a "mutual severing of ties," usually with a reduction in their number and emotional quality. Cumming and Henry do not suggest a biological or instinctual basis for this process, but their theory acknowledges an inner need in the elderly to sever object ties and to reach a new, relatively contented equilibrium when the disengagement process is complete. This hypothesis is supported by the contrast, in the normal aging population sample they were observing, between the continuing conflicts in the 70-year-old group and the relative tranquility of the octogenarians. Cumming and Henry also take issue with other gerontologists for applying their own standards of "healthy middle age" as a criterion for "successful aging," which may not be appropriate to a later developmental phase.

Bernice Neugarten and her associates (1964, 1965), in their extensive psychological studies of normal aging in the middle-aged and elderly, also found an increasing tendency toward introversion with advancing age, a decrease in emotional ties with persons and objects in the outer world, and "a constriction. . . in the ability to integrate wide ranges of stimuli and in the willingness to deal with complicated and challenging situations" (Neugarten, 1965). She noted that these prevailing trends could already be detected in the mid-forties, well before the usual emotional losses of mid-life had occurred, and that the "decreased cathexes for outer-world events seems to precede rather than follow changes in social behavior." These observations led her to suggest that these phenomena had "the characteristics of a developmental change," reflecting an intrinsic process, partly independent of life events, "closer to the biological than to social determinants of behavior."

David Gutmann (1964), a collaborator of Neugarten's, used the TAT to study groups of normal urban Americans in their forties, fifties, and sixties. He found a regular sequence of changes in ego mastery, from active to passive to "magical" styles of coping with the stimulus material. The last of these patterns included forms of denial that enabled these elderly men and women to lead relatively successful everyday lives, in spite of various defects in cognitive and ego functioning. Gutmann interpreted these data in terms of the developmental concepts of Erikson and Hartmann, suggesting that the ego continues to undergo developmental changes in middle and late life. In later studies, he applied the same methods to more primitive societies, to a preliterate Maya village (Gutmann, 1966), and a Navajo Indian reservation (Goldstine and Gutmann, 1972). He found a similar sequence, from active to passive to "magical" mastery, with only moderate differences in emphasis that reflected the influence of contrasting cultures. Interpreting this relatively culture-free age-staging as evidence of a developmental process, Gutmann suggested that "the movement from active to passive to magical forms seems to replicate—though in reverse order—the course of maturation in childhood" (Goldstine and Gutmann, 1966).

Aging, Time Perception, and the Death Instinct

If we accept a developmental concept of aging as an intrinsic biological process that operates in all human beings and all cultures, and if we consider the commonplace phenomenon that time seems to pass more quickly during the aging process, and that there is an increasing reduction in sensory and emotional responsiveness, we can interpret both the changes in time perception and the aging process itself as manifestations of the death instinct. Freud did not refer to the vicissitudes of aging as evidence of its operation, but, as Edward Bibring (1941) has pointed out, Freud considered sleep or, rather, an innate need for alternating periods of rest and activity, as one of the few "clinical" manifestations of the death instinct. Except for manifestations of the repetition compulsion, the death instinct was a "silent force," impelling every living organism to die "for *internal reasons*" (Freud, 1920, p. 38). But Freud also emphasized, throughout his writings on the dual theory of life and death instincts, a constant tendency for living matter to return to an inorganic state, and for sensory stimulation and instinctual excitation to be reduced to the lowest possible level. Thus Freud's dual-instinct theory is both a biological and a developmental one that can be extended to include both ends of our life span — from the timeless, undifferentiated state of the infant at his mother's breast to the abridgment of time in old age and the timelessness of coma and death. With his developmental theory that accepts the evolutionary purpose of a predetermined life span, Freud (1920) thus affirms with Montaigne that "the aim of all life is death" (p. 38), and with Claude Bernard and Weismann that aging and death are adaptive for biological survival. Therefore, Freud's theory of the death instinct finds some meaning in the vicissitudes of aging during the postreproductive years, rather than regarding them as biologically meaningless, as an accidental "running out of program" for accurate cell division, according to recent gerontologists (Comfort, 1964).

Summary and Conclusions

This paper has attempted to connect two aspects of time perception: (1) its origins in the newborn infant's adaptation to the 24-hour biological rhythms of night and day; and (2) the familiar phenomenon that time seems to pass more quickly with advancing years. Between these two developmental phases, certain everyday experiences reflect our conflicting attitudes toward time, our clinging to the protective custody of the 24-hour cycle. We recognize its effects during jet lag, solitary confinement, and experimental isolation, and in our need for a periodic escape into the relative timelessness of weekends, vacations, drug states, and religious ecstasies. The connecting links in this hypothesis are derived from Freud's concepts of the timeless unconscious, early ego development from an undifferentiated phase (in which the infant experiences his mother as part of himself), and "oceanic feelings" as adult echoes of this blissful union with a nourishing mother. An attempt was also made to encompass these phenomena within Freud's biological concept of the life and death instincts, considered as a developmental theory. This implies that the infant is wakened from a timeless state by sensory excitation, and is periodically drawn back by a silent, unceasing force to a less stimulated state and eventually to death, when "Time must have a stop."

In the light of these biological and metapsychological theories, the awareness of time first emerges from repeated experiences of hunger and delay in obtaining satisfaction. In learning to endure deprivation for the sake of future gratification, we acquire our adaptation to the 24-hour rhythms of daily life in early infancy. We return to a relatively timeless, less stimulated state—nightly in sleep and periodically in more attenuated form—during weekends and other ritualized furloughs from the 24-hour cycle. In states of reduced sensory stimulation, and during the gradual withdrawal from emotional ties and intense perceptual experience that occurs with aging, there is a subjective sense of time passing more quickly. Both the apparent shortening of elapsed time and the regressive phenomena of aging are interpreted as manifestations of the death instinct, fulfilling a biologically adaptive purpose in bringing life to its predetermined end.

REFERENCES

Bergler, E. & Roheim, G. (1946), Psychology of time perception. *Psychoanal. Quart.*, 15:190-216.

Berkman, A. (1912), *Prison Memoirs of an Anarchist.* New York: Schocken, 1970.

Bexton, W. H., Heron, W., & Scott, T. H. (1954), Effects of decreased variation in the sensory environment. *Canad. J. Psychol.*, 8:70-76.

Bibring, E. (1941), The development and problems of the theory of the instincts. *Internat. J. Psycho-Anal.*, 22:102-131.

Bibring, G. (1966), Old age: Its liabilities and its assets, a psychobiological discourse. In: *Psychoanalysis: A General Psychology—Essays in Honor of Heinz Hartmann*, ed. R. M. Loewenstein et al. New York: International Universities Press, pp. 253-271.

Bone, E. (1957), *Seven Years' Solitary.* New York: Harcourt Brace.

Burney, C. (1952), *Solitary Confinement.* London: Macmillan, 1961.

Byrd, R. E. (1938), *Alone.* New York: Putnam.

Colson, R. H. (1926), *The Week.* Cambridge, Eng.: Cambridge University Press.

Comfort, A. (1964), *Ageing: The Biology of Senescence.* New York: Holt, Rinehart & Winston.

Cumming, E. & Henry, W. E. (1961), *Growing Old: The Process of Disengagement.* New York: Basic Books.

Deutsch, F. (1936), Euthanasia: A clinical study. *Psychoanal. Quart.*, 5:347-368.

Eissler, K. (1955), *The Psychiatrist and the Dying Patient.* New York: International Universities Press.

Erikson, E. H. (1959), *Identity and the Life Cycle* [*Psychological Issues*, Monogr. 1]. New York: International Universities Press.

Ferrari, G. C. (1909), La psicologia degli scampati al terremoto di Messina. *Rivista Psicol.*, 5:89-125.

Figner, V. (1927), *Memoirs of a Revolutionist.* New York: International Publishers.

Freud, S. (1915), The unconscious. *Standard Edition*, 14:166-215. London: Hogarth Press, 1957.

———— (1920), Beyond the pleasure principle. *Standard Edition*, 18:7-64. London: Hogarth Press, 1962.

———— (1930), Civilization and its discontents. *Standard Edition*, 21:64-145. London: Hogarth Press, 1962.

———— (1937), Analysis terminable and interminable. *Standard Edition*, 23:209-253. London: Hogarth Press, 1964.

Gifford, S. (1960), Sleep, time and the early ego. *J. Amer. Psychoanal. Assn.*, 8:5–42.
_____ (1969), Some psychoanalytic theories about death: A selective historical review. *Ann. N.Y. Acad. Sci.*, 164:638–668.
_____ (1971), Time's wingèd chariot: The origins of time-experience and its fate in later life. Paper presented at Fall meeting of American Psychoanalytic Association, New York, December, 1971. Reported in Panel (1972).
Goldstine, T. & Gutmann, D. (1972), A TAT study of Navajo aging. *Psychiatry*, 35:373–384.
Gutmann, D. (1964), An exploration of ego configurations in middle and later life. In: *Personality in Middle and Later Life*, ed. B. Neugarten. New York: Atherton Press, pp. 115–148.
_____ (1966), Mayan aging—A comparative TAT study. *Psychiatry*, 29:246–259.
Guyau, M. (1890), *La Genèse de l'idée de temps.* Paris: Alcan, 1902.
Hartmann, H. (1950), Comments on the psychoanalytic theory of the ego. *The Psychoanalytic Study of the Child*, 5:74–97. New York: International Universities Press.
Hartocollis, P. (1972), Time as a dimension of affects. *J. Amer. Psychoanal. Assn.*, 20:92–108.
Hoagland, H. (1943), The chemistry of time. *Scient. Monthly*, 56:56–61.
Kates, G. N. (1952), *The Years That Were Fat.* Cambridge, Mass.: MIT Press.
Kleitman, N. & Engelmann, T. G. (1953), Sleep characteristics of infants. *J. Appl. Physiol.*, 6:269–282.
Kropotkin, P. (1899), *Memoirs of a Revolutionist.* New York: Dover, 1971.
Laski, M. (1961), *Ecstasy: A Study of Some Secular and Religious Experiences.* Bloomington: Indiana University Press.
Leach, E. R. (1954), Primitive time-reckoning. In: *A History of Technology*, Vol. 1, ed. C. Singer, E. J. Holingard, & A. R. Hall. London: Oxford University Press, pp. 110–127.
MacLeod, R. B. & Roff, M. F. (1935–1936), An experiment in temporal disorientation. *Acta Psychol.*, 1:381–423.
Mason, J. W. (1959), Psychological influences on the pituitary-adrenal cortical system. *Recent Progress in Hormone Res.*, 15:345–389.
Neugarten, B. L. et al. (1964), *Personality in Middle and Later Life.* New York: Atherton Press.
_____ (1965), Personality changes in the aged. *Catholic Psychological Record*, 3:9–17.
Nilsson, M. P. (1920), *Primitive Time-Reckoning.* Lund: C. W. K. Gleerup.
Palthe, P. M. van W. (1958), Sensory and motor deprivation as a psycho-pathological stress. *Aeromed. Acta*, 6:155–168.
_____ (1968), Time sense in isolation. *Psychiat. Neurol. Neurochirurgia*, 71:221–241.
Panel, (1972), The experience of time, reported by J. S. Kafka. *J. Amer. Psychoanal Assn.*, 20: 650–667.
Pollock, G. H. (1971), On time, death, and immortality. *Psychoanal. Quart.*, 40:435–446.
Rapaport, D. (1960), Psychoanalysis as a developmental psychology. In: *The Collected Papers of David Rapaport*, ed. M. Gill. New York: Basic Books, 1967, pp. 820–852.
Rasmussen, J. E., ed. (1973), *Man in Isolation and Confinement.* Chicago: Aldine.
Scott, R. F. (1923), *Scott's Last Expedition.* London: J. Murray.
Siffre, M. (1965), *Beyond Time.* London: Chatto & Windus.
Spencer, S. (1963), *Mysticism in World Religion.* Baltimore: Penguin Books.
Strehler, B. L. (1962), *Time, Cells and Aging.* New York: Academic Press.
Taylor, B. (1856), *The Lands of the Saracen.* New York: Putnam.
Thompson, J. E. S. (1970), *Maya History and Religion.* Norman: University of Oklahoma Press.
Underhill, E. (1964), *The Mystics of the Church.* New York: Schocken Books.
Vernon, J. A., ed. (1963), *Inside the Black Room.* New York: C. N. Potter.
_____ & McGill, T. E. (1963), Time estimation during sensory deprivation. *J. Gen. Psychol.*, 69: 11–18.
Wood, H. C., Jr. (1880), *A Treatise on Therapeutics, Comprising Materia Medica and Toxicology.* Philadelphia: Lippincott.
Zinberg, N. E. (1972) Rehabilitation of heroin users in Vietnam. *Contemporary Drug Problems*, 1: 263–394.
Zubek, J. P. (1969), *Sensory Deprivation: Fifteen Years of Research.* New York: Appleton-Century-Crofts.

December, 1978

Bion and Babies

SUSANNA ISAACS ELMHIRST, M.D., F.R.C.P.
(Beverly Hills, Calif.)

I was recently surprised but charmed when a colleague, on seeing the title of this paper, asked "What is a Bion?" His natural thought that a Bion was perhaps a biological substance led me to think of "Bionic" and to how often Bion appears in my patients' dreams as a highly desirable alternative to me, more biological (physical) or more bionic (magical). "Beyond the beyond" was a patient's recent association to a dream. My colleague's unawareness of Bion's work led me to realize how little WRB is known in psychoanalytic circles outside the area where he works, Los Angeles, or beyond the more consciously "Kleinian" community, which is strong in South America as well as in England, Italy, and Spain.

Freud was well aware, at times painfully aware, that his work was greeted with a great deal of hostility. He consoled himself with the knowledge that he had merely discovered, not invented, some unwelcome impulses in human beings, young and old. He also knew, as he wrote in the paper about Little Hans, that "when we cannot understand something we always fall back on abuse" (Freud, 1909, p. 27).

His findings about the sexual fantasies of children and about the child unconsciously alive in each and every one of us undermined people's cherished notions of themselves as innocent children developing into that different species — adult. Much of the hostility which Bion's analyst and teacher Melanie Klein faced, and which her work and those developing it are still liable to encounter, is similarly stimulated. She further eroded the cherished illusion of ourselves as the perfect baby, in an ideal relationship with a perfect mother — or at least driven from purity by evil external influences. Many people have found it impossible to believe

The Gerhart Piers Memorial Lecture, presented to the Chicago Institute for Psychoanalysis and the Chicago Psychoanalytic Society on Tuesday, March 27, 1979, and reproduced by courtesy of the Chicago Psychoanalytic Society.

This paper is also being published in *Do I Dare Disturb the Universe? A Festschrift for Wilfred R. Bion*, edited by J. S. Grotstein. New York: Jason Aronson, in press.

that there is an infant alive at all times in every unconscious, let alone one who is not always either contentedly passive or helplessly maligned.

In addition to her work being subject to somewhat the same responses as Freud's, Klein shared with him a not dissimilar geographical and social background. But in other ways they were indeed very different, for she had little formal academic or professional education before becoming a psychoanalyst. She went first to Ferenczi stimulated, as we analysts all have been, both by a personal need for help and a wish to understand others. She was especially interested in child development.

Both Ferenczi and Abraham, to whom she went later for more analysis, encouraged her to do psychoanalytic work with children. She was 39 years old when she approached this task with the knowledge that in small children action, which is more primitive than thought or words, forms the chief part of behavior. She formed the original theory that children's relative lack of free association (which was worrying Hug-Hellmuth and Anna Freud at this time) need not be a barrier to analyzing them because in an analytic setting a child's use of toys in undirected play, considered in conjunction with its spontaneous speech, song, sounds, and movements, can be taken as exactly equivalent to the free association of adults. She also, of course, allowed children the same privileges as adult patients who were, and are, encouraged to say whatever thoughts or feelings occur to them, secure in the knowledge that confidentiality is guaranteed and punishment, moral or physical, eschewed. To this verbal carte blanche and open-minded scrutiny of the details of the child's use of the toys was added detailed attention to its nonverbal sounds, songs, and movements. Each child was given sessions of the same length and was provided with an individual set of simple sturdy toys to use in an uncluttered, relatively indestructible room.

Melanie Klein, in her turn, was as surprised as Freud had been at first by the force and details of the unconscious mechanisms involved. In my opinion one of Freud's mistakes was to use the word "passive" as synonymous with "feminine," and it is just as much a mistake to see babies as passive. Karl Popper (1974), the philosopher of science, writes "there is no such thing as a passive experience" (p. 52). Children do show, with incontrovertible vividness, the strength and variety of their experiences. When the water tap has to be turned off in order to limit the flood to an amount that can be mopped up before the next patient, or scissors temporarily removed in order to prevent a real attack, be it defensive or not, something very intense is evidently going on. In my view Klein's psychoanalytic work with children fully confirmed her basic assumption about the equivalence of the sum total of their activities in a session to verbal free association. Subsequent development of this idea in analyses of adults has led to an expansion of the amount of evidence available for study and interpretation, and thus to an increased likelihood of understanding mental processes. Central to the development in analytic technique resulting from Klein's work with children is the emphasis on what Strachey (1934) has called the "mutative interpretation" (p. 282). By this is meant observation and description of the point of urgency when an id impulse is in a state of cathexis with the analyst as its immediate object, and an interpretive linking of the immediate experience to that with the primary objects (or part objects).

In his paper on the "Two Principles of Mental Functioning," Freud (1911) delineated the theory that primitive mental processes are experienced as "accretions of stimuli" which he thought were evacuated during motor activity. Klein (1930, 1946) confirmed and developed this idea of the concreteness of infantile sensations and responses. She discovered the mechanism of projective identification, whereby parts of the self are experienced as being projected into the object, or part object. Klein found herself confronted with very young and very disturbed children who had become ill in what were, apparently, reasonably nurturing environments. So she was clinically preoccupied at first with the hostile manifestations of projective identification, aimed at greedy possession of, or envious assault upon, the object.

After Abraham died in 1925, Melanie Klein, urged and assisted by Ernest Jones, moved to London. There she undertook a lot of training analyses, teaching, and writing. She did not herself concentrate on the psychoanalysis of the psychoses. She seems to have been a clinical psychoanalyst of extraordinary skill, and her analytic offspring have included Hanna Segal, Roger Money-Kyrle, Donald Meltzer, Esther Bick, Joan Riviere, and Wilfred Bion, who has lived and worked in Los Angeles for the last ten years.

As we turn to Bion himself, it is clear that many of those who have heard of him, or have tried to read his books, will be surprised to learn that he has meant, and will mean, a lot to babies. For it is widely believed that the activities of Bion's complex mind are so abstruse as to be incomprehensible and are thus irrelevant to the day-to-day reality of life, even to that of working psychoanalysts, let alone babies.

In this paper I want to consider the role of Bion's work in furthering our understanding of the interaction between an infant and its environment in mental development. In that sense the title of this short essay may be misleading, for it does scant justice to the importance of those on whom babies depend. However, I hope to be able to demonstrate Bion's contribution to the solution of the nature-versus-nurture controversy as it applies to the growth of the mind from birth onward.

My own first close contact with Dr. Bion was as a candidate of the British Psychoanalytic Society: "Yes, Dr. Bion can take you in supervision for your second training case." These longed-for words were momentarily a source of delighted relief and hope before I was struck with terror at the prospect of discussing my attempts at psychoanalysis with WRB himself. Bion, of the giant frame and master mind. How could I, a practical pediatrician turned child psychiatrist and psychoanalytic trainee, expect to apprehend and comprehend the mental maneuvers of such a man? Should I waste his time with my bumbling efforts? Would I die of fright or be paralyzed with nervousness so that I appeared stupid as well as ignorant? This was in England, in the mid-1950s, before Bion's sequence of books about the growth and functioning of the mind had been initiated with the publication of *Learning from Experience* in 1962. But he was already an impressive figure on the London, and world, psychoanalytic scene. He had also made a lasting impression on psychiatry with his work on groups, which had not then penetrated to pediatricians or to me personally. However, Bion's serious but not censorious demeanor, his capacity to find something benign but perspicacious to say at scientific meetings, and the way in which he drew respect and cooperation from all factions within the British Psychoanalytic Society (of which he was president at the time) did not in any way justify my fears. Yet frightened I was. Luckily for me I was not too frightened to go into supervision with him, and so began one of the great learning experiences of my life.

All that had ever come my way, personally and professionally, had increased my conviction that how babies and children are cared for is of fundamental importance for their psychological, as well as their physical, growth throughout their lives. However, what drove, and drew, me into psychoanalysis was partly a search for answers to the problem of why parents could *not* provide the care they knew was needed and they wanted to give. In other words I was concerned by, and interested in, unconscious factors in abnormal parenting. But over and above that I was intrigued, and at times appalled, by the type of infantile emotional catastrophe which could lead a baby to develop a psychosis, or literally to die, in environments which would be good enough to enable others to make some viable adaptation.

Two babies will serve to illustrate the type of problem I was seeking to comprehend, at least a little more fully. The first was actually of central importance in my decision to train in child psychiatry and psychoanalysis when I returned to work after caring for my own children. I was a pediatric senior resident, and a four-month-old baby was admitted for investigation. She was not brought in by me, for I had already had my own intuition fortified by the view of some of my teachers that a good baby's ward is an empty ward. The suspected diagnosis was pink disease. All went well enough, with mother visiting frequently until she had a miscarriage and was admitted to another hospital. The baby continued to take feedings and appear unperturbed, but she pined until she was near death. We could not reunite mother and baby, but an adaptation in the nursing care, with the crib placed beside the ward nurse's desk, enabled the sick child to revive and survive. What, I wanted to know and am still wondering, happened in her immature mind and how did that affect her body so drastically?

Later I was almost equally struck with the way in which a ten-month-old girl developed an intractable autistic illness. She was a third child, with two normal siblings, who had been thought to be quite alright until her father had an acute illness. Although he could be nursed at home, the mother was very upset and both parents were temporarily very preoccupied with each other. When they emerged after about ten days their baby was gone, as a person, and she remained so.

Less harrowing problems were, for example, how could one understand or help a parent whose conscious plea for dry beds from a seven-year-old was accompanied by a description of a better week, with five continent nights, as "he only did it for me twice last week." What to make of a child or of her pediatrician's unconscious, when she stoutly maintained that "My doctor wants me to put a star on the chart when I *wet* the bed"?

It must have been during the years that I went to him for supervision that Bion was working with, and thinking about, patients with thought disorders. So he was also involved with thinking about the development of a capacity to think. In my first tentative efforts to explain to him what I observed and felt had been taking place in the psychoanalytic sessions I was describing for his supervision I often fell back, in my own view, to memories stirred in me from my work with babies. To my surprise these notions were often enthusiastically greeted by WRB as *models*, to be taken very seriously, and the patients' responses were to be studied for confirmation of their relevance and validity.

The effect could not have been more encouraging, then and in my continuing efforts to study feeling and imagination and give them due weight in each individual personality and its world. Bion was able to show how psychoanalysis was not separate from life, nor a substitute for it, but a method of microscopic distillation, making study possible if one could stand it. He was showing me how to perceive, use, and learn from the transference. He took the view that whatever came into the analyst's mind when he or she was in a state of "free-floating attention" was valid evidence, but that it must be used with sensitivity and continuous scrutiny of one's countertransference. With that proviso my spontaneous memory of a mother and baby could be the basis for an interpretation, which would require validation from the patient's response. At this distance I cannot remember details, but a current example comes to mind. A patient who formerly suffered from a delusion that his guts were hanging out often uses the blanket which is there, folded on my couch, for use if required. He places it over his abdomen, covering the area of the delusion. He uses the blanket a lot less now than he used to. He is a patient who gets severely disturbed or psychosomatically ill when there is an interruption of his analysis. On a recent Thursday morning before I was to make a trip he put the blanket on while complaining of the noise of the heater. I made an interpretation about his need to feel held together by my blanket, which I thought felt to him to be part of my skin; without a skin I am left noisy and attacking (the bad heater). His immediate association was to a sick child who says that someone is eating her skin and feels very threatened when her mother shouts, apparently because mother's noises are felt to be eating into her like the heater had bothered my patient. He also verbalized grateful relief, and showed it by no longer feeling attacked by the heater, or by my voice.

Once when trying to help me see that my overexpectations of what I *should* see were actually interfering with my perceptions, Bion said, "Dr. Isaacs, if you were anywhere else but in a psychoanalytic session you would know what this patient is doing to you." That was a characteristically compact communication with its clear-cut appreciation of one's abilities, and failure to use them, coupled with equally clear warnings against paralyzing fear of, or exaggeration of the importance of, one's role as a psychoanalyst.

It is evident to all those working in child psychiatry that a child's environment is of extreme importance in affecting its emotional development. Before this specialty came into being, the common knowledge of both families and educationalists was in no doubt concerning the importance of nurture for the growth of personality. Since the beginning of recorded knowledge poets have spoken for the work of parents and babies in their descriptions of the ways in which adults are forever influenced by their childhood experiences. However, what has not been so apparent, except to those involved with the continuous care of babies from birth, is that what the child brings to the environment is variable and also vastly important in determining personality growth. Indeed it seems to me that those who, like the Jesuits, claim to be able permanently to mold a person's development and ideology if given their care when young are making the assumption that they will be presented with a child in whom the fundamental steps toward human thought and concern have been taken in an earlier relationship, between the baby and its mother.

To some extent, I think the stance of assuming the inevitability of satisfactory mother/infant relations outside the uterus, as well as during pregnancy, was also taken by Freud. However, Freud took the first, essential, fundamental step in the scientific investigation of the child in us all, when he devised the technique of psychoanalysis. Abraham's application of this method to patients with manic-depressive illness opened the way to the study, in adults, of problems arising in the oral phase of babyhood. Melanie Klein, carrying on from Abraham, took the investigation to the very roots of character, and its disorders, in earliest infancy.

In choosing the names "paranoid/schizoid" and "depressive position" for two essential early infantile developmental states, Melanie Klein had consciously in mind the relation between infant experience and psychotic illness in adults. Winnicott perceptively accumulated and documented convincing evidence of how the basic healthy patterns of childhood personality growth can be distorted by family failure and fostered by family achievement. He coined the phrase "good enough mothering" (1941, 1950). But he called adult psychosis "a deficiency disease of infancy" (1954), deliberately implying that the environment was failing to provide necessary care, as with the vitamin deficiencies. Winnicott misunderstood Melanie Klein's intense preoccupation with her fascinating, but painful, discov-

eries about the fierceness of a baby's hatreds and the anguish of its struggle to resolve its conflict between the life and death instincts. He thought her constitution-
ally incapable of understanding the importance to an infant of the successes and
shortcomings of its environment. This misunderstanding reinforced a defensive
stance, in himself and others, against awareness of the infants' contribution to the
impact of the care being offered to them. In my view Bion's development of Melanie Klein's discovery of projective identification offers a resolution of the Klein-
Winnicott misunderstanding. I think it also makes possible a reconciliation of the
more rigid and vehement nature-versus-nurture protagonists.

Bion worked a lot with psychotic adults, but not with children. He was influenced by Freud's discoveries and linked them with those of Klein to develop his
own views of how early infantile emotional states, pleasurable as well as painful,
are experienced concretely and as such are not available for mental growth.
These concretely experienced states cannot be thought about, imagined,
dreamed of, or remembered (as opposed to being repeated) until they have been
transformed into abstract experiences. An infant cannot acquire this capacity for
transforming its primitive experiences from beta to alpha elements, as Bion has
called them, except by identification with an object capable of performing this
fundamental function.

Bion postulates that such identification is achieved in healthy development via
the use of projective identification as a normal mechanism. In this situation an infant evacuates its unmanageable, indigestible conglomeration of good and bad
experiences into the caretaking part object. This receptive part object offers a realization of the infant's inborn expectation, its preconception, that there is a somewhere in which the unmanageable can be made manageable, the unbearable
bearable, the unthinkable thinkable. For the primary part object, the breast in
Kleinian terminology, does act, by a process which Bion calls alpha function,
upon the projected beta elements and renders them into thinkable, storable,
dreamable alpha elements. These are returned into the baby by the mother, and
introjected by it. The result is an identification with a part object capable of performing alpha function. Perhaps one should speak of a trace identification, for
the word identification can seem to describe too formal and final an activity. It
can seem to imply that with one contact with one manifestation of alpha function
in an object all is well. Certainly, one sees such a misapprehension in young analysts who say, "But I've made that interpretation," to which one can only reply
that it is likely to need making and remaking on a million or more occasions. So it
is with mothers and babies. In my view that nature of a baby's need for repetitive
experience, as though of a theme and variations, is worryingly and increasingly
misunderstood by an influential section of pediatricians and child-care personnel.

The receptive part-object alpha function is usually provided for the baby by the
mother. It may be that this function *can* only be adequately performed for very
young infants by the natural mother, with nine months' experience of ante-

natal involvement with her baby as a background. This is a view Meltzer has expressed at times (personal communications). It may be that only women can tolerate and respond creatively to the impact of a healthy infant's normal projective identifications over a long period of time. It certainly appears to me that even if it should be a man who successfully performs for a baby the onerous task of receiving and responding to its projected experiences, at any time of the day or night that the need arises, the internal representation will nevertheless be of a good breast.

Be that as it may, Bion has given the name "reverie" to the capacity of the object to receive and respond creatively to the baby's projected, concretely experienced chaos and confusion. The word is lovely, with its thoughtful and gentle associations. But I sometimes wonder whether in choosing the word reverie Bion did justice to his own understanding of the emotional intensity of the relationship between mother and baby, or analyst and analysand. For I do not think that amongst the penumbra of ideas commonly associated with reverie we find what Winnicott once called "the white heat" of a session. To me, and I think many others, reverie implies the availability of more time than is the lot of mother and baby when a need for satisfaction arises.

A normal baby's capacity to tolerate frustration is very small. When a normal neonate experiences frustration it is in a terrible state of suffering, which feels endless to the infant. This sense of urgency that an infinite agony must be stopped right away is projected into the mother. She often must, and normally can, react both appropriately and speedily. Reverie, or alpha function, can occur almost instantaneously. But such responses, meeting the baby's preconceptions with appropriate realizations, must be repeated on innumerable occasions and over a long period of time, if normal mental growth is to be built on a firm foundation. So if reverie means prolonged concentration, with patches of musing, and periods of intense attention, then it is indeed a very suitable word to describe the patient preoccupation of a mother with her infant, or an analyst with his patient. For appropriate growth in sensitivity and depth in any relationship depends on the object as well as the subject learning from experience.

One thing that can go wrong in an infant's early life is that its mother has not herself been able to develop an identification with a breast which can tolerate, and transform, the intolerable. Therefore, she cannot respond creatively, with reverie, to the baby's projections but has to rid herself, back into the baby, of unnameable dread. Such a response interferes with growth of the infant's capacity to assess action and reaction, cause and effect, to put one and one together to make two. In other words it hinders the growth of a capacity to think.

A common way of attempting to conceal such a failure in herself is for the mother to take a purely physical approach to an infant's distress. Young babies do need feeding so often that it is easy to see how such a view can be developed and clung to. Yet such an attitude can seriously jeopardize an infant's emotional and mental nutrition, especially when it extends to the material provision being seen as adequate from just any caretaker, babysitter, or housekeeper.

Bion's view is that if reverie is not associated in a mother with love for the child and its father, that fact, like an incapacity for reverie, will be communicated to the infant, albeit in an unmanageable, indigestible way. He is speaking of the mother's unconscious, as well as of her conscious mind. The implications are legion, but this idea certainly suggests some reasons for the difficulties children have when reared in one-parent families or by adults with psychoses or perversions.

Now I want to move the focus of our attention to the variability of an infant's capacity to extract, and use for growth, what good the environment offers. But before doing so it seems relevant to mention that in a psychoanalyst countertransference problems can be the equivalent of those of a mother who cannot perform her function of reverie because she cannot love her baby or its father. An analyst in such a plight may not be able to love his patient, or his patient's parents or former therapists. I don't mean anything sentimental, or sexual, by the word "love." Perhaps "concern" would be a better word to choose, but that too has connotations which need clearing away. What I mean by love in this context is a genuine wish for the independent growth and life of the patient.

I have been trying to show that Bion's idea of the breast as the prototype of the container, the recipient of the projected contents known by him as the contained, is not as static as the words sound or the symbol looks. I have been trying to indicate that throughout life people use each other, their environment, in this active way. They are in search of an active response. In infancy this interaction, with the breast as the container returning the altered contained projections to a baby who then becomes and identifies with the container, is utterly vital to mental growth and can only be achieved if the infant's containing objects are adequately capable of alpha function.

Equally vital are the infant's reactions to the containers' responses. Melanie Klein drew attention to the importance of envy as an innate characteristic which renders good experience bad. This, like other innate traits, is of variable intensity. Envy can be a crippling disability which, in both projective and introjective identifications, distorts good objects and potentially beneficial experiences.

Since no infant can survive at all without some identifications with good part objects, envious assaults result in a desperate sense of deprivation and frustration which increases the need for gratification and the difficulty of achieving any. Clearly, any external deprivations compound the problem. Babies who have a serious innate problem with envy are in need of the most responsive and stable environment. We cannot yet identify these babies at birth or very early in life, nor, if and when we do, is their environment easily enabled to provide the required sensitivity and continuity of care. Excessively envious projective identifications are even harder to tolerate, let alone respond to creatively, than are normal neonatal communications. Even when such high standards of reverie are available, introjective, as well as projective, identifications are interfered with by envious assault in the infant.

Oliver Wendell Holmes, when asked to what he attributed his success in life, put it down to having discovered at an early age that he was not God. To some extent all infants and young children, healthy or not, are strongly influenced by the belief that their mental processes are magical and control the environment. Therefore any real, external damage to hated objects is held by the infant to be its responsibility. Or it would be so held if the baby were not driven to desperate defenses against such an awful state of affairs, with punishment and depression both threatening to overwhelm it. Among situations perceived by *all* infants as damaging to the object, and to the baby, is the object's disappearance externally. For babies "gone, not there" equals "bad, broken," and "broken" to some extent always equals "will break me." The absent object gives no evidence to the contrary, and such evidence is essential. Furthermore, the absence, the unavailability, of an essential object and the anxiety resulting from its disappearance both result in angry, greedy, and envious responses and so lead to further attacks on whatever good internal representation of the object may have been achieved.

There are some personality characteristics which vary innately. Freud called them "constitutional differences." The strength of the belief in personal omnipotence is an important factor in determining an infant's response to the care it is offered. The relation between omnipotence, narcissism, envy, and the death instinct is the subject of a great deal of psychoanalytic study and discussion. Perhaps these are all names for the same inborn quality of disliking, or hating, what is, what exists, because it is not under the infant's, or adult's, control. Whether or not this is so, there does seem also to be an innate variation in the ego's capacity to tolerate the anxieties aroused by helplessness. This in turn clearly affects the extent to which a baby must resort to extreme attempts to defend itself from suffering.

Of particular importance in determining the growth of the human mind is the variable capacity of the individual ego to tolerate what Melanie Klein described as depressive anxiety. If symbol formation inevitably involves an experience of loss of the object as a material possession, which is Hanna Segal's thesis, then it appears that alpha function must do so, too. In my view capacities for alpha function and symbol formation, if indeed they are not one and the same thing, will also turn out to be innately variable. I think a high tolerance of depressive anxiety is a fundamental factor in some babies' capacity to develop more normally in disturbed and disturbing environments which would prove beyond the adaptive capabilities of infants less fortunately endowed.

Among the many interesting facts emerging about the type of environment in which a baby is most likely to be able to develop a capacity for thought are those concerning sound and speech. Thinking is impossible without alpha elements, so is truly symbolic speech. Not only is the sound of the human voice enormously important to babies, whose powers of discriminating one voice from another develop early and detectably. It can also be seen that even newborn babies respond rhythmically, with evident relief of anxiety and often with a manifest sense of pleasurable containment, to the language of an adult speaking to them. This remarkable phenomenon can be explained by the assumptions that introjection of alpha function not only provides the infant with the tools for later pleasurable pattern making, but that from birth onward there is an innate human capacity, probably also varying in strength genetically, to take pleasure in the creative union of alpha elements. Could this last capacity be none other than gratitude and generosity as the basis of love? I think so.

In that remarkable and compact paper, "Formulations on the Two Principles of Mental Functioning," Freud (1911) wrote "it is probable that thinking was originally unconscious, in so far as it went beyond mere ideational presentations and was directed to the relations between impressions of objects, and that it did not acquire further qualities, perceptible to consciousness, until it became connected with verbal residues" (p. 221). Although I am not at all sure that he is correct in the last assumption I quote the passage because of his view of early creative thinking being directed to the "relations between impressions of objects." Bion thinks, and I agree, that there is an inborn awareness of threeness in the human mind. We all arrive in this world with a preconception that two unlike objects, or part objects, will interreact so as to produce a result, be it physical or abstract or both. Realization of this expectation will bring satisfaction, relief, interest, even delight— whatever other emotions are aroused, such as frustrated narcissism or jealousy.

An artist patient of mine, recovering from problems with creativity and low self-esteem, had a dream after watching a program about the investigation of Jupiter. There were many changing swirls, shapes, and colors, but no image more formed than "something inside something." It was interesting, puzzling but not unpleasant. Her associations led to the realization that these patterns were all versions of Paradise, none of which produced the desired result of perpetual bliss. Further, she revealed, through an association to Mars, the epitome of War, that her rage at such deprivation threatened her interest in mixing and relating patterns, seen in this instance as deriving from the relationship of Io and Jupiter. So the hostile impulses were split off into a part-object father, who became the War God. As such he was unconsciously frightening, preventing her full development. The loss of part of the self by projection, albeit an angry destructive part, contributed to her low self-esteem by making her feel incomplete and distressed by the masochistic nature of her relationships, especially with men.

Her capacity to dream of problems of very primitive origin, and to think of them afterward in discussion in a psychoanalytic session, is an indication of her progress toward recovery from an apparently circumscribed, physical, self-damaging "habit" behind which lay an actually crippling, as well as potentially dangerous, personality problem.

Any of the innate or environmental barriers to normal identification with an object capable of alpha function interferes with mental growth and with satisfaction and joy in growth. Beta elements are not capable of constructive conjunctions with each other. The bizarre internal objects resulting from excessive envious projective identification are only capable of bizarre unions. They cannot foster further growth and are inevitably unpleasurable except to the perverse, omnipotent, sadistic aspects of the self. However, they *are* available for defensive evacuation. Alpha elements and alpha function may be rejected in favor of more primitive mental mechanisms for the very reason that they cannot be dealt with in this way.

In 1817 Keats wrote, in a letter to his brothers, "several things dovetailed in my mind and at once it struck me what quality went to form a Man of Achievement. I mean Negative Capability, that is when man is capable of being in uncertainties, mysteries, doubts, without any irritable reaching after fact or reason." Bion is fond of this phrase and uses it to describe the breast's capacity for reverie, and the psychoanalyst's ability to tolerate and sometimes respond creatively to the unknown, the unconscious, without resorting to the therapeutic zeal against which Freud also warned us.

Keats and Bion and Gerhart Piers have all recorded for us, in their different ways, their belief that mental growth is attainable and beautiful but is never effortlessly achieved. All have told us that undue pain can increase the likelihood of distortions in natural growth. So it seems to me appropriate to end this tribute to Bion's work and to Gerhart Piers's life and work, and to their courageously honest attitude, with Keats's (1817) words:

"Beauty is truth, truth beauty," —
       that is all
Ye know on earth, and all ye need to
       know.

REFERENCES

Bion, W. R. (1961), *Experiences in Groups*. London: Tavistock Publications.
_____ (1962), *Learning from Experience*. London: Heinemann.
_____ (1963), *Elements of Psycho-Analysis*. London: Heinemann.
Freud, S. (1909), Analysis of a phobia in a five-year-old boy. *Standard Edition*, 10:3–149. London: Hogarth Press, 1955.
_____ (1911), Formulations on the two principles of mental functioning. *Standard Edition*, 12:213–226. London: Hogarth Press, 1958.
Keats, J. (1817), Ode on a Grecian urn. In: *Complete Poems of Keats and Shelley*, Vol. I. New York: The Modern Library, pp. 185–186.
Klein, M. (1930), The importance of symbol-formation in the development of the ego. *Internat. J. Psycho-Anal.*, 11:24–39.
_____ (1946), Notes on some schizoid mechanisms. *Internat. J. Psycho-Anal.*, 27:99–110.

Piers, G. & Singer, M. B. (1953), *Shame and Guilt*. Springfield, Ill.: Charles C Thomas.

Popper, K. (1974), *The Philosophy of Karl Popper*. Vol. 2, *Unended Quest*. La Salle, Ill.: Open Court.

Strachey, J. (1934), The nature of the therapeutic action of psychoanalysis. *Internat. J. Psycho-Anal.*, 50:275-292, 1969.

Winnicott, D. W. (1941), The observation of infants in a set situation. In: *Collected Papers*. London: Tavistock, 1958, pp. 52-69.

⎯⎯⎯ (1950), Aggression in relation to emotional development. In: *Collected Papers*. London: Tavistock, 1958, pp. 204-218.

⎯⎯⎯ (1954), Metapsychological and clinical aspects of regression within the psycho-analytic set-up. In: *Collected Papers*. London: Tavistock, 1958, pp. 278-294.

April, 1979

IV

CLINICAL
PSYCHOANALYSIS

Adolescent Involvement
with the Supernatural and Cults:
Some Psychoanalytic Considerations

PETER A. OLSSON, M.D. (Houston)

Supernatural Self
Emptiness torments our searching.
The modern self, alone.
No turning back,
To easy comforts of sacredness.
We seek meaning and excitement,
With a cold uneasy gut.
The dawn a familiar haunting.
Departed cocoon-company of sleep.
New day's novel ghosts,
The warmth of self- deception.
We read, believe and view too glibly.
Hold on to favorite truths projected.
The night self-silence returns,
An old familiar God again.
　　　　　—Peter A. Olsson, M.D.

I. Introduction

In recent years adolescent interest in the supernatural and related cults has become heightened and has given a new shape to the already established psychodelism of the 1960s. The by-products of science and technology—the communication media—impinge on the adolescent with an explosive, multidimensioned immediacy. He or she is rapidly presented with widely polarized and highly charged social, cultural, philosophical, religious, and political ambiguities and uncertain-

Presented on October 2, 1979, as the Judith Baskin Offer Lecture co-sponsored by the Michael Reese Hospital Department of Psychiatry and the Chicago Institute for Psychoanalysis.

ties. Parents, teachers, and other adult leaders are fellow strangers in this communally created modern land.

As clinicians working with adolescents in psychotherapy we see many young people obsessed, preoccupied, fused, amused, or apparently just entertained with a geometrically expanding variety of supernatural topics. The popular literature and films of the past decade are permeated with supernatural subjects. These creations vary enormously as to literary or cinematic merit, but their style, form, content, and affect-producing power are often impressive. The adolescent can view or read about haunted or possessed airliners, ships, houses, trucks, bulldozers, animals, fish, or fellow humans. Children or adolescents themselves are often portrayed as possessed, haunted, or abused by the possessed. Just a few examples are *The Exorcist, The Omen, The Manitou, Suffer the Children, Hostage to the Devil, The Sentinel,* and *Rosemary's Baby*, cleverly presented media which exploit, exalt, and entertain with a spectrum of supernatural and uncanny devices.

Burgeoning cults tighten the connection between the supernatural and adolescents. Leading the list are the perpetrators of the ghastly climax in Guyana — The People's Temple — but there are many others as well (appealing to members of all ages), such as Sun Myung Moon's Unification Church, Divine Light Mission, Synanon, Hare Krishna, "The Family," Children of God, and Satanism. All of these cults hold out (1) easy answers to the meaning of life, (2) instant comradeship and a quick sense of communally derived self-worth, and (3) an overly emotional type of persuasion to attract new members. So-called "love bombardment" is "the practice of verbally surrounding a person with 'Love,' until he or she joins the group, and then removing that attention and demanding he or she give it to other members."[1]

These preoccupations with the supernatural and cults are by no means new in history (the Greek Dionysian cult was, of course, referred to by Plato), but the intensity of recent adolescent interest and media coverage is markedly extreme. The cults seem to fall on a wide spectrum of supernatural preoccupation which includes several major types: (1) the traditionally religious supernatural, (2) the nontraditional religious supernatural, (3) the meditative-mystical-philosophic ("Eastern") supernatural, (4) the occult-secular supernatural, and (5) the anti-religious or areligious (purely uncanny) supernatural. They all touch on political-economic issues at times, and at the extremes blend into the frankly sociopathic, delinquent, or criminal behaviors (i.e., the Manson Family).

At a sociohistorical level of conceptualization, the ascendancy of cults and the supernatural seems related to the decline of authoritative forms of traditional religion, as well as to urbanization, rapid shifts in the forms of family life, "feminine liberation," geographic mobility, the mass media, political assassinations, and ever present, but warded-off, reality-based fears of nuclear holocaust.

[1] *Houston Post,* December 13, 1978.

Many adolescents react to these supernatural currents with normal curiosity and sublimated aggressive or sexual excitement without perverse acting out. This paper will focus on the others, whom we as therapists so often see. They seem to entwine the supernatural with neurotic, borderline, narcissistic, prepsychotic, or frankly psychotic symptomatology and processes. In many of the forms of supernatural adolescent preoccupation we see expression of what greatly resembles a perversion or addiction.

My approach will be to present three adolescent cases whose psychopathology blended inextricably with their supernatural beliefs and preoccupations. I believe they will provide clinical data to support the thesis that the adolescent uses the supernatural and uncanny to grapple with and express old and familiar adolescent issues at an intrapsychic level. A final section will attempt to lend some order to our thinking about our adolescent patients who seek the new and the novel from the old and familiar realms of the supernatural through a discussion of theoretical issues.

II. Clinical Case Presentations

ANITA

Anita appeared at her college psychiatric health service when she was nineteen years old. She expressed vague complaints about periodic depression, low self-esteem, and poor self-confidence. After a recent rejection for a position as dorm counselor, she cut both her wrist and arm so deeply as to require emergency-room treatment and subsequent psychiatric hospitalization.

The same fear of feeling rejected had begun early in high school, when she had turned to a deep involvement with Satanism for "a focus of commitment." Her interest had begun with palmistry and moved in a tough progression through Ouija board, tarot cards, and witchcraft readings to a culmination in Satanism. She remarked, "It sets you up to be your own god."

Early in her involvement with the supernatural she had taken Valium (her mother's prescription), dexedrine, mescaline, and, most heavily, marijuana. These chemicals in no way measured up to the excitement of Satanism, so they were discontinued spontaneously.

The patient had experienced intense premonitions prior to her hospitalization. She felt that someone among her family or close friends would be hurt or hospitalized. She felt nauseated and told her friends "something is happening and it is really strange." The next week she learned that a friend's brother had almost drowned, her father entered the hospital for surgery, and she herself was hospitalized as mentioned above.

The patient had been raised in a very "fervent" Protestant fundamentalist church. She attended church regularly and also joined in extra activities such as church suppers and weekly prayer meetings. She was "baptized" at ten years of age. Suddenly, in her last year of grade school her parents quit going to church. They said, "You are old enough to make up your own mind about church." At the same time (sequence blurred), she had her first sexual experience with a boy. She was very aware of guilt about this but also noted "my values going wrong." She regarded all the people at her church as hypocrites and began to mock them in her thoughts and words. She began to be very promiscuous sexually and studied the "Satanic Bible" fervently. (She recognizes now, after thirty-five psychotherapy sessions and carefully adjusted antipsychotic medications, that she was projecting "all the inner turmoil and my feelings onto the church.") At the same time she would chant Satanic, mocking, anti-Christian chants daily. She would make up anti-Christian prayers and was excited by the way the Satanic Bible made fun of Christ at the crucifixion with his "wormwood cross and funny lewd expression." She avoided telling her parents of her sweeping doubts and ruminations, such as: What is the reason to live for a future if there is no eternity? If you just live to die, why not die now? Satan says to make up your own rules. Be independent! It's not what you do, it's how it affects you. You're not past doing anything! You are powerful!

One night late in high school, she found herself in her parents' bedroom in a "kind of trance" with a butcher knife poised above her father's head. She suddenly stopped herself and returned quietly to her room. She noted a gradual personality change from passive aggression to overt, clear feelings of hostility and anger toward "everyone."

Anita described a paradoxical polarity in her life. "I have always been very dependent on authority and always craved a lot of attention. Yet," she went on, "Satanism stresses independence and tells you to make up your own rules." Her self-styled Satanism and witchcraft progressed slowly and relentlessly; it was based, for the most part, on her personal reading of the Satanic Bible and other books. Anita "just knew by the inner senses what Satan wanted me to do." Late in high school she made several suicidal gestures but the attempts were noticed by no one. Upon arrival in college she began to attend religious meetings and loved to sit at the back of the meetings and utter curse words and "mocking comments." A group of Christian girls took an interest in her, and she underwent a religious "reconversion" her freshman year. She became a roommate of one of these young women during her sophomore year. Unfortunately her new roommate attempted to become a controlling, dominating "mother figure." When she criticized the patient for her attraction to boys, the patient felt considerable ambivalence about her rediscovered religion and "heard the distant voices of Satan." She changed her major from music to math. It was then that she was hospitalized after the episode of hypomania and the hallucinations of Satan demanding she cut her arms.

Psychological testing revealed an I.Q. of 120 and documented "thought disorder," strong tendency to intellectualize, self-deprecatory trends, religious preoccupation, guilt, and feelings of unreality along with "bizarre or confused thinking and conduct." She was found at testing to have a chronic, tenuous hold on reality in spite of a strong tendency to respond in conventional ways. "She tends to jump to broad conclusions based on small details of her environment" (overinclusive thinking). She had heavy reliance on fantasy and autistic modes with overincorporation of stimuli to force an ultimate relation between every thought or perception. She projected labile affects onto the outer world with little control over the accuracy or reality of her responses. The psychological testing protocol suggested a broad variety of diagnostic trends (paranoia, hysteria, depression, psychopathy, and schizophrenia). Hostile acting out, intellectualization, autistic withdrawal, symbolization, and phobic-obsessional thinking were major modes of defense.

The Kuder Preference Test revealed an interesting polarity. She had a very high interest in scientific and computational activities (paternal introject) plus high interest in musical and social-service activities (maternal introject and positive high-school music/band activities).

Anita is the eldest of four children, with sisters aged eighteen and seventeen and one brother aged thirteen. Her father is a year younger than her mother and described as "a perfectionist and extremely work-oriented person." The patient said she and her father were alike in looks and personality. He was a rigid and authoritative parent, and moves necessitated by his business both within the United States and abroad forced the patient to enroll in six different public school systems. One of Anita's roles in the family was to stand up to her father in order to divert his attention when he would be angry at another family member. His bad temper led his children to seek gratification in individual rather than family activities. He excelled in math and science, and his constant obsession with work caused constant conflict with her mother. The patient also described chronic conflict between herself and her father.

She described her mother as "real compassionate and caring." Her mother would constantly try to hold down dissension. The patient had been extremely close to her mother in her younger years but experienced her as "smothering" and "really weak." It is of note that her mother was a registered nurse but had not used her training professionally since Anita's birth. Anita really did not "feel feminine" and didn't get much pleasure with sex. She enjoyed "the attention."

Anita has always made good grades and had several close friends; she was never in conflict with teachers and, in fact, frequently idealized them. Her best grades were in math and science (like her father), and she successfully played flute and clarinet in the school band. She was selected drum major in her senior year of high school. When permission was asked for use of disguised material from her life history for this paper, she grew interested and excited, but her therapist recalled how such "special attention" so often evoked "the return of feeling Satan's presence" and compulsions toward self-mutilation. Anita spotted this herself, saying, "I always needed a lot of attention wher. I was committed to Satanism but that has broken down — maybe I'll start a foster home for abused children some day." So far, Anita's treatment continues to progress nicely.

CANDY

Candy was seventeen years old when seen for consultation. Soon after transfer from public school to a strict Catholic high school for her senior year she began to have behavior problems. She had a "poor attitude in class" and often made vague, disruptive comments. She passed notes in class and would giggle inappropriately to herself. She constantly expressed envy of other girls and enjoyed running off during the evening to smoke marijuana or drink beer with older young men who were out of high school and working.

Both Candy and her mother have had periodic, severe asthma attacks since they were three years old. Candy had seen a child psychiatrist at age eight for breath-holding spells and enuresis. Psychotherapy was recommended but the family believed they couldn't afford it. Two other psychiatrists were consulted briefly for family therapy when Candy was ten and twelve years old. On each occasion her father stopped treatment because he didn't like the therapists. Though cooperative on the surface he seemed angry and severely critical toward psychiatry. Candy's parents described her as "emotional and creative" (she began writing poems at age nine). She had always had trouble sleeping at night and until the time of consultation would very frequently be found sleeping on the floor near her parents' bed or require one of them to be beside her until she fell asleep. They seemed to subtly encourage this pattern.

At the first interview Candy described "thinking too much" and "speeded-up thoughts." She would vacillate between writing love poems and "thinking lofty thoughts," and feeling rebellious and "supernatural." She felt she was possessed by some spirit of a poet from "the past." She read about exorcism and felt that a slow process of demon possession prevented her from sleeping, made objects change in size, speeded up her thoughts, and made her fall in love with older men. She obsessed about her middle name really being Zelda. Actually, her middle name was Alice. She thought boys would not really love her if they knew her real middle name. If she married a man and he ever found out that her middle name was Zelda, he would divorce her on the spot. Later the therapist learned that a paternal cousin who carried the name Zelda had been "put in an institution" many years ago. This woman remained chronically psychotic despite psychiatric care and an attempt at exorcism. Her parents alleged that Candy had never been told of Zelda, because she looked so much like her. Candy's father said, "I adored Zelda and couldn't bear to tell Candy the sad story."

In a brief English class essay she shared with the therapist, Candy wrote:

I feel I have some special power or something or someone inside of me. Nature is the only thing we have left to grow on. Why do I feel so bored and alone? I am seeing but I don't like what I see. I am looking at the world through a microscope and not a telescope. I see the people but then again I don't. I cannot identify with them — are they unidentified specimens not yet ready to be studied? I hear the voices of the people and they are telling me to go back to my own little world and watch the world go by . . . So here I am . . . I am behind a glass window and I see the people but they do not see me.

Candy further explained that she felt possessed by some person from the past. "This spirit is both beautiful and sunny but also haunted by dark clouds."
Candy's poems speak for themselves:

Loneliness

I am haunted by loneliness, tortured by
What might have happened. I am alone
Now, no one cares or can they care?
Can they understand I want to be
Something? I wanted to be noticed by
Large crowds of people and admired
By both men and women. And of
Course I want to be loved.

Why are people always living in the past?
Instead of counting your
Mistakes, try counting your blessings.

Death?

Death — that's a word many people are frightened of —
But why should we be?
Sure death is mysterious, it's
Sinister; some say it's wicked
To me death must be a certain
Trip, an adventure, a wonderful
Peaceful feeling with God and the
Universe . . . Death to me must
Be like falling down a huge cliff
And never touching the bottom . . .
Maybe death is like being so free and
So peaceful and so filled with tranquility.
Death — it's what you make your
Destiny is where you choose.

Freedom

My soul is actually moving and I
Can feel the vibrations. I can

Actually "feel" the stereo music — I
Feel as if I am the music. I feel
Like that other person Zelda? that
Has been locked up inside of me
For so long, has finally broken the lock.

Other poems refer constantly to her middle name, a man she almost obtains, and being trapped behind a glass window, "looking out at the world" (perhaps from some distant mental hospital). Her parents could not remember if Candy had gone to see Zelda at the mental hospital when she was young.

Candy's mother almost died of asthma when Candy was twelve years old. Her mother speaks of this often. Candy describes her mother as "nervous, thoughtful, edgy, easily upset, afraid of everything, sort of disturbed, and on tranquilizers all the time." She hovers over me and seems afraid that I can't make it." Candy has a married sister, four years her senior. Candy describes her father as intelligent, understanding, strong, and moody (she describes herself as moody, also). She feels close to her father, talks to him easily, and he often talks soothingly to her late into the night when she can't sleep. At separate sessions her father expressed fear that Candy would be like his first cousin Zelda, who wrote poetry, was intelligent, and "went insane." He wept as he spoke of this cousin who had been like a sister to him.

After the fifth psychotherapy session, Candy quadrupled her dose of Prolixin, and one day while talking to her friends at school between classes she had an acute oculogyric crisis with severe torticollis. Her eyes rolled up into her head so "only the whites were showing," and her neck twisted on itself. The other teenagers at the strict Catholic school felt she was possessed. The movie *The Exorcist* had been very popular at that time, and "everyone had seen it and me." Candy was hallucinating visually and heard "demons cursing me." Later in the hospital she described a feeling that she was behind a glass window, frightened but excited by all the attention during the extrapyramidal drug reaction.

After a brief hospital stay she made slow but steady progress despite overprotective stances by her parents who fought over "how to discipline her" on passes from the hospital. Her father insisted that her mother was "too fearful within herself to help Candy." Candy's mother admitted that she was overprotective, cautious, and "afraid of life."

Despite repeated and gentle confrontation the parents refused therapy for themselves and abruptly terminated Candy's treatment after thirty sessions, when Candy became outspoken and demanded more freedom. They protested that financial problems made further treatment impossible, but turned down referral to the medical-school psychiatry clinic saying, "That was the beginning of the end for Zelda!"

At the five-year follow-up I learned via a colleague that a similar cycle of treatment had occurred with three subsequent psychiatrists. The bonds of symbiotic "love" persist within this family triangle. Here are Candy, Father, and Mother — all possessed by the old and familiar mystery of Zelda.

Lara

Eighteen-year-old Lara was admitted to the acute unit of a psychiatric hospital near the end of her summer vacation from college.

Lara is from a Jewish family but had been on a religious retreat conducted by "The Family," a devout, Protestant sect that believes in the imminent coming to earth of Jesus Christ. Lara grew progressively more excited and would talk to anyone day or night. Adults at the retreat grew concerned when she didn't sleep for two nights and took her to a small general hospital. Sedation was only partially successful, and, very unfortunately, her roommate in the hospital leaped from a hospital window to her death. The patient was convinced she had caused "that poor woman with *breast cancer* to leap to her death." Lara escaped from the general hospital "trying to get back to those kind, loving, caring people in The Family." Her father found her and brought her to the psychiatric hospital. Both her parents and her sixteen-year-old brother were greatly upset by her newfound religion. Her father believed her psychosis was related to upsets with her boyfriend and the recent psychiatric hospitalization of a close cousin. Lara was described as always being too dependent and clinging but also as optimistic, exuberant, and outgoing.

Lara's father was an articulate, brilliant, and benevolently controlling psychiatrist. Numerous family members had had severe psychiatric problems. The maternal great-grandfather died in a psychiatric hospital. A maternal aunt died by suicide at age 39. Her serious mental problems had begun at the patient's age of 18. This aunt had been in and out of hospitals but was able to marry and actually took care of Lara for the first year of her life. When severe marital problems occurred this aunt killed herself. The patient's parents had had a recent recurrence of marital problems. Lara had been promiscuous but enjoyed no pleasure at sex. "I just like to be held."

At first, Lara's mother seemed very passive, distant, and completely subordinate to Lara's father, who articulately described the intricate history and dynamics of the family. Only after several meetings did the therapist learn that six months after Lara's mother became pregnant with Lara she was discovered to have bilateral breast cancer. Her mother waited until Lara's birth before having bilateral mastectomies, and then became profoundly depressed for six or seven months. The deceased aunt (after whom she is named) and her father then acted as mother surrogates. Her father was studying child development at the time and would often stay up most of the night "to feed her at any sign of oral frustration or discomfort." Her father seemed to become mother-aunt-father in the face of her mother's depression and lengthy subsequent psychoanalysis. Lara had rebelled against her father through dating Protestant boys in grade school and hoped her father "would back off and let me live my own life." Lara revealed that in her moments of discouragement her mother had said she would commit suicide if she ever had a recurrence of her breast cancer.

Lara had always been overweight, but she initiated a diet in the hospital and has stayed trim since. Intensive family and individual therapy have helped father to see how overinvolved he had been with Lara. When given freedom, Lara briefly rejoined "The Family," but with a tolerant attitude by the therapist she gradually got involved with her college work. She dropped her major in psychology and did well in fine arts.

After several years in intensive analytic therapy she had worked through "my panicky, manicky guilts about me, my mother, and cancer." When her own family began to shift toward equilibrium she slowly lost interest in "The Family," but she still makes occasional friendly visits to their meetings, "mainly to see some of my friends there—we respectfully disagree about religion."

III. Psychoanalytic Views about the Supernatural, Adolescents, and "Youth Cultures" or Cults

Sigmund Freud on the Supernatural and the Uncanny

The supernatural, the uncanny, parapsychology, the occult, telepathy, and related subjects were always of great interest to Sigmund Freud, and one senses that he had both personal and professional fascination for these unusual topics.

In "Psychopathology of Everyday Life" (1901) Freud compares himself with the superstitious person:

> I believe in external (real) chance, it is true, but not in internal (psychical) accidental events. With the superstitious person it is the other way round. He knows nothing of the motivation of his chance actions and parapraxes, and believes in psychical accidental events. He has a tendency to ascribe to external chance happenings a meaning which will become manifest in real events, and to regard such chance happenings as a means of expressing something that is hidden from him in the external world. The differences between myself and the superstitious person are two: first, he projects outwards a motivation which I look for within; secondly, he interprets chance as due to an event, while I trace it back to an unconscious thought [pp. 257–258].

Freud concludes that in this regard two world views or belief systems emerge in response to experiences of superstition or the supernatural. He calls one of these "The Mythological View of the World" and the other "Our Modern Scientific but as yet by no means perfected Weltanschauung" (p. 258). Freud here connects the mythological *Weltanschauung* in an applied anthropological formulation to the mentality of "pre-scientific peoples." Thus Freud seems to equate the mentality of a person who frequently thinks superstitiously with the mental state of primitive people of past and present cultures. He subtly includes much past and present religious thinking in this formulation:

> In point of fact I believe that a large part of the mythological view of the world, which extends a long way into the most modern religions, is nothing but psychology projected into the external world. The obscure recognition (the endopsychic perception) of psychical factors and relations in the unconscious is mirrored in the construction of a supernatural reality, which is destined to be changed back once more by science into the psychology of the unconscious. One could venture to explain in this way the myths of paradise and the fall of man, of God, of good and evil, of immortality, and so on, and to transform metaphysics into metapsychology [p. 259].

In this, his first published usage of the word metapsychology, Freud draws the battle lines between scientific psychology and superstitious-animistic conceptions of the world.

It is interesting how often the popular literature of the supernatural pits a rational and/or scientific hero against the irrational or demonic spirit from another culture or an earlier, more animistically oriented culture. In *The Exorcist*, the humanitarian priest Merrin and the priest-psychiatrist Damien Karras stand in pitched battle with Pazuzu (a demon from earlier ages and a personification of the southwest wind) who invades the psyche of a preadolescent, sophisticated, contemporary American twelve-year-old, Regan MacNeil (see Blatty, 1971).

Many adolescents today appear to rebel against what seems to be their perception (perhaps valid) that adults worship, animate, or "religify" science or psychology itself. The modern literature of the supernatural and the adolescent joining of anti-intellectual cults are often rebellions against the pseudocertainty of science without humility.

In our cases of Anita, Candy, and Lara we find fathers who were intellectually dominant, preoccupied with "hard-science approaches," and sources of overstimulating conflict to their daughters. Each young woman seemed to use the supernatural in efforts to anger, defy, or create a buffer between herself and a strong father or parental figure. The results were paradoxical for each. It is fascinating to imagine a lively adolescent in animated dialogue with Freud after just having presented his supernatural convictions or experiences.

Freud (1901) responds:

> Whether there are definitely no such things as true presentiments, prophetic dreams, telepathic experiences, manifestations of supernatural forces and the like [I cannot say]. I am far from meaning to pass too sweeping a condemnation of these phenomena, of which so many detailed observations have been made even by men of outstanding intellect, and which it would be best to make the subject of further investigation [p. 261].

The adolescent challenges, "Haven't you ever had one special supernatural experience?" Freud states with a glint of subtle humor in his eye:

> To my regret I must confess that I am one of those unworthy people in whose presence spirits suspend their activity and the supernatural vanishes away, so that I have never been in a position to experience anything myself which might arouse a belief in the miraculous. Like every human being, I have had presentiments and experienced trouble, but the two failed to coincide with one another, so that nothing followed the presentiments and the trouble came upon me unannounced [p. 261].

Freud goes on after these qualifications to link superstition and the supernatural experience with paranoia, obsessional neurosis, and the origins of religion. He says:

> Superstition derives from suppressed hostile and cruel impulses. Superstition is in part the expectation of trouble; and a person who has harbored frequent evil wishes against others, but has been brought up to be good and has therefore repressed such wishes into the unconscious, will be especially ready to expect punishment for his unconscious wickedness in the form of trouble threatening him from without [p. 260].

Thus the mental mechanism of projection comes into play as a central linking concept. The kernel of truth or validity as found in the paranoid who senses his inner aggressive or erotic strivings, but transforms these affects into delusions of external persecution, is clearly described in the Schreber case (Freud, 1911, p. 66).

In each of our cases early symptoms of psychosis seemed to be rationalized or intellectualized in terms of supernatural phenomenology or process. Trances, dazes, feelings of unreality, visual-perceptual distortions, blocking, lability of mood, increasing emergence of primary process, early disturbances in ego functions, such as attention, motility, drive regulation, and impulse control, and later, frank delusions or hallucinations, can all be ruminated about in supernatural terms. In each of our cases these progressive losses in contact with reality were so described and with a sense of mild elation at first.

In the famous "Rat Man" case Freud stresses the peculiarities of obsessional neurotics in their attitudes toward reality, superstition, and death. Of the obsessive's need for doubt and uncertainty, Freud (1909) says:

> The predilection felt by obsessional neurotics for uncertainty and doubt leads them to turn their thoughts by preference to those subjects upon which all mankind are uncertain and upon which our knowledge and judgements must necessarily remain open to doubt. The chief subjects of this kind are paternity, length of life, life after death, and memory [pp. 232–233].

It is interesting that Freud himself frequently ruminated about the length of his life and the immortality of his work. These same ruminations present themselves in the inner thoughts of obsessional adolescent patients and often drive them toward the supernatural for answers.

I hypothesize that one problem in the child rearing of modern adolescents has stemmed from a tragic misinterpretation of Freud's theories over several generations of parents. It has led to a pseudoscientific notion of child rearing where free reign of impulse and all whims of the child seem to be valued, encouraged, and vicariously enjoyed by parents. The superego defects and weaknesses fostered by such misconceptions and failures of empathy are widespread among many adolescents today. "Do your own thing" is so encouraged that many parents abdicate their role of authority. The weird, Satanic, or occult is used to provoke adult authority and also to replace authority abdicated too completely by parents.

Freud's (1919a) basic thesis with regard to the uncanny was that it "is that class of the frightening which leads back to what is known of old and long familiar" (p. 219).

To arrive at his conclusions Freud embarks on a fascinating examination of linguistic usage. The English word "uncanny" means not only "cozy" but also "endowed with occult or magical powers." In Arabic and Hebrew "uncanny" means the same as "demonic" or "gruesome." In English, "uncanny" is synonymous with uneasy, uncomfortable, ghastly, haunted, or repulsive. Freud then goes into exhaustive detail about the German words, *Heimlich* (homely, familiar, agreeable) and *Unheimlich* (the "apparent" opposite—everything that ought to have remained secret and hidden but has come to light). *Heimlich*, however, undergoes a subtle transition of meaning from the idea of "homelike," "belonging to the house," to something withdrawn from the eyes of strangers, something concealed—secret—and this development in the direction of ambivalence leads to an identity with its opposite, *Unheimlich*. In summary, the uncanny is viewed in the same model as the return of the repressed in neurosis.

> The uncanny is in reality nothing new or alien, but something which is familiar and old—established in the mind which has become alienated from it only through the process of repression. Reference to repression enables us to understand Schelling's definition of the uncanny as something that ought to have remained hidden but has come to light [Freud, 1919a, p. 220].

Freud then launches into an in-depth discussion of the things, persons, impressions, events, and situations which arouse feelings of the uncanny. Freud stresses the uncanny aspect of doubt as to whether an apparently animate being is really alive; or conversely, whether a lifeless object might not in fact be animate. Thus, waxwork figures, ingeniously constructed dolls, automata, the uncanny effects of epilepsy and psychotic behavior, or analogous techniques are often used by literary and cinematic craftsmen.

As an illustration of a unique literary figure who is the master of these techniques, Jentsch and Freud discuss E. T. A. Hoffmann's work and his story of "The Sandman" in particular. The recurrent theme is of "the Sandman" who tears out children's eyes. The key character, a late-adolescent student, Nathaniel, despite his present happiness, cannot banish the childhood memories associated with the mysterious and terrifying death of his beloved father. On certain evenings his mother used to send the children to bed early, warning them that "the Sandman was coming." Later Nathaniel hides to try to see "the Sandman." His father barely saves Nathaniel from the Sandman's attack on his eyes. At another visit of the Sandman his father is killed by an explosion. The Sandman is a disturber of love who separates Nathaniel from his betrothed and from her brother, his best friend. He destroys the narcissistic object of his second love, Olympia, a lonely, lifelike doll. Then "the Sandman" drives Nathaniel to suicide at the moment he has won back his betrothed and is about to be happily united to her. Hoffman, the author, was the child of an unhappy marriage. When he was three years old, his father left and never returned.

Freud discusses the uncanny fear of losing or damaging one's eye. Expressions such as "apple of our eye," eyeballs, etc., relate to the study of myths and dreams in which the fear of going blind is often a substitute for the dread of being castrated. The Sandman story also seems to me to be a means by which parents try to scare their children into staying in bed so that they can be alone for sex together. Thus the wish to see and the fear of seeing "the primal scene" seem to be involved as well. Many of the incestuous, sexual, and lewd scenes in the modern, popular literature of the supernatural are permeated with this deeply unconscious theme. A striking example is the scene of the conception of *Rosemary's Baby* as the product of the grotesque intercourse of a demon and a lovely woman.

In many cults that appeal to adolescents there is value in "seeing the light" or in a visual encounter with the leader-hero of the cult. The supernatural eyes of Charles Manson or the Reverend Jim Jones have been described with surrendering awe by their followers. At her oculogyric crisis at school Candy's classmates kept saying, "Look at her eyes! Look at her eyes!"

Freud discusses in detail the notion of projected envy involved in the "Dread of the Evil Eye." My own notion about an unconscious repetition compulsion in children and adults to view the uncanny primal scene is supported by Freud's (1919b) comments on Otto Rank's volume on the incest complex (1912). Rank emphasizes in this work that the working over of the oedipal theme in a great variety of modifications, distortions, and disguises by the dramatist and writer reflects an attempt to master the emotional attitudes toward their mother and father (i.e., family).

Freud (1919a) discusses the extraordinarily strong feelings of something uncanny that pervades the conception of "the double," in which telepathic experiences allow one to "possess" knowledge, feelings, and experience in common with the other. This has been a powerful theme in great literature. "In other words, there is a doubling, dividing and interchanging of the self" (p. 234). Freud also says:

> The theme of the "double" has been very thoroughly treated by Otto Rank. He has gone into the connections which the "double" has with reflections in mirrors, with shadows, with guardian spirits, with the belief in the soul and with the fear of death. . . . For the "double" was originally an insurance against the destruction of the ego, an energetic denial of the power of death, as Rank says; and probably the "immortal" soul was the first "double" of the body [pp. 234–235].

As Freud goes on to relate the notion of the "double" to the idea of primary narcissism and "conscience" we see anticipations and conceptual premonitions of Kohut's psychology of the self (developed 50 years later). It would be tempting to speculate that the vast popularity of literature about twins stems from the uncanny aspect of such relationships. Freud presented what was really an old and familiar idea when he stated that the "double" was an attempt to surmount the narcissism of our earliest developmental times. Only much later would Kohut (1971) describe in more detail the twinship transferences seen in narcissistic personality disorders and help in our understanding of some adolescent patients' preoccupations with the supernatural.

Freud (1919a) reviews in his paper on "The Uncanny" a whole section from "Totem and Taboo," which he offers as a penetrating tool to understand the supernatural in literature and adolescent strivings.

> Our analysis of instances of the uncanny has led us back to the old, animistic conception of the universe. This was characterized by the idea that the world was peopled by the spirits of human beings; by the subject's narcissistic overvaluation of his own mental processes; by the belief in the omnipotence of thoughts and the technique of magic based on that belief; by the attribution to various outside persons and things of carefully graded magical powers, or mana; as well as by all the other creations with the help of which man, in the unrestricted narcissism of that stage of development, strove to fend off the manifest prohibitions of reality. It seems as if each one of us has been through a phase of individual development corresponding to this animistic stage in primitive man, that none of us has passed through it without preserving certain residues and traces of it which are still capable of manifesting themselves, and that everything which now strikes us as "uncanny" fulfills the condition of touching those residues of animistic mental activity within us and bringing them to expression [pp. 240–241].[1]

James Hamilton (1976), in his fascinating paper, "The Exorcist: Some Psychodynamic Considerations," reminds us of Freud's unique paper of 1923, "A Seventeenth-Century Demonological Neurosis." Hamilton's reference to Freud's paper

---

[1] See also Freud (1912), Part III, Animism, magic, omnipotence of thoughts.

is aptly chosen. Freud carefully analyzes the record of the possession of Christoph Haizmann, a painter, who grew depressed and work-inhibited and suffered "frightful convulsions" after his father's death. The subsequent nine-year pact with the devil is seen by Freud as a neurotic solution to the loss of father via obtaining the devil as a father substitute. Freud stresses how God and the devil in Christian mythology are really a psychodynamic unity. The son's affectionate-submissive longing for the father is ambivalently fused with his fear, hostility, and defiance toward him. This is a common dynamic in young adolescent followers in cults. The supernatural father figures found in Satanism often reflect their search for the physically or psychologically absent father of their childhoods. Hamilton also notes the significance of object loss and the use of primitive defense mechanisms of introjection, incorporation, projection, denial, and splitting associated with the failure to mourn in the genesis of so-called demon possession.

We see these same vivid dynamics in Candy and Anita. Lara, who joined a cult, discovered a new "Family" as a replacement for the old family of ambivalent feelings. She had fled, but never mourned or separated from her family intrapsychically. In our three cases, however, the surface power struggles and separation-individuation conflicts of these adolescent girls with their fathers raise questions of earlier, more profound, difficulties with their maternal objects. All three girls were very protective of their mothers when they spoke of them. All three admitted they were closer to their fathers emotionally with greater intensity of affects of love/hate. The maternal objects emerging from between the lines were weak, phobic, narcissistically vulnerable, or potentially enveloping. The fathers then became relatively more stable objects of attachment, attack, distant longing, or rebellion. The supernatural metaphors of preoccupation (Anita and Candy) or the cult (Lara) became compromise arenas to unconsciously portray their difficulties. Preoedipal conflicts seem to have been more prominent in our three cases.

In summary of Freud: I believe he would see the supernatural preoccupations and uncanny experiences of our patients in terms of the return of repressed affects, preverbal experiences, conflicts, and vague traumas from their personal pasts.

Waelder (1951) refines this notion in his discussion of isomorphism. He writes: "If the defense mechanism had the form of denial, the return must have the form of an assertion" (p. 176). As comedian Flip Wilson used to say: "The Devil made me do it." This principle of isomorphism in regard to the relation to inner drive, conflict and symptom, and symptomatic behavior and defense, is heuristically helpful when more primitive mechanisms are present. In all three of our patients, and I think generally in adolescents with severe problems expressed in terms of the supernatural, we find a preponderance of denial, projection, projective identification, paranoid-persecutory ideation, and pervasive splitting mechanisms. Anita said, "I heard the distant voices of Satan again. They told me to cut my arms, and I did." The isomorphism idea might be extended to acting-out behaviors as reflections of the return of old and familiar abusive behavior by parents toward their children (child abuse and incest being ever more in our attention). Though Lara did not act self-destructively she felt she had caused her hospital roommate's suicide (possible maternal object surrogate). Anita and Candy had strong self-destructive and acting-out difficulties. When acting out involves promiscuity, lewd profanity, or self-destructive ritual, we often see adolescents seeking out supernatural or uncanny cults as channels for such expression.

SATANISM, PERVERSION, AND THE SUPERNATURAL

I would like to discuss Anita's case in further detail because some adolescents today go far beyond the point at which her treatment fortunately intervened. These ritualized, truly perverse behaviors reached profound extremes in the "mass murders" (Houston, Chicago, and many other locations) of the recent decade. These activities at the extreme find young adolescents sexually stimulated, tortured in ritualized ways, and then usually murdered. What intrapsychic forces could be at work to bring a young person even near such potential dangers? Some perspectives come from some further exploration of the concepts of Satanism and perversion.

Satanism began in the third or fourth century, and has continued in various forms ever since. Its essential two ingredients are (1) worship of the devil, and (2) reversal of Christian values. D. H. Rawcliff (1975) writes:

> A Satanist has renounced Christ and his church [parent and family intrapsychically], and blasphemously maltreated its sacred objects, symbols and ceremonies; he adores the Devil in the form of a man [parental surrogate] or animal; he sings and dances in the Devil's honor and obscenely kisses and fondles his person [preoedipal-oral] issues; and he revels in child slaughter and cannibalism, indiscriminate sexual orgies, perversion, homosexuality and every species of crime and abomination. This same pattern is described for witches and objects of the irreligious or areligious supernatural. [There is a vivid, illustrative account of the "Black Mass" in J. K. Huysman's novel La'- Bas, probably drawn from real life] [p. 34].

Such supernatural content seems to peculiarly fit the rebellious externalizations or projective identifications of adolescent intrapsychic struggles; they are really recapitulations of preoedipal and oedipal themes and their distortions.

Robert Stoller (1976) writes:

> Sexual excitement depends on a scenario the person to be aroused has been writing since childhood. The story is an adventure, an autobiography disguised as fiction, in which the hero/heroine hides crucial intrapsychic conflicts, mysteries, screen memories of actual traumatic events and the resolution of these into a happy ending, best celebrated by orgasm. The function of the fantasy is to take these painful experiences and convert them to pleasure-triumph. In order to sharpen excitement—the vibration between the fear of original

traumas repeating and the hope of a pleasurable conclusion this time — one introduces into the story elements of risk (approximations of trauma) meant to prevent boredom [p. 899].

Anita described sexual excitement as she obeyed the Satanic command to cut herself. Candy felt exhibitionistic excitement as her classmates watched her apparent demon-possession. For the most part all three young women described severe dissociation of tenderness, orgasm, and deeply felt sexual excitement. None gave much detail about sex. Very late in her therapy Lara was able to get somewhat beyond her intense preoedipal and oedipal conflicts. As her parents resolved their marital conflicts and Lara individuated, she met and really got to know a young man. Tenderness began to combine with sexual excitement for the first time.

In the fully developed Satan cults one finds the full-blown symbolism of perversion. Stoller (1975) writes in his aptly titled book, *Perversion: The Erotic Form of Hatred*: "In men, perversion may be at bottom a gender disorder constructed out of a *triad of hostility:* rage at giving up one's earliest bliss and identification with mother, fear of not escaping out of her orbit, and a need for revenge for putting one in this predicament" (p. 99). Stoller also says: "A phallus is dangerous but not mysterious; the womb's danger comes from silence, secrecy, and growth in darkness — which is mystery" (p. 98).

The bizarre extremes of Satanism that require detached female submission and mocking male cruelty concretize and act out old and familiar mysteries of male/female dilemmas. In the cases of Candy and Anita, Satan as the father/God substitute propounded by Freud seems to have relevance; fortunately neither girl had found a bizarre group cult in which to act out to destructive extremes. Such cases I am sure could be documented. Full discussion of delinquent and criminal groups and behaviors that have implications for study of adolescents in this "supernatural vein" is beyond the scope of this paper, but it clearly has relevance and importance.

Adolescence, Separation-Individuation, and the Supernatural

Peter Blos (1962) says:

Adolescence (as a phase and process) must accomplish the renunciation of the primary love objects, the parents, as sexual objects; siblings and parent substitutes have to be included in this process of renunciation. This phase, then, is concerned essentially with object relinquishment and object finding, and these processes reverberate in the ego to produce cathectic shifts which influence both the existing object representations and self-representation. Consequently, the sense of self or sense of identity acquires a heretofore unknown lability.

During adolescence the drive turns toward *genitality* [a combination in experience of tenderness, maturity, intimacy, generativity, and sexual excitement], the libidinous objects change from the preoedipal and oedipal to the nonincestuous, heterosexual object. The ego safeguards its integrity through defensive operations; some of these are ego restricting and require counter-cathectic energy for their maintenance, while others prove to be adaptive, and to allow aim-inhibited (sublimatory) drive discharge; these become the permanent regulators of self-esteem [p. 75].

In all three cases we can identify severe problems in the renunciation–new-object-finding process described by Blos. The supernatural preoccupations seemed to form or give mental representation to abortive symbolic efforts to effect such shifts away from the parental objects. The preoedipally problematic mothers were all variously weak and narcissistic and thus poor models for identification or full, unambivalent renunciation. The incestuous struggles, then, become in this context uncanny and mysterious for Anita, Candy, and Lara. They are all still in various ways struggling with these issues of identity.

A discussion of Margaret S. Mahler's work in regard to the case histories and implications for a study of the supernatural and uncanny could be voluminous; so I will present some of her comments about the third subphase of separation-individuation which she calls rapprochement. She says:

The rapprochement struggle has its origins in the *species-specific* human dilemma that arises out of the fact that, on the one hand, the toddler is obliged, by the rapid maturation of his ego, to recognize his separateness, while, on the other hand, he is as yet unable to stand alone [Mahler et al., 1975, p. 229].

She goes on:

In some children, however, the rapprochement crisis leads to great ambivalence and even to splitting of the object world into "good" and "bad," the consequences of which may later become organized into neurotic symptoms of the narcissistic variety. In still other children, islands of developmental failures might lead to borderline symptomatology in latency and adolescence.

Fixation at the level of rapprochement may be seen every so often in the widening range of child and adult patients who nowadays seek our help. Their most pervasive anxiety is separation anxiety; their affects may be dominated by narcissistic rage with temper tantrums, which may subside and give way to altruistic surrender (A. Freud, 1936). Their basic conflict is to be sought and found, we believe, in the primitive narcissistic struggle that was acted out in the rapprochement crisis, but that may have become a central internal conflict pertaining mainly to their uncertain *sense of identity* [pp. 229–230].

It seems to me that the polarized supernatural metaphors of God/Satan, White/Black, Saint/Sinner, Angel/Demon, Good/Evil, Heaven/Hell, Found/Lost have a natural fit with the splitting mechanisms and their origin, as Mahler describes them, or, as Freud would suggest, are reminiscent of old and familiar preverbal, primitive, affective cognitive, magical omnipotent states like that of the infant or primitive tribes. The primitive group processes in some cults seem to blend as a natural, old, and familiar interpersonal context for these dilemmas for borderline, narcissistic, or very neurotic adolescents.

Mahler, above, referred to Anna Freud's delineation of the term coined by Edward Bibring—"altruistic surrender." Anna Freud, after her lucid descriptions of "identification with the aggressor" and reversal (primarily love/hate), and their relation to projection in its negative interpersonal connotations, goes on to say:

> But it [projection] may work in another way as well, enabling us to form valuable positive attachments and so to consolidate our relations with one another. This normal and less conspicuous form of projection might be described as "altruistic surrender" of our own instinctual impulses in favor of other people [1936, p. 123].

She points out that "this defensive process has its origin in the infantile conflict with parental authority about some form of instinctual gratification" (p. 130). This mechanism also allows such gratification by sharing vicariously in the gratification of others via projection and unconscious identification. I propose that in some troubled adolescents we see another variation of this process that might be termed "malevolent surrender." Here the unresolved, primitive islands of sadistic, masochistic, and phallic narcissistic strivings find sustained, untamed existence via malignant forms of supernatural preoccupations, obsessions, ruminations, and perverse behaviors. The supernatural in these areas provides a perfect haven for the preservation of the immature, the infantile, and the destructive.

Views from the Therapeutic Dyad Back Out to the Social Field

Heinz Kohut offers some helpful perspectives on our topic. I want to avoid the theoretical and semantic quarrels associated with Kohut's formulations, but rather will assume the reader is familiar with the primary sources or with the four fine, concise reviews of Spruiell (1975), Loewald (1978), Schwartz (1978), and Marohn (1977). Marohn's review presents in detail the implications of Kohut's concepts for understanding and treating the delinquent and criminal adolescent. Giovacchini's (1977) discussion of Marohn's paper provides a rigorously balanced critique of Kohut.

Kohut's (1971) sensitive delineation of the spectrum of so-called selfobject transferences or transferencelike states is very enlightening. It expands on Freud's discussion of the uncanny aspects of "the double" and offers a theoretical perspective on the supernatural as experienced by adolescents. Kohut describes various "mirror transferences" (alterego or twinship, archaic merger, and mirror transference in the narrower sense). The early traumatic disappointments in the maternal object, later disappointments with the fathers, and intense separation-individuation problems of our three cases could be viewed in terms of tremendous problems in the narcissistic sector of their personalities. The implications of the psychology of the self for understanding the inherent grandiosity and uncanny power of supernatural preoccupations in the lives of narcissistically vulnerable adolescents are many (see Loewald, 1973; Schwartz, 1978). For Anita, Satan became a kind of twin, double, or alterego of grandiose power and sustenance. The idealizing transference, established quickly with the therapist, became crucial to sustain the therapeutic work as she examined the selfobject qualities of her relationship to the therapist and his medication. Even to interpret the oral, anal, oedipal, or other traditionally viewed conflict areas, before extensive work with the narcissistic (perhaps preoedipal), selfobject aspects of her case, would lead to precarious situations.

The supernatural, the uncanny, and the primitive belief systems and metaphors of some cults have a unique phenomenological fit with inner narcissistic and borderline dynamics and problems of psychic structure. The supernatural metaphors seem to act as foci for "transmuting externalizations" as compromise formations in these troubled adolescents. It is clear how delicate therapeutic technique must be as the therapist approaches these areas during sessions. It is not unlike the great sensitivity one must use in approaching creative literary-artistic productions of adolescents (Skolnikoff, 1976). The adolescent can indeed be and feel very creative and vulnerable in his use of the supernatural metaphors. Empathic mirroring of the degree of self-cohesion provided by the supernatural must take place if such malignant transmuting externalizations are eventually to be contained and worked through as transmuting internalizations of a well-conducted therapy. The supernatural involvements may be used by the patient as a buffer or desperate defense against overwhelming merger anxiety toward the therapist as the powerful mind reader. Kohut's "bipolar self" was a very helpful concept in attempting to understand Candy as she exclaimed, "I vacillate between seeing myself as thinking lofty thoughts and being a famous poet; and then feeling haunted, bored, rebellious, and depressed."

One final area I wish to explore is nicely put into perspective by Kohut (1977):

But now I shall turn to a field that lies "beyond the bounds of the basic rule": the field where the scrutiny of psychological factors and the scrutiny of social factors converge.

I shall go directly to the heart of the matter by making the claim that the psychological danger that puts the psychological survival of modern Western man into the greatest jeopardy is changing. Until comparatively recent times the dominant threat to the individual was unsolvable inner conflict. And the correlated dominant interpersonal constellations to which the child of western civilizations was exposed were the emotional overcloseness between parents and children and intense emotional relationships between the parents — perhaps to be looked upon as the unwholesome obverse of such corresponding wholesome social factors as firmness of the family unit, a social life concentrated on the home and its immediate vicinity, and a clear-cut definition of the roles of father and mother.

Today's child has fewer and fewer opportunities to observe its parents at work or at least to participate emotionally, via concrete, understandable imagery, in the parents' competence and in their pride in the work situation where their selves are most profoundly engaged.... Today's child can, at best, observe the parents' activities during their leisure hours [p. 269].

Kohut acknowledges that leisure time together has positive aspects, but that the child's forming "nuclear self" does not get the same nutriment as the emotional participation in the activities of real life day to day. Kohut particularly believes that the progressive, limited, optimal, nontraumatic parental failures that can provide the fuel for transmuting internalizations are not available. Kohut further refines this:

The environment which used to be experienced as threateningly close, is now experienced more and more as threateningly distant; where children were formerly *over*stimulated by the emotional (including the erotic) life of their parents, they are now often *under*stimulated; where formerly the child's eroticism aimed at pleasure gain and led to internal conflict because of parental prohibitions and the rivalries of the oedipal constellation, many children now seek the effect of erotic stimulation in order to relieve loneliness, in order to fill an emotional void [p. 271].

This sort of applied analysis is always risky, but I think Kohut frames for us where the troubled adolescent's intense preoccupations with the supernatural, uncanny, and cults seem to fit psychosocially. He states:

[In the narcissistic-defensive sphere], it is clear that children [and adolescents] often undertake both solitary sexual activities and group activities of a sexual, near-sexual, or sexualized nature in the attempt to relieve the lethargy and depression resulting from the unavailability of a mirroring and of an idealizable self-object [p. 272].

Kohut lends some perspective here on the narcissistic, masturbatory-like, and perverse intensity of some adolescents' preoccupations with the stimulation of supernatural and uncanny cults. In the acted-out extremes, Stoller's subtitle, *The Erotic Form of Hatred* (1975) sums it up nicely. Perhaps the children-rearing ethos described by Kohut leads to a relative increase in borderline and narcissistic pathologies, and a society with such extensive mass media available has an increased preoccupation with overstimulating supernaturalism.

Otto Kernberg (1975), in a paper very germane to our discussion, "Cultural Impact and Intrapsychic Change," cautions us against too hasty conclusions. He points out:

I do not think that changes in contemporary morality have effects on the sense of self in the direction of fostering identity diffusion or loss of the sense of self. I think the syndrome of identity diffusion always reflects serious psychopathology related to borderline personality organization, which stems from vicissitudes of very early development; the underlying intrapsychic structures which reflect such psychopathology are probably crystallized within the first five years of life. . . .I do not think that changes in contemporary morality [or perhaps supernatural preoccupations] have effects on patterns of object relationships if we define object relationships not simply in terms of actual interactions between a person and others, but in terms of the intrapsychic structures which govern such interactions, and in terms of the internal capacity to relate in depth with others. Many authors have talked about what has been called this "age of alienation," and it has been implied that social and cultural alienation may foster disintegration of the capacity of involvement in depth with others. I think that clinically speaking this does not hold true.

Keniston's work (1960, 1968) comparing youth in protest with alienated youth has provided important sociological evidence indicating that generalized withdrawal from relationships with others and incapacities to establish deep, lasting relationships are not a direct reflection of youth culture, but stem from very early childhood conflicts and family pathology. By the same token, I do not think that changes in contemporary morality have changed the need and the capacity for intimacy in various forms. This does not mean to say that such changes in the patterns of intimacy could not occur over a period of several generations if and when changes in cultural patterns affect family structure to such an extent that earliest development in childhood would be affected [pp. 39–40].

Several paragraphs later Kernberg continues:

All this does not mean that the deciding factor of where an adolescent stands in the cultural struggle is determined exclusively by the degree and type of his or her personal psychopathology. I feel very critical about the tendency to explain away cultural identities in terms of a purely individual psychology of psychopathology. . . . However, a certain culture selects or highlights certain types of psychopathology because they fit into it better, and thus convey — erroneously — the impression that it has brought about a certain type of individual psychopathology [p. 41].

Kernberg then nicely and concisely summarizes Jacobson's "Levels of Superego Development" (1964) and concludes:

What needs to be stressed is that the main reorganization in adolescence of superego identifications relates to those of the oedipal period, in connection with a definite growing out of the oedipal conflicts of childhood. Jacobson points out that it is only in patients with severe borderline or narcissistic character structures that reprojection of more primitive superego nuclei takes place, which indicates that the superego was poorly consolidated and integrated in the first place. In this case, we find a combination of primitive idealizations which reflect the tendency toward narcissistic self-aggrandizement, general devaluation of value systems and external objects, a chaotic shift in group identifications, and lack of capacity to empathize in depth with other persons. Patients with these borderline and/or narcissistic features may emerge as temporary leaders or predominant exponents of protesting, alienated, or bizarrely oppositional groups, rapidly adapting to the unusual or far out, rationalizing their socially drifting quality and lack of consistency in terms of a chaotic social structure [pp. 41–42].

In summary, Blos, Mahler, Stoller, Kohut, and Kernberg help us toward an awareness of the adolescent at risk for "malevolent surrender" to perverse, supernatural cults. This hypothetical young person has intense unresolved "preoedipal" conflicts. He or she would have (1) major separation-individuation conflicts, (2) gender-role confusion, (3) incestuous attachments, (4) conflicted internalized object relations, (5) defensive structures typical of narcissistic or borderline personality, and (6) a vulnerability to powerful, perverse supernatural overstimulation because of parental understimulation via lack of empathic, collaborative parental contact.

Very careful clinical scrutiny is required to sift out what is really going on with each individual adolescent. This must take into account (1) the cultural milieu, often over several generations, (2) the intrapsychic structure or lack of it as it relates to supernatural preoccupations, and (3) the selfobject aspects of our therapeutic relationship with an adolescent so preoccupied.

IV. Summary

In recent years there appears to be a heightened adolescent interest in the supernatural and in variously related or associated cults. The range of supernatural preoccupations can be arbitrarily divided along a spectrum: (1) the traditionally religious supernatural, (2) the nontraditionally religious supernatural, (3) the meditative ("Eastern") supernatural, (4) the occult-secular supernatural, and (5) the anti-religious or areligious supernatural.

Adolescent responses to the potentially overstimulating media and peer preoccupation with the supernatural varies from normal curiosity and sublimated excitement to devout interest via sudden "conversion" and/or an entwining of these supernatural preoccupations with major neurotic, characterologic, narcissistic, borderline, prepsychotic, or frankly psychotic psychopathology.

Three cases are presented to illustrate how adolescents weave supernatural involvements into their major psychopathology. These cases are used to focus perspectives from prominent psychoanalytic thinkers upon adolescents and the supernatural. The cases presented typify the predominant "preoedipal," borderline, and highly narcissistic trends that the supernatural metaphors uniquely fit into phenomenologically. These images of Good/Bad, White/Black, God/Satan, Saint/Sinner, Angel/Demon, etc., of the supernatural belief systems, relate like friendly bedfellows to primitive intrapsychic defenses such as denial, projection, "malevolent surrender," splitting, and projective identification.

The general conclusion is that adolescent preoccupation with cults and the supernatural is really reflective of old and familiar adolescent psychodynamic, psychoeconomic, and psychogenetic issues. Great care must be taken so as not to glibly assume that sudden surface shifts in varieties of "youth culture" or cults easily affect intrapsychic structure or functioning. On the other hand, over several evolving generations, sociocultural phenomena can lead to significant changes in child-rearing and thus may ultimately affect intrapsychic pathology.

Valuable observations can be made on "youth culture" issues from within the psychoanalytic psychotherapy dyad, to combine with careful sociocultural-historical observation and to contribute to in-depth perspectives on such phenomena as adolescent preoccupations with cults and the supernatural.

The potentially perverse and/or violent extremes of recent supernatural preoccupations and cults is a clear indication for therapists of adolescents to be knowledgeable about such phenomena.

REFERENCES

Blatty, W. P. (1971), *The Exorcist*. New York: Harper & Row.

Blos, P. (1962), *On Adolescence: A Psychoanalytic Interpretation*. Glencoe, Ill.: Free Press.

Freud, A. (1936), *The Ego and the Mechanisms of Defense. The Writings of Anna Freud*, Vol. 2. New York: International Universities Press, 1966, pp. 3–176.

Freud, S. (1901), The psychopathology of everyday life. *Standard Edition*, 6:1–279. London: Hogarth Press, 1960.

_____ (1909), Notes upon a case of obsessional neurosis. *Standard Edition*, 10:153–318. London: Hogarth Press, 1960.

_____ (1911), Psycho-analytic notes on an autobiographical account of a case of paranoia (dementia paranoides). *Standard Edition*, 12:3–82. London: Hogarth Press, 1958.

_____ (1912), Totem and taboo. *Standard Edition*, 13:1–198. London: Hogarth Press, 1955.

_____ (1919a), The uncanny. *Standard Edition*, 17:219–256. London: Hogarth Press, 1955.

_____ (1919b), Preface to Reik's "Ritual: Psycho-Analytic Studies." *Standard Edition*, 17:259–263. London: Hogarth Press, 1955.

_____ (1923), A seventeenth-century demonological neurosis. *Standard Edition*, 19:69–105. London: Hogarth Press, 1961.

Giovacchini, P. (1977), Discussion of: A critique of Kohut's theory of narcissism. In: *Adolescent Psychiatry*, Vol. 5, ed. S. Feinstein & P. Giovacchini. New York: Jason Aronson, pp. 213–235.

Hamilton, J. (1976), The exorcist: Some psychodynamic considerations. *J. Phila. Assn. Psychoanal.*, 3:37–53.

Keniston, D. (1960), *The Uncommitted*. New York: Dell.

_____ (1968), *Young Radicals*. New York: Harcourt, Brace & World.

Kernberg, O. (1975), Cultural impact and intrapsychic change. In: *Adolescent Psychiatry*, Vol. 4, ed. S. Feinstein & P. Giovacchini. New York: Jason Aronson, pp. 37–45.

Kohut, H. (1971), *The Analysis of the Self*. New York: International Universities Press.

_____ (1977), *The Restoration of the Self*. New York: International Universities Press.

Loewald, H. (1978), Review of *The Restoration of the Self*, by H. Kohut. *Psychoanal. Quart.*, 47: 441–451.

Mahler, M., Pine, F., & Bergman, A. (1975), *The Psychological Birth of the Human Infant*. New York: Basic Books.

Marohn, R. (1977), The "juvenile imposter": Some thoughts on narcissism and the delinquent. In: *Adolescent Psychiatry*, Vol. 5, ed. S. Feinstein & P. Giovacchini. New York: Jason Aronson, pp. 186–212.

Rank, O. (1912), *Das Inzest-Motiv in Dichtung and Sage* [The Incest Motif ·in Poetry and Saga]. Leipzig and Vienna: Deuticke.

Rawcliff, D. H. (1975), *The Occult and the Supernatural*. New York: Crown.

Schwartz, L. (1978), Review of *The Restoration of the Self*, by H. Kohut. *Psychoanal. Quart.*, 47: 436–443.

Skolnikoff, A. (1976), The creative process and borderline patients. Paper presented at the Annual Meeting of the American Psychiatric Association, Miami, Florida.

Spruiell, V. (1975), Three strands of narcissism. *Psychoanal. Quart.*, 44:577–596.

Stoller, R. (1975), *Perversion: The Erotic Form of Hatred*. New York: Random House.

_____ (1976), Sexual excitement. *Archiv. Gen. Psychiat.*, 33:899–909.

Waelder, R. (1951), The structure of paranoid ideas. *Internat. J. Psycho-Anal.*, 32:167–177.

April, 1979

The "Monday Crust" in the Disorders of the Self

ERNEST S. WOLF, M.D.   (Chicago)
and JAMES E. WILSON, M.D.   (Chicago)

I

"Even short interruptions have a slightly obscuring effect on the work. We used to speak jokingly of the 'Monday crust' when we began work after the day of rest on Sunday." Freud was the first analyst to note that even the minor interruptions in the continuity of an ongoing analysis which were occasioned by weekends left a mark on the observed analytic process (Freud, 1913, p. 127). He was able to make this observation even though he usually saw his patients six times a week, Sunday being the only day of rest. Since Freud's day, contemporary psychoanalytic practice has become somewhat less tightly scheduled. Analysands now are usually seen four or five times a week, and the weekend interruption has become correspondingly longer. The "slightly obscuring effect" noted by Freud often seems to be magnified into a quite obscuring disturbance. In general analysts are aware that disruptions in the analytic process or changes in regular scheduling leave a discernible impact on the analytic process. Published case reports occasionally call attention to the severe reactions sometimes precipitated in patients by the analyst's vacation. Such reactions — usually associated with an increase in the patient's symptoms — are generally understood to be more or less intense varieties of separation anxiety and may be thought to herald the working-through process which is anticipated for the termination phase of the analysis. Less attention, however, has been paid to the weekend interruption, and the psychoanalytic literature contains few references to Freud's discerning observation of the "Monday crust."[1]

Freud did not discuss the intrapsychic events leading up to the formation of the

[1] Freud (1913) stated that he saw his patients every day but Sundays and public holidays. However, he mentioned certain indications for seeing patients three times per week: "For slight cases or the continuation of treatment which is already well advanced, three days a week will be enough. Any restrictions of time beyond this bring no advantage either to the doctor or to patient; and at the beginning of an analysis, they are quite out of the question" (p. 127).

"Monday crust." Probably he thought of it as a nonspecific manifestation of the ubiquitous phenomenon of resistance to analysis. The word *crust* evokes images of something warm and liquid having cooled off and hardened on the surface leaving the old condition to persist underneath. Perhaps Freud had in mind the protective crust that forms over an oozing wound. At any rate, the implication is that resistance is to be overcome, that the crust is to be penetrated or removed in order to get at the underlying conflicts which are still active.[2] It seems reasonable to assume, therefore, that the phenomena which Freud observed on Mondays were an intensification of resistance against instinctual derivatives. Thus the effects of weekend interruptions on the analytic process in the treatment of disorders of the self have attracted our interest, and we have observed that Monday reactions to the weekend in these disorders were often quite marked and even disruptive. It was our hope that such minor interruptions would allow us to observe the microstructure of the intrapsychic events since the transference relationship, though strained, is essentially preserved. Grossly traumatic macroevents such as disruptions due to vacations or illnesses often grossly disrupt the transference. Such grossly traumatic events and their consequences are easily observed but they obscure the interactions of the finer psychological structures.

II

References in the psychoanalytic literature to the effects of the weekend interruption on analysis are scanty. In a current textbook on psychoanalytic technique (Menninger and Holzman, 1973), twenty-two references to other books on technique are listed. Only four of these have even a peripheral mention of the weekend interruption. In some cases it is seen as fertile ground for an outbreak of dangerous impulses which may lead to a symptom formation. Ferenczi (1919) views the "Sunday neurosis" as the symptom picture presented by the disruption of analysis. He sees these symptoms mostly as hysterical punishments and dangerous impulses which (on weekends) were mobilized by the bad examples of others. The emphasis is on the relaxation of the repression barrier which coincides with the external relaxation induced by the holiday. While Ferenczi does not directly mention Freud's "Monday crust," one could speculate that the resistance implied by the "Monday crust" is provoked by the breakthrough of instinctual material during the "Sunday neurosis." In this vein Abraham (1918) emphasizes the defensive use of work in an elaboration of Ferenczi's 1919 paper. Abraham believed that many persons can protect themselves from neurotic symptoms only through work. Work is viewed as an escape from dangerous libidinal demands. Similarly, Grinstein (1955) makes reference to "changes in the

---

[2] Freud's analogy here is closely related to the geological-archeological metaphors which he used throughout his life (Wolf and Nebel, 1978).

mental apparatus during vacations" (p. 178). The emphasis is on the opposition and compromise between the pleasure principle and libidinal gratification on the one hand, and the reality principle, ego defenses, and superego on the other. A vacation is seen to stimulate the libidinal side of this conflict. Neurotics fear their dangerous impulses. Others with shaky ego boundaries are frightened of dissolution.

Along somewhat different lines, Kubie (1950) states that any interruptions deprive the analyst of the "contact with current events, without which the dynamic significance of the past may be lost" (p. 42). He goes on to say that even weekends can check the momentum of the work and that therefore daily sessions are most valuable. Kubie suspects that the day of rest may become a day in which the patient withdraws from the analysis both intellectually and emotionally to a degree which may jeopardize his progress. He has, metaphorically, added that a day of freedom between analytic sessions gives the patient a breathing spell. Kubie can see advantages, but he fears that the loss of continuity may prove to be too high a price to pay.[3]

Several authors attempt to make use in the analytic process of the phenomena evoked by the disruption of the analysis. Alexander (1950) recommends the introduction of interruptions to facilitate the process. He cites the fact that an unplanned cancellation of a therapeutic hour often has a stimulating effect on the production of unconscious material. He suggests that analysts should not leave this important therapeutic tool to chance. Rickman (1950) sees the patient's response to the weekend interruption as providing both patient and analyst with some indication of the patient's readiness for termination. Peck (1961) points out that dreams recorded by a patient shortly before an interruption of the treatment may be vivid and revealing in terms of the psychopathology and defenses. Observing more prolonged interruptions than mere weekends, Jackel (1966) describes situations in analyses where, under the impact of impending temporary separations due to vacations or holidays, patients express a wish to have a child. He interprets this as an attempt to re-establish the mother-child unit in order to avoid the anxiety that would result from separation from the analyst.

Greenson (1967) makes explicit reference to Freud's expression of the Monday crust. Greenson defines the Monday crust as "the day residues, the experiential events of the separation plus the resistances evoked by the separation which inter-

---

[3] The history of psychoanalysis has demonstrated that what at first seems to be a disadvantage has often been turned into an advantage: e.g., resistance to hypnosis was turned into the free-association method (an advantage). Similarly, at first transference was thought to be a disadvantage. It has now become the major tool for treatment. Perhaps the disruption of the process, Kubie's "breathing spell," which he views as a disadvantage when he says "the loss of continuity may be too high a price to pay" (1950, p. 42), actually may be turned into a good advantage. It gives the analyst an opportunity to demonstrate to the patient what happens during disruptions, to explain the mechanism of what happens and allow the patient to work it through — the best preparation for termination. Glover (1955) states that a continuous analysis can be achieved despite a two-day break. However, interruptions of a longer duration would fall in the category of "short treatment" (p. 21).

fere with the resumption of the therapeutic alliance" (p. 335). He explores a number of typical ways in which patients in analysis react to the weekend interruption in the analytic work. He suggests that for some patients the weekend separation is viewed as an intermission or respite from the analytic process. In these cases the analyst represents a critical superego figure for the patient. As a consequence, the weekend may be utilized as an opportunity for engaging in a variety of pregenital and genital libidinal as well as aggressive activities. Then the Monday hour is experienced as a time for confession and atonement. In other cases, the weekend is experienced as a desertion — either on a pregenital level or on an oedipal level where it becomes a primal scene from which the patient has been excluded. Then, Greenson suggests, one sees affects such as guilt, anxiety, depression, and rage. Patients who are in a relatively regressed state, in the throes of a transference neurosis, or diagnosed as borderline may react to the absence of the analyst as the loss of ego functions: "then the analyst has been functioning as an auxiliary ego" (p. 333). The analyst may also be utilized by the patient to lessen the critical demands of his harsh superego. But, at the time of the weekend interruption, these patients return to their "hypercritical anti-instinctual state" (p. 334). The temptations of the weekend may mobilize severe guilt and shame responses. For them, the Friday hour is the beginning of a dangerous journey and the Monday hour is a return to safety. Greenson states that reaction to the weekend interruption offers a valuable replica in miniature of what one can expect at termination.

Greenson was aware that the disruption reaction was related to the kind of pathology the analysand was dealing with. Greenson apparently tried to differentiate the various types of disruption reactions depending on how the analyst was utilized by the patient — e.g., as a critical superego, as a less than harsh superego, or as an auxiliary ego. In general, Greenson's differentiation of the use of the analyst requires that the analysand has developed tripartite structural relationships. In other words, one is dealing with a structural oedipal neurosis. Greenson does not pursue the use of the analyst as a selfobject — a prominent transference when there has been trauma and fixation during the earliest states of development (Kohut, 1971, 1977).

Some authors emphasize the significance of holidays and certain anniversaries. Inman (1949) notes that some people are especially subject to illness at Christmas and Easter and concludes that such malaises can be seen as derivatives of the Oedipus complex. Cattell (1955) discusses the holiday syndrome as a specific reaction in a certain group of psychoanalytic patients during the period from Thanksgiving until just after New Year's Day. It is characterized by anxiety, regressive phenomena (including feelings of helplessness, possessiveness, increased irritability and nostalgia), bitter rumination about the holiday experiences of one's youth, depression, and a wish for magical solutions. Rosenbaum (1962) emphasizes the oral regression seen at Thanksgiving and suggests that this regression can be used defensively against predominantly oedipal conflicts. Usually the content and specific meaning are stressed in discussing the significance of holidays and anniversaries. We would like to add that the mere disruption of a relationship may evoke a reaction quite aside from the content. Pollock (1971) already made this distinction when he called attention to the significance of anniversary reactions. A specific hour, day, or year may reflect some highly significant intrapsychic experience of the past. Pollock suggests that the ensuing symptoms might result from a break in contact. He emphasizes that "although there was a coupling of symptoms with specific times, dates or holidays, the internal unconscious determinants were the significant factors; the external temporal reference served only as a trigger for the release of the repressed conflicts, which appears as an anniversary reaction" (p. 130).

Fleming (1975) provides some very interesting clinical material to illustrate the impact of weekend interruptions on a patient who suffered developmental trauma during the separation-individuation phase. Fleming demonstrates how patients' reactions are modified by analytic interpretations and by the relationship she offers her patients.

As already noted, Greenson (1967) and Fleming (1975) have called attention to the relationship with the analyst. Greenson designated a particular aspect of this relationship as an "auxiliary ego" function (p. 333). It seems to us that the phenomena Greenson and Fleming observed are similar to those conceptualized by Kohut in describing the role of the analyst as a selfobject. Kohut (1971) has directed our attention to those reactions which certain patients experience when there is a disruption in the relationship with a narcissistically experienced selfobject. In those patients with self pathology, where the analyst is experienced not as a separate center of initiative but as a selfobject, one sees "the strategic role played in the course of the analysis not only by the patient's rage, despondency and regressive retreat when facing extended separations from the analyst (such as the summer vacation) but also by his severe reactions to small signs of coolness from the side of the therapist, or to the analyst's lack of immediate and complete empathic understanding, and, especially to such apparently trivial external events as minor irregularities in the appointment schedule, weekend separations, and slight tardiness of the therapist" (p. 91). These reactions to even minor disturbances in the relationship between analyst and analysand, i.e., to disturbances in the selfobject transference, occupy a central focus in the analysis of disorders of the self. Illustrative case material has recently been published in a collection of case reports (Goldberg, 1978, pp. 270–272, 443).

III

The clinical material we have selected in the form of vignettes from analyses of patients with disorders of the self illustrates a particular kind of selfobject-transference vicissitude. Although other clinical material not shown in these vignettes would provide abundant evidence that selfobject transferences were indeed being dealt with in these cases, a cautionary comment is necessary at the outset. The presentation of detailed clinical material in the form of psychoanalytic vignettes invariably and properly evokes a multitude of responses in the trained psychoanalytic observer who reads or listens to such presentations. Sometimes such responses converge into a semblance of consensual validation. More commonly—and this is what one should expect—the inevitable incompleteness of the presented data together with the distortions introduced by the working and writing styles of the presenter are confronted by the different predilections and styles of the reader: different interpretations of what appear to be the same data emerge and there is a tendency to reject the author's proffered explanations out of hand when they diverge too sharply from long-held and cherished views. Since our conclusions, we believe, are divergent from many long-accepted theories and practices in psychoanalysis, we urge the reader to remember (1) that published analytic material is always incomplete and never can be proof for the correctness of one position or the other; and (2) that the conviction of the correctness of an interpretation in psychoanalysis can only be obtained through the prolonged immersion into and observation of an ongoing psychoanalytic process by a trained psychoanalytic observer.

Mr. A., the oldest of four siblings, is an engineer in his mid-thirties. He decided to seek treatment when once again he found himself losing interest and pulling away from a relationship with a woman just as it became more deeply meaningful. In relationships with both men and women he continually fails to achieve the closeness that he craves. He remains lonely and frustrated. He is easily hurt, and with each new relationship he faces considerable anxiety about the anticipated rejection. Some years ago he was divorced after eight years of marriage. He thought he had been excessively demanding with his wife and unable to achieve the closeness he had desired. She had wished to have children but he did not feel ready.

His manner of working is slow and obsessive. His perfectionistic demands on himself get him caught up in excessive detail. Legitimate requests are experienced as exploitations. He responds with rage and rebelliousness, refusing to do the work or turning it in late.

He describes his mother as a warmly caring and understanding woman with, however, a tendency to be overcontrolling. He feels that he was her favorite child.

His father was either critical or indifferent. Working long hours and coming home tired, he was unavailable to the patient and his sisters. When they did spend time together the patient experienced his father as cold, arrogant, insensitive, depreciating, and exploitative. When working with his son on some project father would lose patience easily and blame him for whatever went wrong. Whereas the father wanted the son around for whatever help the boy could provide, the youngster craved to be loved and accepted. The father also humiliatingly ridiculed any attempts at closeness that the boy made out of his own initiative. "Each time I'd reach out for him, I felt thrust back again and ignored."

Many infantile longings, wishes, and needs persisted into Mr. A.'s adult life. He experienced himself as defective and incompetent both as a person and as a man. He felt himself to be dull, self-centered, weak, and poorly organized. Often he felt empty and depleted. As he put it, "the missing attention from my father is a missing part of me." A developmental arrest had interfered with what should have been phase-appropriate internalization of psychic structure, and he found it necessary to rely on external sources for his self-esteem. To get the necessary affirmation and acceptance he felt that he had to sacrifice his assertiveness by obsequiousness and compliance.

Four analytic hours are now presented to demonstrate the loss of self-cohesion resulting from the weekend disruption and the restoration of cohesiveness as a consequence of the reunion with the analyst.

Hour 152, Monday: "As I walked to the couch I had the same feeling I had last week — best described as wanting to rebel against seeing you — I feel like a big kid who has to do something that is the domain of little kids — come to appointments. Do I still have to do this? Have I outgrown this? Is there something that's bothering me? The obvious answer: the weekend break. There's no sense denying it. I'm feeling a sense of upheaval. It's a sense that my work is. . . not crumbling. . . but eroding around the edges."

Hour 155, Monday: "I want to talk about what the interruption was like. I was disappointed. Time seemed very long. I found myself less effective in projects than I wanted to be — the two days dragged. I felt less effective than ever. The feeling — it was bleak."

Hour 159, Tuesday (after a three-day weekend): "I felt your absence this weekend — especially on Sunday — a return of that old feeling: rootlessness, not having any joy, not having any central purpose. Monday when I returned to work the same feeling from Sunday continued. There was nothing to look forward to, no session. I am continually surprised at how looking forward to seeing you is a subtle thing. It works outside of my awareness at times.

"There is a hesitancy in assuming you are in the same place you were when I last talked with you. It sometimes takes an hour to re-establish that connection; other times, it comes early on in the session. . . I can now recover more quickly from an absence than formerly."

A dream from the night before: It is fall, a college setting, the patient is a freshman. He feels excluded from social activities. He hears the voice of a man who is forty-ish. The voice communicates that the speaker is friendly, understanding, and protective. The patient is lured by this voice into the man's apartment. "I hoped we would strike up a conversation. Maybe a relationship would develop."

The material in the preceding hours really shows the depressing and disorganizing effects of the weekend disruption: "sense of upheaval," "eroding around the edges," "rootlessness," "not having any central purpose," etc. In hour 159 the re-establishment of the selfobject transference with a recovery from fragmentation experience also is evident. The dream may be seen as a hopeful attempt to re-establish the connectedness that gets lost on weekends.[4] The recovery has proceeded well into the next hour.

Hour 160, Wednesday: Mr. A. has been looking for a new apartment, a move which is the result of his increased vitality due to our earlier interpretive work. The night before he was shown an apartment by a woman from a local real-estate office, who apparently demonstrated her positive feelings for him. Mr. A. in commenting says, "It was gratifying. In the past I would tend to apple-polish, bend myself out of shape to get someone to like me. Last night there was very little of this. The last few weeks I've been very positive about the way I've been feeling. It is interesting that when I began looking for an apartment it seemed like a big deal, almost insurmountable. Now it doesn't seem threatening at all. I have a whole different feeling; I feel the center of all of this. I am in control of all these details. I am feeling happy and involved; events aren't controlling me. I want to consolidate this — it's a good feeling. Another thing stands out — almost everything is enjoyable — even things that were tedious. Time seems to go streaking by. I feel so fulfilled. I used to obsess about every little sand pebble. The fact that I talk so positively with you is reflected in how I behave with others outside. This same vitality is operating out there." We can see in hour 160 a full restoration of the selfobject tie; Mr. A. now talks of taking the initiative, being happy, being involved, fulfilled, vital, in control, and consolidated. Even in such an emotionally charged activity as looking for a new apartment he functions well and deals efficiently with the woman from the local real-estate office.

The next case is that of Mr. B.

Mr. B. began his analysis as a thirty-year-old, single, professional-school student who sought help with his depression, shyness, and lack of enthusiasm for work and interpersonal relationships. He was hypersensitive to criticism, usually panicked at exam time, and found it painfully difficult to speak up in class.

As the only child of an unhappy marriage Mr. B. usually felt unwanted. He recalled a comment by his mother that he had been found in a cabbage patch. When the boy was twelve the parents divorced.

---

[4] Of course, this represents only one of a number of possible interpretations for this dream. Each of the dreams in this essay might be interpreted differently when viewed from a different theoretical framework.

The father was a successful businessman who spent minimal time at home. There were painful memories of the patient's coming home from school to an empty house. He wanted to show someone, anyone, his schoolwork but the house was empty. He recalls trying to get his father involved, pleading with him, for example, to come and watch him play baseball. The father would promise to come, but on the day of the game he would be absent. Whenever he made an intercity trip the patient begged to go along, but father would invariably refuse. When Mr. B. was eight he experienced what he called "the most painful event of my life." A paternal uncle swindled his father out of his business, and the father subsequently had a "nervous breakdown." Painful memories of seeing him gaunt and withdrawn at the state psychiatric hospital remain. His mother now found it necessary to work full time, and the ensuing years were empty and lonely for Mr. B. He was "on my own, a good boy, one who never broke the rules." Yet secretly he yearned for guidelines from a man. After the parents' divorce he remembers being almost addicted to the family television show "Father Knows Best," which often brought tears to his eyes.

During the first diagnostic interview Mr. B. reported a dream the night before in which he saw a professor with his son on a ski trip. He associated to the fact that he often gets tearful when he observes fathers and sons together. He also revealed a special pleasure: spending time with the young son of a fellow worker.

A few selected Friday and Monday hours will demonstrate the use of the analyst as a substitute selfobject to replace the missing psychic structure left as a deficit from the unhappy relationship with his father. The weekend interruptions similarly will demonstrate the reactions when the analyst is unavailable as an idealizable selfobject.

Hour 7, Monday:[5] "I felt this weekend I was going it alone. I felt mad Friday night but decided that's the way it is—I'll go it alone. All weekend I felt very much alone—I thought of calling you—I was reluctant to come today." The analyst asks why. Mr. B. replies, "I don't know. On Friday I had a dream. I was under some kind of X-ray machine. I could see that they were examining me. There was a skeleton that appeared on X-ray. It was a horrifying kind of thing [associations to time when father had a nervous breakdown]. I felt I was disintegrating, as if they had taken the life out of me—that some life-sustaining material was being drained out of me. But I have the feeling that something can also be pumped back in so that I won't remain a skeleton. It's up to these people [those doing the exam in the dream]." It seems that in hour 7 Mr. B. experiences himself as a skeleton without flesh and without life-sustaining material. Clearly, however, his hopes and needs for a substitute selfobject tie have created a quick transference readiness. He had already thought of calling the analyst over the

---

[5] Psychotherapy prior to psychoanalysis accounts for the rapid development of transference.

weekend, and he dreamed that the people examining him could also pump back into him the material that would rescue him from his skeletal state.

Hour 19, Wednesday (missed hour on Monday because of Memorial Day): "It seems so long since I've been here. It seems like I have to re-establish this relationship. It has been a major blank space with no carry-over. Yesterday I felt detached. It was the result of no Monday appointment. I felt cut off and alone. I felt lethargic, alone. All the people around me had left. I tried to tell myself that it's normal not to work on a holiday. I didn't want to feel that you'd left and abandoned me."

Hour 21, Monday: "It seems strange to be here. There seems to be a longer period between Friday and Monday than two days, like Friday was a long time ago. After I left on Friday...I couldn't study anymore. I went to a porno movie because I couldn't calm down to study. I asked myself, 'Why am I doing this,' then you came to mind—but not in the sense of my having gone to the movies as good or bad. I had a strange desire to masturbate every two hours. I was startled at some of the things I was saying on Friday, feelings I had about my father [the longing]. Saturday I went to the medical-school skit. I was petrified that they would leave me out or that I would be an afterthought. I felt so sad for those who might have been left out and forgotten." In hour 21 we see Mr. B.'s attempts to deal with the painful emptiness and deadness through the self-stimulation provided by masturbation and attendance at a pornographic movie. These feelings of loss and depletion are reflected in Mr. B.'s attempt to organize his feelings around the school skit. The association to the longings for his father are an indication that points to the location of the structural deficit in his psyche.

Hour 52, Friday (the analysis had been resumed two weeks before after a two-week vacation): "I just completed a book I wanted to tell you about...about the return of Viet Nam veterans...It had to do with the difficulty of their readjustment. I cried when I read it. The central theme was that returning veterans felt alienated, detached, unable to comprehend. The only people they could talk to about their experiences were other veterans. I recall a long time ago I suspected you were in the service. I felt a kinship because of that link...a feeling of closeness, [being] able to talk with you, but also confused, 'out of sight, out of mind.'" The analyst interpreted the experiences described in the book as parallel to the patient's feelings of estrangement and alienation. The analyst then added that by turning to a common experience (military service) the patient was trying to bridge the gap and heal the breach. The patient ended the hour by saying, "This has been an interesting session for me. I feel close to you with what I said and with the way you responded. Your vacation seems far away and long gone." In this hour we see Mr. B.'s anticipation of the pending weekend interruption having become amalgamated with the memory of the recent experience precipitated by the recent vacation interruption. By reference to a common experience the patient hopes to heal the breach in the selfobject transference, and as the hour ends a selfobject tie to the analyst seems firmly established.

Hour 55, Friday: "I have a feeling I have avoided discussing with you how I use my time outside of our sessions. I really don't do anything. I'm very lethargic. I waste my time; I'm very passive, stagnant—not doing anything. Last night I felt bored with Barbara, bored with myself. I had no desire to show affection, so I left. I want you to know I'm doing very little. Last night I had a very upsetting dream. I'm reluctant to talk about it. Essentially the dream was that my penis was detached from me. I guess detachable, removable, stripped from me at various times. I had some degree of reluctance to come. I had a passing thought of cancelling the appointment. I don't know why...I have this feeling you are busy ...I don't want to keep coming up with nagging problems. I fear you'll get bored, tired, fed up. I have this image from childhood. I come home from school and find nobody is home, nothing to do. Mother working, father away." The analyst replies: "You have emphasized how you felt as a boy that you had to do it alone. There was no 'we', no joint effort. You longed for a man to teach you, to help you become a man yourself. There was no sense of his showing you and taking pride in your becoming a man. So you've looked to this relationship as providing another chance. You need us to work together. In the dream, your being without the penis is symbolic of the loss of your masculine self as you anticipate the weekend interruption." In hour 55, the dream of a detached penis is a symbolic expression of the anticipated loss of a part of his self—namely, his masculine self—which during the week is supplied by the presence of the idealized selfobject analyst. There was nothing in this phase of the analysis which would suggest that Mr. B. was dealing with a triadic oedipal constellation or with castration anxiety.

Hour 61, Friday: "I felt angry when you said our time was up Wednesday. I had a dream last night. I called the professor. [Mr. B., having just graduated from medical school, has applied for a fellowship.] The professor said he had not yet decided whom he would select among several applicants. In the dream I told him that it was not fair because he had interviewed me two months ago. I convinced him to give me another interview because my image had diminished over two months. On Wednesday when I left, I had a strong desire to go to a porno movie in order to stop thinking of the session. Since you've returned from vacation I've become more aware of my feelings about interruptions and breaches, even time changes—now even gaps between sessions. I have this assumption: any feelings that I have, which develop over time, will die out and will need to be rekindled." The analyst replies: "I think that's right—two days are experienced as two months. During the interruption you lose yourself. The dream was an attempt to find yourself again." Mr. B. replies: "I think you're right. I'm very afraid this is the end of the session. It will send me out to deal with the weekend not sure who I am. My feeling—you can't send me out of here that way—I don't have myself; I'm somehow lost." (Mr. B. seems near tears.)

In hour 61 we can see the enfeebled self, fragmentation prone, missing the joy of being a whole self, and therefore attemptir.g, in fantasy, to banish the feeling of deadness by substituting the pleasures of the senses stimulated by a pornographic movie. The fear of dying out (that is, of losing the self completely) and needing to be rekindled—in the here and now of the transference by the presence of the analyst, in the past by the appropriately responsive presence of the father—is actively mobilized as a selfobject transference in the analytic process, including its disruptions, and is available for interpretation with resultant transmuting internalizations leading to cure.

IV

The clinical material in the preceding section presents a sampling of data obtained from patients with disorders of the self when the analytic process has been disrupted by weekend or other minor breaks in the continuity of the selfobject transference. In other words, during psychoanalytic treatment both Mr. A. and Mr. B. reactivated those specific needs of an emerging self for confirmatory responses that had remained unresponded to—or had been faultily responded to—in childhood. These reactivated needs found expression in pathognomonic self-object transferences to the analyst.

In our discussion, therefore, our focus will be on the vicissitudes of the self and its disorders (Kohut, 1971, 1977; Kohut and Wolf, 1978). While we will pay particular attention to the relation between weekend disruption and psychoanalytic process—i.e., to Freud's "Monday crust"—we shall first touch upon related issues of self-selfobject relationships.

It is specifically the concept of the selfobject, introduced and elaborated by Kohut (1971, 1977) that has become the cornerstone of the psychology of the self. Most simply, the selfobject is an object that is experienced as part of the self. For example, in observing a mother caring for her baby one may describe the social interaction as between the mother and her object—the baby—or vice versa. In the social field the observer observes objects in interaction. However, at the same time, the child may experience a certain aspect of the mother and the mother's function as part of the child's self. Thus the mother is simultaneously an object and a part of the child's self, depending on whether she is observed in the social field or in the field of subjective intrapsychic experience. Within the framework of the psychology of the self the mother is a selfobject for the child. The selfobject concept bridges the introspected and the extrospected worlds.

To say, however, that an object is experienced as part of the self presents some peculiar difficulties. Part of the problem is inherent in the language of science which objectifies and describes best the events in the world of objects. Words that refer to the nuances of inner experiences are not plentiful, and it is extremely difficult to convey shades of subjective meaning in language: we admire poets precisely because of their skills and talents in evoking and communicating mental states. If we were poets we might be able to convey the particular joyous experience of feeling whole, good, together, blissfully functioning, like a well-tuned engine — an experience which implies, in Kohut's terminology, a cohesive self. It is perhaps a little easier to convey the experiences of tension, depression, anxiety, awkwardness, disconcertedness, frazzled crabbiness, or just plain ineffectiveness or irritability that have generally been denoted as fragmentation states of the self.

Our everyday language has trained us to pay attention to the world outside, the world of objects, by not providing us the linguistic tools to clearly apprehend and express inner experiencing.[6] The statement of experiencing an object as part of the self, therefore, may appear to some as illogical nonsense and, indeed, in the world of extrospected objects it is an impossible absurdity for self and object to be the same.

The difficulty seems compounded when we turn to the world of subjective experience. In the foreground of our mental processes are thoughts, fantasies, memories, images, and emotions — all the ways in which our perceptions and knowledge of the world and the objects in it manifest themselves to our awareness. But behind this foreground, so to speak, we are also, more or less consciously, aware of a background of feeling and experiencing — self-esteem, well-being — which does not refer to any specific content of our psyche but to its total state of being. Borrowing words from the world of extrospected objects, we may describe the introspected experience of this background on a scale between continuity-cohesion in time and space, on the one hand, and disintegration-fragmentation, on the other; or between dissonance-confusion and harmony-order; or between vigor and depletion. Normally, we are no more aware of this constant background of our psychological self experience than we are of our breathing in the background of our bodily self experience. We forget, if we ever knew, that the continuous presence of a certain environment with which to interact psychologically and physiologically is a condition for survival. But let the oxygen in the air we breathe suddenly diminish to, let us say, half its usual proportion: our bodily discomfort and loss of proper functioning as well as our desperate gasping for air will soon signal that all is not well with us. Similarly, the sudden removal of those aspects of the environment which sustain us psychologically results in a state of psychological dis-ease.

Unfortunately, most of the time we are as unsophisticated in recognizing the essential self sustainers in our total environment as mankind was ignorant of the sustaining fraction of air before the discovery of oxygen in 1774. Often we are totally mystified when we feel absolutely miserable psychologically, or when we

---

[6] Of course language is not the real culprit. Psychoanalysis has discovered weighty psychological reasons for not becoming aware of certain inner events: Freud constructed the model of the psychic apparatus, including the function of repression, to account for this. The inadequacy of the language may, indeed, be a result of repression when viewed in the historical context of human development.

find ourselves compelled into the most irrational behaviors—such as various addictions to food, drugs, rituals, or perversions—or into certain relationships with people. It is as if we were blindly gasping for some psychological oxygen, the lack of which we feel inside ourselves. It is our imperative need to seek relief which pushes us into symptomatic behavior. In the light of this need for environmental psychological sustenance for the maintenance of the psychological self we speak about the self's need for selfobjects.

A brief historical overview of the development of the selfobject concept may provide further clarification. The accumulation of psychoanalytic experience with patients suffering from disorders of the self has corroborated Kohut's early and decisive observations again and again. Analysands who develop a stable relationship with the analyst have, in general, a sense of relative well-being merely by being in the presence of an empathically tuned-in analyst who understands their needs for confirming responses; nothing more is needed, in fact. Most of the time the analyst's understanding of the need is the equivalent of the confirming responses. Conversely, the absence of the analyst's understanding—e.g., because of ignorance, emotional handicap, absent-mindedness, or actual physical absence for whatever reason—is experienced as a loss of well-being, sometimes only minimal, sometimes of near-psychotic proportions. It is these clinical observations that led Kohut to the conceptualization of the analyst as a selfobject for the analysand, a selfobject whose continuous availability lent cohesion to the analysand's self whereas unavailability resulted in degrees of fragmentation. Reconstruction of the analysand's childhood history, particularly of the ambient responsiveness or lack thereof, led Kohut to the further conclusion that the selfobject phenomena observed during psychoanalytic treatment were the reactivated, specific selfobject needs that had remained unresponded to in the specific faulty interactions between the nascent self and the selfobject of early life—i.e., that a selfobject transference had become established in the analysis.

One more possible misunderstanding must be avoided. In the selfobject transferences the analysand transfers *archaic* selfobject needs which had been arrested in their development, or to which the child had regressed at the time of the childhood trauma. These archaic selfobject transferences must be distinguished in the analytic situation from the *age-appropriate* needs for a mature and healthy selfobject relationship. In the normal course of development of the self the need for selfobjects to maintain cohesion does not diminish. Rather, the nature and quality of the selfobject need changes in the direction of becoming less concrete and more symbolic, less individual and more group oriented, less focused on specific persons and more easily displaceable to other individuals (cf. Wolf, 1976b, 1980). Thus, for example, an analysand's requirement for the average acknowledgments prescribed by contemporary social intercourse is not a transference but a healthy expectation of a confirming selfobject response. The absence of such normally given responses are not only experienced painfully as coldness or even rudeness but are normally accompanied by minor and transient yet uncomfortable episodes of fragmentation which may be misunderstood as pathological symptoms—e.g., instinctual aggression—when in fact they are merely artifacts produced by inappropriate withholding of needed average expectable responsiveness (cf. Wolf, 1976a).

V

We are now ready to return to our consideration of the analyses of Mr. A. and Mr. B. Both analysands developed selfobject relationships with the analyst and suffered degrees of fragmentation symptoms when the selfobject relationship was disrupted by the weekend or vacation suspension of the analytic work. The need for the continuous availability of the selfobject analyst, even on weekends, in order to maintain the analysand's self-cohesion cannot be judged as a normal, age-appropriate selfobject need but must be understood as the reactivation of archaic selfobject needs, i.e., as a selfobject transference. Genetic material obtained in associational data corroborates this conclusion by providing evidence of the childhood trauma which would account for the persisting presence of archaic residues which could be reactivated and observed in the transference.

Close attention to the effects on the analysand's intrapsychic state and on the psychoanalytic process of the impact of the weekend disruption suggests the possibility for using this data for clinical evaluation and for guiding therapeutically effective interpretations. The reactivated selfobject needs which often can be observed quite vividly in analysands who suffer from disruptions in the selfobject transference may differ from the reactions of analysands whose transferences reflect repressed and reactivated oedipal conflicts. As reported in the psychoanalytic literature, oedipally structured transference reactions to weekend disruptions frequently demonstrate shifts in the conflict toward increased defensiveness or increased acting out, depending on the structure of the neurosis and the strength of the ego. We have ourselves noted, for example, with certain women during the time of intense transference neurosis that there may be a diminution of anxiety during weekends, perhaps with a displacement then of the incestuous instincts from the analyst to less emotionally invested men. On the Monday following one may then see increasing anxiety as the newly remobilized sexual impulses strive for breakthrough of the transference to the analyst.

These clinical considerations may lead to different therapeutic interventions. In oedipally structured transferences, interpretations of both defense and drive strengthen the ego with some resolution of conflict and anxiety. No such response is observed when the analytic transference is of the selfobject variety. Here it is necessary, through interpretation, to help the patient recognize his need for selfobjects and his inevitable tendency to experience "mini-fragmentations" when the absence of the needed selfobject deprives him of the "glue" that holds his self together (Wolf, 1979). Although massive disruption and fragmentation are therapeutically not fruitful, the mini-fragmentations precipitated by such mini-disruptions as weekends, when repeatedly experienced and interpreted, lead to the gradual accretion of psychic structure through the process of transmuting internalization (Kohut, 1971, 1977). In this way selfobject needs are not given up but become modified into more mature forms.

REFERENCES

Abraham, K. (1918), Observations on Ferenczi's paper on "Sunday neuroses." In: *The Psychoanalytic Reader*, ed. R. Fliess. New York: International Universities Press, 1948, pp. 312–315.

Alexander, F. (1950), Analysis of the therapeutic factors in psychoanalytic treatment. *Psychoanal. Quart.*, 19:482–500.

Cattell, J. (1955), The holiday syndrome. *Psychoanal. Rev.*, 42:39–43.

Ferenczi, S. (1919), Sunday neuroses. In: *Further Contributions to the Theory and Technique of Psychoanalysis*. London: Hogarth Press, 1950, pp. 174–177.

Fleming, J. (1975), Some observations on object constancy in the psychoanalysis of adults. *J. Amer. Psychoanal. Assn.*, 23:743–759.

Freud, S. (1913), On beginning treatment (further recommendations on the technique of psychoanalysis I). *Standard Edition*, 12:121–144. London: Hogarth Press, 1958.

Glover, E. (1955), *The Technique of Psychoanalysis*. New York: International Universities Press.

Goldberg, A., ed. (1978), *The Psychology of the Self: A Casebook*. New York: International Universities Press.

Greenson, R. (1967), *The Technique and Practice of Psychoanalysis*. New York: International Universities Press.

Grinstein, A. (1955), Vacations: A psychoanalytic study. *Internat. J. Psycho-Anal.*, 36:177–186.

Inman, W. S. (1949), Clinical observations on morbid periodicity. *Psychoanal. Quart.*, 18:536–537.

Jackel, M. (1966), Interruptions during psychoanalytic treatment and the wish for a child. *J. Amer. Psychoanal. Assn.*, 14:730–735.

Kohut, H. (1971), *The Analysis of the Self*. New York: International Universities Press.

_____ (1977), *The Restoration of the Self*. New York: International Universities Press.

_____ & Wolf, E. (1978), The disorders of the self and their treatment: An outline. *Internat. J. Psycho-Anal.*, 59:413–425

Kubie, L. (1950), *Practical and Theoretical Aspects of Psychoanalysis*. New York: International Universities Press.

Menninger, K. & Holzman, P. (1973), *Theory of Psychoanalytic Technique*. New York: Basic Books.

Peck, J. (1961), Dreams and interruptions in the treatment. *Psychoanal. Quart.*, 30:209–220.

Pollock, G. (1971), Temporal anniversary manifestations: Hour, day, holiday. *Psychoanal. Quart.*, 40:123–131.

Rickman, J. (1950), On the criteria for the termination of an analysis. *Internat. J. Psycho-Anal.*, 31: 200–201.

Rosenbaum, J. (1962), Holiday symptom and dream. *Psychoanal. Rev.*, 49:387–398.

Wolf, E. (1976a), Ambience and abstinence. *This Annual*, 4:101–115. New York: International Universities Press.

_____ (1976b), The family as selfobject. *Proceedings of the Annual Meeting of the American Political Science Association*, Chicago, September 1–5.

_____ (1979), Transferences and countertransferences in the analysis of disorders of the self. *Contemp. Psychoanal.*, 15:577–594.

_____ (1980), On the developmental line of selfobject relations. In: *Advances in Self Psychology*, ed. A. Goldberg. New York: International Universities Press, pp. 117–130.

_____ & Nebel, S. (1978), Psychoanalytic excavations: The structure of Freud's cosmography. *Amer. Imago*, 35:178-202.

October, 1979

The Developmental Significance of Affective States: Implications for Psychoanalytic Treatment

FRANK M. LACHMANN, Ph.D.   (New York)
and ROBERT D. STOLOROW, Ph.D.   (New York)

Despite the central therapeutic importance of affective states and the voluminous literature that exists on that subject (see Arlow, 1977; Green, 1977), numerous authors have indicated that psychoanalysis lacks an adequate theory of affects (Arlow, 1977; Brenner, 1974; Green, 1977; Jacobson, 1971; Rapaport, 1953; Ross, 1975). The roots of this felt inadequacy can be found in the intellectual history of psychoanalytic affect theory, in Freud's choice of an economic or drive-discharge model for affect expression. By postulating a topographic separation of affect from cognition, which in turn precludes a developmental view of affects, the drive-discharge model has obstructed the theoretical understanding of affective states. Hence, until recently, the evolving knowledge of the development of self and object representations was prevented from contributing significantly to the theory of affects. In this paper we shall suggest a point of view through which the postulated schism between affect and cognition can be mended and the significance of affective states in the structuralization of the representational world (Sandler and Rosenblatt, 1962; Stolorow and Atwood, 1979) can be comprehended.

Rapaport (1953) aptly summarized the evolution of Freud's thinking about affect. Prior to the formulation of the structural theory, affects were seen solely as drive-discharge processes, safety valves which dissipated dammed-up drive cathexes (Freud, 1915a, 1915b). Within the structural theory, affects could still occur as drive-discharge phenomena, but a second view of affects (specifically, anxiety) as anticipatory signals produced and utilized by the ego became pre-eminent (Freud, 1926). Rapaport attempted to integrate these two conceptions, proposing that in the course of ego development affect discharges are "tamed" through alterations of their discharge thresholds which render them suitable as signals. In contrast, we suggest that the two theories are not only incompatible, but derive from different levels of discourse (G. Klein, 1976). The drive-discharge conception of affect is an experience-distant, mechanistic theory in which affects are viewed as blind discharge processes entirely divorced from ideas—i.e., from meanings. The affect-signal concept is an experience-near, personalistic theory in which affects are inseparable from ideas and, indeed, are defined in terms of their meanings—e.g., as anticipatory signals of impending intrapsychic danger. Whereas the drive-discharge conception maintains an artificial disjunction between affects and the developing person, the affect-signal concept is inherently developmental.

Despite its inadequacies, analysts continue to find the drive-discharge conception of affects compelling, perhaps because of its resonance with the unconscious anal riddance fantasies that dominate our thinking about feelings, as Schafer (1976) has so persuasively demonstrated. As a consequence, the unfortunate separation of affect from cognition has been perpetuated—a theoretical trend which, as Ross (1975) has pointed out, can lead to a fallaciously fragmented view of human experience. As an antidote to this fragmenting tendency, Ross posits a primal infantile experience in which affect and cognition are one—amalgamated and indistinguishable. He further suggests that, optimally, affect and cognition remain indissoluble throughout life (see also Lewin, 1965; Novey, 1959; Schur, 1969), becoming dissociated *only* in psychopathology. Through this unified view of affective states, Ross hopes to "integrate the concepts of ego autonomies and the roles of perception, motility, cognition, and indeed all other ego functions with the origin and growth of affects in the individual" (p. 81).

Those authors who anchor their conceptions of affect in the structural theory tend to eschew the drive-discharge model and to emphasize the affect-signal concept in which affect and cognition are inseparable. Particularly lucid examples of this approach are found in the contributions of Brenner (1974, 1975) and Arlow (1977).

Brenner (1974) states that affects are "complex mental phenomena which include (a) sensations of pleasure, unpleasure, or a mixture of the two, and (b) thoughts, memories, wishes, fears—in a word, ideas. Psychologically an affect is a sensation of pleasure, unpleasure, or both, plus the ideas associated with that sensation. *Ideas and sensations together,* both conscious and unconscious, *constitute an affect*" (p. 535; italics added). Thus affects "can be *defined* or distinguished from one another only on the basis of the amount and intensity of pleasure, unpleasure, or both, and of the *nature of the related ideas*" (Brenner, 1975, p. 10; italics added). For example, depressive affect is defined as "unpleasure associated with the idea that something bad has happened" (p. 10), whereas anxiety is defined as "unpleasure associated with the idea that something bad is about to happen" (pp. 11–12). Brenner stresses that, in his definitions, the major difference between anxiety and depression is in their *ideational content.* We would add here that the differentiation of anxiety from depression, as defined by Brenner, presupposes a number of developmental prerequisites, including the consolidation of a self representation organized along a time perspective of past, present, and future, a dimension of affective experience stressed by Hartocollis (1976).

Arlow (1977) aptly summarizes the theoretical and clinical difficulties inherent in a drive-discharge concept which separates affects from ideas ànd proposes that in the psychoanalytic situation affects "are compromise phenomena shaped by contributions from each of the major components of the psychic structure, in conformity with the principle of multiple function" (p. 160). In line with Brenner's formulations, Arlow argues that "In order to re-establish the organic unity in affect of ideational content, feeling tone and physiological response, it is necessary to place each of these individual components in its appropriate relationship to the unconscious fantasy which is the usual concomitant and determining influence of what is experienced consciously. This approach...stems from Freud's (1926) elucidation of anxiety as a danger signal" (p. 163). Affect is viewed here as feeling tone evoked by unconscious fantasy, with differences in the quality of affects depending on the details of the unconscious fantasies.

By stressing the role of ideas or fantasies in determining the differentiation of affective qualities, Brenner and Arlow open the door to a developmental approach to affect. Extrapolating from their formulations, we would emphasize that distinctive affective states could be experienced *only* when the requisite mental representations have become consolidated. Brenner (1974) touches on this proposition when he states that "the ideas which are part of an affect are wholly dependent on ego development and ego functioning..." (p. 535). This statement recalls the earlier work of Zetzel (1949, 1965), who emphasized that the capacity to experience and tolerate both signal anxiety and depressive affect is contingent on the maturation of basic ego functions such as the ability to recognize and accept realistic limitations.

The complex interplay between affective and representational development is stressed by Jacobson (1964, 1971), who points out, for example, that it is the establishment of stable self and object representations that makes possible a variety of "warm, affectionate feeling qualities and...rich feeling shades" (1964, p. 85). More recently, Basch (1975), utilizing the viewpoint of general systems theory, has elucidated the dependence of affective life on the development of symbolization and of a "symbolic world" in which subject and object are conceptually distinguished. Similarly, it is strongly suggested in Kohut's (1971, 1977) work that all those affective states (e.g., true longing and grief) which can be experienced only in relation to a more or less separate and whole object (i.e., one that does not serve predominantly as a selfobject) presuppose the consolidation of a cohesive self structure achieved by way of the requisite developmental transformations and "transmuting internalizations" of archaic selfobject configurations.[1] Our work on

---

[1] Our view of the relations between the structural-conflict model utilized by Brenner (1974, 1975) and Arlow (1977), the representational world framework (Sandler and Rosenblatt, 1962; Stolorow and Atwood, 1979), and the selfobject concept (Kohut, 1971, 1977) may be stated as follows: Developmental transformations and transmuting internalizations of archaic selfobject configurations consolidate the representational structures which are a prerequisite for the experience of intrapsychic structural conflict (see Stolorow and Lachmann, 1980).

the developmental prestages of defenses (Lachmann and Stolorow, 1976; Stolorow and Lachmann, 1975, 1978, 1980) also invites a complementary view of the developmental prerequisites of affective states.

Among analytic writers, it is Krystal (1974, 1975) who has provided the most detailed examination of affects from a developmental perspective. He states that "the maturation of affects involves their separation and differentiation from a common matrix, as well as their verbalization and desomatization" (1974, p. 98). Drawing from the work of Novey (1959, 1961) and Schmale (1964), he then develops an ontogenetic framework in which the separation, differentiation, verbalization, and desomatization of affects are rooted in the progressive development of self and object representations. In Krystal's view, the establishment of self-object differentiation and of self and object constancy is a crucial step in affect differentiation and in the development of affect tolerance and the ability to use affects as signals to oneself. He notes that affect tolerance and the ability to use affects as signals also depend on the internalization of the mother's soothing, comforting functions, a point also stressed by Tolpin (1971). Krystal describes patients who, as a consequence of early trauma, remain arrested at, or vulnerable to regressions to, the "ur-affect" states experienced prior to the establishment of self and object representations. In such states affects are undifferentiated, inchoate, overwhelming, unverbalizable, and somatized; there is a lack of affect tolerance and an inability to utilize affects for self signaling. Krystal (1974) suggests that in the treatment of such arrests and regressions, a preparatory phase may be necessary in which the "recognition, verbalization and separation of various affects are emphasized" (p. 124).

When one turns from the general theory of affects to the psychoanalytic conceptualization of particular affective states, numerous examples can be found wherein the developmental prerequisites for the affective experience have been recognized. The developmental implications of the concept of affect signals have already been discussed. Classically, the concept of guilt has always presupposed the structuralization of superego functions through oedipal identifications. Indeed, Freud's (1926) entire ontogenetic sequence of infantile danger situations speaks to the contribution of the development of self and object representations to the content of anxiety experiences, as Brenner (1974) and Gedo and Goldberg (1973) have pointed out. Child observational studies (Mahler, Pine, and Bergman, 1975; Spitz, 1965) have documented the dependence of separation anxiety on the structuralization of the maternal object representation. Similarly, the appearance of death anxiety can be seen to presuppose the establishment of a sense of self whose loss can be anticipated and feared (Stolorow, 1979; Stolorow and Lachmann, 1980). Hypochondriacal anxiety and depersonalization experiences can signify as yet fragile consolidations of the self representation (Stolorow, 1979; Stolorow and Lachmann, 1980), whereas castration and penetration anxiety can issue from a newly acquired and thus precarious sense of gender identity (Stolorow and Lachmann, 1980).

Mahler (1966) found that depressive affect can emerge in children as a consequence of developmental steps in self-object differentiation and the corresponding struggle to accept intrapsychic separation, a phase that may be regressively
revived in adult mourning (Miller, 1977). Blatt (1974) has postulated two types
of depression — anaclitic and introjective — which are distinguished by the developmental level at which the capacity for object representation has been impaired.
Analogously, Basch (1975) has classified depressive states developmentally on the
basis of whether a symbolic concept of self has or has not been attained. In the developmental scheme proposed by M. Klein (1935), the experience of depressive
affect per se requires the synthesis of good and bad part-object images into a representation of the whole object, an achievement which Winnicott (1963) believes underlies the capacity for feeling concern. According to Kernberg (1976),
this integration of the object representation is the structural foundation for all
those affective attitudes which comprise "mature love." Curiously, although
Klein and Kernberg recognize the developmental prerequisites for certain affective states, such as depressive anxiety and mature love, certain others, such as envy, are regarded as instinctual givens. Yet, as Frankel and Sherick (1977) have
shown, even the capacity to experience primitive envy presupposes a certain
minimal attainment of self-object differentiation and self and object constancy.
The developmentally more advanced experience of jealousy requires further
structuralizations which underlie the capacity for triadic object relationships.

Having reviewed the pertinent literature, we can now summarize the theoretical point of view which has guided this paper. Once it is recognized that affective
states are *configurations of emotional experience* rather than isolated discharge processes, a developmental perspective is inescapable. The capacity to organize and
represent experiences of increasing complexity is the product of development.
Configurations of emotional experience can be conceptualized in terms of both
the consolidation of self and object representations and the affective qualities
which color them. Hence, any affective state must be viewed not only in terms of
the multiple functions it may serve, but also as the *endpoint of a series of developmental achievements* in the articulation and structuralization of the subjective representational world.

At least two important implications for psychoanalytic treatment follow from
this formulation. The first pertains to those patients who present vague, diffuse
affective states which are apparently unconnected with any representational content. It is essential in the treatment of these patients to make a careful diagnostic
judgment on whether the diffuse affective states are (1) the product of a defensive
separation of emotional experiences into affective and cognitive fragments, or (2)
the result of a developmental arrest at, or regression to, the inchoate, undifferentiated "ur-affect" states experienced prior to the structuralization of self and object
representation (Krystal, 1974, 1975). In the former situation a classical analysis of
the defensive dissociation of affects from ideas would be sufficient. In the latter

situation the analyst might for a period of time be required to assume a function analogous to that of the mother who helps the child to perceive, differentiate, interpret, and verbalize his feelings and to recognize their signal function, as Krystal (1974, 1975) has suggested. In addition to Krystal's recommendations, the general principles that we have outlined in earlier contributions (Stolorow and Lachmann, 1978, 1980) for treating arrests in the development of the representational world would also apply here. Specifically, the analyst would focus consistently on the archaic states or selfobject configurations which the patient needs to maintain or restore, rather than on what he needs to ward off (see Stolorow and Lachmann, 1978, 1980 for clinical exemplification of this approach).

The second implication following from our developmental point of view is that under certain circumstances the occurrence of an affective state may be seen not only as a signal evoked by an unconscious fantasy or conflict, but also as an "indicator" (Spitz, 1965) that certain requisite developmental tasks have been accomplished. When an affective state become available as a result of developmental milestones achieved in the analysis, it is essential for the analyst to recognize and interpret its developmental significance *before* analyzing its other functions vis-à-vis the patient's intrapsychic conflicts.

Clinical Illustrations

The clinical material which follows is not intended as proof or demonstration of the validity of our thesis concerning the significance of affective states as developmental indicators. This could be accomplished only by a series of detailed, systematic developmental studies correlating representational and affective development. Instead, we present these clinical illustrations to exemplify the clinical application of our developmental point of view and the therapeutic principles that derive from it.

DEATH ANXIETY

We have presented elsewhere (Stolorow, 1979; Stolorow and Lachman, 1980) the case of Bill, as an illustration of the significance of death anxiety, and it is necessary only to summarize it here. Central to his psychopathology was the extreme fragility of his self representation and his vulnerability to states of self-fragmentation. Early in the treatment he attempted to restore his sense of self-cohesion by indulging in primitive, perverse, sadomasochistic, and exhibitionistic fantasies and acts.

Bill was gradually able to form a stable selfobject transference of the mirroring type and thereby increasingly experienced a buttressing of his precarious self representation. As a result of the uncovering, partial working through, and gradual tempering of his grandiose fantasies and expectations within the transference, toward the end of the fourth year of analysis he began to show evidence of having acquired the beginnings of a cohesive, autonomously maintained self representation. Correspondingly, narcissistic insults no longer evoked states of total self-disintegration, and hence the florid pathological fantasies and acts which earlier had served a narcissistic function in restoring his crumbling self representation were no longer necessary and faded into the background. During this same period, however, he began to experience an acute dread of death, which centered on the idea of the extinction of his existence. According to his recollections, it was the first time that he had either feared death or confronted its inevitability.

Although the death anxiety had multiple meanings for Bill, he and the analyst came to understand that its appearance at this juncture in the treatment was a direct consequence of his having achieved an important developmental milestone. The appearance of death anxiety was an indicator of his having attained a firmer structuralization of his self representation. Prior to this achievement, the experience of acute death anxiety had been largely beyond the scope of his capacities, since he lacked the representation of an integrated and valued self that would be lost as a result of his death. With the beginning establishment of a cohesive, stable, and positively colored self representation, the experience of death anxiety had become a possibility. He now felt, perhaps for the first time, that he had a self to lose.

The acuteness of Bill's dread and the urgency of his preoccupation with death were clearly a measure of the precariousness of his newly germinated sense of self. Yet it would have been a breach of empathy had the analyst focused only on the pathological implications of the death fear, rather than recognizing with the patient that his anxiety was a manifestation of a pivotal developmental achievement.

DEPERSONALIZATION AND CURIOSITY

When Mary began her analysis (described briefly in another context in Stolorow, 1979; Stolorow and Lachmann, 1980) at the age of 30, she had been rendered nearly homebound by acute panic states and multiple, severe agoraphobic symptoms. Prominent in her personality disorder were sexual inhibitions, depressive and dependent trends, and a pervasive narcissistic vulnerability which contributed to her extreme self-consciousness and frequent, searing feelings of shame, embarrassment, and self-hatred. The extent to which her sexual and agoraphobic difficulties were rooted in a masochistic, symbioticlike bond to an invasive, sadistically controlling, and binding mother was dramatically depicted in a dream reported early in the analysis, in which an older woman was cutting out a young girl's vagina so that the girl would remain with her rather than venture out to have relations with men. Interferences with self-object differentiation were shown in the immediate, total "empathy" she experienced for the feeling states of her mother, and of mother-surrogates such as her husband, and in the silent, trancelike, mystical mergings with the analyst that she experienced early in the treatment.

Toward the end of the first year of treatment, a disturbance in the transference occurred which demonstrated that the analyst was becoming established for Mary as an archaic selfobject. As a result of being caught in a traffic jam, he had arrived for the session with Mary, his first patient of the day, about twenty minutes late. During the session, she commented that when he spoke to her he seemed edgy and impatient. The analyst decided to confirm that her perceptions had been correct. Unaware of the nature of Mary's growing tie to him as a self-object, he benignly explained that she was not to blame for his bad behavior and that he was in an irritated state from having been in a traffic jam and having his schedule disrupted. The impact of this disclosure on Mary was profound. She did not show even a trace of the mixture of pleasure and anxiety at being permitted a forbidden glimpse into the analyst's private life that one might expect if an oedipal conflict were structuring the transference. Instead, she began to weep profusely and to describe feelings of deep hurt, utter worthlessness, and self-disgust. Exploration of these feelings led to the understanding that the analyst had inflicted a traumatic narcissistic injury by telling Mary that his affective state had not been evoked by her but by something else, for this had abruptly confronted her with his separateness as an object who could have thoughts and feelings that did not pertain to her. He had, as they came to understand, ruptured an archaic tie in which her newly germinating but fragile sense of self-esteem was becoming solidified around an illusory feeling of union with him as an idealized selfobject who thought only and continuously about her. When he disturbed this developing tie by introducing his separateness, her self-esteem literally disintegrated. In the context of the archaic selfobject bond that she was attempting to revive and maintain at this time, curiosity about the analyst's existence as a separate object was beyond her developmental capacities.

Partly in consequence of the understanding and working through of this disturbance, Mary was able, during the second year of treatment, to become immersed in a stable selfobject transference with both mirroring and idealizing components. During this period, the contribution of her narcissistic disorder to her agoraphobic symptoms was systematically explored—for example, her fears of exposing humiliating weaknesses and flaws and evoking unendurable ridicule while "trapped in the spotlight." The origins of these fears were in turn traced to repeated early narcissistic traumata in which her independent grandiose-exhibitionistic strivings and her actual accomplishments were consistently met by her mother with complete unresponsiveness, undermining belittlement, or relentless criticism, which seemed to discourage intrapsychic separation, strengthen the masochistic, symbioticlike bond, and interfere with the consolidation of a nuclear self structure.

As a result of the solidification of the selfobject transference and the insights gained during this period of the analysis, Mary achieved a marked improvement in her agoraphobic symptoms and began to engage, during the third year of treatment, in a variety of autonomous activities which previously had been unimaginable to her. With each successful mastery of a new activity, Mary experienced a transitory spell of depersonalization. She described an uncanny feeling of unreality, as if the activity were being performed by someone else — a stranger, not herself. Although there were certainly defensive components in these depersonalized states, they were seen primarily as temporary disturbances in the sense of self which signaled a crucial developmental step in self-object differentiation, and were so interpreted to the patient. Mary become depersonalized, in part, because each independent performance of a novel activity constituted an experience of intrapsychic separation from her mother and mother surrogates (such as her husband and the analyst) and hence a beginning loss of her symbiotic identity. At the same time, her newly differentiating self was most precarious and indeed seemed like a stranger to her. To feel distinct, self-reliant and competent seemed uncanny, strangely unfamiliar, and fleetingly severed her sense of self-continuity.

In the fourth year of analysis Mary dreamed that she found and looked through the analyst's wallet. There were pictures of a dark-skinned woman, assumed to be his wife, and two dark-skinned children with blond hair. This dream and Mary's associations to it signaled a decisive shift in the transference. It indicated that sufficient self-object separation had been consolidated in the transference so that she was now capable of feeling curiosity about the analyst's personal relationships with others. Her curiosity showed that sufficient structuralization of her representational world had occurred so that she no longer experienced the existence of other objects in his world as a shattering narcissistic injury. It was a sign that the analyst had become less an archaic selfobject and more a separate and whole object — and, as shown by the dream, an oedipal object. *Both* the developmental milestone and the emerging oedipal conflict required interpretive responses from the analyst.

Envy

At the age of 37 Anita began her third attempt at treatment for a number of difficulties which could be understood in terms of arrests in the structuralization of self and object representations. She was experiencing rapid and unpredictable fluctuations in her self-esteem and in her evaluations of herself and certain significant people in her life. She alternated between viewing herself as "shit" and as "unassailable," and similarly between viewing her husband and certain friends with contempt and with awe. As long as Anita viewed these people with reverence — enthralled by their patience, wisdom, and capabilities — she felt connected to them and valued herself as well. At such times she felt comfortable in her work as a teacher and in her social interactions. When she felt contemptuous of these others and "shitty" about herself, she also became despondent about her professional and social functioning.

Her recent marriage and the recurrence of her "old" problems had prompted Anita once again to seek analysis. Early in the analysis she established a selfobject transference of the idealizing type. During the third year of treatment, an acquaintance from Anita's past was, by chance, referred to the analyst. When Anita learned that this woman would be seeing "her" analyst, she immediately imagined that he would prefer the acquaintance over her. In this context certain new details of familiar historical material were uncovered. Anita's father had abandoned his family (which included Anita, her mother, and her younger sister) when Anita was five years old. However, even prior to this time he was periodically absent from the family, supposedly looking for work. With intense, anxious excitement, Anita now recalled how her father would carry her and play with her. She also recalled her mother's warnings, from a later period, that she should not trust men because they would leave her and take with them every penny she owned.

These memories were recovered during several sessions in which evidence of Anita's idealizing transference continued to emerge. She described feeling anxious in anticipation of each session. The sessions had a subtly disorganizing effect on her self experience. After her analytic hours she was at first "energetic," but the feeling of anxious excitement gradually turned into "inertia." During weekend breaks in the analysis, she became "depressed" and then, anticipating her return to the analyst, would begin to feel more anxious again. Concurrently, she described her acquaintance in the most derogatory terms, as a shallow person who substituted sentimentality for feelings and talked endlessly about trivialities. Anita was convinced that this description was accurate and yet wondered how she could at the same time imagine that the analyst would prefer this woman over her. She felt undeserving of the analyst's attention and anticipated his rejection of her.

The analyst commented that feeling accepted and chosen by him had been having a disorganizing effect on her experience of herself, and that to avert this painful sense of disorganizaton she was now anticipating rejection and was becoming unassailable. Anita responded, "When you say something right, I have mixed feelings. I feel 'thank God' you understand, but I've also begun to envy your ability to connect with people." Further inquiry highlighted the novelty for Anita of her envy of the analyst. It meant that she could now at least imagine that she, too, might someday be able to "connect" with people. She described a new-found sense of parity with the analyst and said she could imagine separations from him without the usual disturbances in her self-esteem.

Although this material could be understood in a variety of ways, it will be discussed only from the standpoint of the pivotal role of envy as it emerged here in the analytic relationship. It should be noted that Anita did not at this point express envy of her acquaintance — for example, as a displacement from her younger sister. Her envy was understood primarily as a developmental indicator signaling a shift in the transference toward experiencing the analyst as a separate object. Anita's "thank God" reflected her awe and reverence for the analyst and her continuing partial reliance on his idealized qualities for her sense of wholeness and value. However, her newly acquired capacity to envy the analyst indicated that now she could also experience his idealized qualities without having to feel entirely merged with them. The envy, that is, signaled a developmental advance in self-object differentiation, in that the analyst was now viewed as the possessor of valued qualities which she currently lacked but conceivably could acquire in the future. When she envied the analyst the therapeutic relationship became enlarged from one in which merger with him had predominated to one in which she and the analyst could at times be endowed with distinct qualities. This developmental significance of the envy was directly conveyed to the patient, facilitating further, groping steps toward still greater intrapsychic separation.

Penis Envy

Sandra, whose treatment has been discussed in greater detail in another context (Stolorow and Lachmann, 1980), began her six-year analysis at age 25 because feelings of anxiety, shame, and humiliation, along with fears of having these feelings, inhibited her work as an actress. She suffered from considerable performance anxiety which affected her ability to control her voice.

Sandra was groomed by her mother to be a performer from the age of five on. Her mother coached her, pushed her, and applauded her until Sandra's talents clearly enabled her to make her own way. At that point the mother-daughter relationship became severely strained. During the earlier, formative years, conflicts between mother and daughter rarely surfaced, with Sandra habitually complying with her mother's expectations and values. In turn, Sandra's image of herself as perfect, good, pure, unambitious, and uncompetitive was supported, and a mergerlike tie to her mother was perpetuated.

Viewed from the standpoint of psychosexual development, Sandra's stage fright could be seen as a displacement from an anal-phase struggle. One line of associations during the analysis led to the understanding that to be observed performing meant to be observed on the toilet. The conflict over who controlled the content of her body — what she produced through her bowels or her voice — had clearly been resolved in favor of her mother's supremacy. From the standpoint of the structuralization of Sandra's representational world, a firm differentiation between the self and maternal object representations was impeded. Her sense of self-esteem became grounded in a pattern of compliance and submission which maintained the mergerlike bond with her mother as an archaic selfobject and sustained the image of herself as her mother's pure and innocent young girl.

Interpretations of Sandra's defenses against aggression toward her mother evoked unbearable anxiety. It became apparent that such interpretations produced an intolerable dilemma in which she felt pressured to separate from her mother at a time when her self representation was not sufficiently differentiated or structured. Pursuing this line of interpretation further would have created within the analysis a repetition of the traumatic anal struggle which had already brought her productivity to a halt.

Rather than implicitly encouraging the expression of aggression toward her mother as a way of fostering separation, the analytic work focused on the recognition and verbalization of her need to feel merged with her mother as a source of power, magical protection, and self-esteem, and her need to avoid experiences of separation. She was then able to express fears that she could become a helpless victim of her mother's envy and retaliation. Exploration of the power and control attributed to her unveiled her unconscious fantasy of a phallic mother.

In the course of the analysis Sandra became professionally more successful and was able to acknowledge the satisfaction she derived from both her work and the applause of her audiences. In turn, her tie with her mother and the required image of herself as unambitious, unaggressive, and uncompetitive—i.e., as pure and innocent—were increasingly placed in jeopardy. Conscious fantasies during sexual intercourse of being raped and degraded, which had appeared sporadically in the past, now became more frequent, occurring typically in connection with successes or the anticipation of a successful performance. Primarily, these fantasies served a narcissistic function by restoring a positively toned self representation. The "rapist" in the fantasies was derived from the image of the phallic mother. The fantasies revitalized this image and averted separation by enabling Sandra, once again, to feel controlled by and merged with the powerful maternal object. Hence, through these fantasies Sandra reinstated the image of herself as her mother's pure and innocent young girl, an image that she still required for her self-esteem.

After this material was partially worked through, Sandra produced dreams in which she possessed a penis. These dreams could have been interpreted as a defensive identification with the aggressor—i.e., with the phallic mother—but from the standpoint of the differentiation and consolidation of her self representation another line of interpretation seemed germane. The dreams were interpreted as reflecting the attainment of a developmental step. She could now imagine herself as powerful and less vulnerable. Her vulnerability to regressive mergers had passed. The dreams suggested that her mother had been demoted from the position of power and supremacy that she had once occupied. At this point, for Sandra to have a penis meant that her mother did not have it. The imagery was interpreted as signaling that a degree of self-object separation had been attained, a developmental advance beyond Sandra's earlier states of merger with the powerful and controlling maternal object (cf. the case of Miss V [Kohut, 1977]).

Working through the fantasy of possessing a penis ushered in a period of homosexual fantasy with some homosexual activity. The actual homosexual experience was "marred" for Sandra by her constant awareness that she lacked a penis. In turn, her feelings of disappointment led to the emergence of intense, pervasive penis envy. Although the envy was open to various interpretations, in terms of the development of her representational world, the emphasis was placed on her painful recognition and acceptance of genital differences and her integration of a gender-specific limitation (i.e., the lack of a penis) into her self representation. In short, her self and object representations were becoming more realistic and less vulnerable to regressions.

For Sandra, the progression from rape fantasies to penis envy signaled a developmental step in the structuralization of her representational world — in the articulation and differentiation of self and object images and the consolidation of self-object boundaries. Specifically, it indicated a firming of a body image which included genital features — albeit to her regret. In the imagery which accompained her envy (at first, fantasies of men dominating women with their penises; later, ideas about various male prerogatives), Sandra acknowledged genital differences and placed the penis on the man, with the painful realization that both she and her mother lacked one. This heralded a firming of her gender identity and a definitive shift toward heterosexuality, i.e., toward her father as her principal love object. As her self representation gradually became more consolidated, Sandra was able to relinquish her mother as an archaic selfobject and establish a more or less realistic relationship with her.

Recognition and acknowledgment of the developmental significance of Sandra's penis envy were pivotal for the progress of her treatment. Had the analyst interpreted the penis envy as merely reflecting pathological fixations and defenses, the patient's developmental thrusts toward greater self-object separation would most probably have been aborted, as they had been in her early "anal" struggles with her mother. By understanding and interpreting the significance of the envy as a developmental indicator, issuing from advances in the structuralization of the patient's self and object representations, the analyst was able to facilitate the further evolution and consolidation of her representational world.

Summary

In this paper we have extended a developmental framework to an exploration of the significance of affective states in the structuralization of the representational world. Any affective state must be viewed not only in terms of the multiple functions it may serve, but also as the endpoint of a series of developmental achievements. Hence, an affective state can occur not only as a signal evoked by an unconscious conflict, but also as an indicator of developmental advances in the articulation and consolidation of self and object representations. Case material was presented in which affective states traditionally understood solely as products of intrapsychic conflict were seen to emerge as indicators of such developmental steps. In each instance, the understanding and interpretation of this developmental aspect were pivotal to treatment.

REFERENCES

Arlow, J. (1977), Affects and the psychoanalytic situation. *Internat. J. Psycho-Anal.*, 58:157–170.
Basch, M. (1975), Toward a theory that encompasses depression: A revision of existing causal hypotheses in psychoanalysis. In: *Depression and Human Existence*, ed. E. J. Anthony & T. Benedek. Boston: Little, Brown, pp. 485–534.
Blatt, S. (1974), Levels of object representation in anaclitic and introjective depression. *The Psychoanalytic Study of the Child*, 29:107–157. New Haven: Yale University Press.
Brenner, C. (1974), On the nature and development of affects: A unified theory. *Psychoanal. Quart.*, 43:532–556.
⸻ (1975), Affects and psychic conflict. *Psychoanal. Quart.*, 44:5–28.
Frankel, S. & Sherick, I. (1977), Observations on the development of normal envy. *The Psychoanalytic Study of the Child*, 32:257–281. New Haven: Yale University Press.
Freud, S. (1915a), Repression. *Standard Edition*, 14:146–158. London: Hogarth Press, 1957.
⸻ (1915b), The unconscious. *Standard Edition*, 14:166–215. London: Hogarth Press, 1957.
⸻ (1926), Inhibitions, symptoms and anxiety. *Standard Edition*, 20:87–174. London: Hogarth Press, 1959.
Gedo, J. & Goldberg, A. (1973), *Models of the Mind*. Chicago: Unversity of Chicago Press.
Green, A. (1977), Conceptions of affect. *Internat. J. Psycho-Anal.*, 58:129–156.
Hartocollis, P. (1976), On the experience of time and its dynamics, with special reference to affects. *J. Amer. Psychoanal. Assn.*, 24:363–375.
Jacobson, E. (1964), *The Self and the Object World*. New York: International Universities Press.
⸻ (1971), On the psychoanalytic theory of affects. In: *Depression: Comparative Studies of Normal, Neurotic, and Psychotic Conditions*. New York: International Universities Press, pp. 3–41.
Kernberg, O. (1976), *Object Relations Theory and Clinical Psychoanalysis*. New York: Jason Aronson.
Klein, G. (1976), *Psychoanalytic Theory: An Exploration of Essentials*. New York: International Universities Press.
Klein, M. (1935), A contribution to the psychogenesis of manic-depressive states. In: *Love, Guilt and Reparation and Other Works 1921–1945*. New York: Dell, 1977, pp. 262–289.
Kohut, H. (1971), *The Analysis of the Self*. New York: International Universities Press.
⸻ (1977), *The Restoration of the Self*. New York: International Universities Press.
Krystal, H. (1974), The genetic development of affects and affect regression. *This Annual*, 2:98–126. New York: International Universities Press.
⸻ (1975), Affect tolerance. *This Annual*, 3:179–220. New York: International Universities Press.
Lachmann, F. & Stolorow, R. (1976), Idealization and grandiosity: Developmental considerations and treatment implications. *Psychoanal. Quart.*, 45:565–587.
Lewin, B. (1965), Reflections on affect. In: *Drives, Affects, Behavior*, Vol. 2, ed. M. Schur. New York: International Universities Press, pp. 23–37.
Mahler, M. (1966), Notes on the development of basic moods: The depressive affect. In: *Psychoanalysis—A General Psychology: Essays in Honor of Heinz Hartmann*, ed. R. Loewenstein et al. New York: International Universities Press, pp. 152–168.
⸻ Pine, F., & Bergman, A. (1975), *The Psychological Birth of the Human Infant*. New York: Basic Books.
Miller, I. (1977), On sadness. *This Annual*, 5:121–140. New York: International Universities Press.

Novey, S. (1959), A clinical view of affect theory in psychoanalysis. *Internat. J. Psycho-Anal.*, 40: 21-104.

——— (1961), Further considerations on affect theory in psychoanalysis. *Internat. J. Psycho-Anal.*, 42:21-32.

Rapaport, D. (1953), On the psychoanalytic theory of affects. *Internat. J. Psycho-Anal.*, 34:177-198.

Ross, N. (1975), Affect as cognition: With observations on the meanings of mystical states. *Internat. Rev. Psycho-Anal.*, 2:79-93.

Sandler, J. & Rosenblatt, B. (1962), The concept of the representational world. *The Psychoanalytic Study of the Child*, 17:128-145. New York: International Universities Press.

Schafer, R. (1976), *A New Language for Psychoanalysis*. New Haven: Yale University Press.

Schmale, A. (1964), A genetic view of affects: With special reference to the genesis of helplessness and hopelessness. *The Psychoanalytic Study of the Child*, 10:287-310. New York: International Universities Press.

Schur, M. (1969), Affects and cognition. *Internat. J. Psycho-Anal.*, 50:647-653.

Spitz, R. (1965), *The First Year of Life*. New York: International Universities Press.

Stolorow, R. (1979), Defensive and arrested developmental aspects of death anxiety, hypochondriasis and depersonalization. *Internat. J. Psycho-Anal.*, 60:201-213.

——— Atwood, G. (1979), *Faces in a Cloud: Subjectivity in Personality Theory*. New York: Jason Aronson.

——— & Lachmann, F. (1975), Early object loss and denial: Developmental considerations. *Psychoanal. Quart.*, 44:596-611.

——— ——— (1978), The developmental prestages of defenses: Diagnostic and therapeutic implications. *Psychoanal. Quart.*, 47:73-102.

——— ——— (1980), *Psychoanalysis of Developmental Arrests: Theory and Treatment*. New York: International Universities Press.

Tolpin, M. (1971), On the beginnings of a cohesive self: An application of the concept of transmuting internalization to the study of the transitional object and signal anxiety. *The Psychoanalytic Study of the Child*, 26:316-352. New York: Quadrangle.

Winnicott, D. (1963), The development of the capacity for concern. In: *The Maturational Processes and the Facilitating Environment*. New York: International Universities Press, 1965, pp. 73-82.

Zetzel, E. (1949), Anxiety and the capacity to bear it. In: *The Capacity for Emotional Growth*. New York: International Universities Press, 1970, pp. 33-52.

——— (1965), On the incapacity to bear depression. In: *The Capacity for Emotional Growth*. New York: International Universities Press, 1970, pp. 82-114.

May, 1979

Metaphor, Affect, and Arousal:
How Interpretations Might Work

FRED M. LEVIN, M.D.   (Chicago)

Introduction

Mr. D., a middle-aged, narcissistically disturbed social scientist, had a dream of a composer and a lyricist. The metaphorical transference interpretation was that the patient had appreciated the extent to which his analyst had been able to acknowledge his feelings — like a lyricist puts words to the music of a composer. Especially useful had been his analyst's ability in the previous session to identify the patient's intense loneliness. The naming of this feeling, which even the patient had failed to recognize, gave him a powerful sense that he was capable of understanding himself and of being understood by someone else, and more specifically by his analyst. He was *not* "psychotic," as he had accused his analyst of thinking of him and as he had secretly felt about himself.

It is my purpose here to explore one of the key issues of technique and theory — namely, the mechanisms of psychoanalytic interpretation. It is my impression that metaphorical language plays a crucial role. If we can be explicit about our interpretive actions and words, we will learn more about what makes interpretations work. This might suggest something to us about our models of the mind, at least as systems for encoding (remembering) and (affectively) organizing experience.

To Freud (1914), "the theory of repression is the corner-stone on which the whole of psycho-analysis rests" (p. 16). The various models of classical psychoanalytic theory can be viewed as systems for the organization of memories, which function as enduring psychic structure. Psychoanalysis is the process which un-

An earlier version of this paper was presented at the Colloquium on Deafness at the annual meeting of the American Psychoanalytic Association, December 17, 1978; and at the Psychosomatic and Psychiatric Institute of Michael Reese Hospital, Chicago, on June 5, 1979. I am grateful to Drs. David Dean Brockman, John Gedo, and Meyer Gunther for their encouragement and criticism.

does repression—often expressed by the patient as a "failure of memory"—by dealing with transference and resistance, "which emerge whenever an attempt is made to trace symptoms of a neurotic back to their sources in his past life . . ." (p. 16). But the questions remain: How precisely does one trace symptoms back to their source? And before, during, or after interpretations are given the patient, what actually happens that results in the opening up of the gates of memory and affect?

Strachey (1934) has suggested a general answer to the question of what makes an effective ("mutative") interpretation: (1) There is an effective *preparation* of the patient for the interpretation. In this "a portion of the patient's id-relationship to the analyst is made conscious by virtue of the latter's position as auxiliary super-ego . . ." (p. 283) (a point I shall return to later); (2) the interpretation is aimed with *specificity*, "that is to say [it is] detailed and concrete" (p. 287); and (3) there is the effect of the particular *language* of the interpretation. Here Strachey writes, for example, of the "blunting effect" of tacking onto interpretations an "ethnological parallel or . . . a theoretical explanation. . . ." In essence, this paper is an attempt to be still more specific about these insights of Strachey.

The vastness of the general literature on interpretation precludes a comprehensive review here. So as to narrow the scope of this paper to manageable proportions, I would like to concentrate on that stage of analysis when transference is in the fore. I would also like to avoid, so far as possible, issues that relate to analytical style. The question at hand is rather: What is it in what each of us does, independent of our unique personality, that effects the analytic process in an effective way? What can be said about the state of the patient at the time an interpretation is made—i.e., about the patient's readiness for experience, affect, insight, etc.— as suggested by Strachey (1934)? How does the analyst recognize and/or create the patient's "receptivity" for interpretations? If some interpretations are more effective than others, there must be specific reasons for this. This paper, then, represents an attempt to explore some aspects of the preparation, "specificity," and language of interpretations.

Metaphor in Interpretation

Many psychoanalysts and psychoanalytically informed scholars have become interested in metaphor (Arieti, 1974; Arlow, 1969; Fine et al., 1972; Forest, 1973; Leavy, 1973; Lewin, 1969, 1970; Litowitz, 1975; Reider, 1972; Rogers, 1973; Rosen, 1977; Rubinstein, 1972; Shapiro, 1971; Sharpe, 1940, 1950). However, these perspectives differ in emphasis significantly from my own. Most prominently, each deals with the role of metaphor in the patient's speech rather than in the analyst's. They also tend to treat metaphor as strictly indicative of relations within a semantic field (Rubinstein, 1972). They do, however, indicate how metaphorical language involves "switching" functions, ambiguity, multiplicity of meanings, symbolism, ease of comprehension, and thinking by similarities: thus they appear aware that metaphorical language is a complex behavior relatively poorly understood but richly deserving of study.

Poets and literary artists speak to us in metaphor. They touch us emotionally. Perhaps one of the reasons for this effectiveness in their use of language is that by employing metaphors the artist is unwittingly tapping the richness of meanings that is a fundamental property of experience. Our work also is based upon this ordering process of the central nervous system. But analysts and artists operate in fundamentally different ways, although there may be some similiarities. For example, no matter how artistic, the analyst's creative product (his analytic activity) is meant to be appreciated only for its value in facilitating an analytic process in the patient.

I believe a reading of Freud's prose shows an active use of metaphorical language, which requires, in fact, a separate index (of "analogies") in the *Standard Edition* of his works. Metaphors continuously enriched Freud's writings, and possibly his interpretations as well. There was no point in Freud's commenting upon this in discussions of technique because its role was probably not apparent, and because it was such an intrinsic part of his method that it seemed more stylistic than methodological.

In the *Webster New International Dictionary*, the Merriam Edition (1958), the word "metaphor" is defined as a derivative of the Greek *metaphora* = meta (beyond, over) and *pherein* (to bring, bear). It represents "the use of a word or phrase literally denoting one kind of object or idea in place of another by way of suggesting a likeness or analogy between them" (p. 1546). At a more fundamental level, at least part of what is carried or brought over from one sensory modality to another are the memories of the experience; that is, metaphors create bridges between sensory modalities. I shall return to this point in more detail toward the end of this paper.

When a transference is interpreted in the language of an apt metaphor (apt for the patient) the evocative power seems enhanced and the analytic process is more likely to be accelerated. This is in part the result of the metaphor's having rewoven together for the patient a unique here-and-now experience, the parts of which connect past and present, but in a particular way. It is the particularity that is the subject of this paper on technique. Additional strands of detailed recollection are thus suggested to the patient in an open-ended manner. (These strands themselves become bridges for, and catalysts of, further synthetic activity, a point which I will clarify later under the headings of the special and the general effects of the analyst's affectivity.) The memories of past and present can then be connected with a sense of vividness that convinces and allows for additional remembering and working through.

At this point it will be useful to consider some clinical examples so as to better illustrate the meaning of a metaphorical (transference) interpretation.

Some Clinical Vignettes

Mr. A. has an advanced degree in engineering. We are now entering the fourth year of our collaboration. As his analysis unfolded, we have understood the effects of a devastating series of early losses which involved an uncle (at age 5), father (at age 8), and a grandfather (at age 18) who had become a father-substitute. The patient is now approaching 40. He began his treatment with a phallic-narcissistic character defense against his unresolved dependent longings and with a history of relationships with women in whom he would readily lose interest. Against the backdrop of the years of our work the interpretations with metaphorical implications seem to have been the most effective.

Our most recent work involved the continuation of his mourning in the following way. Having had some of his clothes stolen from a laundry, he spoke one day of his outraged embarrassment and his impulse to immediately replace the lost articles. Unfortunately, he would have had to order new clothes in a slightly larger size since he felt he had gained weight. He mused about having someone assist him in relation to this loss. I suggested that he needed a tailor and asked him if he knew of any way to mend the situation. This ambiguous metaphor was a reference to his major loss in childhood (father), who was a tailor; to his recent loss (of clothes, etc.); and to myself in the transference as one who mends or helps him mend himself, etc. He recalled with vivid details for the first time a particular garment his father had made for him, just before his terminal illness. He remembered his giving it to him; and with affect he continued with new details of the situation involving the later loss of the grandfather who had served *in loco paternis* for years. Shortly after this remembering and working through, he was able to mobilize himself to obtain a job after months of having been paralyzed in this regard.

Miss B., a 25-year-old prelingually deafened woman with an advanced degree, entered intensive psychotherapy approximately five years ago because of her feeling that in many ways her life had ground to a halt. She has been described by this writer elsewhere (Levin, 1977, 1980), especially with regard to the role of sign language in the defense transference. In a recent session she began by communicating an impulse to turn off the light near her "to save electricity." The previous session dealt with her sexual feelings toward me and her boyfriend, difficult feelings for her to acknowledge. I reminded her of this last session. She said, "You know what happens when the light is turned off," then moved on to more neutral subjects. After a while I brought her back to her remark and interpreted that she wished she could turn off her sexual feelings of excitement here, just as easily as she could turn off my lamp. She agreed and went on to discuss in a so-

phisticated manner her situation with her lover and her plans for eventually resolving that situation in a manner favorable to her (in a way that sounded more
realistic to me than some of her past plans). Toward the end of the session she
said she had decided the room light did not really need to be turned off. I commented that now she felt more in control of her excited, "electrical" (sexual) feelings and did not need to turn them off. She nodded and with a warm glow remembered for the first time how she felt entering (hearing) junior high school.
She had previously been only in schools for the deaf. After a few weeks with hearing classmates she felt years behind in her work. For a while her father had helped
her regain her equilibrium (as I just had), and before long she had felt relatively
caught up, although never fully comfortable.

The Patient's "Language"

Over time we learn how a patient uses words, and over years we develop a vocabulary of his fantasies, feelings, impulses, inhibitions, dreams, neuroses, etc., to
which we call the patient's attention when they can be used to illustrate or organize a pattern near, but just out of, the patient's awareness. The reliable and apt
recall of details from the patient's previous discourse is part of what convinces
him that we hear, think, and care about him, so he can now begin to experience
himself as worth paying attention to, understanding, and caring about.

A patient's language probably also involves his particular blend of sensorimotor experience. Presumably, each of us has preferential combinations of sensations which excite, interest, or bore us. The verbal imagery that reaches us emotionally probably bears a relation to this mix. I shall return to this important
point later.

Shannon's communication theory suggests another critical element in any
transfer of information—namely, the predictability of what is transmitted next.
To the extent that the receiver of a message can predict what is coming, the value
of the information derived approaches zero. The mathematics involves Markoff
chains of a special class called "ergodic" processes (Shannon and Weaver, 1949).
*Metaphors thus have a capacity to surprise the listener in part because of their novelty. The im-
probable and therefore unexpected combination of ideas, sensory modalities, meanings, etc.,
arouses the patient's interest; without it I do not believe synthetic activity can occur.* With the
use of metaphor the informational value of the message rises to a maximum (cf.
Shannon's communication theory). If the reader has any doubts about this property of metaphors to surprise us, he should ask himself how often, when he is
trying to communicate some difficult or important idea, he resorts quite spontaneously to a novel metaphor.

Transference and the Therapeutic Process

Valenstein (1961) quotes Anna Freud as suggesting that the psychoanalytic process is like a dinner, "where in Smorgasbord fashion a number of foods are set on
the table for the choice of the diner. He selects foods in proportion and sequence
according to his needs and the progress of the meal" (p. 315). Valenstein quotes
Bibring to the effect that five psychotherapeutic principles are at work: suggestion,
abreaction, the intentional use of the transference for support, insight through
clarification, and insight through interpretation (p. 319). James Strachey (1934)
writes of "mutative interpretations" (p. 283) in which the patient is prepared, details are specified, and wording can help or hinder the effectiveness of the interpretation. In his role as "auxiliary super-ego" the analyst interprets an id impulse the
object of which is the analyst himself. Thus, with the analyst's permission the patient becomes aware of his impulses and defenses (in optimal dosage), and simultaneously of the contrast between the character of his feelings about the analyst
and the real nature of the analyst; i.e., the patient becomes aware of his archaic
fantasied objects in the transference situation. Strachey thus regards transference
as the patient's superego projected onto the analyst. What gets mutated is the superego which is reintrojected, based upon a less harsh view of the analyst-as-
archaic-imago and the remodeled view of the parent-as-archaic-imago.

Zetzel (1956) points out another view, that of Sterba and Bibring, in which an essential feature of the transference is an identification with the analyst. The superego
is seen to have precursors, the development of which becomes relevant to the analytic work. There are a variety of ways to handle this situation of preoedipal problems
theoretically. To Zetzel the rubric of the "therapeutic alliance" covers what others
(Kohut, Gedo) represent as manifestations of archaic transference states. With this
in mind, however, we can understand her feeling that the therapeutic process depends almost exclusively on transference interpretation; i.e., analysis involves a regression in which there is a revival (re-experience) of primitive stages of development, which can be interpreted as "here-and-now" experience.

Kohut has painstakingly and explicitly expanded the definition of "transference"
(1966, 1971, 1977) to include the continuation of an "unstructured" situation. In
one of his earlier papers (Kohut, 1959), he indicates that "introspection in the case
of narcissistic and borderline disturbances shows the analyst is not [merely] the
screen for the projection of internal structures (transference), but expresses with the
patient the direct continuation of an early reality that was too distant, too rejecting,
or too unreliable to be transformed into solid psychological structures . . ." (p.
471).[1] In the more recent terminology of the self, the descriptive term selfobject
"transferences" has been used.

---

[1] It would seem that theoretically, at least, such arrests might also occur in every neurosis to some extent; why would one have trouble traversing the oedipal conflictual experience unless one already had
had some difficulty, however minor, in a preoedipal stage of development?

There is thus general agreement that the analyst's attention to transference through observation, introspection, and vicarious identification (empathic means) and the interpretation of the transference are the *sine qua non* of an analysis. The question now is: is there any contradiction between my preceding remarks on the details of interpretation — more especially, on the use or role of metaphor — and the value of keeping one's eye principally on transference and its vicissitudes? I think not. The preceding remarks have been aimed at the detailed wording, the structure of the interpretations, but I think it should be clear that these will primarily be transference interpretations. When the analyst, using a metaphorical style, tells the patient that he feels more whole because the analyst has been able to put words to his feelings in the same way a lyricist puts words to the music of a composer, this is a transference interpretation. The same is true when the analyst tells a patient, as in the foregoing example, that he is thinking of (re)finding a (father) tailor to mend himself. The discussion regarding metaphor must not be seen in any way as an attempt to propound a new theory in opposition to the one which has served us satisfactorily and which is confirmed daily in our work: regressions set in motion by the analytic arrangements result in transferences based upon fixations or arrests, which we then interpret in a timely manner, because they now constitute current affective/cognitive experience.

It seems to me that when metaphor can be found naturally and without artifice it has many benefits: it treats with respect the patient's intelligence; it arouses the patient's interest, which will be understood *a priori* to facilitate probable synthetic activity; it generally makes the transference interpretation easier to understand; and it has an ambiguity that allows for simultaneous relevance at multiple levels of experience and meaning. I would like to elaborate on this latter point in the following sections.

The Specific Effect
of the Analyst's Affectivity

The Freudian models of the mind, along with some neurological models which preceded them (e.g., those of Hughlings Jackson in the previous century), implicitly contain the idea of memory as functional systems of the brain with hierarchical ordering. Whatever the current disagreements as to whether self is super- or subordinate mental structure, there seems to be general agreement that the brain is characterized by simultaneous multiple levels of functioning, with potential for the emergence of ontogenetically earlier modes of adaptive experiencing when later (higher) levels of the CNS become disabled for whatever reason.

Such a view is supported implicitly by clinicians who talk of addressing the patient's "observing ego" as opposed to his "experiencing ego"; it is also the explicit perspective of mathematicians interested in computers and the brain — for example, John Von Neumann (1967), who points out that unlike the brain the digital computer operates linearly and at only one level.

The question remaining is how to relate the earlier perspectives with regard to the role of metaphor in transference interpretation to the prevailing view of the brain as such a hierarchical system. I believe that this can be accomplished relatively easily, if we keep in mind that the diagrams which follow as well as the descriptions associated with them are meant only as maps to facilitate understanding—not as causal explanation. The fundamental problem is not in our models (which are understood to be temporary and tentative approximations, by definition) but in our tendencies to reify them (e.g., see Feldman and Toulmin, 1974–1975).

Interpretations that are effective provide bridges of various kinds. I have attempted to illustrate some of this bridging in Figures 1 and 2. In Figure 1 I have superimposed upon a view of the left hemisphere of the brain a triangle representing a linking up of three major sensory modalities: touch, hearing, and sight. Next to each letter I have placed numbers in an inverted series to indicate the layering of functions according to a hierarchy within the framework of Piaget, but entirely compatible with psychoanalysis (Basch, 1976a, 1976b). The details of this layering appear in Figure 2 and will be described in what follows. The triangle represents a "horizontal" bridging.

The dotted lines in Figure 2 attempt to portray "vertical" bridging within a particular sensory-modality-pattern complex. By this is meant some unique tying together of experience so as to involve each of the four (arbitrary) levels indicated, in some way. At the lowest level (1) our metaphorical transference interpretation has touched upon some important sensorimotor schema, which represents the encoding of autonomic affective experiences organized into idiosyncratic rhythm patterns. At the next level (2) our interpretation is effective in the sense that its words serve to elicit evocative recall of still more complex and variegated memories of experience in which objects and subjects are named, but in which essential characteristics of the classes to be named are superseded by accidental properties. Because of this latter fact, the recall is bound to be highly idiosyncratic or even disorganized to the extent that any recall evoked by our interpretation is influenced by this level of organization of experience. Finally, at the last two levels (3 and 4), presentational symbolism and discursive symbolism, respectively, are capable of being evoked. Although I am using Suzanne Langer's (1967) terminology here these levels coincide with Piaget's two highest levels. Time qualities (past/present) and essential rather than accidental properties of things are characteristic of the former (3), so that objects can now be considered in terms of their properties. In the latter symbolic level (4) propositions of if/then, either/or, hypothetical and deductive logic, etc., are now possible and will be manifested especially in secondary-process kinds of recall (discursive symbolism). In contrast to this, the primary-process characteristic of the presentational symbolism of level

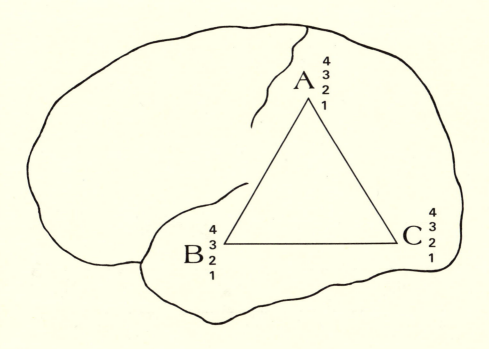

FIGURE 1

(3) activation will be substantially harder to verbalize to the extent that it contributes to the patient's response to our interpretation. However, it might be easier for us to decode, inasmuch as it might present itself as a purely visual memory (much like a dream) to which the patient and we can begin to associate.

The above description is of course highly schematic, but it should communicate to some extent the capacity of interpretations (when effective) to make us feel as though complex, internal chain reactions of falling dominoes have started which run in several directions simultaneously and involve some reactivated memory processes that can possibly reorder our thinking and feeling. The nature of metaphor allows it some special effectivity in the direction of creating horizontal and vertical bridges of the types described above.[2] A good metaphor, when

[2] Past and present are also connected, but general issues of time and timing have been deferred to a future essay. Time bridging could be referred to as "diagonal" bridging.

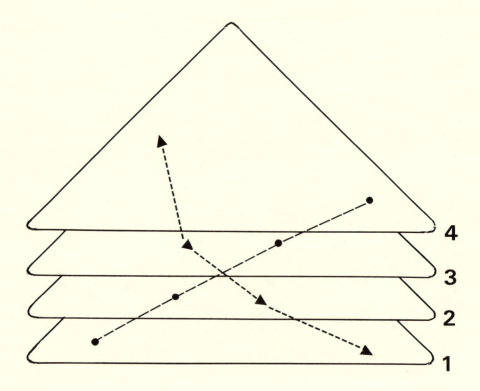

FIGURE 2

tied to a transference interpretation, is like a four-pronged plug that makes contact with each level of the patient's experience simultaneously. At the highest level (4) of conceptualization verbal propositions are independent from sensory-modality quality (Basch, 1976a, 1976b). At the lowest level (1) of sensorimotor schema there are imprints of the unique blend of sensory-modality experience. As Basch (1976b) says of this latter period (the first 18 months of life), "the parent's attitudes towards him are conveyed to the infant through tone of voice, rhythm of action, sureness of touch and other [sensory] signals which are to a greater or lesser extent not in the adult's awareness. The infant [in this stage] in responding to the kind and quality of the messages sent to him lays down the aforementioned [sensorimotor] action patterns that form the basis of his personality and are a response, so to speak, to what his parents are 'telling' him about himself and the world he has entered. This form of communication remains basic throughout life, though, for the most part, people continue to remain unaware of it" (p. 9). I interpret that by "this form of communication" Basch is referring to what we encode in our transactions with patients (without being aware of doing so) which addresses itself to the sensorimotor experience of the infant. I agree with Basch that this in large part accounts for Freud's observation that the unconscious of one person can communicate with that of another. And my suggestion is that in part this is accomplished by reaching for metaphors with our patients—metaphors that will tap multiple levels of experience in ourselves and in them.

Metaphors cross modalities; they relate one sensation to another and the various hierarchical levels of experience to each other. In this manner metaphorical language contributes to the specific effects of the analyst's affectivity; i.e., it seems to create the general affective arousal level that is required for synthetic activity to occur. Our continuous problem is that the patient's changing moods require us to be flexible and not rigid or repetitive in our interpretations.

The General Effect of the Analyst's Affectivity

In the foregoing sections I have attempted to outline schematically what I believe to be the importance of metaphor in making transference interpretations effective. When used naturally and without artifice, when not an end in themselves, and when apt (to the patient), metaphors will resonate with the highest and deepest layers of the patient's functional hierarchy of experience. I should now like to present some additional data from a related field that tends to confirm the observation that metaphor can function as a bridge, and particularly as a bridge across the lines of various sensory modalities.

A recent article in *Scientific American* (Lassen et al., 1978) reports work that might be of interest to us as analysts. Using radioactive scanning techniques to study regional blood flow in the human brain in awake subjects, Lassen et al. have been able to draw conclusions about the ongoing metabolic activity of the cerebral cortex. Their apparatus allows the visualization of the brain's surface cortical activity, as it occurs! One of their most central observations relates to the role of the general level of arousal (of nonspecific pathways) of the brain. *When the arousal level is below a certain threshold of excitement, the patient's cortical activity appears to be limited to only one cortical (sensory) association area at a time.* Thus, for example, a relatively unaroused subject instructed to imagine himself listening to a Beethoven sonata will activate only the auditory associative cortex in the temporal lobe. However, if a threshold of interest is exceeded, the brain becomes activated *as a whole*, and (importantly for this discussion) the various associative cortical (and presumably also the subcortical) parts of the brain come into communication with each other.

Lassen et al. assume—I think correctly—that learning about the world (and one would have to add, the self) can then occur; i.e., synthetic activity of the brain would appear to be a function of this general level of arousal of the brain's nonspecific pathways. It seems to me we have here a general explanation as to how our interpretations might work (Levin, personal communication). We could say, preliminarily, that the general effect of the analyst's affectivity[3] is to help bring about this state of arousal of the brain as a whole (or to recognize when it has occurred). As already stated, it seems likely that synthetic activity occurs when the patient's mind is aroused and in communication with itself. Moreover, as noted in the preceding section, this general state of arousal appears to be facilitated by specific interpretations, and more especially by linguistically coded, metaphorical interpretations that tap multiple levels of meaning, including (affect-laden) sensorimotor schema.

The Role of Sensory Modalities

An important aspect of synthetic activity as it is understood by Lassen and his associates is the functional isolation of the various sensory modalities according to the topography of the cerebral cortex. Memories for each sensory modality are in all likelihood not neatly localizable topographically in any simple manner, but seem to have some functional dispersal.

The role of sensory modality in the organization of memory was implicit, and often explicit, in Freud's early theoretical thinking. (For example, the rungs in the reflex-arc model were meant to be the various sensory modalities.) It even played a role in Freud's thinking about one of the basic subjects of this paper—namely, repression—which Freud (1897) defined as follows in a letter to Fliess: "To put it crudely, the current memory stinks just as an actual object stinks; and just as we turn away our sense organ (the head and nose) in disgust, so do our preconsciousness and our conscious sense turn away from the memory. This is *repression*" (p. 269). In *Studies on Hysteria* (Breuer and Freud, 1893–1895), Freud described the case of Lucy R., who was tormented with subjective sensations of smelling "burnt pudding." Freud states: ". . . I only needed to assume that a smell of burnt pudding had actually occurred in the experience which had operated as a trauma" (p. 107) in order to begin to unravel its meanings. References to the complex fabric of sensory modalities as mnemic organizers occur repeatedly throughout Freud's work and apparently played an important role in his own organization of psychic data.

---

[3] I refer here to affectivity rather than simply to interpretive technique, because I believe along with John Gedo (1978) that there is no communication without affect.

Without our realizing it, in our work with patients we take advantage of the principle that memory is organized along the lines of the different sensory modalities. Again, taking clues from the work of Lassen et al., we must in some way, through our interpretations, be fostering a process in which a general state of arousal occurs. Since this would appear to involve bringing the various psychical agencies into communication with each other (bringing, for example, the memories that are organized according to various sensory modalities into functional connection with each other), our interpretive activity might be seen as inviting a transfer across sensory modalities.[4] How might this occur?

A tentative answer is that *one of the crucial elements in an effective interpretation is metaphor.* Here *metaphorical language may even serve as a functional bridge between various psychical agencies that might not be otherwise connected at the time, and in a manner that would allow transfer and creative synthesis of information.* Some of our best (most effective) interpretations might be those that have clear metaphorical aspects, at times implicitly, but preferably, perhaps, explicitly; and our use of metaphor in these cases will not be accidental or incidental, but will probably be a reflection of some decisive role of metaphorical language in the coding and in the transfer of information within the mind.

Functionally organized mental structures work in concert as well as in conflict. The descriptions of "functional bridging" given above use some linguistically coded means (e.g., metaphor) which focuses on the need to understand better the internal communicative and relational aspects of mental systems. Metaphor in this paper is being used both concretely and abstractly to denote the complex subject of the hierarchical organization of the mind, and its regulation.

Summary

In this paper I have attempted to begin to describe the complex subject of the role of metaphor in the analyst's interpretations. The original insights of Strachey about the specific mechanisms of effective interpretation are pursued. When apt, metaphors appear to play a crucial role for the patient, first of all in producing in him a state of general psychical arousal which allows for synthetic activity. (I have characterized this threshold shift in terms of the general effect of the analyst's

---

[4] There is a fascinating reference to what may be a similar or related phenomenon—namely, *"transfert"*—in the sense of hysterical transferring of sensibility, which appears in the preface to Freud's (1888) translation of Bernheim's book on hypnosis (pp. 78–79). The "transfert" is from one side of the body to another. Freud sees this as "proving the suggestive origin of hysterical symptoms" (p. 79). Later he states: "It is merely an exaggeration of a relation which is normally present between symmetrical parts of the body." This raises the question of the role of the different functions of the two hemispheres of the brain, a subject about which much has been written; and the way in which this splitting of function between the hemispheres is related to the subject of transfer of sensory experience across modalities, transfer of learning, etc. This paper could not hope to discuss these subjects comprehensively; they are richly deserving of a separate presentation.

affectivity.) This is part of the meaning of Strachey's point that interpretations require a "preparation." Second, the metaphorical language (of the analyst's transference interpretations) has precise "specificity" in this arousal of the patient's interest by creating specific or idiosyncratic "vertical," "horizontal," and time-dimensional ("diagonal") bridges within his mind which tap his unique hierarchical ordering system of encoded experience. (This detailed bridging activity, in all its complexity, constitutes the specific effect of the analyst's affectivity, much as a specific key works in a specific lock.) Metaphors thus cross sensory modalities and address the patient in a manner which respects his intelligence and which is concrete and abstract, comprehensible as well as integrating. Their novelty is part of what evokes arousal; their familiarity is part of what evokes synthesis; and their relation to the transference is what makes the whole thing go.

REFERENCES

Arieti, S. (1974), The rise of creativity: From primary to tertiary process. *Contemp. Psychoanal.*, 1: 51–68.

Arlow, J. A. (1969), Unconscious fantasy and disturbances of conscious experience. *Psychoanal. Quart.*, 38:1–27.

Basch, M. F. (1976a), Psychoanalysis and communications science. *This Annual*, 4:385–422. New York: International Universities Press.

———— (1976b), Psychoanalytic interpretation and cognitive transformation. In press.

Breuer, J. & Freud, S. (1893–1895), Studies on hysteria. *Standard Edition*, 2:1–305. London: Hogarth Press, 1955.

Feldman, C. F. & Toulmin, S. (1974–1975), *Logic and the Theory of the Mind*. Proceedings of the Nebraska Symposium on Motivation. In press.

Fine, H. J., Pollio, H. R., & Simpkinson, C. H. (1972), Figurative language, metaphor and psychotherapy. *Psychother. Res. & Pract.*, 10:87–91.

Forest, D. V. (1973), On one's own onymy. *Psychiatry*, 36:266–290.

Freud, S. (1888), Preface to the translation of Bernheim's *Suggestion. Standard Edition*, 1:73–85. London: Hogarth Press, 1966.

———— (1897), Letter to Fliess, November 14. *Standard Edition*, 1:268–271. London: Hogarth Press, 1966.

———— (1914), On the history of the psycho-analytic movement. *Standard Edition*, 14:3–66. London: Hogarth Press, 1957.

Funt, D. (1973), The question of the subject: Lacan and psychoanalysis. *Psychoanal. Rev.*, 60:393–405.

Kohut, H. (1959), Introspection, empathy and psychoanalysis. *J. Amer. Psychoanal. Assn.*, 7:459–483.

———— (1966), Forms and transformations of narcissism. *J. Amer. Psychoanal. Assn.*, 14:243–272.

———— (1971), *The Analysis of the Self*. New York: International Universities Press.

———— (1977), *The Restoration of the Self*. New York: International Universities Press.

Langer, S. (1967), *Mind: An Essay on Human Feeling*, Vol. 1. Baltimore: Johns Hopkins.

Lassen, N. A., Ingvar, D. H., & Skinhoj, E. (1978), Brain function and blood flow. *Scientific American*, 23:62–71.

Leavy, S. A. (1973), Psychoanalytic interpretation. *The Psychoanalytic Study of the Child*, 28:305–330. New Haven: Yale University Press.

Levin, F. (1977), How sign-language is used in the service of resistance: Approaches to psychoanalytic psychotherapy with deaf adults. Colloquium on Deafness, American Psychoanalytic Association Meeting, New York, December 14.

———— (1980), Psychoanalytically-oriented psychotherapy with the deaf. In: *Mental Health Needs of*

Deaf Adults and Children, ed. L. Stein & G. Mindel. New York: Grune & Stratton.

Lewin, B. (1969), The train ride: A study of one of Freud's figures of speech. *Psychoanal. Quart.*, 39: 71–89.

―――― (1970), Metaphor, mind and manikin. *Psychoanal. Quart.*, 40:6–39.

Litowitz, B. E. (1975), Language: Waking and sleeping. In: *Psychoanalysis and Contemporary Science*, Vol. 4, ed. D. P. Spence. New York: International Universities Press, pp. 291–328.

Pribram, K. (1971), *Languages of the Brain*. Englewood Cliffs, N.J.: Prentice-Hall.

Reider, N. (1972), Metaphor as interpretation. *Internat. J. Psycho-Anal.*, 53:463–468.

Rogers, R. (1973), On the metapsychology of poetic language: Modal ambiguity. *Internat. J. Psychiatry*, 54:61–74.

Rosen, V. (1977), *Style, Character and Language*, ed. S. Atkin and M. D. Jucovy. New York: Jason Aronson.

Rubinstein, B. B. (1972), On metaphor and related phenomena. In: *Psychoanalysis and Contemporary Science*, Vol. 1, ed. R. R. Holt & E. Peterfreund. New York: Macmillan, pp. 70–108.

Shannon, C. & Weaver, W. (1949), *The Mathematical Theory of Communication*. Urbana: University of Illinois Press.

Shapiro, T. (1971), The symbolic process: A colloquium. *Amer. Imago*, 28:195–215.

Sharpe, E. F. (1940), Psycho-physical problems revealed in language: An examination of metaphor. *Internat. J. Psycho-Anal.*, 21:201–213.

―――― (1950), *Collected Papers on Psychoanalysis*, ed. M. Brierly. London: Hogarth Press.

Strachey, J. (1934), The nature of the therapeutic action of psychoanalysis. *Internat. J. Psycho-Anal.*, 50:275–292, 1969.

Valenstein, A. F. (1961), The psychoanalytic situation. *Internat. J. Psycho-Anal.*, 43:315–324.

Von Neumann, J. (1967), *The Computer and the Brain*. New Haven: Yale University Press.

Webster New International Dictionary (1958), Merriam Edition.

Zetzel, E. (1956), Current concepts of transference. *Internat. J. Psycho-Anal.*, 37:369–376.

March, 1979

INTERDISCIPLINARY RESEARCH

Amazonian Interviews: Dreams of a Bereaved Father

WAUD H. KRACKE, Ph.D.   (Chicago)

Anthropology and psychoanalysis are both founded on methodologies which embody epistomological paradoxes of a rather similar nature. Psychoanalysis is devoted to the study of what man does not know about himself, what is repressed or otherwise rendered inaccessible to the observing ego which is its main instrument of observation. Anthropology is devoted to the study of ways of life and systems of belief that are incomprehensible to us because they are based on cultural presuppositions incompatible with our own, yet must be studied by individuals whose perceptions are profoundly molded by the cultural presuppositions of our society. Both enterprises require a long and taxing period of piecing together the mute assumptions of the person one is intimately and intensely engaged in understanding — mute in one case because the assumptions are warded off and often rooted in childhood modes of thought no longer accessible, and in the other case because they are so ingrained in a culture's perception of reality that they are not perceived as assumptions — not perceived, that is, as having alternatives. Both enterprises might be compared to Archimedes trying to move the earth without a fulcrum.

If one goes one step further, and tries to apply psychoanalytic modes of studying the psyche to an individual of a culture very different from one's own, the two paradoxes compound one another — Archimedes without either a fulcrum or a lever. Indeed, it has been argued — and not just by armchair methodologists — that the psychoanalytic study of individuals in non-Western cultures is impossible, at least by the conventional psychoanalytic method of interviewing. The grounds on which this has been argued are several. It is argued that another culture's perception of psychic and external realities is so different from ours that we have

A shorter version of this paper was presented at the January 22, 1980, meeting of the Chicago Psychoanalytic Society. Some of the material in this paper has also been used in a paper submitted to *Ethos: Journal of the Society for Psychological Anthropology*, entitled "Kagwahiv Mourning I." I am indebted to George Pollock, Kay Field, John Gedo, and the discussants of the paper at its January 22 presentation, George Moraitis and Mark Gehrie, for stimulating and provocative comments. Valuable suggestions made at the Bennington South American Indian Caucus (August 1980) unfortunately came too late to be incorporated.

no way of evaluating how much a particular individual's perception or idea may be influenced by his private unconscious fantasy. It is also argued that affective cues may differ from those we are accustomed to reading, and so mislead our intuitive judgments of a person's state of mind. It is even suggested that different concepts of self in other societies may utterly preclude the kind of introspective reporting that is essential for psychoanalytic understanding: if certain affective experiences are culturally perceived as being external to oneself rather than of the self, one cannot reflect and report on the precursors of the experience in one's own life.[1]

Some of these objections do not hold at all, at least for the Kagwahiv Indians with whom I worked in the Amazon Basin of Brazil. I have argued elsewhere (Kracke, 1979) that the Kagwahiv do have a concept of an autonomous thinking and experiencing self, even if that self and some experiences are conceived differently from our way of thinking about them; if anything they give more thought than we do to the part that day residues and nocturnal thought processes play in dreams. The challenge is to discover the concepts in the culture or language in which such introspective observations can be discussed. Some of the other epistemological objections do point to certain real difficulties in the way of such investigations, yet do not render such knowledge impossible. It is not infrequently the case that what can be shown by the philosophical purist to be epistemologically impossible is in reality merely difficult, and one needs only the determination — or blind foolishness — to proceed, to listen and observe carefully, without being dissuaded by the logical objections (cf. Kracke, 1978a).

Still, this is not to deny that there are difficulties in the way of cross-cultural psychoanalytic understanding. Although I do not agree with the position taken by some anthropologists that only a psychologist brought up in a culture can achieve an empathic understanding of his compatriots' psychic processes — or even that such a person is necessarily in a privileged position in this regard (LeVine, 1973, pp. 221-223) — I do believe that it is essential for a psychoanalyst or a psychoanalytic researcher working with a person of a widely different culture from his own to achieve some level of competence in his patient's or subject's culture, especially if he is working in that person's own cultural setting. Freud (1918) spoke of the "laborious task" of feeling one's way into the psychic reality of a patient of a "national character that was foreign to ours" (p. 104), even as little different (on a world scale of cultural differences) as Greater Russian from Viennese. It is my purpose in this paper to explore the possibility of achieving psychoanalytic understanding of psychic processes in someone of a very different culture, and to examine some of the barriers, not all of them by any means purely cognitive, which impede such understanding. I will conduct this exploration in

---

[1] These points are expressed, somewhat more tentatively than I have stated them here, in LeVine, 1973. I am not sure to what extent LeVine may have modified his views more recently (cf. LeVine, 1977; LeVine and LeVine, 1979).

the context of my relationship with one Kagwahiv Indian.

Despite the difficulties—which as Freud showed in another context may themselves prove illuminating and even of positive value, at least for the understanding of human psychic processes—there is a major value in such an undertaking. If psychoanalysis is a general approach to the understanding of human psychic life, we need not only to expand it to embrace a wider range of pathology and normal experience in our own society, but also to test the limits of its extension in the experience of individuals in cultures very different from our own. Takeo Doi (1973) has shown us how different the intrapsychic world—our own intrapsychic world as well as a Japanese one—looks through Japanese eyes. If I differ from Doi in strategy, I still believe that the psychological insights *of* other cultures, as well as insights *about* the psychic reality of individuals of other cultures, should both be integrated into psychoanalysis, as should insights into what it is that makes communication and mutual understanding difficult between individuals of different cultures.

In this broad project, it is essential to apply the psychoanalytic method of investigation directly with individuals of different cultures, and not simply depend on secondhand materials gathered by anthropologists with different methods and for different purposes. In my experience, free-flowing interviews modeled on psychoanalytic interviews can explore an aspect of cultural phenomena that standard anthropological methods cannot reach: such interviews can show something of how cultural beliefs and imagery are used by individuals to express personal fantasies that are unique and individual—that is, to articulate and resolve personal conflicts.

I will here present a sketch of a series of interviews I had with a Kagwahiv Indian, a young headman I will call Jovenil, in his settlement. I will focus on his mourning of two children he had recently lost, which in retrospect (though I was not at the time fully aware how much) was quite understandably a focus of our interviews. I also choose to illustrate my topic with an instance of mourning because it is a familiar process, facilitating comparison. It is also a process which is both intrapsychic and socially regulated, and thus it brings out especially well the interplay between the two levels. Indeed, it has already been the subject of one of the most important recent contributions to bridging psychoanalytic and anthropological theory (Pollock, 1972). Although I will allude to some of the ways Jovenil uses cultural forms in expressing and regulating his feelings, I will concentrate on the intrapsychic aspect of his mourning, raising the question to what extent it is possible to understand the feelings and psychic processes of someone of so different a culture, and what obstacles need to be overcome in order to do so.

I did not immediately begin my depth interviews when I began my fieldwork with the Kagwahiv in February of 1967. It was only in the last three-month stretch of that period of fieldwork, July to September, 1968, that I did carry them through. Some good and valid reasons for such postponement can certainly be adduced. The familiarity I gained with Kagwahiv culture in six months of contact prior to starting the interviews, and the fluency I gained in Portuguese, and at least a beginning command of Kagwahiv were essentially prerequisites for establishing a coherent conversation. Where one is an uninvited guest, too, it is necessary to establish one's reliability as a sensitive and concerned person before people will confide in one. But beyond these good reasons, there was also an element of procrastination in my delay in undertaking such intimate contact as these interviews involved. Some of the motives that contributed to this procrastination are relevant to the problem of cross-cultural understanding, and I will come back to them before concluding this paper.

Before turning to Jovenil's interviews, I need to sketch something of his culture and the Kagwahiv beliefs and values that affect his mourning process, and also say something about Jovenil as a person and the development of my relationship with him.

The Kagwahiv live in the Western part of the Brazilian Amazon region along the Madeira River, a southern tributary to the Amazon that flows from the Bolivian border to join the Amazon just below Manaos. Their language is of the Tupi family, a group of languages widely spread south of the Amazon, but the younger men especially, who have to deal economically with Brazilians, have also become quite fluent in Portuguese. They live in sturdy beam-and-palm-thatch houses in small settlements of three or four families each, located on the banks of tributaries to the right bank of the Madeira, and annually clear fields from the jungle during the dry season, by the slash-and-burn method, for their corn and root crops — manioc or cassava and several kinds of potato and yam — as well as bananas and other tropical fruits. They still fish primarily with bow and arrow (or in the dry season by poisoning dammed-up pools with the timbo vine), but now hunt with shotguns.

Dreams are an important part of their culture, a fact which may have considerably facilitated my interviews with them. A dream will often be recounted in the morning for general discussion of its meaning. I have sketched a variety of Kagwahiv theories of dreaming in another paper (Kracke, 1979); the most frequent interpretations of dreams have to do with symbolic predictions of the future, but Kagwahiv are also very aware of the role of day residues in dreams, and of the relation of dreams to nocturnal thinking. Some dreams are explained as wish fulfillments.

A few comments on the beliefs and values that regulate the mourning process are essential background. Although the immediately bereaved person is supported in the period of initial shock by a sympathetic gathering of close neighbors and relatives, the general effort thereafter is to dampen the experience of grief. It is not considered appropriate to talk to a bereaved person much about the loss, or to remind him of the deceased person. One avoids arousing painful feelings. The bereaved person is permitted to withdraw from social life for a few days or weeks, however. Indeed, a bereaved parent in particular should refrain from eating too much and from going to parties, lest death be visited on another of his or her children. Excessive weeping is anathema; it exposes one to supernatural dangers. The way to deal with loss is to forget the deceased person as rapidly as possible: you give away all the person's belongings or any utensils they used that remind you of them. You dismantle the house you have lived in with the person—if it was a child, by minimally removing the thatch and rethatching it, or, if an adult, by taking all the beams apart and rebuilding the house at a new spot—or even by relocating the whole settlement, in order not to be reminded. The rationale for this in Kagwahiv belief is that, since the person's ghost (*añang*) might return to familiar spots and seek familiar objects, everything associated with the deceased person is *pojy*, supernaturally dangerous. But informants also give another explanation in free variation with this one, as if it were synonymous: "We move so as not to remember, because it makes us sad." Everything possible is done so as to push away the memory of the deceased and the immediacy of the death. Under these conditions, mourning is a difficult and problematic process, and understandably became a focus for my interviews with Jovenil.

Jovenil is one of seven men with whom I conducted extended series of free-associative interviews—seventeen interviews in his case, each one to two hours long—which are more fully reported in my recent book (Kracke, 1978b). Jovenil, in his thirties when I interviewed him, was the second of five children. His older brother and his next younger sister, along with their spouses, had died some fifteen years before, working for Brazilians far from home. His younger brother and youngest sister lived in Jovenil's settlement, the latter with her husband. So did their elderly and ailing father, Ukarepuku, a notoriously temperamental but respected man. Their mother, whom Jovenil remembered as a hard-working woman—even when sick, she did the heavy work with manioc while Ukarepuku went fishing—had died of tuberculosis some six or eight years before the interviews, just before the missionaries arrived with their medications which saved many others from similar deaths. Himself the father of ten children, Jovenil had just three months before the interviews lost two of them to an epidemic, his approximately one-year-old daughter and his six-year-old son, Alonzo. The latter loss was especially painful to him. This undoubtedly contributed to the introspectiveness and attunement to his inner life that he showed in his interviews, but even before the loss these qualities distinguished him among the Kagwahiv—and others—I have known. He is not to be taken as a "typical" Kagwahiv, any more than any of the other informants I interviewed; each is as unique an individual as anyone in our own culture, and the differences among them are as great. I describe my interviews with him not to present a "representative" Kagwahiv, but to bring up the question of understanding psychic processes in an individual of so different a culture from ours.

I liked Jovenil from the time I first met him in his settlement. His immediate outreaching hospitality met my needs as I was beginning my fieldwork in his settlement, still rather helpless both in language and in jungle adaptation after only one month spent in a neighboring settlement. In contrast to the headman of the first group I stayed with, Jovenil was solicitous about arranging my lodging and making sure I was fed for the first day or two. Although our roles led to some tense periods in the development of our relationship — as when my desire to preserve a dwindling supply of canned meat, which took on a symbolic and emotional importance to me far beyond its caloric value, came into conflict with his responsibility to see that all food in his settlement was duly and equitably distributed — I felt warmly toward him, and he showed warm feelings toward me, throughout most of my stay. He expressed reciprocal curiosity about my culture and my family, and sometimes we sat companionably together on the porch of an evening listening to BBC concerts on my transistor radio — he was especially fond of Bach. In short, the interviews I had with him in the last three months of my fieldwork took place in the context of an already developing relationship. The oedipal memories that emerged in his sixth interview are not to be seen as coming up abruptly in the second week of an interview relationship, but rather, after four months of intimate coresidence in a small settlement, stretched in segments over a year.[2]

Some of the themes that were later to develop in the interviews were articulated in the very first conversation I ever had with Jovenil, the night after I arrived for the first time in his settlement for a month's stay in July of 1967. He was about to leave for a week's hunting trip, but showed solicitous concern that I should be kept comfortable. As I recorded in my notes, "He kept repeating that anything I wanted I should ask his wife for." (The ambiguous overtones of this offer of his wife's services anticipated a later theme in the interviews.) In that conversation, he showed some skepticism about the firmness of my commitment to spend an extended period with him. After telling me something of his life history, he remarked that I probably would get married and never return, like another American visitor they had liked, who shared his catch of fish with them but never came back. As the time of my departure neared toward the end of that month's stay, he showed some distress over it. Shortly before I left, he told me a dream — I think it was the first one he told me — that he was defending me from the attack of a Brazilian who wanted to kill me, a man he portrayed in his associations to the dream as a friendly, humorous, lively fellow who never drank: "I don't know why he didn't get along with you." After a pause, Jovenil mused "Estados Unidos," and asked

[2] I was based in Jovenil's settlement for one month, July-August of 1967, and for three more months, November, 1967 through February, 1968, before the last three-month period of that field trip, July-September of 1968. During these periods, I made forays of a few days at a time to the neighboring settlement. I spent an additional two months visiting Kagwahiv settlements distant from these two. In the summer of 1973, my wife and I spent a further two months in Jovenil's area, dividing our time between Jovenil's settlement and the neighboring one.

some questions about my impending departure. Evidently, he had to protect me from his anger at my leaving him, and/or feared that it was his anger, or his demands, that were driving me away.[3] Later I learned that it was very important for him that I left my baggage with him for safekeeping when I left; it was a guarantee of my return.

One of the most important stages in the development of my relationship with Jovenil, and with the rest of the group of which he was head man, was the illness of Jovenil's children during my next extended stay in his settlement, beginning in November. Before that, my role was that of a curious visitor with a rather peculiar interest in Kagwahiv ways of life, and a periodic source of relatively cheap trade goods. After the episode of illness and my involvement in it, I became more a part of the group, or at least someone who cared, who valued their lives and evidently shared some of their concerns and feelings. I took on a more medical or paramedical kind of role in the group from then on. This diatrophic role, I think, greatly facilitated the kind of interviewing I was to carry on later in the last three months of that field trip.

When I arrived that November for a three-month stretch of fieldwork, several of Jovenil's children were sick, in the aftermath of a measles epidemic. But the climax came around Christmas, when his one-year-old daughter became ex-tremely ill. He was at first reluctant to have me give her injections, fearing that in her weak state the strong medicine would be too much for her. At one point, she reached the unresponsive state the Kagwahiv call death, and her mother started wailing. Antibiotics did pull her through that crisis, however, and with continued treatment she gradually improved. Had she not, Jovenil's sister warned me, they would have "reported me to the sheriff." I also treated Jovenil's cherished six- or seven-year-old son, Alonzo, who had not reached quite the same extremity. For a few weeks in December and January, my research activities nearly came to a halt as I spent my time giving what medical attention I could from the medical sup-plies I had with me. When I had to leave to replenish my supplies at the end of February, both children were on the mend and seemed well on the way to recovery; but a month or two later, both had relapses (or in their weakened state contracted new illnesses). Alonzo died, and then shortly his younger sister followed.

It was in my next three-month stint of fieldwork, after a four-month break, that I began the intensive interviews. I learned of the children's deaths as I was returning at the end of June. I went in with some anxiety, with vivid images of what their reaction to the deaths might be. My worst fantasies were not realized,

[3] A childhood memory he told me early in 1968 may be relevant here. While I was discussing food taboos with him — or more exactly, the state of *paném*, an unlucky state that prevents success in hunt-ing or fishing and is precipitated by the infringement of rules about the sharing and respectful treat-ment of meat and fish — Jovenil recalled having made his father *paném* by quarreling with his brother over the prized head of the fish. In consequence, "Papa went fishing every day, but didn't kill anything for two weeks — until [the fish] became accustomed to him again." His demands, he feels, may have disastrous consequences.

or at least were never verbalized to me. But I realized later, when I had learned more about Kagwahiv values of mourning, that I had committed something of a faux pas in sympathetically asking Jovenil's wife Aluza about the deaths, reminding her of the painful loss she was trying to forget.

Jovenil was the first informant with whom I began intensive interviews when I got to his settlement. I established a pattern of daily interviews with him (except on Sunday) varying in length from a half hour to nearly two hours—"fifty minutes" would of course have no significance whatever to a Kagwahiv—asking him to tell me whatever he felt like talking about, including dreams, childhood memories, or whatever thoughts he had. We sat on the open platform of the unwalled house I was staying in, which afforded much greater privacy than would any more enclosed spot, at which children would indubitably gather to listen.

Jovenil did not explicitly mention the deaths of his two children for the first two weeks of our interviews. But he did drop an uncharacteristically discouraged remark the day I arrived back in his settlement in early July: he mentioned that he did not want any more children. Pressed for a reason, he would only say that he had enough children. And he remarked in the fourth interview, when he was telling me about an adolescent affair he had had with a clan sister, that the punishment for such incest was that "one's father dies, or else one's child."

The deep personal significance for him of this remark, however, came out only in a dream which Jovenil reported five days later, in his sixth interview. He closed the intervening interview—which had been a difficult one, full of silences—with an account of the myth about a woman named Kagwahivahẽ, whose jealous husband, with the help of his daughter, slaughters the tapir who has been carrying on an affair with his wife. The wife, in grief, takes the children and jumps into the river, all turning into porpoises. His resistances were little in evidence in the following, sixth interview. I jotted in my field notes: "He seems especially eager today to respond to challenge."

He began the interview, which was late in the afternoon after interviews with two other informants, with a series of dreams he had had the previous night, including one in which his gun failed him in defending himself against a group of Brazilians. The third dream he told me was even more strikingly open:

José Bahut [an older man, of the opposite moiety] was having intercourse with his wife [Camelia]. Everyone saw it. Suddenly his dick was very big. Patricio [Camelia's younger half-brother] grabbed his dick and pulled it, and it snapped. "Why did you break my dick?" "Because you were screwing my sister!" Patricio was fixing José's dick, with a vine thong, and it got real thin. —It's funny, my dream!—Aí, they said "Did your dick snap?" Aí, a lot of blood came out, his dick got rotten. Patricio fixed his dick, it got real thin. Homero [Patricio and Camelia's father] scolded Patricio, "Why did you snap his dick? He'll die!" "No, he won't die," he said.

He followed the dream with a series of associations that underscored the danger to the dreamer of such a dream — "If you dream of a woman's genital, it's a wound you are going to get, you cut yourself" — suggesting that the wound represented in the dream may be his own.

I pointed out that this was the second time in two days he had mentioned to me a dream of José Bahut's big penis: in the previous interview, he had told me of a dream he had had upriver that "José Bahut had a dick this long!" Could it be, I asked him, that he had at some time seen a grown man's big penis when he was little? Yes, he replied, he had. At five years of age, he saw José Bahut's penis, when he went swimming in the river as José was there bathing. He had asked José how he got such a big penis, and José responded: "No, I make my wife a lot, that's why it gets so big." Excitedly, Jovenil ran back to report his observation and new knowledge to his mother, only to receive a severe scolding: "When you see someone else's dick like that," his mother told him, "when you get older, you will go blind!" "She scolded with a stick, a belt," Jovenil recalled, "for me not to ask him anymore." Further memories led him to recollections of a childhood phobia of pigs and cows: "It seemed as if they wanted to eat me." (His mother reassured him: "Sometimes a dog bites if it is angry, but pigs don't eat people.") At times he couldn't sleep at night for fear of ghosts, and needed the reassurance of his father bringing him a drink of water, or of going to sleep in his father's hammock.

All of this shows a remarkable access to memories of his own childhood phobias and conflicts; his pig phobia seems similar to Little Hans's, and we may note from the dream that he seems to have interpreted his mother's warning of blindness as a castration threat. Indeed, on the surface one might think this dream a virtually undisguised expression of a childhood memory, without repression. Yet there *are* repressed thoughts in this dream, and this latent content brings us back to the mourning of his children. The disguise in the dream becomes apparent when we compare the dream's content with an episode in Jovenil's past. The woman José Bahut was making love with in the dream — José's current young wife at the time of the dream, not his wife of the time of Jovenil's five-year-old memory — was the very same parallel cousin of Jovenil's with whom Jovenil had had an incestuous affair in adolescence. In Kagwahiv terminology, she was his "sister." If we put Jovenil himself, the dreamer, in the place of José Bahut in his dream, then some of the comments in the dream take on new significance: "Because you were screwing my sister!" may be an echo of Jovenil's own self-accusatory guilty conscience; and Homero's exclamation: "Why did you do that? Now he'll die!" may refer to the punishment for such incestuous activity, the death of a close relative — perhaps that of his child. The dream, then, is a self-accusation, saying that he himself was responsible for his young son's death, represented in the dream as a castration. In the imagery of the dream, it was his own incestuous desires that brought about his "castration."

Two interactions Jovenil engaged in during this interview reveal transference

derivatives[4] of the childhood memory that emerged during the interview — or
more accurately (as we shall see) derivatives of the childhood fantasy for which
the memory was a screen memory. First, late in the interview Jovenil's wife
Aluza wandered over with their four-year-old son Louro and joined the conversation. Conscious of the child's presence, and of the intimate nature of what we had
just been talking about, I steered the discussion toward more neutral topics. But
Jovenil would have none of it. After politely answering my questions, he turned
to his wife and excitedly recounted for her, in rapid Kagwahiv, all that he had
just told me — the castration dream, the memory of childhood sexual curiosity,
and his mother's blindness threat. When we were alone again, he resumed with a
tale of how Daniel Aguarajuv (a neighbor and close friend of Jovenil's) at the age
of six had been mistreated and almost killed by his stepmother (his mother's co-
wife), then concluded the interview with a series of questions about the notes I
had been taking on the interview:

> How many pages did I fill today? (Ten.) Not many today, because I didn't
> remember much. I only beat Daniel — he told eight pages, wasn't it? I didn't
> beat Francisco — he told eleven. [But he pointed with pride to the nearly com-
> pleted notebook.] Tomorrow I'm going to fill it almost all!

It takes but a small leap to surmise from this competitive comparison what was
going through his mind as a child as he inspected José Bahut's penis, and in-
quired how it got so big. Given José Bahut's answer, one suspects that he may
have run to his mother with something more in mind than simply telling her about
his discovery. Jovenil is a man of action, and likes to try out his newly gained
knowledge.

The fact that Jovenil was so ready to communicate to Aluza his newly found
self-knowledge should not be taken as detracting from the dynamic importance
of the conflicts behind the dream and the screen memory. On the contrary, his
telling her is itself an enactment of the memory, if in a more benign context:
she does not threaten him with blindness. Where I had misjudged Jovenil's
response was in attributing to him a strong desire for privacy of intimate
thoughts. Such a value on privacy, and especially on protecting children from
"adult" sexual discussions, is something appropriate to my own culture and
defenses, but not to his.

To return to the thread of mourning in the interviews: My guess that the
dream of castration is a representation of his child's death (an understanding, incidentally, that I reached much later in retrospect; I was not aware of it at the
time) is confirmed by the somewhat more open expression of the idea in a dream
he reported the next day. Daniel Aguarajuv and his older Brazilian wife had a pet
monkey which, since they were childless, was like a child to them. In the dream,

---

[4] This is not the place to enter a discussion of the concept of transference, but I here follow
Loewald's view (1960) that transference is an element of all meaningful human relationships.

Daniel went out hunting and shot what he thought was a wild monkey—but it turned out to be his own pet monkey, which had run away. He had inadvertently killed his own child. Jovenil's associations, just to confirm this, went back to his first child, who had (many years earlier) died young, his wife almost dying at the same time; then to the various prohibitions that surround the birth of a child: "When he is born, you don't go working...If you do, the child won't grow up—he'll die." And he listed the animals one should not hunt—including monkey—if one is to avoid bringing harm to one's infant. The mood of the interview was sad, and it was clear that his thoughts were returning to his lost children.

The next day, he elaborated much more on his teenage affair with Camelia, who was then single, vividly describing the incident that terminated his relationship with her: the dog barked as he and his companion sneaked into her settlement, and they were almost caught. In that interview, he also described a recent fight in which José Bahut almost killed a man who had slept with his wife—Camelia. And, toward the end of the interview, he commented on a dream he had reported at the beginning, in which Aureliano teased him about his tattered clothes:

> When you dream that your clothes are all torn, you dream your own death.... You're afraid in the morning, because sometimes something can happen to you. Sometimes you can get sick. You get sad when you dream like that. If you dream of a house, it's a bad dream like that, [a house] full of holes, it's a child of yours that's going to die.

(The traditional Kagwahiv interpretation of a falling-down house in a dream is that it predicts that *a close relative* will die.)

It was the next day, in his ninth interview, that Jovenil finally brought up his son's death explicitly—through a dream. "I had a dream," he said right off. "A bad dream."

> My son died. Alonzo. They drowned him in the deep—in the water. "Why did you guys kill my son?" "No, he died." "Where did you bury him?" "In the bank." They buried him in the bank.

He elaborated that it was three Brazilians who had drowned him—then revised it; they hadn't intentionally drowned him, it was that Alonzo went out in a canoe with them and and the canoe turned over.

The drowning in the "deep water" is a punning reference to the sin Jovenil felt he was being punished for. When he first told me of his incestuous relationship with Camelia, he had used a Kagwahiv word for "incest"—*typyowý*—whose literal meaning is "deep green/blue water." But what of the three Brazilians in the dream? They could refer to the thought that came out toward the end of the interview, his suspicion that a woman jealous of his healthy family had hired a Brazilian sorcerer. But they also may be an allusion to my treatment of the children, holding me responsible (in the end) for not saving them. (The "three" Brazilians may include two missionary linguists stationed in the neighboring settlement, who also had a part in the treatment.)

In the rest of this interview, he went on to describe the children's deaths in detail, with deep affect. It was the first time, with me at least, that he had fully experienced and expressed his grief. It would seem that he had to deal with his conflicts over it, his sense of guilt and remorse over having as he felt caused his own children's deaths—and, in this last dream, his anger at me for not saving them—before he could go on with the mourning.

In subsequent interviews, he went on to mourn further and deal with other facets of these conflicts. In the next (tenth) interview, in association to a dream with a theme of being lost in the jungle, he acknowledged another feeling that contributed to his guilt over Alonzo's death: some ambivalence toward the child. I suggested that some planks he was carrying in the dream might be for a coffin, which he agreed was a conventional interpretation of that dream image; and I suggested that they might refer to Alonzo's death, to which he replied: "I dreamed of Alonzo, too."

He went to the Festa with me, "Ah, Alonzo, there you are, after so much time!" Alonzo said, "I died at first, now I came alive again."

The Brazilians [Jovenil went on] say it is God who gives the orders. If you scold your child too much, He kills him. If you scold your child too much, God is watching and says, "He doesn't like his son, I'm going to kill him, to see if he will be sad." (Did you feel you scolded him too much?) I scolded him a lot. Afterward, Papa said to me: "One doesn't scold one's son."

First I thought one's children didn't die. That's why I married, to have children. A single woman doesn't have children. It happens a lot when you are married: If your wife doesn't die, your child dies.

Here, he remarked on a plane passing over: "Púxa! One after another, the airplanes!" and a moment later, returning to this theme, observed: "From Pôrto Velho, you took a plane to Rio." This referred to my movements after I left his settlement in February; so his noticing the plane flying over, just as he was talking about Alonzo's death, was an allusion to my leaving before Alonzo was fully recovered. If I had not left, he may have been thinking, I might have been able to save his children's lives with my medicines. By leaving, I let them die. In addition, a week hence I was to go to a neighboring settlement where I was doing other interviews—the first interruption since I had started these interviews with Jovenil—and there await a small float plane that would take me out for a two-week sojourn in Pôrto Velho. It would be just a three-week interruption (after three intense weeks of interviews), but it no doubt reminded him of my permanent departure planned for two months later, as well as of my previous absence which had been so disastrous for him. He felt he was about to be deserted.

In casual conversation later on that morning, he mentioned that Maria, a

Kagwahiv girl who had flirted with me in earlier field trips and was jokingly regarded as my amour and bride-to-be, had gotten married. *Opohi hẽ nde-hugui,* he said: "She discarded you." But this husband was too jealous for her taste; she left him to go to Pôrto Velho, at which he cried piteously. "He was old and crippled, that's why she didn't like him." These further spontaneous associations, though after the interview, again express the theme of abandonment and anger—perhaps a fear that his anger, like the husband's jealousy, might drive me away as it had "driven" Alonzo away—or led to his being taken away.

These interviews, a situation decidedly out of the ordinary in Kagwahiv society (as it would be in ours), seem to have given Jovenil significant help in carrying through the mourning process (although that was not their intent, nor was I fully aware to what degree Jovenil was using the interviews in this way until I reviewed the interviews in the perspective of later psychoanalytic training). That his uncompleted mourning had been affecting his life was suggested by the remark he had made to me early in July, before we started the interviews: "I don't want any more children." For Jovenil, usually immensely proud of his prolific family, this was a very unusual remark. I asked him why, but he only said: "It seems I already have enough." The source of these feelings of discouragement and anger over the loss of a favorite son comes out clearly in the remarks just quoted: "If your wife doesn't die, your child does." His depression over the loss of his child had thus at first interfered with his full emotional involvement with his children, and his pleasureful anticipation of having more. By the end of the summer, he had recovered some of his good spirits and enjoyment of life. After I left, Aluza became pregnant again, and has since had three more children.

But it was not only the conflicts immediately pertaining to the loss of his child that he had to work through before he came to experiencing the loss directly in his interviews. The first dream alluding to the loss—the castration dream—was one directly modeled on a childhood memory: seeing José Bahut's big penis and learning that its size (erectness, perhaps?) had something to do with "making his wife." The conflicts he needs to work out over his current loss are related, then, to interests and feelings he had when he was five years old. His guilt feelings about his incestuous experimentation in adolescence may be derivatives of guilt over childhood curiosity in the same area, perhaps related to the blindness his mother threatened him with in punishment for his curiosity. The loss of his child in punishment for incest is represented in his dream as castration—the loss of that about which he was so curious at age five. Perhaps the threat of loss of eyesight for his visual curiosity may have suggested the loss of another member in punishment for illicit pleasures involving it. This representation suggests, too, why he felt with special intensity the loss of his *male* child.

The nature of his childhood conflicts is further clarified in a frightening dream that he very reluctantly recounted to me in the eleventh interview. He was watching a family of forest spirits (*añang*) from behind a tree, while the father *añang* was making love with the mother *añang*, teaching their five-year-old son ("the age of Josinho, of Louro," said Jovenil, naming his six-year-old and four-year-old) how it was done. Terrified at the sight, Jovenil ran back to the settlement and told about it. His brother-in-law Miguel was all for going out to hunt the *añang* family and kill the father; Jovenil tried to dissuade him, but he went ahead and did it.

This dream is a blatant portrayal of a childhood fantasy which, to judge by the age of the onlooking child in the dream, Jovenil must have had at around five years old—the same age as his earlier reported memory of seeing José Bahut's penis, which also involved watching and learning about sex. (Indeed, when I asked him to repeat the dream, he added an image of the *añang* wife pulling her husband's penis until it was a yard long—a child's mechanical conception of erection, perhaps, and surely an allusion to José's information about how he got his big penis.) The fantasy was a little *too* openly expressed for Jovenil's comfort; even the last-ditch distancing device of presenting the action, as it were, "on stage" (Jovenil was *watching* the scene enacted before him) was not enough to allay his anxiety, and in the dream he ran away. He was also very reluctant to tell me the dream, and his associations were primarily to the danger of *añang* and the unmanliness of running away: "A man confronts everything."

If we regard this as a "second edition" of the castration dream which embodies childhood memories from the same age, one intent of his fantasy of pulling José's penis off becomes clearer: If the two dreams are parallel, then Jovenil's fantasy was of *borrowing* José's penis (or his father's) for his own use, just as in this dream he learns from his father how to use it. And it was with his mother that he wanted to practice, just as he later shared a woman with Aureliano when the latter taught him the joys of sex. (Compare the overtones of his offering me his wife's services in the first interview.)

The theme of *learning* in the dream has a direct reference to me. Two days earlier, I had suggested in casual conversation that he learn to give injections, so that he could continue the tuberculosis treatment I was giving his wife. The next morning, I woke up to an animated discussion between Jovenil and his sister as to whose shots hurt more, mine or the missionaries'. (Jovenil maintained that mine did.)[5]

This childhood fantasy, whose reconstruction requires only the juxtaposition of its expression in the two dreams and associated transference expressions, further

[5] The situation of his children's deaths, in which I first saved their lives with injections, then later in my absence they died, creates a situation of defeat for him as a father who cannot protect the lives of his children, as John Gedo pointed out in a discussion of this material. This is a real situation which he experienced as an oedipal defeat; and my offer to teach him to use the syringe in this context contains an especially poignant and ironic parallel with his oedipal fantasy expressed in the dream. However real the defeat may be, though, it is still Jovenil who construed it (unconsciously) as an *oedipal* defeat.

clarifies the conflicts that interfered with Jovenil's mourning. His just-postoedipal son Alonzo, aged six or seven when he died, had evidently stirred up old oedipal conflicts in Jovenil (as Alonzo's successors, represented in the *añang* dream, still did). His death raised these conflicts to critical intensity — especially their competitive and hostile components, the only aspects not represented undisguisedly in the dreams: it is Miguel who kills the father, and over Jovenil's protests. (Compare, again, Jovenil's early dream of protecting me from the Brazilian neighbor's aggression.) He had to work through these conflicting feelings from childhood that were stirred up by his child's death — as well as his adult guilt feelings, closer to consciousness, about having contributed to the child's death through his incest — before he could begin fully to experience his grief. Only after recalling his conflict-laden childhood experiences could he have his first dream directly expressing his sense of blame for Alonzo's death, the dream of shooting the monkey. Articulating these childhood conflicts helped him to sort them out — separating past fantasy from current reality — and freed him to face the present mourning task. It was his needs in mourning, then, that prompted his relating to me these deep childhood conflicts; this is why his interviews are so rich in childhood memories.

These interviews were of course not carried out for therapeutic purposes; I engaged in them strictly for research purposes, and it is only in retrospect that I have become aware of some of the therapeutic processes that were occurring in them. Yet every informant who engaged in these interviews, not just Jovenil, used them to express and sort out conflicting feelings in some area of his life, and to work out personal problems.

Let me return to the question of cross-cultural understanding. When I shifted during my fieldwork from asking predominantly ethnographic questions to a psychological approach, asking my informants to report introspectively rather than to explain their social traditions, I was struck not only by the ease with which fantasies were reported to me, revealing a side of their experience of which I had hardly been aware while I questioned as an anthropologist, but also by the apparent familiarity of the kinds of childhood fantasies that they told me. It was an impressive confirmation for me of the discoveries of psychoanalysis, and convinced me on some issues about which I had remained skeptical.

But there were some things that surprised me, and these points give an opening for some reflection on the differences between the experience of being Kagwahiv and our own experience. One surprise was the comfort with which Jovenil related conflictful childhood memories, not only to me but also to his wife, and especially in the presence of a child of close to oedipal age. It was mainly in deference to the child's presence that I tried to steer the conversation away from such charged topics as Jovenil had been talking about, but Jovenil showed no embarrassment about discussing such things in front of him. This revealed a much more accepting attitude toward infantile sexual fantasies than I was prepared for, although I might have expected it from the openness with which sexuality is talked about—and with which Kagwahiv children themselves inquire into the nocturnal activities of their older siblings. Sexuality is simply part of life for the Kagwahiv child, and he learns about it the way he learns most of the skills he will need as an adult: by watching adults engaging in it, and/or listening to them talk about it. This mode of learning is very nicely dramatized in Jovenil's *añang* dream. Kagwahiv openness both toward sexuality as an aspect of life and toward childhood fantasies pertaining to sexuality is carried over into their folklore, which is full of sexual themes, some transparently reflecting childhood fantasies.[6] It is not, I should stress, that these myths are in any sense infantile, for they are elaborately and poetically constructed. It is rather that the myth tellers, as Pinchas Noy (1969) put it so well, have refined and developed these areas of primary-process forms to a level of complex mythic and artistic thought, just as we refine secondary-process thought into scientific language.[7]

The openness in talking about topics which are spoken of guardedly in our own culture must not be confused with an absence of repressions; nor must the conscious availability of *some* fantasies that we usually repress be taken for a total absence of repression of infantile fantasies, as one discussant of this paper was tempted to do. Despite Jovenil's candid recollection of childhood sexual curiosity and open dream of castration, many of his dream thoughts were unconscious and expressed in disguised form. Though he mentioned guilt feelings over his adolescent incestuous escapade, he did not seem conscious, at least at first, of the connection with his feelings about his children's deaths. This connection appeared only in his dream, heavily disguised. Even more clearly, his castrating and murderous oedipal impulses toward his father remained unconscious, appearing only displaced and projected in his dreams, and in the phobic symptoms he remembered from his childhood. Jovenil is not free of repressions, nor does he necessarily even repress less than someone in our culture might. Rather, the accent in his repressions is different from what one would expect in our society; the thoughts and feelings *most likely* to be repressed are different. It is in this sense that I say the distribution of repressions may differ from society to society.

In particular, I was struck by the length of time it took Jovenil in the interviews

---

[6] The Kagwahivahē myth appears as manifestly oedipal when one notes that the son who accompanies his mother on her assignations with the tapir, and is left on the bank as she crosses the river, is invariably noted to be about the age of five; and that the daughter helps her father attract the tapir by imitating the mother's seductive call.

[7] I would also take issue on but one point with Noy: our scientific models also derive ultimately from primary-process metaphors. We use anal-discharge metaphors in our energy theories (in physics *or* psychology), and compulsive or paranoid ideation is quite compatible with our germ theory of disease. All thought develops out of infantile fantasies, and if the thought of other cultures looks "infantile" to us it is only because it is derived from fantasy roots that are different from those which give rise to the dominant imagery of our theories. What makes these theories rational is integration into adult logical thought, and primitive men think as rationally (or as irrationally) in terms of their world views as we do in terms of ours.

to come to any explicit mention of his child's death. At times, like Kenneth Read with the New Guinea headman he writes of in *The High Valley* (1965), I was tempted to mistake this for callousness or shallowness of emotional involvement; but this did not fit with my experience of Jovenil, or with his deep concern when his children fell sick. At one level, this avoidance might be "explained" by the Kagwahiv value on muting the feelings of grief by avoiding thoughts of the deceased. But the sequence of developments in the interviews shows that it was not so much the value on muting grief per se that led to his inhibition in talking about his loss; it was his deeper conflicts over destructive wishes, partly of oedipal origin, that interfered with his experiencing grief. The value on muting grief became a cover for his conflicts, perhaps supporting his repression of them by keeping him from coming to grips with them.

Still, Jovenil's conflicts (for all that their ontogenetic origins remain somewhat obscure, since these brief interviews did not permit any extensive reconstruction of his childhood development) are not unrelated to Kagwahiv values. His difficulties with aggressive wishes are in tune with the very strong value in Kagwahiv society on inhibiting the expression of face-to-face aggression toward relatives — i.e., in practice, toward any other Kagwahiv. In situations of interpersonal contention, the appropriate course of behavior is withdrawal from the situation, psychically or physically, and children are discouraged from engaging in competitive play or roughhousing with one another, which is viewed as "fighting." Numerous myths, such as the story of Kagwahivahẽ which Jovenil referred to, convey the message that aggressive expression leads to abandonment — a message which certainly found resonance with Jovenil's feelings, whatever their origin in his childhood psychic life.

A particular aspect of Jovenil's mourning which may be noted is that his manifest dreams and reported memories relate almost exclusively to his six-year-old son, to the neglect of his one-year-old daughter. This may partly reflect a degree of condensation in the interviews, as there are certainly hints that his grief extended to his daughter as well. Jovenil had certainly shown deep concern over his daughter's illness before she died; and the pet monkey Daniel shot in his dream seems to have been female ("he thought it was a mother").[8] But the preponderant focus on memories of Alonzo certainly also reflects a bias on Jovenil's part in favor of sons, whom he considers more "useful" than daughters. This bias is ambiguously related to general Kagwahiv social values. On the one hand, it is consistent with a marked ethic of male dominance in this formerly martial society, but on the other hand, it is quite inconsistent with the importance of daughters in traditional Kagwahiv social organization: daughters bring in sons-in-law, who are the core of a headman's following. It is possible that Jovenil's disparaging attitude derives from early ambivalent feelings toward his mother, perhaps related to the

---

[8] This could also, of course, refer to unresolved guilt feelings about his mother's death six or eight years earlier.

strong paternal identification which Jovenil plays up in his childhood memories (Kracke, 1978b, pp. 207–208, 215–217), but his depreciation of women's usefulness is inconsistent with the picture he draws of his mother as always having been the hard-working member of the family who kept them fed. This aspect of his character is another which remains unclear.

Mourning his child, is, of course, not the only issue of the interviews, and perhaps not the principal one. The same conflicts that came up over his children's deaths were also expressed in relation to me, and indeed were expressed in communications at the very beginning of our relationship, before his children had died. Separation from me was a recurring issue from the beginning. This of course is a reality of the fieldwork situation—one of Dorothy Eggan's (1949) informants expressed it nicely by portraying her in a dream as a "white wife" who eagerly participates in Hopi ritual, but "gets homesick" and wants to leave (pp. 182–183). But the same concerns over the consequences of his anger appear in relation to me as they do in relation to his child's death.

This brings me back to an issue I mentioned early in the paper, my procrastination in beginning the interviews. As I said, there were of course many quite good reasons for delaying them until the end of fieldwork, including the necessity of learning enough of Kagwahiv culture and language to be able to follow my informants' train of thought. Yet there was also an element of anxiety about beginning them, at least one source of which is, I think, directly related to the current topic. When I was discussing the question of difficulties in cross-cultural communication with Kay Field, the Director of the Teacher Education Program at the Chicago Institute, she mentioned a factor I had not thought of: the fear of difference. Some of the difficulty I felt in shifting from my anthropological role of studying formal beliefs to the more intimate communication entailed in my interviewing certainly involved such anxieties—anxieties about whether I would be able to follow my informant's train of thought based on different cultural assumptions, among other things. One source of such anxiety, I think, stems from one's awareness of the different distribution of repressions in a culture different from one's own. Whereas individual fantasies and the degree to which one is aware of them vary widely, of course, according to one's particular childhood experiences and endowment, cultural values may influence which fantasies or aspects of them may be closer to acceptability and less apt to be repressed, and which may be more liable to deep repression. The degree of accessibility of fantasies depends not only on cultural values, of course, but also on the degree to which certain fantasies may be elaborated in the culture's conscious literary tradition and beliefs, as a model for integrating fantasies into adult thought and experience. Fantasies that are relatively accepted or openly elaborated in another culture may stir up similar ones in oneself that are not so readily dealt with, whereas with respect to wishes and feelings that are more strongly condemned and suppressed in the other culture, and thus perhaps more liable to repression, one may fear being a bull in a china shop.

The last issue was sensitively addressed by Jean Briggs (1970) in her book *Never in Anger*. All these sources of anxiety may compound the difficulties other anthropologists have reported in establishing intimate relationships with informants of very different cultures.

In sum, it has been my experience that, once one has mastered enough of another culture and language to establish an intimate and communicative relationship with an individual of that culture, the cultural differences themselves seem to present surprisingly little interference with the understanding of the conflicts and fantasies of that person. Where barriers do arise, either affective barriers or surprises in one's expectations of the other's reactions, the examination of those barriers can contribute to the understanding of oneself, of the culture of the person one is in communication with, and of the part that cultural assumptions play in thought, in communication, in character, and in the expression of childhood fantasies.

REFERENCES

Briggs, J. (1970), *Never in Anger*. Cambridge, Mass.: Harvard University Press.

Doi, T. (1973), *Anatomy of Dependence*. Tokyo: Kodansha International.

Eggan, D. (1949), The significance of dreams for anthropological research. *Amer. Anthropol.*, 51: 177–197.

Freud, S. (1918), From the history of an infantile neurosis. *Standard Edition*, 17:3–122. London: Hogarth Press, 1955.

Kracke, W. (1978a), A psychoanalyst in the field: Erikson's contributions to anthropology. In: *Childhood and Selfhood: Essays on Tradition, Religion and Modernity in the Psychology of Erik Erikson*, ed. P. Homans. Lewisburg, Pa.: Bucknell University Press, pp. 147–188.

_____ (1978b), *Force and Persuasion: Leadership in an Amazonian Society*. Chicago: University of Chicago Press.

_____ (1979), Dreaming in Kagwahiv: Dream beliefs and their psychic uses in an Amazonian Indian culture. *Psychoanalytic Study of Society*, 8:119–171.

LeVine, R. (1973), *Culture, Behavior and Personality*. Chicago: Aldine.

_____ (1977), Psychoanalysis and other cultures: An African perspective. Lecture at the University of Chicago, January 26.

LeVine, S. & LeVine, R. (1979), *Mothers and Wives: Gusii Women of East Africa*. Chicago: University of Chicago Press.

Loewald, H. (1960), On the therapeutic action of psychoanalysis. *Internat. J. Psycho-Anal.*, 41:16–33.

Noy, P. (1969), A revision of the psychoanalytic theory of the primary process. *Internat. J. Psycho-Anal.*, 50:155–178.

Pollock, G. (1972), On mourning and anniversaries: The relationship of culturally constituted defensive systems to intrapsychic adaptive processes. *Israel Ann. Psychiat.*, 10:9–39.

Read, K. (1965), *The High Valley*. New York: Scribners.

January, 1980

VI

APPLICATIONS

Regulation of Self-Esteem in Some Political Activists

ALAN J. STERN, Ph.D.   (Chapel Hill, N.C.)
and JOHN RHOADS, M.D.   (Durham, N.C.)

I

Harold Lasswell was the first student of politics to apply psychoanalytic theory and methods to his subject. He also pioneered in focusing attention on the relation between participation in politics and the maintenance of an integrated self-concept. In Lasswell's books, *Psychopathology and Politics* (1930) and *Power and Personality* (1948), he asked why political activists participate in public life.

The answer he offered, based on pioneering adaptations of the psychoanalytic clinical interview, was in the form of a hypothesis that has been the center of much attention ever since. Lasswell proposed that the political activist is essentially a power seeker, who pursues political involvement to overcome low self-esteem (Lasswell, 1948).

With Lasswell as a benchmark, a complex literature has grown up around the subject. But investigation has been hampered by a loose definition of what a political activist is and by lack of agreement about how best to study the relation between political involvement and self-esteem.

"Activists" as different as American presidents and casual, intermittent campaign workers have been seen as subjects appropriate for study. And the methods employed in these researches have varied just as much as their subjects—from short, survey-type formats utilizing fixed-choice items to rather extended interviews. Two examples may suffice to delineate the range of methods and findings. One investigator (Sniderman, 1975) used data drawn from large groups of people peripherally involved in politics who responded to short survey interviews including items on self-image. This scholar claims that the people he studied have a more positive sense of self-esteem than nonparticipants in public life. Sniderman argues that political life demands a considerable measure of self-confidence and assertiveness and repeated contact with others including strangers from unfamiliar backgrounds. By contrast, Barber (1965), using more open-ended interviews with state legislators, suggests that political leadership strata include large, definable subgroups of individuals with both higher and lower self-esteem than the population at large.

The available material on self-esteem and politics (Putnam, 1976) makes plain that some of the confusion in findings may be attributed to the broad and diverse categories of individuals referred to as activists. In the present study the term activist is used narrowly. "Activists" are grass-roots leaders. All of the subjects reported on are now, or have been, local officeholders, or officials in political campaign organizations or other community-based, mass political movements. Many of them were paid for their work. But none are full-time professional politicians, and none expressed a desire to hold high political office.

Research to this point does not dispute that a portion of those who choose to devote considerable time to political life use such involvement to help regulate an unstable sense of self. The intention of this report, in which we have adapted what appear to us to be the unique possibilities of the psychoanalytic research interview, is to begin to specify *how* some grass-roots leaders use efforts in the public sector to grapple, often unconsciously, with problems of the self. In what follows an attempt is made to clarify methods of self-esteem regulation that have been unclearly distinguished in the past because of the unavailability of theoretical or methodological tools. The efforts of what might loosely be called more neurotic political activists are contrasted with the patterns employed by activists with marked narcissistic problems. There is also some discussion of which patterns seem likely to grow more common in the future.

II

A deliberate effort to adapt the psychoanalytic therapeutic interview for research purposes in social science can also be traced to the pioneering work of Lasswell. On his return to the University of Chicago in the early 1930s after a period of study and brief training analysis in Vienna and Berlin, Lasswell (1939) employed what he called the prolonged interview. But he did not fully elaborate his techniques.

More recently, a few analysts and social scientists have done further work in this area with varying efforts to adhere to the psychoanalytic model (Hendin et al., 1965; Hendin, 1965, 1975; Lane, 1962; Keniston, 1965). A landmark in these efforts is the work of Daniel Offer (1969) and his colleagues who develop an environment of trust between investigator and subject which they call the research alliance and which is modeled closely on the therapeutic alliance.

Our work attempts to adhere to the psychoanalytic model inasmuch as limited transference material is utilized. For this reason the interviewing was pursued at somewhat greater depth with fewer individuals than was the case with most of the projects cited above.

We draw on a group of five people involved in local politics selected from a larger pool who volunteered for a series of research interviews on "politics and personality" advertised in a local newspaper. The five where chosen after an initial discussion which allowed the investigator to discourage inappropriate subjects and which made it easy for some people to reconsider participation.

In this screening process the investigator employed rough analogues to criteria used to assess analyzability. The hope was to have subjects who could work well within the research alliance. During the screening talk, first of all, potential subjects were given the opportunity to learn something about the work in a face-to-face meeting, in which it was made clear that in the planned, loosely structured discussions personal material was likely to come up and that confidentiality was absolutely guaranteed. Most of the people we talked with wanted to go ahead; a few, upon being reminded about the personal discussions, decided immediately against participating in the project.

It was easy to screen out those who were obviously deeply disturbed, although only a few such individuals appeared. Those selected for participation had good verbal skills and appeared to have a reasonable degree of psychological mindedness. The talks that preceded the interviewing proper were certainly not exhaustive. But it is important to remember that we were not looking for individuals with clear prospects for good analyses; our object was to find local political leaders with certain basic psychological capacities that, we hoped, would facilitate a measure of resilience and some introspective bent.

It is possible that the people who answered the advertisement and were subjects in the project after the screening interviews are not representative of local political activists. The research subjects had to have some strong motivations to cooperate, beyond the $2 per hour paid to them, a payment designed to underscore the nontherapeutic aspect of the work.

The subjects seemed motivated by an interest in learning more about themselves and, in some cases, by the conscious or unconscious desire to change something in their lives. For many, the interviews appeared to be a way of discussing some material that was personally disturbing without fully acknowledging a need for therapy.

Because the research subjects inevitably sought some relief from personal concerns in the course of the project, the investigator was obliged both at the outset of the work and periodically thereafter, in as diplomatic a manner as possible, to make clear that although it was hoped that helpful insights would arise in the talks, the work did not have therapeutic goals. To accent such a leitmotif puts a strain on researcher as well as subject, but the problem can be surmounted.

A series of ten to fourteen hour-long interviews, spread over a two-month period and never exceeding three talks per week, were conducted with each subject. The aim in the first session was to establish the mode of interaction. The investigator told the subject that he was interested in the way political concerns and personality intermingled. We began with a question about early political memories. The subjects were encouraged to respond in an associative fashion and to try not to censor material. As might be expected, with some of the subjects little more than an occasional question or request for expansion or clarification kept the interviews in motion; with others more questioning was necessary. In these latter instances specific queries posed by the investigator were often experienced as intrusions.

Within the research alliance the relationship between investigator and subject inevitably brings about transference. That is to say, the physical and psychological atmosphere of this kind of research technique makes it likely that the subjects' defenses will weaken and that the investigator will be experienced within the framework of earlier ties.

Especially because of the built-in power inequalities in the research setting, however freely — even eagerly — they may be accepted, subjects are likely to develop transference feelings that have special relevance for their political activities and ideas. Sensibilities relating to the exercise of authority both in hierarchical situations and in regard to peers are likely to be activated (Le Guen, 1974).

Properly utilized, the recapitulation of developmental relationships in the transference and the tracing of them to characteristic patterns of political actions and beliefs are the core of research work of this kind. To be responsibly utilized, the transference must be limited. Fostering the expression of some rather intense transference feelings in the research setting was no problem. What called for attentive management, and may deserve some comment, was the forestalling of the conditions leading to the development of a full transference neurosis.

The simplest and most obvious technique was to restrict the number of interviews. A subject prone to much intellectualization centering around political ideology could easily withstand a very large number of sessions without developing intense transference, whereas another subject with more available affect could more appropriately participate in a more limited schedule of interviews.

Another useful means of limiting the transference was the regular but polite accenting of the research nature of the relationship through the weekly or biweekly payments to the subjects by the investigator. The size of the checks seems rather inconsequential. But even these modest payments from a small university grant provoked resentment in many cases. This reversal of the cash flow in the therapeutic setting stimulated comments like, "If you have nothing better to do with it . . . it really can't matter . . . I'll give it to my children." Many subjects appeared rather embarrassed as they took the checks. No one ever asked for payment. And this low-key exchange was also a useful reminder to the investigator as well as the subjects. The investigator realized that his neglect (once or twice) to make a payment when it was scheduled was often an indication of some countertransference problem, at times of joining the subject in hoping to be able to work for a therapeutic goal.

A third means of limiting the transference was the shifting of subject matter during the interview. The posing of a particular political question, often about a safe, easy-to-handle substantive matter, was utilized when the subject seemed to be regressing in a way that was intense and disturbing. At times, the question would allow for a shifting of levels of association upward, without the necessity of saying directly to the subject that it would be better to avoid getting involved in a sensitive area we could not handle responsibly. But this was a tactic that proved difficult to employ. Often the question was resented as an intrusion. At other moments, the question was ignored or dealt with summarily. Usually, the price for abruptly changing the intensity of an exchange was the damaging of rapport during the rest of the talk.

Although it is not directly related to limiting the transference, the place of interpretation in these research interviews might be noted, since its proper use lies at the heart of the psychoanalytic therapeutic process. In this project interpretation was used only to try and bring certain forms of resistance to the attention of subjects in an effort to better understand still-obscure political motivations. And interpretations were always put in the form of questions to allow the respondents a quick dodge. For example, an endless discussion of the ideological nuances of a political stance might be met at a moment of pause with a question as to whether we were getting away from feelings about a political leader, an employer, or a sibling. There was no interpretation of transference.

Is the concept of limited transference viable? Is there a definable psychological state that allows considerable understanding of developmental patterns but still falls short of a transference neurosis? And can this psychological zone be explored by researchers with scholarly profit without emotionally endangering cooperating subjects?

To a considerable degree these must remain open questions awaiting further work. Certainly, we know that the data obtained in the deliberately constrained transference is not equivalent to clinical data obtained from analytic hours (Gehrie, 1976). But the advantages of this utilization of the transference relationship with a number of individuals offer unique scientific opportunities in applied analysis, work that usually relies on noninterview material.

III

The psychoanalytic literature that discusses the need for mastery, when brought together with the important developments in understanding the psychology of the self, allows us to build on and refine the work that Lasswell began on the regulation of self-esteem through political participation.

Whether one takes the position that a need to adjust the environment to satisfy personal goals can be incorporated with the classical dual-drive paradigm as a transformation of aggression, or the position that a need for competence comprises a distinct and independent drive of its own, it is agreed that from infancy onward human beings display needs to explore, understand, and deal competently in an active way with the widening environments they encounter.

In his expansion of Freud's ego psychology, Hartmann (1939) sets out a framework wherein mastery is incorporated within the dual-drive paradigm. And Stone (1971), Parin (1972), Joseph (1973), and Anna Freud (1972) utilize the same conceptualization. Work begun in the 1940s by Ives Hendrick (1942, 1943) and the more contemporary writings of Robert White (1963) and Jane Loevinger (1976) exemplify thoughtful approaches wherein the relative independence of the mastery effort is maintained.

More important than their differences is the fundamental agreement of scholars that striving for mastery and seeking the goal of subjective competence are broad and complex ego activities that are not restricted to one stage of the life cycle. Political activity in any of its many variations in scope and intensity is a readily available field of activity that can allow an individual to achieve or repair, or attempt to achieve or repair, a sense of mastery, and perhaps relative autonomy, by facilitating the sense of being able to manipulate and change a significant environment.

The deepening analytic understanding of the formation of the self and its pathologies makes clear that those with narcissistic disorders often search for idealizable figures and, in other situations, for individuals who will furnish admiration, often within the context of selfobject relationships (Kohut, 1971, 1977; Goldberg, 1978; Forman, 1976; Reich, 1960). This new work alerts the investigator to watch patiently for the emergence of some forms of narcissistic transferences in the analytically modeled research interviews.

Political life may be especially attractive, at least for a time, to those with serious self deficiencies. Without a great deal of preparatory effort, involvement in politics allows the activist to be both ardent follower of an exalted figure and respected leader of a small circle. The appeal of combining these possibilities in public life may be a special attraction for those with narcissistic problems. The interviews with the five activists in our study confirm the general insightfulness of Lasswell's early work. These research subjects either unconsciously or with considerable awareness used their political work to grapple with self estimates. But the limits of Lasswell's efforts and the theory he drew upon are also apparent.

The problems involving the self were quite diverse. One kind of problem that took different forms involved the bolstering of what the activist termed a weak self, a self that was too passive. The other kind of self problem centered around a chronically unstable self, with long histories of oscillating feelings ranging from the grandiose to the enfeebled. The activists who are representative of the latter group, as the case material will show, had periodic difficulties with self integration.

The activists, however small their number in the study, seemed to fall quite clearly into two groups in terms of their efforts to regulate self in political life. One group consistently expressed a need to overcome a sense of curtailed autonomy. In their actions in the political realm, these activists sought to assert themselves as authoritative in an environment in which they could grow to feel skilled and confident. Other grass-roots leaders searched in political life for a leader and a set of values to idealize, around which they could regulate many different kinds of conflict-producing stimuli. In presenting evidence that tries to differentiate these two different kinds of self difficulties as expressed in politics, we will draw on patterns of political behavior, forms of political belief systems, the qualities of the hierarchy within the political organizations, and the limited transference material generated within the relationship with the investigator.

IV

Presentation of the research case material tries to highlight (1) the conditions that lead some individuals who have problems in the area of self-evaluation to turn toward public arenas in their search for compensatory resources; and (2) the conditions that allow some people to succeed in using their brand of political activism (whatever its scope and intensity) to enhance in a relatively stable, long-term fashion their sense of self-esteem, whereas others ultimately fail in this effort. First, two ineffective efforts:

RESEARCH SUBJECT #1

Mr. A. is a 31-year-old civil servant who is unmarried. He is the younger of two sons of Jewish, lower-middle-class parents.

Glamor is a word that figures prominently in the early interviews. Politics these days, he says, is not glamorous. In the deliberately serene mood he tries to maintain through most of the talks, Mr. A. says this is all right. But almost immediately he launches into a discussion of his nonglamorous job and his readiness to pursue another career.

Mr. A. became involved in politics when he believed it was deeply exciting. He was a great admirer of first John and then Robert Kennedy. He saw in them an amalgam of the best possible features of American political leadership. Mr. A. idealized the Kennedy brothers. Working in a Kennedy campaign gave him a feeling of satisfaction. Indeed, this rather brief, though intense, experience seems to have had a deep impact on him, and he tends to exaggerate his role.

After Robert Kennedy was assassinated, Mr. A. established what has become his basic orientation to politics: he withdraws from the day-to-day interaction and sits back as an observer. He is in fact a knowledgeable person. He believes he has a better sense of political strategy than those who are actively engaged. For example, though he is sympathetic to the efforts of the professional association of civil servants in his state to press for better salaries, he sees their program as ill-conceived and likely to fail. But he does not offer to work. At present he perceives his great interest in politics as still stimulated by the "refreshing," "amusing," or "humorous" aspects of public life.

But very close to the surface — in his attitude toward the then-emerging Jimmy Carter, for example — is the continuing need to idealize. Mr. A. is proud that he saw Mr. Carter as a comer. He is deeply impressed, he says, by the moral tone Carter injects into politics. But, in his disillusionment, Mr. A. still cannot imagine actively working for the new president in local politics.

The desire to idealize and to be allowed room to express grandiose ideas was apparent in the relationship Mr. A. established with the interviewer. From the outset, although he answered a clearly stated advertisement and said he needed the token payment, Mr. A. treated the investigator as a colleague. He assumed, he said, a sharing of interests and outlooks. As he saw it, circumstances had somehow made it difficult for him to get a doctoral degree and become a college professor.

Mr. A. wanted opinions about many subjects, including the academic department of the interviewer, and was clearly annoyed when not answered. At such moments of frustration he began to talk, again mostly in the slightly amused "tolerant" fashion he utilized, of his fury at the excessive charges imposed by the auto industry and by certain professionals like eye doctors.

Another aspect of Mr. A.'s underlying search for approval and admiration involved the question of his life style. Mr. A. talked many times of his pleasure in living as a "tolerant" person in a "tolerant, tranquil way," in an especially pleasant setting. Again, when he did not receive full approval, he showed a small flash of rage covered over with a weak smile when he said, "You find out what you want, then you're through with me." Here he seems to be experiencing again the kind of rejection he felt when Robert Kennedy was assassinated and the followers of Lyndon Johnson dominated Democratic party politics.

RESEARCH SUBJECT #2

Mr. B. is a 28-year-old man of considerable intelligence and sensitivity who has had chronic difficulties in sustaining either a line of occupational development or enduring personal ties. At present he is earning a barely adequate salary as a laborer, and after a divorce and a series of fly-by-night relationships with other women, is living with a girlfriend he has been with for some months. Mr. B. has a serious drinking problem and from time to time finds himself engaging in violent, antisocial behavior.

Mr. B., like Mr. A., seeks an idealized leader in political life. Mr. B.'s most intense, concentrated political experience came in the early 1970s when he worked first as a paid professional in the campaigns of George McGovern, and then in a related effort to get poor blacks to register to vote. Both experiences, in the context of his rural, border-state hometown, required courage and ingenuity. For a short time he expended enormous amounts of energy for political goals in some imaginative ways, but on the whole his account of his efforts sounds more like an impulsive assault than a planned strategy mobilizing transformed drives.

What is more, Mr. B. could not sustain his commitment after the overwhelming McGovern defeat. In the first place his hero had lost. Furthermore, the efforts of the candidate's staff to get a permanent organization started in the area showed Mr. B. that even McGovern workers made deals and wanted patronage. As a consequence of what he describes as his disillusionment — it sounds more like rage — Mr. B. gave up his job. Soon thereafter, this time angered by the obstacles involved in trying to work with poor blacks, he gave up a position as a social-service worker.

Mr. B.'s material reflects again and again a pattern of sporadic, intense efforts aimed at instant success in one tremendous push. These attempts are mixed in with, and ultimately supplanted by, a sense of hopelessness and personal unworthiness, often punctuated with fist fighting, change of residence, surrender of responsibility, promiscuous sexual behavior, and alcoholic binges.

Mr. B. wanted to please the interviewer. In the early sessions he tried courteously to convey the impression that he wanted to supply the kind of information sought so as to justify the $2-per-hour payment. But as the meetings continued it was less his desire to earn his wage and more his wish to make the interviewer like him that dominated the transference. Mr. B. used his considerable charm and event-filled life to advantage. With the guess that dreams would interest the interviewer Mr. B. brought in several flying dreams where glorious soaring was followed by disastrous collapse.

Another transference theme was a search for encouragement, a desire for the interviewer to accent the great talents Mr. B. really commanded, could salvage, and could put to good use. Mr. B. bewailed his fate but talked repeatedly of the difficult academic work he had undertaken from time to time with great success. And he frequently commented on the teachers who had seen fit to praise his work.

Although the limited number of interviews makes the need for caution in interpretation essential, it is obvious that Mr. A. and Mr. B. display characteristics prominent in those afflicted by narcissistic personality disorders. In fact, a careful assessment of attitudes of individuals toward public life, communal commitments, and political leaders may provide one more tool in the assessment procedure for the identification of pathological narcissism.

In any case, in both men there is an absence of deep or enduring object ties. Evidence of preoedipal difficulties is present in family histories and reoccurs to some degree in the limited transference. The impulsive use of food (Mr. A.), alcohol (Mr. B.), and sex (Mr. A. and Mr. B.) underscores the common recurrent sense of emptiness and the need for supplies in individuals with narcissistic problems. The chronic instability in concepts of self-worth expressed by these men is also abundantly documented.

Again with appropriate tentativeness, it would seem possible, even in the context of the research alliance and limited transference, to detect rather easily differences between mainly neurotic and mainly narcissistic individuals while in no way ruling out overlapping problems (Kohut, 1977; Forman, 1976).

Idealization of political figures did not work to stabilize successfully over the long term the serious problems of self suffered by these two men. This in no way suggests that a temporary stabilization or even inflation of self-esteem is not available to the narcissistically disturbed political activist. Indeed, we would hypothesize that narcissistic problems might be rather common among the highest group of political officeholders. In those cases the accolades and privileges and powers of office might, for a time — even a long time — sustain exaggerated perceptions of grandiosity, certainly provide admirers by the dozens, and, again for extended periods, conceal the shallowness of object relationships in the constant press of events.

But in the present research, and perhaps for many narcissistically disturbed people, the usual rewards of grass-roots politics do not provide the resources necessary to repair chronically unstable self concepts. Their psychological deficits in terms of structuralization are not amenable to the balm that local political life makes available.

Then who can use the psychological rewards of grass-roots politics to deal relatively successfully with the regulation of problems with self-esteem? The answer, as we will try to illustrate in the research case material in the next section, appears to be people with more structured personalities, whose problems of low self-esteem grow predominantly out of neurotic conflicts rather than narcissistic difficulties. The following cases will serve as examples:

RESEARCH SUBJECT #3

Mrs. X., a married woman in her forties, is the only daughter of affluent parents. She is an obviously intelligent and articulate person, extremely well informed about the public issues of the day. Her style of presenting herself is that of an energetic, engaged woman. Mrs. X. used the years of a privileged childhood for many physical and intellectual achievements. Horseback riding was a special source of pride, providing an excellent arena for the opportunity to compete as an equal with male peers, especially her brothers.

This sense of freedom and pride was curtailed rather abruptly in early adolescence by her parents, particularly her father. He reminded her pointedly that she was a woman, not a man, and he demanded an end to unladylike activities. The subject conveys a sense of being unfairly restrained in contrast to men. She reports being forced to act like a lady and subsequently being ridiculed for lack of female graces. She feared being forced into an identification with her mother, who was neglected and derided by her father.

After some years of embittered compliance enforced by rewards and strict sanctions, Mrs. X., unhappy within the confines of a fashionable education, defied parental authority by entering into marriage at a young age. This union, instead of providing new freedom, saw a repetition of an established pattern: deep dissatisfaction, but submissive behavior, overseen this time, the subject reports, by a domineering husband. Though Mrs. X. mentioned that she thought about divorce constantly, she "didn't know how to act," and added, "I couldn't walk out." This sounds very much like a theme she reiterates throughout the interviews: she sees herself as a woman who, from circumstance, has to make a series of sacrifices for others — parents, siblings, mates, or children — and has to be a "pillar of strength," "a rock."

Mrs. X. is aware that "community work was an excellent outlet. . . ," "a substitute for home recognition." At another point in our talks she referred to political work as "a reserve, if put down. . . it made homelife easier." So this woman who could not act to liberate herself from intimate tyrannies found the resources to help lead an eventually successful opposition to the hegemonic political party in her town and to run for local political office in circumstances that required an extraordinary expenditure of effort and exposure to quite a bit of public criticism. The political participation provided an alternative channel to counter the stifling, oppressive authority situations in the family. "That's what allowed me to survive: picking myself up and going in another direction."

Mrs. X. provides an unusually clear example of someone with a sense of assertiveness and competence that can be sustained in extrafamilial roles. Throughout her adult life public activism seemed to grow most intense when private dependent passivity caused the greatest number of problems. Throughout the many trials of her private life, now more tranquilly centered about a second marriage, Mrs. X. needed to think of herself as durable, strong, and capable of independence, even if she was somehow trapped and subject to domination. Effective political activism was central to the successful maintenance of a relatively positive self-image.

RESEARCH SUBJECT #4

Mr. Y. is a 24-year-old unmarried man who appears initially as rather reserved and shy. This general tendency toward quiescence and inhibition proves to be an important personal characteristic. Mr. Y. does not like dancing, loud clothes, noisy parties, or flamboyant personal styles. During the interviews he reported discomfort when seeing people skinny-dipping in a student swimming hole, and in general he finds anyone "who makes a spectacle of himself" objectionable.

Throughout his childhood, Mr. Y. acted quietly and obediently. His family life was pleasant although his mother and especially his older brother were dominant figures. Yet unlike Mr. A., Mr. Y. did not feel alienated from family members. He reports the situation matter-of-factly with some affection. Indeed, one gets the sense from Mr. Y. that even though he was physically rather small and performed only in average fashion in schoolwork and sports, he felt more capable, forceful, and colorful than he allowed himself to appear in family or peer-group life. Politics provided the vehicle and acceptable legitimation for the development of a sense of subjective competence and a power-oriented occupational goal.

While still in grade school and in more sophisticated fashion later, Mr. Y. was attracted to the conservative Republican banner. The coherent encompassing set of principles espoused by conservatives was especially appealing. Mr. Y. became, and still is, a fluent and informed ideological conservative, a stance which fits in well with his traditionally oriented religious convictions. Currently, Alexander Solzhenitsyn is the man Mr. Y. admires most in the world.

In college Mr. Y. eventually helped lead a drive to force a leading university official to resign, and in various local and national elections he supported candidates in favor of the Vietnam War, against pornography, and in favor of men like Senator Goldwater and Governor Reagan, even though he was often derided for such positions. In what may be a key line for others as well as himself, Mr. Y. told me, "politics has risks, but not of any consequence."

For Mr. Y., assertion and free expression in the private arenas where other people might feel more protected and secure have not been possible. The publicity, even notoriety, that his rather extreme conservatism gives him seems to be pleasing. This quiet, likable young man has a difficult time acting or speaking intimately or being forceful in private situations. He would like, most of all, to be a "public-safety officer," where duty allows extremely authoritative aggressive behavior, or the editor of a small, crusading right-wing newspaper, where similar, if more intellectualized, forceful behavior is sanctioned by political principles.

Research Subject #5

Mrs. Z. is a 35-year-old divorced black woman. Political activism came to be the central focus of her life, overshadowing all private ties. Beginning in the early days of the civil-rights sit-ins in the South, Mrs. Z. has remained deeply engaged. And for at least ten years, she worked as a professional community organizer. During this long period of intense commitment to public life, Mrs. Z. has become more theoretical and systematic in her approach to political problems and has moved from an optimistic, pragmatic stance of being able to reform the present system to benefit underprivileged groups to a quasi-Marxist position where she believes the whole of the present socioeconomic structure needs a thorough-going revision.

Mrs. Z. grew up as an only child. Her father died when she was three months old. The capable and determined mother took over her husband's business and moved with her daughter to an apartment over it. Mrs. Z. grew up as a spunky, street-wise little girl who operated outside the confines of the usual family atmosphere and without other children as playmates. She was comfortable in the busy downtown section of the city, accustomed to successfully fending for herself as a little black girl in a mostly white environment still regulated by the rules of segregation. Elementary school was experienced as an annoyance to be gotten over with as quickly as possible so she could return to the adventures of downtown.

This life pattern of "content autonomy" was abruptly terminated when her mother announced remarriage when Mrs. Z. was eleven. Mrs. Z. remembers suddenly feeling afraid of the dark, wanting to sleep between her mother and her mother's new close companion. This major disruption was followed by another that Mrs. Z. calls "traumatic": Mrs. Z.'s mother and stepfather purchased a long-dreamed-of house in the black, upper-middle-class section of town. Mrs. Z. was miserable in the new location and bewildered by her mother's stricter discipline and insistence on the instant feminization of some of her daughter's habits which were considered unsuitable in their new neighborhood. Mandatory, resented piano lessons were a sign of the new regime. But Mrs. Z. never challenged her mother's authority, and when she was home alone she spent many hours staring out of the window.

Only when she had finally gotten away from her mother's scrutiny at college did Mrs. Z. try to break loose. She spent much of her first year partying and dating and drinking: activities either severely regulated or altogether forbidden at home. Expulsion from college was followed by an emotional confrontation when for the first time Mrs. Z.'s mother expressed deep disappointment and talked of all the sacrifices she had made for the daughter's benefit. Mrs. Z. then obediently moved back home and enrolled in the local black college.

Almost by chance, or as Mrs. Z. says, because of "the times," she came to political activism — a young woman searching again for a chance to feel personally independent and competent in her behavior, as she had been as a preadolescent girl. One day the daughter of a prominent leader of the movements of the sixties came to the college Mrs. Z. attended and recruited a group of students for a movie-theater sit-in. Thus began a three-year commitment to civil-rights peaceful protest which included five or six brief arrests.

After a two-year nonpolitical postgraduate stint in New York City, Mrs. Z. returned home again to her mother's house. She soon married and simultaneously began her years of deepest political activism. Mrs. Z. began to fashion a new ideological approach. "In New York I didn't have that kind of eyesight. It wasn't until community work that I came to political analysis."

Even as she renewed her sense of personal competence by striving long hours and weekends to effect local social change by instilling a new consciousness in poor citizens, Mrs. Z. submitted to many of her mother's wishes—for example, in attending her weekly Sunday dinners and in agreeing to a fancy wedding reception. In fact, it appears that Mrs. Z.'s marriage was more a gesture toward her mother and her maternal aspirations for an only daughter than a union based on deep feeling.

From the outset work, not married life, had priority for Mrs. Z. Always available to her poor constituency and fellow community-activist cadre, Mrs. Z. was exhausted at home, caring little for domestic chores. More and more she attributed difficulties in getting quick results to "the system," "a universal interconnected series of economic forces." Mrs. Z. grew excited and read a great deal as she saw "connections" between social events she earlier had felt were unique or happenstance. An intensification of ideological orientation took Mrs. Z. through a Pan-African period to an involvement in what she calls "scientific socialism." Here the emphasis is on "objective" analysis.

In the last few years, Mrs. Z. has faced two important changes. One, a divorce, seems to have, on the surface, affected her little. The other, being forced out of her job because the director of the agency accused her of having "become useless in her job role," was in Mrs. Z.'s words "the greatest shock in my life." Mrs. Z. struggled to retain her job—her characteristic response in times of personal stress—with her mother's aid. (Mrs. Z. calls her "my National Guard.") But final resignation was inevitable. Now, feeling "on hold," but still deeply committed to political work, Mrs. Z. wishes her political ideas were more coherent, "because then it would be clear what to do." Mrs. Z. was badly shaken by a man in authority who implied that her work, her source of competence, and her means to personal mastery were faulty. Mrs. Z. still takes refuge in her political beliefs. She considers herself as being part of a temporary "downward spiral" and wishes her ideology could be stronger to provide surer predictions for the future. Mrs. Z. is presently rather uncomfortable with so much time for herself and may have agreed to the research interviews so as to have a "scientific" rationale to do some needed talking out of problems.

The transference relationship is distinguished as a research tool by the repeated opportunities it gives to validate a hypothesis informally (Gedo and Pollock, 1967). In all three mostly neurotic political activists, in repeated instances, the limited transference relationships with the interviewer reflected an inability to confront authorities directly in intimate settings.

Mr. Y., for example, in a suppressed competitive relationship, reminiscent of ties to his father and older brother, wanted the investigator to invite sharp dialogue about deeply held political beliefs. When this was not forthcoming he obliquely suggested that our interviews were perhaps not accomplishing their purpose, and then at the end of the talks he admitted he withheld material such as dreams, which probably would have been of interest.

Mrs. X. wanted nurturance and sometimes eroticized the transference. When wishes were not fulfilled, especially as the interviews drew to a close, she commented that child psychologists are a bunch of "bachelors writing about Swiss children," that a Ph.D. running for public office is a "funny spectacle," etc. Mrs. Z. alternated in the transference between a desire to lean on the investigator in times of stress and a defiant stance bolstered by ideology. Both reactions reflected uneasy feelings about authority and were repetitious of patterns developed with her mother. In a job crisis she wanted the investigator to provide immediate help. When she became angry in the interviews, she derogated the discussions and referred to her token interview payments as "gas money," comparable to political funds she could extract at will from "guilty liberals"—a display in some way of an indirect manipulation of powerful figures.

V

Why the turn toward political life? After all, family and friends are more accessible. Why did the people studied here, who presumably closely resemble many other individuals who suffer from problems of low self-esteem and avoid the public arena, move toward political participation?

There is some evidence to indicate that political activism is not a primary resource for problems of self-regard. Both the more neurotic and the more narcissistic research cases had made an effort to seek a solution within the family setting before they turned to public life.

Mrs. X. entered into a disapproved first marriage. Mrs. Z. had a year of wild behavior away from home at the outset of college. Mr. Y. rarely contested parental rule-making, but, significantly, he sought intense political ties at an earlier age than any of the other research cases. For these research subjects, early efforts at assertion of autonomy in the home environment were episodic. After instilling a very brief sense of freedom, these futile acts of rebellion served, if anything, to weaken rather than strengthen self-esteem.

The rebellions did not contribute to a sense of being able to reshape or remold a meaningful environment. Repairing self-esteem by working toward mastery requires an arena that can accommodate long-term constructive effort. This is not to suggest that a private-sphere solution to the problem of thwarted autonomy is impossible. Certainly, work in this intimate setting would yield the most positive outcome. But the sustained effort to restructure self-esteem through the reordering of internal familial authority relationships was a demanding psychological task which none of the research subjects could manage.

The choice of the political arena as a forum for the expression of autonomy can in part be traced to the values socialized by the very family setting that worked to thwart the expression of autonomy in the home. Strikingly, the more neurotic, but not the more narcissistic, subjects report a pattern of intense parental interest in political life which is similar to reports collected from many levels of political leadership (Putnam, 1976). Turning to political involvement to some degree reflects an identification with a parental model, even if that identification is marked with ambivalence. Subjects talk about this kind of identification rather proudly in terms of family political traditions that often are generations old. Such politically patterned identifications help to stabilize the self-concepts of subjects X., Y., and Z.

In the United States, especially for individuals of middle- or upper-middle-class backgrounds, political opportunities abound. There are multiple points of entry into a vast array of overlapping local and national spheres of operation. And so long as one does not aim for the most powerful and/or most remunerative positions, there is a very good prospect of being able to hold a position that brings with it the ability to exercise authority and have visible impact on zoning regulations, school policy, or recreational facilities, to cite only a few of the arenas of public life that do not attract many participants.

None of our subjects reported any problem in gaining a toehold in politics. Several discussed being pressured to do more in public life than they believed they could manage. The research subjects reported easy movement in and out of activist phases, which may suggest another of the attractions of the political rather than the private arena. Because participants are scarce, civic organizations often tolerate uneven involvement.

For the more narcissistic individuals, too, political discussion was not absent from familial conversations, but with them the movement to political participation was more a matter of seeking a replacement for a parental figure to idealize than a modeling of parental values and activities. For the narcissistic subjects, political life appeared to present new heroes; but setbacks, inevitable in the rough and tumble of public life, caused disillusionment and quick retreat.

Mr. A., as a young boy, greatly admired his father. He remembers how strange it felt to sense that his father could not protect him from religious slurs in a new neighborhood. At about the same time he brings up material about his father working simultaneously at what he remembered as three jobs. He was never at home.

Similarly, Mr. B. experienced an overly rapid disenchantment with a parent and parental values. After what he says were close ties to his parents, Mr. B., at four, suffered through a temporary separation of father and mother. From that period on he saw his father as a kind of backwoods bigot with distorted values that included condoning violence and supporting the KKK.

This study indicates that although persons with evident narcissistic disturbances may seek to regulate self-esteem through political involvement, their ability to sustain participation in grass-roots organizations is weak. The narcissistic subjects were drawn to politics by prominent national figures, and they seemed rapidly frustrated when the distant, idealized figures were not victorious and when working at the local level did not yield both spectacular results and widespread admiration for the individual activist within a short time span. They also had some difficulty in managing the stimuli of political life.

By contrast, the activists who sought a sense of mastery within the political arena had more elaborated ego and superego structures. In the main, they did not seek figures to idealize or followers who admired them, though there are elements of these desires present. Mostly, they seemed content to dedicate themselves to the slow, often unpublicized, hard work of small-scale politics. Here they gained from the knowledge that they worked effectively to make a change in a direction that they preferred — whether it was to oust a university official (Mr. Y.), to reorient a school board (Mrs. X.), or to encourage poor people to organize for the first time (Mrs. Z.).

And the values that they elaborated within the political sphere — civic responsibility for Mrs. X., conservative Republicanism for Mr. Y., and increasingly radical ideologies for Mrs. Z. — were consistent with, not antagonistic to, the values that were partially internalized in the home, although in the family setting superego development promoted conflict because of problematic resolutions of oedipal situations. The ideological continuity thus furnishes another opportunity for a distanced identification with parental figures.

Overly rapid disenchantment with parents in early childhood made it difficult for Mr. A. and Mr. B. to internalize in any coherent fashion a set of family values, including appropriate political norms. In a search for idealizable figures they turned to politics, expecting rather perfect leaders with unimpeachable policy positions. But neither Kennedy nor McGovern nor their prinicipal spokesmen provided models for satisfactory life patterns. In fact, in many ways the tragic assassinations of the Kennedy brothers traumatically repeated the overly rapid disenchantment with his father that Mr. A. experienced as a child. This may partially explain the defensive, withdrawn quality of his narcissistic stance.

Mr. A.'s later search for inspiring cultural models in the northeastern suburbs and Mrs. B.'s similar quest in the southern and western countercultures were unsuccessful. Increasingly, Mr. A. and Mr. B. showed some desperation in their need for a reassuring set of ready values. Mr. B. literally moves across the country trying different movements and groups. Mr. A. adopts the brittle defense of relativism, trying with little evident success to turn tolerance of all values (hence the suggestion that no special set of them is important for anyone) into a way of life.

The political ideologies that have dominated local American politics in the past, even the recent past, can help the activist who has a relatively well-integrated personality to regulate self-esteem. At best, the loose, decidedly pragmatic ideologies facilitate ego adaptation and stability. Almost always, they provided good material for intellectualizing defenses. Political life can provide a suitable arena for the improvement and stabilization of self-worth for individuals who have rather well-structured, if conflictual, personalities. Political participation can help nourish an enhanced positive sense of self by providing an appropriate arena for the continuance of efforts toward mastery — especially in regard to authority — truncated during childhood. In this way political life can be used to overcome, to some degree, the sense of passivity experienced early in life.

But political activists with marked narcissistic difficulties, this exploratory study would suggest, are not able to sustain commitment in public life that is patterned by traditional political ideologies. For political ideologies in the United States are not as inclusive, dogmatic, or demanding as many political belief systems — especially certain totalitarian or utopian political movements or some religious cults with political components. In these latter ideologies ready identification of heroes, enemies, direction, and promises about a wonderful future abound. Such ideologies might well appeal to men like Mr. A. and Mr. B.

Although it is extremely difficult to make confident statements about changes in the frequency of psychopathological problems in a given population, there is accumulating evidence that changes in family structure, occupational patterns, and value orientations have contributed to an increase in the number of individuals, at least in the United States, suffering from narcissistic problems. It is likely that such an increase has contributed to the growing disinterest in local political life. Both psychoanalysts and social scientists have begun to explore this development (Kohut, 1971; Sobo, 1977; Lasch, 1977, 1978; Sennett, 1976). By itself this possible change in the distribution of psychopathologies is a serious challenge to the vitality of American grass-roots politics. Perhaps even more ominous is the possibility that new political movements will grow in which leaders try deliberately to tap the pool of potential activists with marked narcissistic problems.

REFERENCES

Barber, J. D. (1965), *The Lawmakers*. New Haven: Yale University Press.
Forman, M. (1976), Narcissistic personality disorders and the oedipal fixations. *This Annual*, 4: 65–92. New York: International Universities Press.
Freud, A. (1972), Comments on aggression. *Internat. J. Psycho-Anal.*, 53:163–171.
Gedo, J. E. & Pollock, G. H. (1967), The question of research in psychoanalytic technique. In: *Psychoanalytic Techniques*, ed. B. B. Wolman. New York: Basic Books, pp. 562–563.
Gehrie, M. (1976), Aspects of the dynamics of prejudice. *This Annual*, 4:423–443. New York: International Universities Press.
Goldberg, A., ed. (1978), *The Psychology of the Self*. New York: International Universities Press.
Hartmann, H. (1939), *Ego Psychology and the Problem of Adaptation*. New York: International Universities Press, 1958.
Hendin, H. (1965), *Suicide and Scandinavia*. New York: Anchor.
———— (1975), *The Age of Sensation*. New York: Norton.

_____ Gaylin, W., & Carr, A. (1965), *Psychoanalysis and Social Research*. New York: Anchor.

Hendrick, I. (1942), Instinct and the ego during infancy. *Psychoanal. Quart.*, 11:33–58.

_____ (1943), Work and the pleasure principle. *Psychoanal. Quart.*, 12:311–329.

Joseph, E. (1973), Aggression re-defined — its adaptational aspects. *Psychoanal. Quart.*, 42:197–213.

Keniston, K. (1965), *The Uncommitted*. New York: Harcourt, Brace.

Kohut, (1971), *The Analysis of the Self*. New York: International Universities Press.

_____ (1977), *The Restoration of the Self*. New York: International Universities Press.

Lane, R. (1962), *Political Ideology*. Chicago: Free Press.

Lasch, C. (1977), *Haven in a Heartless World*. New York: Basic Books.

_____ (1978), *The Culture of Narcissism*. New York: Norton.

Lasswell, H. (1930), *Psychopathology and Politics*. Chicago: University of Chicago Press.

_____ (1939), The contribution of Freud's insight interview to the social sciences. *Amer. J. Sociol.*, 45:375–390.

_____ (1948), *Power and Personality*. New York: Viking Press, 1962.

Le Guen, G. (1974), The formation of the transference: Or the Laius complex in the armchair. *Internat. J. Psycho-Anal.*, 55:503–513.

Loevinger, J. (1976), *Ego Development*. San Francisco: Jossey-Bass.

Offer, D. (1969), *The Psychological World of the Teen-Ager*. New York: Basic Books.

Parin, P. (1972), A contribution of ethno-psychoanalytic investigation to the theory of aggression. *Internat. J. Psycho-Anal.*, 52:251–257.

Putnam, R. D. (1976), *The Comparative Study of Political Elites*. Englewood Cliffs, N.J.: Prentice-Hall.

Reich, A. (1960), Pathologic forms of self-esteem regulation. *The Psychoanalytic Study of the Child*, 15:215–232. New York: International Universities Press.

Sennett, R. (1976), *The Fall of Public Man*. New York: Knopf.

Sniderman, P. (1975), *Personality and Democratic Politics*. Berkeley: University of California Press.

Sobo, S. (1977), Narcissism as a function of culture. *The Psychoanalytic Study of the Child*, 32:155–175. New Haven: Yale University Press.

Stone, L. (1971), Reflections on the psychoanalytic concepts of aggression. *Psychoanal. Quart.*, 40:174–244.

White, R. W. (1963), *Ego and Reality in Psychoanalytic Theory* [*Psychological Issues*, Monogr. 11]. New York: International Universities Press.

July, 1979

Michelangelo's Moses: "Madonna Androgyna" (A Meaning of the Artist's Use of Forefingers)

JEROME KAVKA, M.D.   (Chicago)

No piece of statuary made a stronger impression on Sigmund Freud than Michelangelo's *Moses*. He regarded this deeply moving work as inscrutable and requiring interpretation as to the basis for its strong effect as well as for the sculptor's intentions (Freud, 1914b, pp. 212–213). The many interpretations that had been offered did not satisfy him.[1]

The statue portrays Moses in a particular posture and with a terrible expression of mingled anger, pain and scorn. It is evidently meant to represent a particular moment in his life, and most writers have connected this with the moment when on his descent from Mount Sinai bearing the Tables of the Law under his arm he catches sight of the backsliding Israelites dancing around their Golden Calf. But at that point interpretations diverge. Freud followed his usual method of delving deeper, not through the general impression of the whole, but through searching for minute and apparently casual clues. These he found by observing, which no one else had, that the Tables were held upside down, and that the right hand, clutching the majestic beard, had some puzzling features in its details [Jones, 1955, p. 346].[2]

Presented before the Chicago Psychoanalytic Society, January 24, 1978. Other versions presented before the Faculty, Chicago Institute for Psychoanalysis, the Denver Psychoanalytic Society, the Departments of Psychiatry of the University of Cincinnati and the University of Wisconsin (Madison), the Department of Psychology of the University of Illinois (Chicago Circle), and the St. Louis Psychoanalytic Society.

Grateful acknowledgment is made to the publishers for permission to use material from: *The Standard Edition of the Complete Psychological Works of Sigmund Freud*, translated and edited by James Strachey, Vol. 13, London: Hogarth Press, 1960; "The Moses of Michelangelo," in Vol. 4 of *Freud's Collected Papers*, New York: Basic Books; and Herbert Friedmann's *The Symbolic Goldfinch*, Bollingen Series VII, Copyright 1946 by Princeton University Press.

[1] "...[N]ever, or scarcely ever, do modern scholars look at Michelangelo's works and ask themselves how they came into being and why" (*Times Literary Supplement*, 1973, p. 1585).

[2] Critics (Rosenfeld, 1951; Worbarsht and Lichtenberg, 1961; Marmor, 1971; Bremer, 1976) have noted Freud's injudicious use of scriptural texts as the basis of his study and have commented on

Freud (1914b) directs our attention to specific features of the *Moses* statue:

These are the attitude of his right hand and the position of the two Tables of the Law. . . . the thumb of the hand is concealed and the index finger alone is in effective contact with the beard. It is pressed so deeply against the soft masses of hair that they bulge out beyond it both above and below. . . [pp. 222–223]. We have assumed that the right hand was, to begin with, away from the beard; that then it reached across to the left of the figure in a moment of great emotional tension and seized the beard; that it was finally drawn back again, taking a part of the beard with it [p. 225].

There are some difficulties involved in this interpretation since the right hand is responsible for the tables which are upside down. The Tables are stood on their heads and practically balanced on one corner [Rothgeb, 1971, p. 89].

To continue with Freud's description of the statue:

The upper edge is straight, whereas the lower one has a protuberance like a horn on the part nearest to us, and the Tables touch the stone seat precisely with this protuberance. . . [p. 226]. It is to *prevent* this that the right hand retreated, let go the beard, a part of which was drawn back with it unintentionally, came against the upper edge of the Tables in time and held them near the hind corner, which had now come uppermost. Thus the singularly constrained air of the whole — beard, hand, and tilted Tables — can be traced to that one passionate movement of the hand and its natural consequences [p. 228].

Jones (1955) has written about Freud's observations regarding this posture:

The conclusion he came to was that the statue was not intended to represent Moses as about to start up and punish the disobedient people below, as so many commentators had assumed. On the contrary, Freud thought it could only be understood by postulating a *previous* movement, not a future one. Moses had been, it is true, on the point of starting up to denounce the rabble, and moreover had made certain movements in that direction. Then, however, observing that the precious Tables were about to slip from his grasp he con-

---

its significance. To Bremer (1976), Freud's creation is that of a nonbiblical Moses and is consistent with Freud's own identification with the heroic figure; Marmor (1971) regards the presence of horns on the Moses as proof of Freud's erroneous interpretation. Worbarsht and Lichtenberg (1961), also on the basis of the horned Moses, agree that Freud selected the wrong, i.e., the first, descent of Moses, but conclude that Freud nevertheless intuitively sensed what Michelangelo was trying to portray, namely, "the feeling of an oppressive, solemn calm" (p. 265). To Rosenfeld (1951), "the image of Moses hewn in marble by Michelangelo's master hand represents the children of Israel's internal image of their murdered father, transfigured, 'sitting there in his wrath forever.'. . . the moment which Michelangelo caught was not only that of conflict between impulse and sublimation of impulse, but was still more that of transition from the earthly to the divine figure, from the living man to the spiritual hero" (p. 87).

tained himself with a mighty effort. The desire to preserve the Tables proved stronger than his anger (the contrary of the version in the Bible) [p. 364].

Freud (1914b) continues:

As our eyes travel down...the figure exhibits three distinct emotional strata. The lines of the face reflect the feelings which have won the ascendancy; the middle of the figure shows the traces of suppressed movement; and the foot still retains the attitude of the projected action...[p. 230]. The Moses of legend and tradition had a hasty temper and was subject to fits of passion.... But Michelangelo has placed a different Moses on the tomb of the Pope, one superior to the historical or traditional Moses...[p. 233]. In his creations Michelangelo has often enough gone to the utmost limit of what is expressible in art; and perhaps in his statue of Moses he has not completely succeeded, if his purpose was to make the passage of a violent gust of passion visible in the signs left behind it in the ensuing calm [p. 236].

Jones (1955) summarizes the statue's meaning for Freud:

[Michelangelo] has added something new and more than human to the figure of Moses; so that the giant frame with its tremendous physical power becomes only a concrete expression of the highest mental achievement that is possible in a man—that of struggling successfully against an inward passion for the sake of a cause to which he has devoted himself [p. 364].

Freud hesitated to publish his essay for a long time[3] "probably because of his doubts about the correctness of his interpretation" (p. 365). He insisted on anonymity for what to Jones seemed thin reasons. " 'Why disgrace Moses by putting my name on it? It is a joke, but perhaps not a bad one.' To Abraham he gave three reasons: (1) 'It is only a joke'; (2) Shame at the evident amateurishness of the essay; (3) 'Lastly because my doubt about my conclusion is stronger than usual; it is only because of editorial pressure (Rank and Sachs) that I have consented to publish it at all' " (p. 366).

[3] In the year 1914, there appeared in *Imago*, a European journal of applied psychoanalysis, an anonymous essay titled "The Moses of Michelangelo." The following footnote was attached:

"Die Redaktion hat diesem, strenge genommen nicht programmgerechten, Beitrage die Aufnahme nicht versagt, weil der ihr bekannte Verfasser analytischen Kreisen nahe steht, und weil seine Denkweise immerhin eine gewisse Ahnlichkeit mit der Methodik der Psychoanalyse zeigt" [Freud, 1914a, p. 15n].

Strachey, in Freud (1914b), translates this passage:

Although this paper does not, strictly speaking, conform to the conditions under which contributions are accepted for publication in this Journal, the editors have decided to print it, since the author, who is personally known to them, moves in psycho-analytic circles, and since his mode of thought has in point of fact a certain resemblance to the methodology of psycho-analysis [p. 211].

Ten years later, in 1924, when his *Collected Papers* were being published, the disguise was lifted, revealing the author to have been Sigmund Freud, a sponsor of the journal and, it was later disclosed, also the author of the apologetic footnote.

Ernest Jones concluded that "Freud had identified himself with Moses and was striving to emulate the victory over passion that Michelangelo had depicted . . ." (pp. 366–367). Just as Moses had bent all his strength and will to preserve the precious Tablets, Freud had an overriding need to save something of his life's work, psychoanalysis, since many of his supporters had deserted him.[4]

Freud's analysis of the *Moses* statue has impressed even art historians over the years and has become something of a classic in the realm of aesthetics. On the other hand, a modern art historian (Rosenthal, 1964) characterizes Freud's zealous interpretation as "cinematographic" and suggests that when the statue is seen from a worm's-eye view, as it was meant to be,[5] "Moses seems to look slightly upward with a suggestion of melancholy. He seems to be distressed and grieved rather than angry and scornful." Furthermore, suggests Rosenthal, the "awesomeness of the prophet" is greatly enhanced by an upward view (p. 546).

This dispassionate professional counterproposal contrasts sharply with the almost violent rejection of Freud by his unauthorized biographer, Emil Ludwig (1947). Depreciating Freud's explorations into the analysis of art, he writes:

> After assuring us he knows nothing of art, Freud turns to Michelangelo's Moses. This profound work of sculpture had the greatest effect on him, seemed to fill him with lasting excitement. He writes little of the statue itself, however, or the masterful creativeness and composition it demonstrates; and he waits many years before he goes into the actual personality of the mythical Hebrew leader. He does fill twenty pages with remarks on the meaning of the position of hand and fingers. The principal thing to him about the statue seems to be that 'one of the four fingers' is placed so as to make a deep groove in the long beard [p. 243].

[4] M. Bergmann (Angel, 1975) agrees with Hans Sachs (1942) that the *Moses* represented Freud's new ego ideal, but goes a step further.

> If we translate the change of Ego Ideal — from Conquering Hero to Self-Conquering Hero — into developmental language, we may say that the Freudian Moses has renounced an immediate satisfaction (the punishment of the idolaters) for the sake of a delayed, more lasting and valuable one. The emphasis here is on ego-control, on the primacy of reality. In this sense, the *preservation* of the Tables in Freud's Moses interpretation appears as an early signpost pointing to the advent of Ego Psychology.
>
> By the same token, Moses' nearly yielding to his rage brings into focus the problems of hate and aggression which could not much longer be seen as mere products of ambivalence or wounded love. Thus, the threatening *destruction* of the divine Tables may have had links [to] Freud's new theory of Aggression, independent of Libido [p. 3].

[5] John Addington Symonds (1893), who did not find the statue aesthetically satisfying, had noted it was to have been observed from below:

> The Moses, which Paul and his courtiers thought sufficient to commemorate a single Pope, stands as the eminent jewel of this defrauded tomb. We may not be attracted by it. We may even be repelled by the goat-like features, the enormous beard, the ponderous muscles, and the grotesque garments of the monstrous statue. In order to do it justice, let us bear in mind that the Moses now remains detached from a group of environing symbolic forms which Michelangelo designed. Instead of taking its place as one among eight corresponding and counterbalancing giants, it is isolated, thrust forward on the eye; whereas it was intended to be viewed from below in concert with a scheme of balanced figures, male and female, on the same colossal scale [p. 354].

Freud's critic is correct in the sense that Freud paid little attention to the artist himself, except to note Michelangelo's relationship to his patron Pope Julius II, for whose tomb the statue was commissioned. Freud's critic is also correct in that the psychoanalyst focused on the idiosyncratic aesthetic effect the statue had on himself rather than on why the artist was compelled to express himself in precisely the way he did. Perhaps Freud's emphasis on the forefinger detail in the light of his solipsistic interpretation needs augmentation from the standpoint of the artist rather than from that of the imaginative observer alone.

A careful examination of all the works of Michelangelo gave me my first clues regarding the artist's finger representations — in particular, his deployment of the forefinger. I was aided in my quest for answers regarding the artist by an observation of the Michelangelo scholar De Tolnay (1969), who had noted some similarity of composition between the *Moses* statue conceived when the artist was thirty years of age and an early sculptural piece, *The Madonna of the Stairs*, executed when the artist was sixteen years old: ". . . [T]he gestures of her hands are found in the Moses of the Tomb of Julius II" (p. 79).[6]

When I compared Michelangelo's first extant piece of sculpture, *The Madonna of the Stairs*, with the *Moses*, the hand positions seemed almost identical (see Fig. 1). The left hand of the mother resembles the left hand of the Moses almost to an exact reproduction of the fingers. The right hands of the mother and Moses also resemble each other. I took an imaginative leap. Photographically, I superimposed *The Madonna of the Stairs* onto the *Moses* statue and I got the baby in the bosom of Moses (see Fig. 2). This gave me my first clue that there was a hidden pregenital aspect to the Moses statue and a lead as to why so much passion was evoked in Freud and his critic by the finger positions. It seemed that the beard of Moses could represent a fetishistic substitution of the mother's garment. The left arm is the baby-holding arm, and the right arm is used for uncovering the garment to expose the underlying breast. Could the white marble tablets then represent breasts? Would this explain why they are double? In another context, the Sterbas (1956) had already equated white marble and breasts and milk, just as Eissler (1963) had done for Newton with white light.

At this point, I conjectured to myself that in the sculptor's fantasy there was an unconscious identification with an angry mother who denies her breasts (tablets) to the idol (penis) worshipers, but recants and again offers the breasts — a theme consistent with Freud's thesis.[7] In his paper Freud had an artist depict those pen-

[6] Fehl (1968) regards the Pope Julius tomb as "a significant structure in its own right" rather than the ill-fitting frame burst asunder by the splendid *Moses* statue. "Without the Moses the work not only is in scale in all its parts, it also introduces into a fitting central position the reclining effigy of the Pope. This work has been much maligned, but its quiet dignity becomes apparent when it is seen on its own and not as an appendage to Moses" (p. 86).

[7] Watkins (1951), like Freud, emphasizes the issue of restraint and sees the statue as the embodiment of one of man's greatest needs, i.e., the prevention of the more or less universally feared paternal punishment and the retention of an intact, prized body ego. He sees Michelangelo "portraying the

FIGURE 1

Similarity of hand positions in *The Madonna of The Stairs* and *Moses.* (Photo, courtesy of Alinari/Editorial Photocolor Archives.)

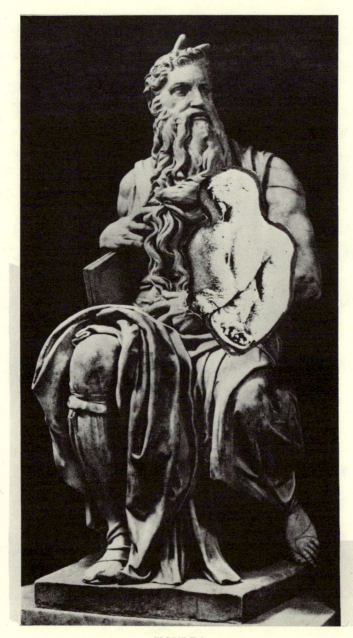

FIGURE 2

Moses as "Madonna Androgyna." (Photo, courtesy of Alinari/Editorial Photocolor Archives.)

ultimate stages which could have anticipated the statue's final form. As it happens, copies do exist of two early sketches for the *Moses* statue by the artist himself; in the earlier conception only one tablet was drawn, but in the later sketch, two tablets were drawn, each on a separate knee — this bilateral placement may be even more suggestive of tablets as breasts than the final form of the statue.

Since these sketches of Michelangelo's plans for the Moses figure itself were in print (Wilson, 1876) at the time of Freud's writing, one wonders whether his perusal of them would have altered his ultimate theoretical speculations and his need for intervening examples. In his 1927 postscript to the original paper, Freud was confirmed in his earlier views by the discovery of a seated Moses figure from the twelfth century executed by Nicholas of Verdun, which to Freud's mind demonstrated "an instant during his storm of feeling" (1914b, p. 238).

Decades later, Servadio (1951) came into possession of another *Moses* statue which to him supported Freud's original theory and whose "face is that of an inspired and saintly man, not that of an angry leader." The face "seems to look imploringly towards Heaven, as if asking of God the relief and consolation which his people have refused him" (p. 95).

It appears to me that the search for a corroboration of Freud's original thesis by finding actual examples of those intervening stages postulated by Freud is a forced line of research and that a more fruitful approach would lead to the artist himself.

Most observers, including Freud, have responded to the *Moses* as a fearsome male authority with overtones of a deity or a primitive brute. My view of the statue as a concealed representation of a nursing mother led in another direction, seemingly contradictory but (as I realized as I learned more about the artist) consistent with his psychosexual development and character structure. An identification with an ambivalently loved and hated maternal figure could be projected into the *Moses* statue as well as into those madonnas of his who obviously appear so isolated from the child.

The arm positions of *The Madonna of the Stairs* and the *Moses* statue and Michelangelo's particular use of the forefinger — i.e., indenting it into a soft mass — suggested parapractic revelations of the artist's oral deprivation and longing for warmth in the infant-mother relationship as well as of his unconscious maternal identification. The artist's homosexuality began to make sense. In fact, the theme of androgyny helped to explain another puzzling iconologic feature of this Moses representation: i.e., why did Michelangelo depict the great leader in a seated position when the usual depiction of the hero is in a standing position?[8]

---

father as *not* dropping the tablets, hence not castrating for the indulgence in infantile gratification in his absence" (p. 63). To him, the two tablets represent testes, and shattering would be castration. By the same token, the calf worship represents infantile oral dependence on the mother.

[8] Moses is not commonly represented in a seated position, and it has been suggested that the seated position of Michelangelo's *Moses* is inconsistent with Freud's interpretation (Bremer, 1976).

Assuming that a pregenital maternal trait was imposed onto Moses by the sculptor, the seated position of Moses makes more sense because that position is customary for nursing.

The ambiguity achieved in the artist's incomparable bisexual synthesis might help to explain the unusual fascination of this work, commonly regarded as man's greatest sculptural attainment.[9]

If my interpretation of Michelangelo's indentation of the forefinger into a soft mass as evidence of unconscious memories (Ricoeur, 1976) relative to breast indentations accomplished by both mother and child in a breast-feeding situation is correct (Eisenbund, 1965; Linn, 1955; and Hoffer, 1949), could there be more evidence from the artist himself and possibly from others as to the validity of such equations? This question led to further scrutiny of the artist and of other sources.

When your attention is drawn to Michelangelo's forefingers, you are inclined to recall his vivid depiction of life itself being passed from Jehovah to Adam in the famous Sistine ceiling mural. However, should you then carefully peruse all of Michelangelo's known drawings, paintings, and sculpture, you may be impressed — as I was — by a uniqueness in Michelangelo's use of this digit which I would characterize as a parapraxis.[10] He persistently represented the forefinger as indenting a soft mass or inside a fold. His forefingers stand out in his various media — drawings, paintings, and sculptures — and are consistent throughout his lifetime (see Fig. 3); I regard this as an idiosyncratic overcathexis and unlikely to have been executed consciously.[11] How can we apply this interpretation more usefully in extending our understanding, and increasing our appreciation, of the artist?

That Michelangelo was aware of the direct importance of the forefinger in relation to breast feeding is revealed in a number of his works in which the forefinger is brought into relation to the madonna's breast. In these instances, was he fol-

[9] Theodor Reik (1964) writes in connection with the vicissitudes of the ancient mother-goddess of the Hebrew tribes: "She became a victim of the great religious and social reform we connect with the name of Moses. This tyrannical and intolerant leader of the Hebrew tribes and his followers banned the figure of the mother-goddess into that nether world. That removal was performed so radically that scarcely any trace of her previous existence remained in the official Hebrew religion. Occasionally Yahweh, the victor, took over her functions, saying 'As one whom his mother comforteth so will I comfort you; and you shall be comforted in Jerusalem.' Even the root of the goddess-idea was torn out: there is no feminine form of Adon, the name of the Lord." That there is a Mother Goddess concealed in the figure of Yahweh is the thesis of a work by Rollenbeck (1949). See also Rosenfeld (1951).

[10] In discussing Shengold's (1972) paper on Freud and Abraham regarding plagiarism, Sterba (1971) preferred the translation "slip-action" to the word parapraxis, which he would regard as an oversight of minor importance. Massive repression is operative in the gross slip-action and plagiarism discussed in that paper.

Perhaps the same could be said with regard to this repetitive detail I am speaking of — it is too important a style of expression in its consistency and chronicity to be regarded as a parapraxis, a term which is used here simply to refer to an unconsciously determined repetition-compulsive action although not a slip-action in the strictest sense.

[11] It should be mentioned that other artists have exaggerated the forefinger in their paintings, particularly the Mannerists, of whom Michelangelo was one of the earliest. In addition to using the Mannerist style, Michelangelo was copied by followers. See, for example, Arnold Hauser (1965).

FIGURE 3

Typical forefinger deployments. Details from *The Bruges Madonna* (left) and *The Last Judgment* (right). (Photo, courtesy of Alinari/Editorial Photocolor Archives.)

lowing the example of other artists; were they his own spontaneous creations; or, most likely, was he copying actual models?

Numerous artists, current and past, depict the importance of forefinger-breast relations: they show the use of the mother's forefinger to help press milk from the breast nipple, to facilitate sucking by proper placement of the nipple in the infant's mouth, and to help keep the baby's nasal passages clear. Likewise, in many works, the forefinger of the nursling is seen grasping or touching the breast during that intimate contact with the mother.

Focusing on hand positions in a random series of madonna paintings permits a crude but unique form of classification of such paintings depending on the form of breast displacement depicted. These divisions are arbitrary, but can be a meaningful way of looking at the art materials pertinent to my original thesis.

The Madonnas Lactata: This group includes all madonnas where the infant is either suckling at or touching the breast. The forefinger's importance is evident in both mother and child.

The "Breast-Reacher" Madonnas: I call these reachers because the infant's hand is reaching for or toward the breast, whereas the breasts themselves are not evident. The meaning, however, seems clear.

The "Fruit" Madonnas: These pictures illustrate the close association of breast and fruit and appear to suggest that the artist symbolically elaborates breast into fruit. In Christian iconography (Ferguson, 1961) "fruit is often used to suggest the twelve fruits of the Spirit: love, joy, peace, long-suffering, gentleness, goodness, faith, meekness, patience, modesty, temperance, and chastity" (p. 31). Each specific fruit, such as apple, cherry, fig, grape, lemon, orange, peach, pear, plum, pomegranate, and strawberry, is associated with a variety of spiritual and ethical qualities and certainly not with secular breast feeding. (A sagittal section of the human breasts with their lobular arrangements suggests their affinity to the pomegranate.)

The "Breast-Garment" Madonnas: This group of madonnas reveals a further move in displacement from a whole organ, the breast, to an organ part or function. In these depictions, imagine the flowing lines of the mother's garment as representing the skin of the breast or the flow of breast milk. ("Whenever we bring a foreign body into relationship with the surface of the body — for it is not in the hand alone that these peculiarities are developed — the consciousness of our personal existence is prolonged into the extremities and surfaces of this foreign body, and the consequence is — feelings, now of an expansion of our proper self, now of the acquisition of a kind and amount of motion foreign to our natural organs, now of an unusual degree of vigour, power or resistance, or steadiness in our bearings" [Flaccus, 1906, quoted in Flügel, p. 34]. Another quote from Lotze is pertinent: "clothing, by adding to the apparent size of the body in one way or another, gives us an increased sense of power, a sense of extension of our bodily self — ultimately by enabling us to fill more space" [quoted in Flügel, 1930, p. 34]. An outstanding example of skin as garment is Michelangelo's self-portrait as St. Bartholomew in *The Last Judgment*.)

In Christian iconography, "the cope, the richest and most magnificent of ecclesiastical vestments, is a large cape fashioned in the form of a half circle. Its symbolic meaning is innocence, purity, and dignity" (Ferguson, 1961, p. 157). "The morse, or brooch, is a clasp used to fasten the front of the cope" (p. 158). In my view, the brooch may also be seen as a displaced breast.

"Book" Madonnas: Learning, Tablets, and Breast Feeding: The penultimate series of book madonnas illustrates the displacement from the breast to the book.

A series of medieval German Sophias (Neumann, 1955) permits us to draw an equation between breast-feeding and learning, flowing garments and the flow of milk, to an ultimate identification of tablets as breast representations. In these depictions one may note the flow of lines from the madonna's cope directly into the mouths of the supplicants. By the same token, a close relationship between the bird and the book is demonstrated by the art historian H. Friedmann (1946) in his detailed analysis of goldfinch madonnas. It is noteworthy that he finds this connection puzzling and concludes that the symbol of fertility links the scroll, the bird, and the mother.

In a relatively small number of paintings, the goldfinch is placed near or directly in contact with a small scroll or piece of paper on which a variety of legends is inscribed. The fact that there is no basic similarity in the wordings on these scrolls indicates that it is not the message that is compositionally or symbolically related to the bird, but the scroll itself. As pointed out elsewhere in this work, the goldfinch is, to some extent, a substitute object for the little scroll or scroll box usually held by the Christ Child in early pictures done under Byzantine influence. Not a few of the earliest goldfinches are decidedly cylindrical in shape, as though the artists still had the scroll case form in mind...

It is, of course, quite possible that the juxtaposition of bird and paper is without particular significance, but it is more likely that some connection did exist in the mind of the painter or the patron in each case. The only connection that I can suggest is the fact that the Italian words for goldfinch, the bird with a 'message' — cardellino, and for scroll [a message] — cartellino, are so very similar that they probably appealed to the pun loving, anagramatically inclined Renaissance mentality and may have been placed together for this reason. Italian art is certainly not wanting in instances of this kind.

Possibly related to the bird-and-scroll motif is the placing of the goldfinch close to an open book as we find in the lower foreground in Fungai's "Madonna and Child, with the young St. John and Angels." In this connection, it may also be recalled that in Raphael's "Madonna of the Goldfinch"..., the goldfinch has temporarily taken the attention of the group away from the book which the Virgin had been reading. This is, however, apparently not intended as a conflict or competition between the goldfinch and the book (apparently Holy Writ) but as a naturalistic bit of genre serving as a vehicle for the introduction of one of the bird's many symbolic meanings — in this case, Fertility [pp. 118–119].

To confirm the pregenital theme in the artist's depiction of Moses, I will draw one more analogy — the hair-breast equation to be discussed later in this paper.

With regard to the *Moses* statue, De Tolnay (1970) had noted: "This Moses was unconsciously prepared for a long time in the work of Michelangelo himself: the two hands of the statue are anticipated a quarter of a century earlier in the Virgin of the Stairs" (pp. 41–42). Moreover,

> it is not unusual for an artist to reveal in his earliest creative attempts the whole essence of his genius in embryonic form. Only in the second stage does he try, through the acquisition of technical ability, to make his personal conceptions conform to the requirements of his age, although sometimes this at the expense of his originality; and in the final period he may achieve a true integration of external ability with his original artistic vision [De Tolnay, 1969, p. 75].

My question is: What can the psychoanalyst contribute to the understanding of the "original artistic vision"? First, a few words about my style of approach.[12] I agree with Wollheim (1973) that "the psychology of gesture is sadly underdeveloped" (p. 196).[13]

"Freud believed that all human behavior is meaningful and explainable and that every gesture, slip of the tongue, every mannerism, is a valid expression of personality" (Spector, 1969, p. 78).[14] Freud compared his analysis to the work of the Italian connoisseur, Giovanni Morelli, whose contention was that

> Every true artist is committed to the repetition of certain characteristic forms or shapes. . . . To identify the characteristic forms of an artist, we must go to those parts of the painting where . . . conventional pressures are likely to be relaxed. . . . We must take seriously the depiction of the *hand,* the drapery, the landscape, the ball of the thumb, or the lobe of the ear [quoted in Wollheim, 1973, p. 181; italics added].

Because trifles can more readily slip past the barriers of attention, they may be

---

[12] It was, indeed, an art historian (Panofsky, 1939) who in his distinction between iconology and iconography provided the rationale for my amateur efforts as art historian. ". . . [W]e need a mental faculty comparable to that of a diagnostician — a faculty which I cannot describe better than by the rather discredited term 'synthetic intuition' and which may be better developed in a talented layman than in an erudite scholar" (pp. 14–15). This point of view is echoed by a sociologist of art (Deinhard, 1970): "Where progress. . .has been made. . .to achieve a deeper understanding of art or new insights into its significance for human existence. . .it has not come from the ranks of the 'professionals' in the art field in the narrower sense of the word" (p. 2).

[13] My interest was primed by exposure to some earlier research on hand gestures under the tutelage of a Freudian psychologist, Krout (1933, 1939). According to Spiegel and Machotka (1974), "Though Krout's experiments were ingenious, their yield of information was low" (p. 68).

More recent emphasis on the language of desires and related vicissitudes of meaning (Sawyier, 1973, p. 221), along with the renewal of interest in matters of empathy which had been explored earlier toward the end of the last century (Spector, 1972, p. 124), now permits some broadening in our analysis of plastic works of art and their creators.

[14] However, according to Ricoeur, "Freud's phrases about every move being a gesture needs spelling out; gestures are for someone even when the message is covert and out of awareness" (quoted in Sawyier, 1973, p. 221).

revelations of expression (Wollheim, 1973, p. 215). According to Morelli, "every painter has his own peculiarities which escape him without his being aware of it" (quoted in Wollheim, 1973, p. 194).

Freud saw Morelli's method of inquiry as closely related to the technique of psychoanalysis: "It, too, is accustomed to divine secret and concealed things from despised or unnoticed features from the rubbish-heap, as it were, of our observations" (quoted in Wollheim, 1973, p. 183).

Actually, however, both Freud's approach and mine diverge from that of the connoisseur; the value of the overlooked detail for Morelli was for its elucidation of the artist's style,[15] whereas for the psychoanalyst it represents a clue betraying the artist's repressed feelings and ideas.[16]

Freud himself paid little attention, however, to the personal motivations of the artist[17] and concentrated his major attention on the subject, Moses,[18] and on the artist's successful aesthetic accomplishment.

It is now over six decades since Freud's essay on Michelangelo's *Moses* was published, and there has been no re-analysis of the *Moses* statue from a psychoanalytic perspective. This is hardly surprising since little new data about the artist which would be psychologically impressive have been discovered. We have many poems and letters of the artist, but anamnestic data remain limited. Two very old biographies by Vasari (1568) and Condivi (1553) and those more recent ones by Grimm (1896), Symonds (1893), and Rolland (1912) provide the somewhat insubstantial basis for the trickle of references we do have to the artist's psychodynamics, and psychopathology. The paucity of the kind of biographic data which might even allow for speculation has obliged interested psychoanalytic investigators to turn to the art works themselves, much as I am doing.

The Hair-Breast Equation

Earlier, I suggested that the *Moses* beard was a fetishistic substitute for the maternal garment in *The Madonna of the Stairs*. I will now strain your credulity by making a symbolic equation between hair and breast milk in order that the

[15] Iannarelli (1968), of the University of California (Hayward), has developed a system of personal identification using the external ear as a supplement to fingerprinting.

[16] ". . . [A] statue may be treated exactly like a dream. In both cases interpretation involves the same attention to unnoticed *details*, the same sort of separate treatment — analytic in the strict sense of the word — of each of these details taken in themselves, especially those that are disregarded or ignored ('the rubbish heap, as it were, of our observations' [Freud, 1914b, p. 222]). This is true of the position of the Moses' right-hand finger in relation to the draping of his beard . . ." (Ricoeur, 1976, p. 17).

[17] According to Spector (1972), Freud "treated the drives and motivations of Moses as seen in Michelangelo's statue without the slightest allusion to sexual matters" (p. 99).

[18] Kohut (1977) thought it characteristic of Freud to respond "most deeply to the Moses statue — the finished rendition of a strong, fully cohesive self" (p. 289, n. 11).

forefinger's indentation of the beard of Moses may constitute evidence for Michelangelo's concealed feminine identification.[19]

De Tolnay (1969), when he establishes a connection between the flowing-beard representation and the flow of water, is the bridge; he describes the flow of the *Moses* beard as a "cascade." I would like to extend the analogy to the flow of breast milk.

Although this analogy seems, at first, far-fetched, it can be supported by the close embryological association between the developing hairs and sebaceous glands: mammary glands, as it happens, are a variation of sebaceous (i.e., sweat) glands (Arey, 1940).

Veszy-Wagner's (1963) study of the bearded man gives evidence of the defensive role of this type of hirsutism in protecting against feminine wishes in the male and against the outbreak of a dominance of the bisexual (female) component and the feminine identification in the male.

My emphasis is not so much on the defensive use of the beard, but rather, on the expressive, though disguised, use of the beard as a simultaneous representation of the flowing breast and as a phallic representation.

Perhaps at this point, a clinical example of the hair-breast equation from the clinical analysis of an actual patient will help clarify my meaning regarding such bisexual representations in mental life.

A rare opportunity presented itself in the case of an analysand who became a father for the second time. Two weeks after the birth of his second daughter, and during the night while his wife got up to breast-feed the baby, he had what he called a peculiar dream; in that dream, a hair was growing in his mouth.

Associations to that "peculiar" dream detail led to a penis-hair equation, a penis-breast-hair equation, and penis-baby in mouth-vagina associations. He himself had been breast-fed until nine months of age. He felt his first daughter was breast-fed "too long"—until eighteen months of age. He had been impatient as a child and became irritated when he didn't get what he wanted. He recently recognized feelings of being neglected by his wife, feelings which he shares with the older daughter who also feels somewhat neglected and mildly resentful. He recalled that this daughter used to snuggle up to his breast and try to suck on it, complaining of the hairs around his nipple. He associated this to the hair in the dream.

He declares in his further associations that he wants his wife to breast-feed the new baby—he is almost fanatic about it, and he notes with ambiguous envy that when the baby cries his wife's breasts automatically begin to flow and drench the front of her dressing gown. Ultimately, he vainly equates the creativity of the wo-

---

[19] I owe the phrase "hair-breast equation" to the imagination of one Fabius Zachary Snoop, probably a pseudonym, who in his monograph on the breast formulated the words for the idea I had been grappling with.

man to his own creative hobbies. Thus, this patient not only demonstrates the hair-breast equation, but the reactive identification with the creative woman, much as I postulate about Michelangelo himself.

Michelangelo's Psychology

Except for idiosyncratic emphasis, psychoanalytic students of Michelangelo's character agree in their general formulations. Preoedipal trauma and oral and anal fixation stand out, and the artist's homosexual character is seen as a perverse solution to his unresolved maternal loss in childhood. His creative work is seen as an identification with his substitute caretakers and as a reparative effort to undo these early traumata and later ones, too.

It is agreed that enforced early separation from his sickly mother made him a unique sibling in engendering feelings of rage over abandonment and that these feelings became fixed in his character as oral rage. Some actually saw his career choice as positively related to living with the foster parents — stonecutters — and believed that to some extent furiously carving into marble represented a sublimated destructive rage toward the abandoning breast. Sterba (Sterba and Sterba, 1956) noted that the only warm madonna done by Michelangelo is *The Doni Madonna* in which the stone quarries of his childhood are depicted in the background. His conclusion is that to the stepmother, Michelangelo was grateful. In general, it is agreed that he made a hostile identification with the abandoning mother which was re-enacted in his homosexuality and creativity, ascribed by some as envy of women's power to create.

The trauma of maternal separation, cruelly enhanced by the death of his biological mother at six and the loss of his stepmother at ten, along with the influence of an unempathic father, forced upon him an isolation and loneliness never to be overcome.

Frank (1966) saw him as a depressive, whose unresolved mourning for his mother losses is evident in his last work, the *Pietà Rondanini*, representing the old and dying artist's poignant reunion with the mother, now represented as death. Mohacsy (1976) saw the last work in a similar fashion. "In this final work of Michelangelo's old age, we have come full circle: to a representation of genuine infantile fusion with the mother, as a final appearance of the need for symbiotic union that accompanies us as a driving force from birth to death" (pp. 512–513).

Peto (1979) essentially agrees with Frank and Mohacsy but emphasizes the artist's conflict. He calls Michelangelo "a life-long depressive who feared independence from and fusion with the mother" (p. 184).

The Sterbas (1978), in their most recent reflections on the artist, attest to his "deeply ambivalent relationship to his mother" (p. 170).

Stubbornness, money grubbing, slovenly habits, and inability to finish work suggested anal fixations to Clark (1927), who characterizes the artist as a compulsive neurotic. Other emphases on his paranoid, masochistic, and hypochondriacal nature suggest pregenital fixations which prevented the development of an oedipal state and resulted in the failure of heterosexual achievement even without marriage. Eissler (1971) goes so far as to suggest heterosexual immaturity as rather characteristic of great and creative men (p. 533).

It is hard to escape the conclusion that the taming of intense aggression played a prominent role in Michelangelo (Sterba and Sterba, 1956). His vengefulness and narcissistic rage alienated him from many who considered him obnoxious and hateful. He was highly perfectionistic and idealistic and capable of the highest achievements, which are regarded by some discerners as reparative efforts to overcome inner destructive urges.

Michelangelo's grandiosity may have reached the proportion of an identification with Christ late in life.

The unsuccessful struggle to personal individuation on a psychosexual axis reflected a deep symbiotic attachment to cold, unempathic caretakers. One author (Liebert, 1977) saw "the yearning for eternal union with an idealized powerful paternal transformation of early maternal figures. . .lost in early childhood" (p. 517). Oremland (1978) saw in the Pietàs the way in which "Michelangelo portrayed a continuing evolution of the themes of return to, reunion, and union with the mother of infancy" (p. 565). These notions closely approach what I have suggested as depicted in the androgynous madonna, Moses.

Michelangelo's Narcissistic Character

Earlier attempts to place the artist's personality in the oedipal-conflict framework have afforded us the diagnosis of a latent (or overt) homosexuality, as if perverse formations and acting out would explain his character.

As in the case of other geniuses, there was extensive arrestation of libidinal and aggressive development and therefore little, if any, oedipal conflict. The nuclear psychopathology of our subject is related more to the development of the self. The nature of his object ties was essentially narcissistic, and he was caught in the grip of chronic narcissistic rage.

It is not clear that Michelangelo was ever psychotic; at worst he was borderline, and at best he suffered from a narcissistic personality disorder. Undoubtedly, he experienced early trauma related to the nature of the mothering. His real mother's sickliness seems to have had a particular impact on this second of five boys, the only one to be farmed out to a stepmother, at least for longer than the usual length of time.[20] His real mother, who presumably visited him and then aban-

---

[20] It may not have been uncommon for children to be put out to wet-nurse in fifteenth-century Italy (Ross, 1974). However, the historian Trexler (1973–1974) recalls the realities of infanticidal deaths and threats of abandonment children had to live with.

doned him on weekends, was finally lost through death altogether when he was six years old, and he was forced to abandon his stepmother at ten when he returned to his father and brothers.

Delayed in his education, he exhibited an early capacity for drawing which was fiercely resisted by an unempathic father who finally yielded to his son's artistic career by providing that he be well cared for financially.

Michelangelo began a lifelong series of vulnerable attachments to idealized males, including Lorenzo the Magnificent whom he also lost prematurely. His relationships to authorities remained tentative so as to avoid further narcissistic injury through abandonment. The only close attachments he could maintain were those in which young men functioned as selfobjects whom, in a sense, he mothered as he would ideally like to be mothered.

His poetry gives convincing evidence of his narcissistic attachments to boys, though in the past this work has been seen only as a perverse formation based on structural conflict.

My contention is that he never escaped from a symbiotic attachment to the frustrating maternal objects with whom he identified. Furthermore, my analysis of the *Moses* statue as an androgynous madonna is in support of a self structure which did not see others as separate and autonomous, but rather as extensions of himself.

This diagnosis would explain his rages — they were consequent to seeing others as flawed, imperfect, and thus offensive and to be blotted out whenever they did not succumb or yield to his grandiose expectations.

Michelangelo had great empathy for himself but little for others, except insofar as they provided him with a kind of support which filled an inner emptiness and despair caused by early trauma. How he was able to transform his misery into such masterful creativity remains mysterious. I dare not go beyond those connections I have made and seriously attempt to explain his creativity.

Like other geniuses, Michelangelo was able at times to withdraw his narcissistic investment from his ideals and from the self and employ them in the service of creative activity. Students of Michelangelo will recall that he openly stated that he owed his artistic capacity to the deity, indicating the he (i.e., his self) was not the initiator, source, or shaper of his products.[21]

Having been alone, abandoned, and unsupported as a child, perhaps he was better prepared than most to enter into those lonely areas that had not previously been explored by others.

Oral Trauma, Aggression, and Scoptophilia

It is not my intention to ascribe the artist's choice of career or his creativeness en-

[21] Perhaps this is a personal variant of what Kris (1952) refers to as "the divine ascent of genius" and which he relates to the myth of the birth of the hero. As an example, he cites Vasari's mythologi-. cal style in his biography of Michelangelo (pp. 73-74).

tirely or directly to preoedipal, particularly oral, traumata and the unsuccessful resolution of infantile conflicts.[22]

The question I wish to consider is whether it is possible for ambivalence toward mothering figures to become incorporated into a stable defensive structure, or even better — and going beyond defensive synthesis — into creative adaptations which may, under close scrutiny or under lapses such as parapraxes, reveal those underlying components which exist even in noncreative individuals in greater or lesser degrees. This in no way detracts from the greatness of the artist or his accomplishments.

Michelangelo certainly had the background for severe oral trauma and reactive rage. All character descriptions attest to his irritability and tension. Furthermore, we have evidence from his life style and his poetic creativity that genital cathexis was retarded by the intensity of his preoedipal fixations. Some scholars (e.g., Eissler) sense intense struggles not to succumb to passivity, a factor that is exemplified in the creative works themselves.

What may have begun as oral, biting rage toward the breast could have been diverted into claw chiseling into marble, a breast symbol (Sterba). If this is so, it is suggested as preconscious in the artist himself when he said that if he was good for anything, it was because he suckled among the chisels and hammers of stonecutters, an obvious reference to the nurturant stepparents. Michelangelo's humorous remark, "I sucked in marble dust with my mother's milk" represents to my mind a hypnagogic determinant in his art work, a memory trace inherent in the blank hallucinations described by Stern (1961).[23]

Indeed, one student of the artist's life (Besdine, 1968, 1970) suggests, under the title "The Jocasta Complex," that Michelangelo was overwhelmed by an intense intrusiveness characteristic of those mothers who facilitate the development of homosexuality in boys who may also eventually become paranoid-masochists.

To my mind, the repetitive pattern of forefinger indentations, which I regard as a parapraxis, suggests such a degree of oral frustration and consequent fixation as

---

[22] Coltrera (1965) points to a pertinent issue from the analysis of the other great Renaissance artist, Leonardo. "Even more interesting is Leonardo's phenomenological understanding of his cognitive style which encompasses a broader view of orality than the narrower view of orality taken by Freud and Eissler in the case of Gioconda's smile. The master's consideration of the eye and the hand as a conjoined cognitive event is compatible with the role assigned to the trinitarian relation between the eye, hand and mouth by Piaget and Hoffer in beginning cognitive epigenesis during the oral stage" (p. 661).

[23] One may wonder whether the artist's description is a reflection of his having experienced those "blank hallucinations" described by Stern (1961), i.e., stereotyped sensory perceptions without appropriate external stimuli and which may include "sandy, gritty, and doughy feelings in the mouth" (p. 205). These hallucinations represent defensive repetitions of responses to oral deprivation, the sensations reflecting the subjective experiences of the traumatized infant.

In this same regard Spitz (1955) saw all perception as beginning with the oral cavity and refers to Isakower's assumption "that the combination of the oral cavity with the hand corresponds to the model of what he defines as the earliest postnatal ego structure, and that the sensations of the oral cavity are probably unified with those of the external cutaneous covering" (p. 220).

to make neutralization impossible and to result in a permanent narcissistic vulnerability. The highly creative person, or genius like Michelangelo, is perhaps able to synthesize a relatively stable character structure and style of work so as to make it appear almost autonomous and independent of instinctual conflict. In his case, ego factors predominate. We are impressed by his ability, almost harmoniously, to depict fierce aggression, exquisitely controlled. It is precisely this exquisite control which Freud saw in his favorite, the *Moses* statue. It must have coincided with a similar resolution within Freud himself, a brother artist in a sense, since Freud was obliged to restrain his own potentially destructive aggression in the face of organizational squabbles, so as to maintain the viability of psychoanalysis as a movement.

When I mentioned earlier the oral destructive rage toward the abandoning mother, I did not suggest that claw chiseling into marble is a substitutive displacement and sublimation of breast-biting. Rather, it constitutes a regression in the service of creativity in the service of the ego (Kris); or, perhaps more accurately, a transmutation of primitive drive energies along with archaic grandiose configurations (Kohut).

Researchers of the early mother-child relationship have related hand erotism and tactile perception to the nursing situation, and connect aggression with oral frustration: according to Spitz (1955), "the child learns to grasp by nursing at the mother's breast and by combining the emotional satisfaction of that experience with tactile perceptions. He learns to distinguish animate objects from inanimate ones by the spectacle provided by his mother's face in situations fraught with emotional satisfaction."

Spitz is further quoted in Almansi (1960), who writes that "at the age of three months, when the child is deprived of the nipple, its eyes deviate from the mother's face in the general direction of the breasts thus leading to the superimposition of these two percepts which then become fused. At this age level the aggressive drive comes to the fore as a consequence of the repressed frustration experienced at the breast" (p. 68).

Almansi demonstrated in all four of his face-breast-equation cases that the phenomena involved were indissolubly bound to the liberation of large amounts of aggression — specifically, aggression reactive to oral deprivation. He adds two considerations which may have special relevance for the origins of scoptophilia. "Three cases were strongly scoptophilic, and their scoptophilia was indissolubly linked with early visual sensitization due to the feelings of oral deprivation and object loss" (p. 69). Moreover, Almansi's "material sheds some light on the origins of the process of incorporation through the eye and of the equation of 'to look at' and 'to devour' which have been discussed by Fenichel (1935) and others" (p. 69).

Herrman (1924), in a presentation before the Hungarian Psychoanalytic Society in 1924, referred to "manifestations of hand erotism in sucking infants, the origin of these phenomena (the act of clinging to the mother), and their connection with oral erotism" (p. 506).

Phyllis Greenacre (1959) has referred to the rhythmic use of the object as reflecting the nursing situation.[24] Sculpture can be regarded as a rhythmic use of the object.

My suggestion is that the artist's work reflected memory traces of both mothers and his interaction with them. These memory traces remained repressed, but were later elaborated into a sublimation through a process of creative transformation and resulted in a product which could permit the original experiences by others through an empathic capacity.[25]

While finishing the preparation of my thesis, I was delighted to find support for my idea in a brilliant re-examination of Freud's views on works of art by the philosopher Ricoeur (1976). He disavows Freud's disclaimers regarding the understanding of creativity and shows how psychoanalytic interpretation of art works and the artist's intentions can be justified by the psychoanalytic theory of dream formation, including the concepts of representability, staging, substitution, and the sign effect. To Ricoeur, "the same interplay of representability and substitution which is already functioning in dreams and memory continues in esthetics" (p. 21).

Thus, he clarified for me my concept of mnemonics in regard to Michelangelo's early breast-feeding experiences and presumed traumas. As he puts it, "...humanity *had* to create works of art just as it has to dream....If primal 'representation' is impossible, if a *lived* institution is impossible, perhaps the only way to rediscover one's childhood, which is behind one, is to create it before oneself, in a work" (p. 23).

In a way, what Freud did with a memory of Leonardo, I try to do with "the marble statue of Moses...treated...as a fantasy objectified in stone" (Ricoeur, 1976, p. 16).

Summary

Freud's aesthetic analysis of the *Moses* of Michelangelo attends largely to the emotions of the viewer and contains elements of his projective identification with the mythical Hebrew leader. Those gestures and postural elements upon which

[24] "...[D]uring even such mild strain as that of prolonged nursing, many babies develop rhythmical playful movements which accompany the nursing. Thus the baby, simultaneously with sucking at the breast or bottle, may play with its hands over the mother's breast or clothing, may later develop a rhythmic touching of its own cheek or pulling at the lobe of its own ear, or touching a lock of its hair, or the edge of the blanket. This seems to be an early manifestation of the use of the transitional object which is both me and not me (Winnicott, 1953). What I would emphasize now is not especially the intermediate quality of the object but the playful comforting rhythmic use of it which is also significant" (Greenacre, 1959, p. 70).

[25] We are, of course, in the realm of theory with regard to the role of empathy in aesthetic appreciation. For some divergent views see Kris (1952, p. 55), Robinson (1963), and Worringer (1953).

Freud based his theory, when examined as to the sculptor's intentions, may reveal the artist's idiosyncratic personal development. An overcathexis of the forefinger and a repetitive deployment of that digit in the art works of Michelangelo are related to unresolved infantile tensions of an oral and narcissistic nature.[26]

The *Moses* statue, when compared with his earliest sculptural work, *The Madonna of the Stairs*, suggests it may be an "androgynous madonna" which conceals within it evidences of the artist's bisexuality. This aesthetic conclusion contrasts sharply with the usual appreciation of the figure as masculine, even brutish.

Repetitive elements in the style of an artist as well as un-self-conscious overcathexes may yield clues to the character structure of the artistic creator; in the past they may have been interpreted in a formal art-historical sense or for the purpose of connoisseurship.

REFERENCES

Almansi, R. J. (1960), The face-breast equation. *J. Amer. Psychoanal. Assn.*, 8:43–70.

Angel, E. (1975), The taming of Freud's passions: Notes in the wake of Martin Bergmann's lecture: "Moses and the evolution of Freud's identity" at the Jewish Museum in New York. *Council News*, 207 (March). Published by the Council of Psychoanalytic Psychotherapists.

Arey, L. B. (1940), *Developmental Anatomy*. Philadelphia & London: Saunders.

Besdine, M. (1968), The Jocasta complex, mothering and genius. *Psychoanal. Rev.*, 55:259–277; 574–600.

――――― (1970), Michelangelo: The homosexual element in the life and work of a genius. *Medical Aspects of Human Sexuality*, May, pp. 127–140.

Bremer, R. (1976), Freud and Michelangelo's Moses. *Amer. Imago*, 33:60–75.

Clark, L. P. (1927), A psychohistorical study of Michelangelo in studies of some aspects of the art of the Renaissance. *Archiv. Psychoanal.*, 1:767–832.

Coltrera, J. T. (1965), On the creation of beauty and thought: The unique as vicissitude. *J. Amer. Psychoanal. Assn.*, 13:634–703.

Condivi, A. (1553), *Michael Angelo Buonarroti and Three Dialogues from the Portuguese by Francisco D'Ollanda*, trans. C. Halroyd. London: Duckworth, 1903.

De Tolnay, C. (1969), *Michelangelo*, Vol. I: *The Youth of Michelangelo*. Princeton, N.J.: Princeton University Press.

――――― (1970), *Michelangelo*, Vol. II: *The Sistine Ceiling*. Princeton, N.J.: Princeton University Press.

Deinhard, H. (1970), *Meaning and Expression: Toward a Sociology of Art*. Boston: Beacon Press.

Eisenbund, J. (1965), The hand and the breast with special reference to obsessional neurosis. *Psychoanal. Quart.*, 34:219–248.

Eissler, K. R. (1963), *Goethe: A Psychoanalytic Study — 1775–1786*, 2 vols. Detroit: Wayne State University Press.

――――― (1971), *Discourse on Hamlet and Hamlet: A Psychoanalytic Inquiry*. New York: International Universities Press.

Fehl, P. P. (1968), The final version of Michelangelo's tomb of Julius II. Abstract in: *Renaissance Papers 1968*, ed. G. W. Williams. The Southeastern Renaissance Conference, 1969, pp. 85–87.

Fenichel, O. (1935), The scoptophilic instinct and identification. In: *The Collected Papers of Otto Fenichel, First Series*. New York: Norton, 1953, pp. 373–397.

[26] Focusing on a small detail in an artist's work and extracting broad meanings therefrom may violate some Gestaltist preferences. With regard to the limitations of isolating repetitive elements in an artist's work, see Kanter and Pinsker (1973) and Kris (1952).

Ferguson, G. (1961), *Signs and Symbols in Christian Art.* New York: Oxford University Press.

Flaccus, L. W. (1906), Remarks on the psychology of clothes (based on the questionary of G. Stanley Hall). *Pedagog. Seminary*, 13:61–83.

Flügel, J. C. (1930), *The Psychology of Clothes.* London: Hogarth Press.

Frank, G. (1966), The enigma of Michelangelo's pietà Rondanini: A study of mother-loss in childhood. *Amer. Imago*, 23:287–315.

Freud, S. (1914a), Der Moses des Michelangelo. *Imago*, 3:15–36.

―――― (1914b), The Moses of Michelangelo. *Standard Edition*, 13:211–238. London: Hogarth Press, 1960. Reprinted in: *Freud's Collected Papers*, Vol. 4. New York: Basic Books, 1959.

―――― (1924), Der Moses des Michelangelo. *Gesammelte Schriffte*, 10:257–286.

Friedmann, H. (1946), *The Symbolic Goldfinch.* New York: Pantheon.

Greenacre, P. (1959), Play in relation to creative imagination. *The Psychoanalytic Study of the Child*, 14:61–80. New York: International Universities Press.

Grimm, H. (1896), *Life of Michelangelo*, trans. F. E. Bunnett. 2 vols. Boston.

Hauser, A. (1965), *Mannerism*, 2 vols. London: Routledge & Kegan Paul.

Herrman, I. (1924), Report from the Hungarian Psycho-Analytical Society. *Internat. J. Psycho-Anal.*, 5:506.

Hoffer, W. (1949), Mouth, hand and ego integration. *The Psychoanalytic Study of the Child*, 3/4:49–56. New York: International Universities Press.

Iannarelli, A. V. (1968), Ear identification. *Internat. Criminal Police Rev.*, p. 226.

Jones, E. (1955), *The Life and Work of Sigmund Freud*, Vol. 2. New York: Basic Books.

Kantor, M. & Pinsker, H. (1973), Musical expression of psychopathology. *Perspectives in Biology and Medicine*, Winter, pp. 263–269.

Kohut, H. (1977), *The Restoration of the Self.* New York: International Universities Press.

Kris, E. (1952), *Psychoanalytic Explorations in Art.* New York: International Universities Press.

Krout, M. H. (1933), *Major Aspects of Personality.* Chicago: College Press.

―――― (1939), Understanding human gestures. *Scientific Monthly*, 44:167–172.

Liebert, R. S. (1977), Michelangelo's dying slave: A psychoanalytic study in iconography. *The Psychoanalytic Study of the Child*, 32:505–543. New Haven: Yale University Press.

Linn, L. (1955), Some developmental aspects of the body image. *Internat. J. Psycho-Anal.*, 36:36–42.

Ludwig, E. (1947), *Doctor Freud: An Analysis and a Warning.* New York: Hellman, Williams.

Marmor, J. (1971), Book Review of *The Horned Moses in Medieval Art and Thought*, by Ruth Mellinkoff. *Amer. J. Psychiat.*, 128:508–509.

Mohacsy, I. (1976), Fusion and anxiety: Children's drawings and Renaissance art. *J. Amer. Acad. Psychoanal.*, 4:501–514.

Oremland, J. D. (1978), Michelangelo's Pietàs. *The Psychoanalytic Study of the Child*, 33:563–591. New York: International Universities Press.

Panofsky, E. (1939), Introduction, *Studies in Iconology.* New York: Oxford University Press, pp. 3–17.

Peto, A. (1979), The Rondanini Pietà, Michelangelo's infantile neurosis. *Internat. Rev. Psycho-Anal.*, 6:183–199.

Reik, T. (1964), *Pagan Rites in Judaism.* New York: Noonday Press.

Ricoeur, P. (1976), Psychoanalysis and the work of art. In: *Psychiatry and the Humanities*, Vol. 1, ed. J. H. Smith. New Haven and London: Yale University Press, pp. 3–33.

Robinson, G. (1963), Empathy and identification on the first developmental level. *J. Asthma Res.*, 11:2, 77–92.

Rolland, R. (1912), *The Life of Michael Angelo*, trans. F. Lees. New York: Dutton.

Rollenbeck, E. (1949), *Die Magna Mater im Alten Testament Darmstadt.* Claassen und Röther.

Rosenfeld, E. (1951), The pan-headed Moses―A parallel. *Internat. J. Psycho-Anal.*, 32:83–93.

Rosenthal, E. E. (1964), Michelangelo's Moses, Dal Di Sotto in Sie. *Art Bull.*, 46:544–550.

Ross, J. B. (1974), The middle-class child in urban Italy, fourteenth to early sixteenth century. In: *The History of Childhood*, ed. L. de Maure. New York: Psychohistory Press, pp. 184–228.

Rothgeb, C. L., ed. (1971), *Abstracts of the Standard Edition of the Complete Psychological Works of Sigmund Freud.* Rockville, Md.: U. S. Department of Health, Education and Welfare, Public Health Service, Health Services and Mental Health Administration.

Sachs, H. (1942), *The Creative Unconscious.* Cambridge, Mass.: Science Art Press.

Sawyier, F. H. (1973), Commentary on *Freud and Philosophy*. *This Annual*, 1:216–231. New York:

Quadrangle/New York Times.

Servadio, E. (1951), An unknown statuette of Moses. *Internat. J. Psycho-Anal.*, 32:95–96.

Shengold, L. (1972), A parapraxis of Freud. *Amer. Imago.* 29:131–132.

Snoop, F. Z. (n. d.), *From the Monotremes to the Madonna: A Study of the Breast in Culture and Religion.* Chicago: Argus Books.

Spector, J. J. (1969), The method of Morelli and its relation to Freudian psychoanalysis. *Diogenes,* 66:63–83.

———— (1972), *The Aesthetics of Freud.* New York: Praeger.

Spiegel, J. & Machotka, P. (1974), *Messages of the Body.* New York and London: Free Press & Collier Macmillan.

Spitz, R. (1955), The primal cavity. *The Psychoanalytic Study of the Child,* 10:215–240. New York: International Universities Press.

Sterba, R. (1971), Discussion of L. Shengold's "A parapraxis of Freud's in relation to Karl Abraham." American Psychoanalytic Association, December 17.

———— & Sterba, E. (1956), The anxieties of Michelangelo Buonarroti. *Internat. J. Psycho-Anal.,* 37:1–6.

———— ———— (1978), The personality of Michelangelo Buonarroti: Some reflections. *Amer. Imago,* 35:158–177.

Stern, M. (1961), Blank hallucinations: Remarks about trauma and perceptual disturbances. *Internat. J. Psycho-Anal.,* 42:205–215.

Symonds, J. A. (1893), *The Life of Michelangelo Buonarroti,* ed. J. C. Nimmo. 2 vols. New York: Modern Library.

Times Literary Supplement (1973), Book review of *Michelangelo,* by Herbert von Einem. December 28, p. 1585.

Trexler, R. C. (1973–1974), Infanticide in Florence: New sources and first results. *Hist. Childhood Quart.,* 1:98–116.

———— (1973–1974), The foundlings of Florence 1395–1455. *Hist. Childhood Quart.,* 1:259–284.

Vasari, G. (1568), *Lives of the Most Eminent Painters, Sculptors and Architects,* trans. G. Duc DeVere. London: Warner, 1912–1915.

Veszy-Wagner, L. (1963), The bearded man. *Amer. Imago,* 20:133–147.

Watkins, J. A. (1951), Concerning Freud's paper on "The Moses of Michelangelo." *Amer. Imago,* 8:61–63.

Wilson, C. H. (1876), *Life and Works of Michelangelo Buonarroti. The Life Partly Compiled from that by the Commend. Aurelio Gotti.* London: John Murray.

Winnicott, D. W. (1953), Transitional objects and transitional phenomena. *Internat. J. Psycho-Anal.,* 34:89–97.

Wollheim, R. (1973), *On Art and the Mind.* London: Allen Lane.

Worbarsht, M. L. & Lichtenberg, J. D. (1961), Freud and the Moses of Michelangelo. *Amer. Imago,* 18:263–268.

Worringer, W. (1953), *Abstraction and Empathy.* London: Routledge & Kegan Paul.

July, 1978

Mourning and Its Effect on Michelangelo's Art

JEROME D. OREMLAND, M.D.   (San Francisco)

In a previous paper, I discussed the evolution of certain themes depicted in Michelangelo's *pietà* sculptures (Oremland, 1978). I conjectured that the striking curiosity in the first *pietà,* the *Pietà* in St. Peter's, of the mother's being the same age or even younger than the dead son, is, in fact, an important component of the statue's enormous evocative capacity (Fig. 1). I suggested that the statue is a dreamlike condensation pictorializing allegorical man at the end of life's travail returned to the young mother of his infancy — the eternal cycle of birth and death. The *Rondanini Pietà*, his last sculptured work, was seen as an artistic intensification of the first *pietà.* The paper asserted that Michelangelo's earliest portrayals of the *madonna*, characterized by the infant's struggling to return to the body of the mother, were the forerunners of the last sculptured work, which in a remarkably abstract manner depicts the fusion of the adult dead son into the body of the mother (Fig. 2).

Though the earlier paper, modeled after Freud's study of the *Moses* statue (1914), largely concerned itself with the study of the artistic depictions and their evocative power, biographical data concerning Michelangelo's early experience were central to the thesis. In short, I suggested that Michelangelo's *pietàs* and *madonnas* reflected the fact that Michelangelo was taken from his ill mother shortly after birth, sent to live with a wet nurse, and returned to his mother shortly after being weaned — a very early loss. Furthermore, he was to suffer a second, more profound loss, the death of his chronically ill, often pregnant mother, when he was six.

The present paper is an attempt to refine this hypothesis. The emphasis shifts to a study of the central importance that aborted and distorted mourning of the mother(s)[1] may have played in Michelangelo's *madonna* and *pietà* sculptures and drawings.

---

[1] Throughout the paper I utilize the term mother(s) to indicate my supposition that the two losses were condensed into one. Of course, it is impossible to know which is of greater importance, the loss of the initial nursing "mother" or the death of the mother. My inclination is to place greater significance on the loss of the initial nursing "mother" which was subsequently organized, intensified, and screened by the death of the true mother, Francesca.

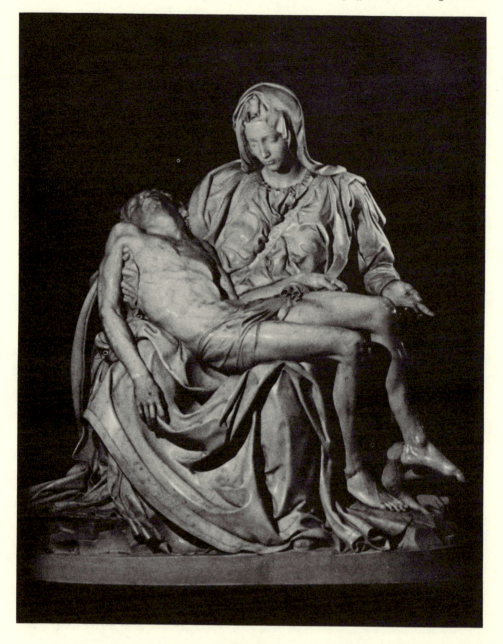

FIGURE 1

St. Peter's Pietà, St. Peter's, Rome. (Reprinted with the kind permission of R.F.S.P., Vaticano.)

FIGURE 2

Rondanini Pietà (side view), Castello Sforzesco, Milan. (Reproduced with the permission of Archivio Fotografico, Castello Sforzesco.)

Loss and Creativity

Ever since the publication of *Mourning and Melancholia* (Freud, 1917), the importance of object loss and the subsequent mourning restitution has been recognized
as one of the most productive areas of study of the relation of experience to personality development and the formation of pathological structures. Of special interest has been the study of the mourning process of the immature ego—that is,
the study of early loss (Barnes, 1964; Bowlby, 1960; Furman, 1964; Gauthier,
1965; Laufer, 1966; Wolfenstein, 1966; Shambaugh, 1961).

Though the subject is complex, it seems clear that the resolution of mourning
with its eventual identification with and integration of the lost object depends on
the age of the survivor and the circumstances of the loss. Early loss alters greatly
the important progressions which in full mourning result in the systematic
decathexis of the lost object with gradual and integrated superego and ego identifications which enhance and augment the mourner's personality. Simply stated,
with early loss the child maintains to varying degrees an introjected and
unintegrated concept of the lost object (Bowlby, 1960; Furman, 1964; Wolfenstein, 1966). This aborted mourning may be related to various disturbances in
personality structuring, often with symptom formation and/or persistent behaviors such as perpetually searching for the lost object. At times, the aborted
mourning may be resumed to varying degrees in adolescence or adulthood with
some subsequent resolution.

Another area of special interest has been the relation of mourning to creativity.
Studies by Pollock (1975, 1977) and others (Hamilton, 1969; Robbins, 1969;
Weissman, 1971) have indicated the importance of the loss of loved objects in
determining themes for creative works. The thesis advanced is that creative people may use their creative productivity as part of the mourning process. The
creativity provides a kind of "working through" of the loss akin to the stepwise
progressive process in mourning. Though it is tempting to say that the mourning
produced creativity, it is more accurate to say that creative people can at times
utilize their creativity in the service of mourning. In this sense mourning provides the ordinary person in the face of loss with an opportunity to enhance and
enrich himself; whereas mourning provides the creative person in the face of loss
with the opportunity to enhance and enrich the world.

In an interesting discussion of the relation of mysticism to creativity Lubin
(1976) makes an additional point. He notes that though the creative process may
be akin to mourning, it is different in that the result is external to the creator's
personality. Because of the external rather than the internal result, there is less
potential for intrapsychic resolution of the loss via creativity than in mourning.
Lubin suggests that this may be a factor in explaining the ongoing nature of
creativity in truly creative people. His investigations point to at least two
different kinds of relations of mourning to creativity. In one, the creative person

suffers a loss which results in the production of a specific creative product — a particular piece of work as a particular resolution. In the other, the process is ongoing and without resolution, and it manifests itself in stylistic characteristics and/or ongoing themes. In general, it is tempting with creative people to link the former to late losses and the latter to earlier losses.

Traditionally, the studies of the relation of mourning to creativity have utilized biographical events which are chronologically related to subsequent work. At times, one can find letters or other documents to substantiate the thesis that the particular work was related to the particular loss. Sometimes the creative person labels his work in such a way as to suggest — sometimes establish — the linkage. In some specific circumstances, the work is an anticipation of the death of the creative person, in effect, the mourning of the impending loss of the self (Pollock, 1975, 1977).

Attempts to make correlations between biographical events and subsequent creative work are fraught with difficulties and must be viewed cautiously, particularly when the creative person lived a long time ago. Old documents, with their translation problems, changes in the meaning of words, styles of expression, and artistic influences and conventions, pose many problems. These difficulties and the limitations in establishing facts and in interpreting them have been extensively documented in Schapiro's (1956) criticism of Freud's (1910) Leonardo monograph and Eissler's (1961) responses.

All of these factors prevail when it comes to studying Michelangelo, and what is more they are complicated by the fact that he lived a very long and remarkably productive life. Because of his extensive *oeuvre*, it is possible to propose almost any thesis and develop evidence for it by selecting those elements which substantiate the proposition advanced.

I attempt to obviate this difficulty by restricting my study to Michelangelo's depictions of the Holy Mother and Child through the years, beginning with the *Madonna of the Stairs* (Fig. 3), sculpted when he was 15, and ending with his last work, the *Rondanini Pietà*, unfinished when he died at 89. Even though I select but one sector of his monumental productivity, I suggest that for Michelangelo the relationship of the Holy Mother and Child was an especially important artistic preoccupation, particularly in his later life. It is striking that this theme was dealt with not only in his last sculptural work, the *Rondanini Pietà*, but also in his last known drawing, *Standing Virgin with the Child* (ca. 1560) (Fig. 4).

Michelangelo's Early Losses

We have a remarkable amount of correlating biographical data about Michel-

FIGURE 3

The Madonna of the Stairs, Casa Buonarroti, Florence. (Reproduced with the permission of Alinari.)

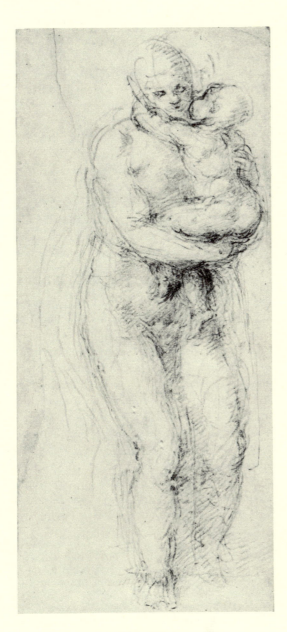

FIGURE 4

Standing Virgin with the Child, the British Museum. (Reproduced by Courtesy of the Trustees of the British Museum.)

angelo, considering that he was not of high nobility. There are the accounts of two students and fellow artists. Vasari's first biography was written during Michelangelo's life and modified (1568) after his death, and there is the semi-autobiographical account developed by Condivi (1553).

In addition, we have a large number of letters written to friends, relatives, and patrons and, most important, a good deal of poetry, chronologically sorted by Girardi (1960) and beautifully integrated and interpreted by Clements (1966). Further, we have major studies of these records in English (Hibbard, 1974; Symonds, 1892; De Tolnay, 1975).

My thesis is that early loss of the mother(s) had a profound influence on Michelangelo's artistic depiction of the mother-child interaction and that the relationships with, and especially the deaths later in his life of, the revered and loved Cecchino, Vittoria Colonna, and Urbino reactivated the heretofore aborted mourning process. In this regard, the relationship with Vittoria Colonna was of pivotal importance, and his mourning of her death manifested itself in significant changes in Michelangelo's artistic depictions of the Holy Mother and Child.

Michelangelo was the second of five children. As mentioned before, it is generally agreed that shortly after his birth, Michelangelo was taken from his sick mother and given to the daughter and wife of stonecutters in Settignano, a village near Florence where the family held property. Though it is uncertain at what age he was returned to his family, in default of evidence I theorize an early return, perhaps shortly after weaning. This seems likely in that it is known that his favorite brother, Buonarroto, was born two years after him. His birth suggests that the mother had probably recovered enough to care for Michelangelo by the time he was one and a half since it was then that she became pregnant with Buonarroto. Two other babies followed shortly thereafter. I suggest that Michelangelo was returned to his home to be reared by his mother when he was weaned — an early loss (the nursing "mother") — and that he was to suffer a second significant early loss when his chronically ill and frequently pregnant mother died when he was six.[2] Returned early or late, psychodynamically Michelangelo in effect had two mothers, the nursing mother and the real mother, and suffered two early significant losses.

[2] This reconstruction is somewhat supported by Ross's (1974) review of the early childhood rearing practices in urban Tuscany during the Renaissance. He indicates that the common practice was to place the newborn with a wet nurse (*balia*) outside of the home until weaning at one and a half to two years, at which time the infant was returned.

However, it most be noted that De Tolnay (1969), admittedly without evidence, proposed that Michelangelo was returned at age ten, possibly after his father's second marriage. This would mean that Michelangelo alone of the five boys spent his entire childhood in a foster home. It seems unlikely that if he alone of the five was so treated, this would not have been specifically mentioned; nonetheless, most psychoanalytical writers utilize this late-return hypothesis (Frank, 1966; Liebert, 1977a, 1977b; and Sterba and Sterba, 1956).

The *Madonnas* and the *Pietàs*

From the outset of his artistic career, we find evidence that Michelangelo was struggling with the issue of early maternal loss. De Tolnay (1969) commented that there is a distinctive quality to Michelangelo's *madonna* portrayals. He notes that the infants are characteristically centrally placed on the body of the mother. Referring to the *Madonna of Bruges* (Fig. 5) he noted, "because of this exceptional positioning, the Child still seems to be contained within the protective womb" (p. 16). This is clearly evident in the *Madonna of the Stairs* (ca. 1480), *Medici Madonna* (ca. 1520) (Fig. 6), and the beautiful black and red cartoon of a *Madonna* (ca. 1520) (Fig. 7). I would add to De Tolnay's important observation additional characteristic qualities: the distant gaze of the mother, the Herculean quality of the infant, and the infant's frequent burrowing, grasping, and/or holding-onto tendency. Even in the early, highly romantic *Doni Madonna* (ca. 1503) the mother seems to be tossing the infant away while the infant links himself to her by holding onto her hair (Fig. 8).

I suggest that the depiction of the muscular infant's turning to, grasping for, burrowing into, being a part of, and literally finding the mother is a defensive reversal. Rather than passively experiencing being left as Michelangelo was, the baby strives to regain. The infant's active striving for contact, symbolized by the detailed muscularity, gives the depictions a uniquely dynamic quality remarkably different from the serene, rounded, passively-attended-to concept of the infant so characteristic of most *madonna* and child portrayals. Perhaps, as a reflection of a continuing attempt to master his early experience, Michelangelo pictorializes an aspect of human development seldom portrayed—*the intensity inherent in the infant's seeking object relatedness*. The evocative capacity is enormous, for in it we re-experience primal feelings, the infant's struggling attempt to make contact with the distant, preoccupied mother, a kind of loss known at times to us all.

I suggested that the theme of the unmourned mother(s), the maintained introjected imagery of the young, never-aging mother, is a biographic explanation for the depiction of the inordinate youthfulness of the mother in the first *pietà* (Oremland, 1978).[3] Michelangelo provides us with a son at the end of life (approximately the age of Michelangelo himself when he sculpted him) held by a *madonna*-like mother, the mother(s) he lost in early childhood. The theme of the *pietà*, the adult at the end of life returned to the mother, was not to reappear in Michelangelo's work until his late sixties, during his relationship with Vittoria Colonna, and it was strikingly to reach great eminence following her death.

---

[3] I suggested a parallel between this hypothesis and Freud's (1910) hypothesis regarding the age-sameness of St. Anne and Mary in Leonardo's *St. Anne and Two Others* in the Louvre. This painting apparently had special significance to Michelangelo, for one of his *madonna* sketches (ca. 1501) is clearly based on it and utilizes the same iconographic representation; in *Madonna with St. Anne* the bodies of the two mothers are fused.

FIGURE 5

Madonna of Bruges, Church of the Notre Dame, Bruges. (Reproduced with the kind permission of Canon V. Laridon, Church of the Notre Dame.)

FIGURE 6

Medici Madonna, Medici Chapel, Florence. (Reproduced with the permission of Alinari.)

FIGURE 7

Cartoon of a *madonna*, Casa Buonarroti, Florence. (Reproduced with the permission of Alinari.)

FIGURE 8

Doni Madonna, Uffizi, Florence. (Reproduced with the permission of Alinari.)

Late Loves and Late Losses

It is generally acknowledged that the people Michelangelo loved were Urbino, Febo di Poggio, Tommaso Cavalieri, Vittoria Colonna, and Cecchino. Of these, the most important were the latter four, all of whom came into his life in his sixth decade, and all of whom, except Tommaso, he was to lose through death. Of these, the relationships with Urbino and Vittoria Colonna were clearly asexual and truly characterized by mutual devotion.

HOMOSEXUAL THEMES

A great deal has been written, and even more has been unwritten, about Michelangelo's homosexuality (Clements, 1966). It seems clear to the psycho-analytically trained that there is ample evidence in the letters, the artistic depictions, and the poems that Michelangelo had intense sexual feelings toward and sexual relations with young men. In a poem to Tommaso Cavalieri, Michelangelo wrote:

> What from thee I long for and learn to
>   know deep within me
> Cannot be well understood by outward
>   acts and signs.
>   [Clements, 1966, p. 207]*[4]

When studied in conjunction with the sculptured works, drawings, and letters, the poetry suggests that these relationships were characterized by adoration of and subjugation to the young man. The intensity of the desire to possess with its oral-incorporative component is graphically portrayed in the *Ganymede* drawing (ca. 1532) done presumably for Tommaso Cavalieri. The subjugation is poetical-ly expressed in two sonnets written in the early 1530s for Tommaso Cavalieri.

> If capture and defeat must be my job,
> It is no wonder that, alone and naked,
> I remain prisoner of a knight-at-arms.[5]
>   [Linscott, 1963, p. 71]

> With thee, my groveling thoughts I
>   heavenward raise.
> Borne upward by thy bold, aspiring wing:
> I follow where thou wilt—a helpless thing.
> Cold in the sun and warm in winter days.
> My will, my friend, rests only upon thine;

---

[4] Poems from *The Poetry of Michelangelo* by Robert J. Clements, Copyright © 1965 by Robert J. Clements. Published by New York University Press. Those poems that are original translations by Professor Clements are marked with an asterisk (*).

[5] "Knight-at-arms" is a pun on the name *Cavalieri*.

Thy heart must every thought of mine supply:
My mind expression finds in thee alone.
Thus like the moonlight's silver ray I
    shine.
We only see her beams on the far sky.
When the sun's fiery rays are o'er her
    thrown.
                            [Clements, 1966, p. 187]

In 1540 he wrote:

Therefore because I cannot shun the blow
I rather seek, say who must rule my breast,
Gliding between his gladness and his woe?
    If only chains and bands can make me blest,
No marvel if alone and bare I go
An armed Cavalieri's captive and slave confessed.
                            [Clements, 1966, p. 110]

The subjugation motive is nearly actualized in *Victory* (Fig. 9) in which the kneeling victim is seen by many as a self-portrait (Clements, 1968).

The intensity with fusion overtones of his desire to possess and be possessed is clearly articulated in *The Two Dialogues* published by Donato Giannotti in 1540. "Whenever I see some one who possesses some virtue, who shows some quickness of genius, who can do more, say something more fittingly than others, I am constrained to fall in love with him, and I give myself to him as booty, for I am no longer my own, but all his. . . I . . . [am] quite diminished and lost: for many days after I should not know in which world I was" (Clements, 1968, p. 152).

The relationship with the handsome, young Tommaso Cavalieri began in 1532 and that with the beautiful adolescent, Cecchino Bracchi, probably around 1541. Both were extraordinary relationships in which an old man adored the handsome perfection of young men. The letters and the poems seem to document the fact that Cecchino was the lover of many men, including his uncle, Riccio, and Michelangelo (Clements, 1968). It is less clear whether Michelangelo's relationship with Tommaso Cavalieri was sexually consummated.

Michelangelo's worship of Cecchino in all of its manifestations dominates the 51 poems written at the insistence of Riccio at the time of the boy's death in 1544. There is reason to believe that Michelangelo revealed himself beyond the dictates of discretion, probably in response to Riccio's pressure and partly through the intensity of grief.

Do yet attest for him how gracious I was in bed
When he embraced, and in what the soul doth live.
                            [Clements, 1966, p. 147]*

It tends to go unrecognized that Cecchino was a nickname, the diminutive of Francesco, the masculine form of Francesca, Michelangelo's mother's name. I suggest that as the masculine bearer of his mother's name, Cecchino represented

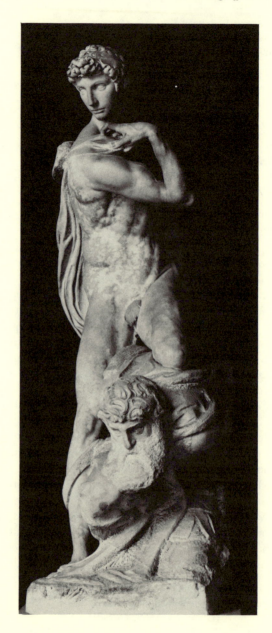

FIGURE 9

Victory, Palazzo Vecchio, Florence. (Reproduced with the permission of Alinari.)

at once the young mother with whom Michelangelo was attempting to reunite and the young, beautiful boy he adored as he wished his mother had adored him.[6] Cecchino's death in 1544, tragically premature, allowed the idealization to continue and further linked him with the lost young mother.

In the funereal poems, we see complicated metaphorical descriptions of an introjected type of identification.

> I was born Bracci; after the first wail
> My eyes saw sunlight only a short space.
> I am here forever, nor would wish it less,
> In him who loved me greatly living still.
> [Linscott, 1963, p. 122]

Here we see a remarkable poetical description of the lost loved object—"alive" as it were, within the survivor. The lost Cecchino (little Francesco) with his symbolic psychological ties to the lost early mother(s) is internalized and being mourned. In the poem we can see, perhaps, progressions toward the integrated internalization of the lost love object which characterized the poems following Vittoria Colonna's death three years later.

How very different this is from earlier poems dealing with loss in which there was a characteristic subjugation-to-the-object response as in the following:

> About here it was that my love, with his usual mercy,
> Took my heart and what is more, my life;
> Here with his beautiful eyes he promised me solace
> And with those very eyes he chose to deny me
> There beyond he bound me, here he loosed me,
> I wept for myself, and with infinite grief,
> From this rock I saw him take leave
> Who took me from myself and then wished me not.
> [Clements, 1966, p. 194]*

VITTORIA COLONNA

De Tolnay (1953, 1971) has carefully presented the profound influence that Vittoria Colonna had on Michelangelo's religious reawakening and the way in which this was manifested in his art. As part of an important Reformation movement, she advocated the direct giving of oneself to God with salvation being achieved through faith alone. This mystical surrender was symbolized by Christ on the Cross—the Crucifixion.

---

[6] Clements (1966) and Sterba and Sterba (1956) have independently pointed to Michelangelo's identification with Cecchino. Both noted that in the mourning poetry, Michelangelo adds the particle *de* to Cecchino's last name, Bracci. They note that having a noble lineage was very important to Michelangelo, and in their view his elevating Cecchino to nobility is evidence of his idealizing and identifying with him. I would add that it was his doing for Cecchino what he wished had been done for him.

Vittoria Colonna's emphasis on the elimination of mediators seems paradoxical because through her instructions she in fact became the mediator. Through a woman Michelangelo finds a way toward acceptance (grace) and eternal life (salvation). I suggest that her persuasive emphasis on acceptance initiated a change in the nature of Michelangelo's relationships which is evidenced in his poetry and his art.

As we have seen, prior to her, his love poetry was dominated by the desire to submit to and fuse with an idealized yet identical (homosexual) object, i.e., Febo or Tommaso.

> It was not necessary to thy dear beauty
> To find me vanquished with any cord;
> For, if I remember well,
> By but a single look was I made prisoner and prey.
>   [Clements, 1966, p. 117]*

His poetry to her became strikingly different — admiring, tender, and at times, loving.

> Madrigal to Vittoria Colonna
>   (ca. 1538)
> While still I shun and hate myself and the more,
> The more, Lady, with proper hope I call
> On you; in me the soul
> Is less afraid, as I to you draw near.
> In your face I aspire
> To what I am pledged from Heaven,
> And in your beautiful eyes, full of all safety.
> And often I see clear,
> At all the others gazing,
> Eyes without heart possess no potency.
> Lights that I never see,
> Nor shall see, and my wish is more than that,
> For rarely seen is neighbor to forget.
>   [Linscott, 1963, p. 107]

Or the beautiful:

> Thus I to both us twain long life can give,
> In paint or marble, as my wish may be
> The semblance of thy face and mine to show.
> A thousand years hence after we have lived,
> How fair thou wert, and I how sad, they'll see;
> And that I was no fool to love thee so.
>   [Clements, 1966, p. 72]

But what is more central to my thesis is that during the period of intense relationship with Vittoria Colonna there was a marked reworking of mother-infant and mother-child themes. Presumably for her, he created three extraordinary drawings: *Crucifixion* (ca. 1539) (Fig. 10); *Madonna del Silenzio* (ca. 1540) (Fig. 11); and *Pietà* (ca. 1546) (Fig. 12).

There is another comparison to be made: the mystical poetry emphasizes the relationship with Christ or God with a striking absence of reference to the Virgin Mary, whereas the drawings and sculptures on the theme of that period frequently are various depictions of the Virgin Mary in relation to Jesus. To me this suggests that on the verbal level, Michelangelo conceptualized an abstract God as that with which he seeks unity; on the more primitive, visual-image level, we see the more fundamental meaning—longing for the mother.

The *Crucifixion* is of special interest for he chose to depict the moment of loss of faith, the looking upward and the calling out in despair immediately preceding death. Like the infant in his *madonnas,* the adult Jesus is turning toward and attempting to gain contact. It is, indeed, tempting to see it as Michelangelo's crying out for contact—but with whom?

Perhaps the answer is in the *Pietà* drawing, the first *Pietà* of the later period, executed shortly before Vittoria Colonna's death in 1547. In the drawing, the cross is replaced by the body of the mother, and the son is pressed up against her lower abdomen as in the *Madonna of Bruges* and the *Medici Madonna.* Here we see the forefunner of the wish for fusion with the mother and its ultimate expression in the *Rondanini Pietà.*

The *Madonna del Silenzio* executed between the two drawings clearly unites *madonna* and p*ietà.* The infant's oversized body is positioned similarly to the *St. Peter's Pietà* in a deathlike pose with his arm hanging lifeless as in the *Florentine Pietà* and strikingly reminiscent of the infant's arm in the *Madonna of the Stairs.* Two side figures—a coifed man and a woman in disguise—are shown in a ghostly manner. Here we see the reawakened image of the two mothers. The man is to become the Nicodemus-Michelangelo of the *Florentine Pietà* watching with us from above; and the woman, the second Mary. The hourglass to the lower left reminds us that time has run out. Although this is a *madonna,* it also is a *pietà.*

These drawings, I suggest, reflect an important shift in Michelangelo's concept of mother. In them we can see Vittoria Colonna's doctrine of the absence of mediators being translated into ontogenetic terms. Grace and salvation become oneness with mother. Rather than depicting return to the unintegrated introject of his early childhood, the *madonna*-mother of the *St. Peter's Pietà,* Michelangelo begins his struggle to depict wished-for fusion with the mother.

It is of interest that there seems to be a reciprocal relation between Michelangelo's poetry and his plastic productions (Clements, 1968). To some extent, his poetic development began ca. 1531, a time, I propose, of great change in the nature of his relationships, following which there was a relative decrease in his

FIGURE 10

Crucifixion, The British Museum. (Reproduced by Courtesy of the Trustees of the British Museum.)

FIGURE 11

Madonna del Silenzio, National Gallery, London. (Reproduced with the kind permission of The Lady Anne Bentinck, daughter of The Duke of Portland.)

FIGURE 12

Pietà, Isabella Stewart Gardner Museum, Boston. (Reproduced with the permission of the Isabella Stewart Gardner Museum, Boston.)

plastic productions. I am tempted to conjecture that his beginning to "play with" words (poetry) as opposed to visual images (sculpture and painting) reflected an increasing desire to reach out for contact with objects in a more differentiated sense.

> O lady, who through fire
> And water leadest souls to joys eterne,
> Let me no more unto myself return.
>   [Clements, 1966, p. 198]*

Vittoria Colonna's Death

Vittoria Colonna's death in 1547 had a profound influence on Michelangelo. For the first and only time in his letters we hear about his love for a woman. It is particularly touching to read Condivi's (1553) account "and he in return bore her so much love that I remember hearing him say that his only regret was that, when he went to see her as she was departing this life, he did not kiss her forehead or her face as he kissed her hand" (p. 102).

This face-to-face touching wish, so typical of early and spontaneous love between infant and mother, now appears in Michelangelo's portrayal of the Holy Mother and Child for the first time. It becomes a conspicuous part of the adult son-to-mother depiction in the *Florentine Pietà* (Fig. 13), and it is intensified in the *Rondanini Pietà* (Fig. 2).[7] In the Windsor drawing, *Virgin and Child* (Fig. 14), ca. 1555, it is overtly expressed in a tender kiss. The Windsor drawing and Michelangelo's last extant drawing, the *Standing Virgin with the Child* (Fig. 5), ca. 1560, a highly mobile sketch of exceptional closeness and intimacy between mother and infant, contrast markedly with the first *madonna*, the *Madonna of the Stairs*, and all the subsequent *madonna*-infant portrayals — drawings and sculptures alike. This is, to my mind, compelling evidence of how much change had taken place in his concept of mother and child. She no longer is distant and preoccupied; he no longer grasps with intensified muscularity. It is no longer all infant *to* mother. There is intimacy and reciprocity.

Following Vittoria Colonna's death there is documented evidence that Michelangelo suffered severe depression of near-psychotic proportions (Condivi, 1553). The poetry mourning her loss is poignantly beautiful and extends over a number of years. The poems become increasingly mystical. Under her influence, he seeks union with an abstract God to achieve acceptance (grace) and eternal life (salvation). He finds through her the primal mother.

> Rapt above earth by power of one fair face,
> Hers in whose sway alone my heart delights.

---

[7] Peto (1978) carried this point one step further. He notes that the Jesus in the *Rondanini Pietà* is bearded. He suggests that the *Rondanini* Jesus is a self-portrait, giving further weight to the idea that the statue expresses Michelangelo's wish for union with his mother.

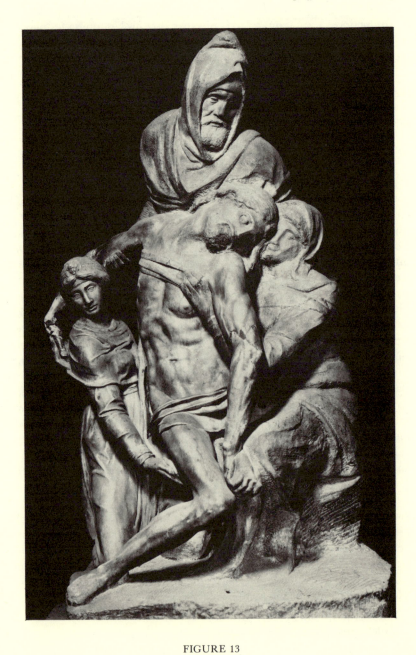

FIGURE 13

Florentine Pietà, Cathedral of Florence. (Reproduced with the permission of Alinari.)

FIGURE 14

Virgin and Child, Windsor Castle. (Reproduced by gracious permission of H. M. the Queen.)

I mingle with the blest on those pure heights
Where man, yet mortal, rarely finds a place.
With Him who made the Work that Work accords
So well, that by its help and through His grace
I raise my thoughts, inform my deeds and words,
Clasping her beauty in my soul's embrace.
Thus, if from two fair eyes mine cannot turn,
I feel how in their presence doth abide
Light which to God is both the way and guide:
And kindling at their luster, if I burn,
My noble fire emits the joyful ray
That through the realms of glory shines for aye.
[Clements, 1966, p. 200]

and

Sonnet (ca. 1555)
Foolish and blind, while others can perceive,
My own mistake tardily understood,
Hope growing less, desire is magnified
That you will loosen me from my self-love.

Cut down by half the road, O my dear Lord,
That climbs to Heaven! You will have to aid me
If I am going to climb even that half.

Cause me to hate the value of the world
And what I admired and honored in its beauty,
So before death to taste eternal life.
[Linscott, 1963, pp. 160–161]

The mourning for Vittoria Colonna is not without ambivalence, for there are three curious drawings accompanying a particularly touching poem lamenting her loss. In these, Michelangelo draws himself devoured within a boar, an obscene sexual gesture, and most important, he presents a distorted portrait of a woman, usually considered Vittoria Colonna, ugly in face with spent, sagging, lumpy breasts, ca. 1547 (Clements, 1966) (Fig. 15). I suggest that this expression of ambivalence at the time of her death further establishes her relationship to the earlier and more profoundly disturbing losses, the mother(s) of his infancy. Intensely filled with longing and antagonism, he directly expresses the linkage by caricaturing Vittoria Colonna's breasts.[8]

---

[8] It is of relevance to this thesis that the only direct reference in correspondence or poetry to any aspect of his mother(s) is the often quoted statement to Vasari in which Michelangelo acknowledged the importance of being nursed by the wet nurse. "If I possess anything of good in my mental constitution, it comes from my having been born in your clear climate of Arezzo; . . . I drew the chisel and the mallet with which I carve statues in together with my nurse's milk" (quoted in Symonds, 1892, p. 6).

FIGURE 15

Sketch of Michelangelo coiffed in a boar's head, Vittoria Colonna with sagging breasts, and vulgar gesture, Biblioteca Medicea Laurenziana. (Reproduced with the kind permission of C. De Tolnay, Director, Casa Buonarroti. Photographed by Dr. G. Pineider.)

Following her death, Michelangelo is to think about death in a new way. Although he has been preoccupied with his death since his mid-forties, he now begins to plan for his tomb. The Oxford Sketches (ca. 1550) (Fig. 16) are of particular importance in understanding this period for they are widely regarded as preliminary to the *Rondanini Pietà*. In the sketches we see a remarkable progression. The initial sketches, done perhaps as early as 1547 (De Tolnay, 1934), are of an Entombment: two men (presumable Joseph of Arimathea and Nicodemus) are carrying the dead Jesus to his tomb. Around 1549, the theme changes to a Lamentation depicted in its most intensified form—the mother mourning the dead son. The Lamentation sketches show considerable revision with increasing closeness between the son and the mother. They suggest a shift from the narcissistic-homosexual position (he with idealized but identical versions of himself) to the higher level dyadic mother-son relationship, and prefigure the *Windsor* and *Standing Virgin with the Child* drawings.

Vasari (1568) reports that Michelangelo began sculpting this dyadic depiction, ca. 1552, but apparently put it aside to work on the four-figure *Florentine Pietà* (Fig. 13). As this was progressing, he suffered another important loss, the death of his faithful servant Urbino in 1555.

Urbino, by far the most important and cherished of Michelangelo's assistants, came to work for Michelangelo in 1530 when he was fifteen. He was considered a *creato*, which implies that he was adopted as a protégé, even though he was of limited talent. He also became servant, companion, and nurse. After Urbino married, one of his children was Michelangelo's namesake and godchild, and on his death Michelangelo became guardian to them all. There are many letters and poems attesting to the depth of Michelangelo's love for and devotion to this man.

> Wherein I evermore with thee do stay
> And of my dead Urbino speak and weep,
> Who living would be with me by thy side,
> As once I thought: his death another way
> Doth draw me now, where he his watch doth keep,
> Till coming thither I with him abide.
> [Clements, 1966, p. 257]

Perhaps this interesting relationship takes on a different emphasis when we realize that Urbino's name was Francesco. He was called Urbino as a nickname because of the town he was from. Like the beloved Cecchino, Urbino was the male name carrier of Michelangelo's mother, Francesca.

I would place great emphasis on the importance of Urbino's "adoption" in understanding a fundamental shift in the nature of Michelangelo's relationships. It does seem significant that all of the intense relationships of Michelangelo that have been documented followed Urbino's coming into Michelangelo's life in 1530: Febo di Poggio entered his life in 1532; Tommaso Cavalieri in 1532; Vit-

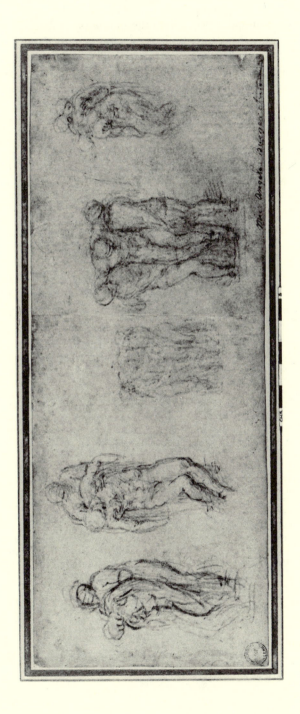

FIGURE 16

Oxford sketches for *pietà* and entombment, Ashmolean Museum, Oxford. (Reproduced with the permission of the Ashmolean Museum, Oxford. Reading left to right, the third and fourth sketches were earlier sketches for an entombment depiction; according to De Tolnay [1934], the first sketch was the last of the group, the second was the first, and the fifth was the second.)

toria Colonna in 1537; and Cecchino in 1541.[9]

Urbino was of crucial importance, for as the mother(s) in disguise, his adoption changes the passive to the active. He was the mother gained (adopted) rather than lost. He was to nurse Michelangelo and, ironically, to be nursed by Michelangelo. At some deeper level, perhaps, he was Michelangelo adopted as the nursing mother had adopted him. He, like Cecchino (little Francesco), was both the mother regained and the boy treated as he wished he had been treated by the mother. I would suggest that the "adoption" of Urbino was the beginning of the reactivation of the mourning process for the lost mother(s) and that the subsequent relationships in various ways participated in it.[10]

During the time the *Florentine Pietà* took shape, Urbino became ill. Though he was scarcely 40, it was clear that he was going to die, and it is reported that Urbino repeatedly implored Michelangelo to finish the statue before he, Urbino, died. There is considerable evidence that it was in a fit of rage at the dying, nagging Urbino that Michelangelo smashed the statue (Liebert, 1977a).

The smashing of the *Florentine Pietà* is one of many interesting psychological mysteries surrounding Michelangelo and one about which there has been considerable psychoanalytic speculation (Liebert, 1977a; Steinberg, 1968; Sterba and Sterba, 1956). Liebert in particular emphasized the psychological role of Urbino in the incident. He hypothesized that Urbino's insistence that Michelangelo finish the statue before he, Urbino, died provided Michelangelo with a magical way of controlling Urbino's death. Michelangelo's destruction of the statue was a magical attempt to keep Urbino alive. Though I agree with Liebert's emphasis on the

[9] Of Michelangelo's four relationships of profound significance we can thus consider that three were with "females": one with a loving, spiritual (safe) woman, and two with Francescas in disguise; in short, all were "mothers." The relationship with the handsome nobleman, Tommaso Cavalieri, is different from the others. Although adored and loved, he represented no symbolic tie to the mother. His perfection and acknowledged nobility (protections against being abandoned?) probably represented Michelangelo as he wished he were. More important, he never participated in any aspect of the mourning process, for he was the only one to survive Michelangelo and remained a good, loyal friend to the end.

[10] However, it should be noted that in 1531 Michelangelo's father, Lodovico, died in his late eighties. It is usually noted that Michelangelo was devoted to his father since there are several poems (not many when compared with those mentioning Vittoria Colonna or Cecchino) mourning Lodovico's death with considerable profundity of feeling. This raises the question of the significance of the father in the progression I am suggesting.

The lifelong correspondence does not bear out the contention that Michelangelo was close to or respected Lodovico, although he probably feared him as a boy. What is clear from the correspondence is that Michelangelo became the head of the family at an early age, probably around age nineteen, when the oldest brother, Lionardo, became a monk. In fact, in the correspondence, Michelangelo usually addressed Lodovico by his first name.

The correspondence suggests that the relationship with his father was marked by disappointment because of the father's lack of achievement and heavy reliance on Michelangelo for advice and even more for financial help. Clearly, Michelangelo early became the father (and in some ways, mother) to his father and his brothers. From a psychoanalytic perspective, he seems to have been a boy who lost his mother and who ambivalently bolstered a disappointing though punitive father, eventually becoming both mother and father to his family.

role of Urbino in the strange fate of the *Florentine Pietà*, I would offer a different conjecture regarding its destruction based on an interpretation of the statue itself. I propose that it represented the nadir in his changing relation to death. It was attacked and abandoned because of its meaning as a portrayal of the finality of death. Michelangelo's final years were to be spent attempting to depict monumental changes occurring within him.

The Final Mourning Phase and the Final *Pietàs*

In my previous paper, I emphasized the importance of the *Florentine Pietà* in the stepwise artistic progression from Michelangelo's portrayals of reunion (*St. Peter's Pietà*) to those of fusion with mother (*Rondanini Pietà*). I now suggest that this progression reflects a changing concept of mother as part of the mourning process initiated by Urbino's adoption, intensified by the relationship with Vittoria Colonna, and culminating in their deaths.

Following Vittoria Colonna's death, Michelangelo became deeply depressed and began planning for his tomb. At first, he envisioned two men (narcissistic objects) carrying the naked body to its garden sepulcher, the Entombment theme of the earliest Oxford Sketches. Under the impact of the continued mourning of Vittoria Colonna, he abandoned this theme for a *madonna*-son (dyadic) portrayal. The revisions of the sketches indicate his increasing desire for closeness with the body of the mother, a desire first given expression in the earlier *Pietà* drawing for Vittoria Colonna.

He began the dyadic *pietà*, but abandoned it to work on the four-figure *Florentine Pietà*. As noted before, it became a literal biographical portrayal of his two mothers with the coifed Michelangelo-Nicodemus figure seeming to move the son from one to the other. Their tenderly touching faces are a marked change in *madonna*-son portrayal. Now Michelangelo strikingly reflects the expressed wish toward Vittoria Colonna after her death, which is to be lovingly depicted in the *Windsor* and the *Standing Virgin with the Child* drawings and intensified in the *Rondanini Pietà*.

During the same period, 1550–1560, his poetry also changed in content and in form. There is a marked shift from fearing the Christ of *iracundia* (the wrathful Christ) to seeking the Christ of *caritas* (the Christ of charity). This seeking became markedly mystical with expressions of transcendence and oneness—perhaps reflecting an identification with Vittoria Colonna, the poetic form became that of hers; his effusive, elusive content is constrained in the rigid form of the sonnet (Clements, 1966).

The Nicodemus-Michelangelo

Vasari (1568) referred to the coifed figure in the *Florentine Pietà* as Nicodemus, which suggests that Michelangelo had so designated it. One cannot help speculating why Michelangelo called it Nicodemus when the most important male at the Crucifixion other than Jesus is Joseph of Arimathea.

By portraying Nicodemus, Michelangelo clearly links this Lamentation to the Gospel of John, for it is only in John that Nicodemus is mentioned as a mourner. This is significant, for the presence of the Virgin Mary at the Crucifixion is also only in John. Further, it is John who most fully elaborates the Resurrection. By labeling the figure Nicodemus, Michelangelo has marked this Lamentation as being the most mystical. From a psychoanalytic perspective, it, like the first *pietà* with its emphasis on the return of the son to the mother, is ontogenetically primitive. Is there a further significance to the Nicodemus?

Nicodemus figures in the life of Jesus prior to the Crucifixion. In John, 3:1-20, he enters into a fascinating dialogue with Jesus in which the aged Nicodemus asks, "How can a man be born when he is old: Can he enter the second time into his mother's womb, and be born?" Jesus answered cryptically, "That which is born of the flesh, is flesh; and that which is born of the spirit, is spirit. . . Whosoever believeth in Him [the Son of Man], should not perish, but have eternal life."

Thus, in the *Florentine Pietà* Michelangelo, by portraying himself as Nicodemus, is asking curiously literal questions regarding eternal life: "Can he enter the second time into his mother's womb and be born?" At the very end of his life, Michelangelo, fearful of death like the aged Nicodemus, seeks hope in the primal relationship of death to birth. As he wrote earlier:

> I believe that nature takes back unto itself
> All that which day by day disappears from thee,
> That it may serve *for the birth from a greater womb*
> With a better fate and with more extreme care
> *To form anew* another person
> Who will have thy angelic and serene face.
>   [Clements, 1966, p. 236; italics added]*

Under the impact of the impending death of Urbino (mother) the statue was smashed because it depicted the finality of death. It is the son returned tenderly to the mother, as is the first *pietà;* however, in the first *pietà*, the dead son is returned to the mother of infancy — a symbolic depiction of beginning again. This Resurrection theme is underscored in an iconographic representation under Jesus' dead foot, a sawed-off tree stump symbolizing a life cut off but with potential for growth anew.

In contrast, in the *Florentine Pietà* there is no return to a beginning; there is no iconographic representation of eternal life (Resurrection); there is only unresolved questioning. Psychoanalytically, it is a depiction of loss without internalization — death without mourning. It is grief without resolution.[11]

---

[11] There is some support for this thesis of a change taking place in a letter to Vasari written two

Compelled toward resolution, Michelangelo returned to the dyadic (*Rondanini*) *pietà* and in successive revisions increasingly made the body of the son of the mother. The final version expresses a more complete mourning of the dead mother(s). Now the infant is no longer grasping and burrowing to make contact as in the early *madonnas;* instead of a return to the mother of childhood, as in the first *pietà*, Michelangelo expresses the feeling that she (they) is (are) part of himself. Here is a dynamic depiction of Michelangelo's terminal experiencing of the primal meaning of Resurrection—explicit fusion with the mother with its mystical promise of rebirth as the two seem to rise as one. In the final *pietà* the wish for eternal life is depicted in its naked ontogenetic form.[12]

Summary

Whence the affectionate fantasy
Which made of art my idol and monarch,
I recognize well now how laden it was with error,
and *what in spite of himself every man desires.*
        [Clements, 1966, p. 296; italics added]*

This late poem epitomizes in many ways what I propose as being Michelangelo's essential conflict. The aborted mourning resulted in an absence of an integrated sense of the lost mother(s) within. Many aspects of his life including his homosexuality can be seen as conflicted, distorted attempts to gain relatedness to counteract this lifelong feeling of loss. The tenuous sense of relatedness made him fear his own finiteness, his longstanding preoccupation with impending death. His works, his true immortality, though he thought of them as "my children" (Clements, 1968), served only incompletely, as do "real" children (via identifications for the noncreative), to assuage this fear.

As his internal relationship to the lost mother(s) changed as a result of the relationships with, the loss of, and the integrated internalization of Vittoria Colonna and

---

months following Urbino's death. "The mercy is that, as in his life he [Urbino] kept me alive, dying he taught me to die, not against my will but welcoming death" (Linscott, 1963, pp. 305–306).

In elaborating on this, Michelangelo described Urbino's peaceful acceptance of impending death as a reassurance that there was an eternity and that they would be reunited. The statement that knowing that he would be forever reunited with his Francesco (mother) made death easier would to my mind suggest an increased capacity to sense him (her) within.

[12] There is suggestive evidence of regressive re-experiencing of the mother(s) during these terminal years. As part of a series of letters to his nephew, there are a number of letters beginning in 1550 and continuing through 1555 urging him to buy "that farm that borders on ours at Settignano" (Linscott, 1963, p. 298). The urgency of the interest is not explained, but it does seem strange that such an aged, ill man would have been so interested in obtaining the property from "that woman" in Settignano. I conjecture that the property was related to the family of the wet nurse and that the urgency reflected an attempt to begin again—at the very least—to make contact with the early experience.

Urbino (a furthering of the mourning), his quest for relatedness and the portrayal of this quest changed. He realized that there could be no substitute ("art, my idol and monarch") for "what in spite of himself every man desires": relatedness to the mother. He came to know that it is on the basis of her and her subsequent integrated internalization (and the related repetitions) that each person achieves a sense of satisfaction now and a sense of continuity into the future (immortality), the absence of which is depression and despair, lifelong feelings he knew so well. In keeping with this, his final depiction of the wish for immortality (relatedness), ironically yet inevitably designed for his tomb, represents the fusion of son and mother.[13]

REFERENCES

Barnes, M. J. (1964), Reactions to the death of a mother. *The Psychoanalytic Study of the Child*, 19: 334–357. New York: International Universities Press.

Bowlby, J. (1960), Grief and mourning in infancy and early childhood. *The Psychoanalytic Study of the Child*, 15:9–52. New York: International Universities Press.

Clements, R. J. (1966), *The Poetry of Michelangelo*. New York: New York University Press.

———— (1968), *Michelangelo: A Self-Portrait*. New York: New York University Press.

Condivi, A. (1553), *The Life of Michelangelo*, trans. A. S. Wohl. Baton Rouge: Louisiana State University Press, 1976.

De Tolnay, C. (1934), The Rondanini *Pietà*. *Burlington Mag.*, 65:146–157.

———— (1953), Michelangelo's *Pietà* composition for Vittoria Colonna. In: *Record of the Art Museum*. Princeton, N.J.: Princeton University Press, pp. 45–62.

———— (1969), *The Youth of Michelangelo*. Princeton, N.J.: Princeton University Press.

———— (1971), *The Final Period*. Princeton, N.J.: Princeton University Press.

———— (1975), *Michelangelo: Sculptor, Painter, Architect*. Princeton, N.J.: Princeton University Press.

Eissler, K. R. (1961), *Leonardo da Vinci*. New York: International Universities Press.

Frank, G. (1966), The enigma of Michelangelo's *Pietà* Rondanini. *Amer. Imago*, 23:287–315.

Freud, S. (1910), Leonardo da Vinci and a memory of his childhood. *Standard Edition*, 11:59–137. London: Hogarth Press, 1957.

———— (1914), The Moses of Michelangelo. *Standard Edition*, 13:211–238. London: Hogarth Press, 1955.

———— (1917), Mourning and melancholia. *Standard Edition*, 14:237–260. London: Hogarth Press, 1957.

Furman, R. A. (1964), Death and the young child: Some preliminary considerations. *The Psychoanalytic Study of the Child*, 19:321–333. New York: International Universities Press.

Gauthier, Y. (1965), The mourning reaction of a ten-and-a-half-year-old boy. *The Psychoanalytic Study of the Child*, 20:481–494. New York: International Universities Press.

Girardi, E. N., ed. (1960), *Michelangiolo Buonarroti, Rime*. Bari: Laterza.

---

[13]From the standpoint of a terminal regressive re-experiencing of the mother(s), there is a particularly moving letter to his nephew, Lionardo, dated June 27, 1562. In it he discusses the pregnancy of the nephew's wife, suggesting that if the baby were a girl, perhaps she could be named Francesca. In the prior correspondence, there was much discussion as to the naming of Lionardo's children, Michelangelo's only heirs. However, whenever he had previously discussed girls' names, Michelangelo had always deferred to his nephew's wife, though he made definite suggestions for boys (usually the names of his brothers). His mother's name, though it was not so acknowledged, appears for the first time in this letter which he wrote when he was close to death — a suggestion that at some level, perhaps, she was on his mind.

Hamilton, J. W. (1969), Object loss, dreaming, and creativity: The poetry of John Keats. *The Psychoanalytic Study of the Child*, 24:488–531.New York: International Universities Press.

Hibbard, H. (1974), *Michelangelo*. New York: Harper & Row.

Laufer, M. (1966), Object loss and mourning during adolescence. *The Psychoanalytic Study of the Child*, 21:269–293. New York: International Universities Press.

Liebert, R. S. (1977a), Michelangelo's mutilation of the Florence *Pietà*. *Art Bull.*, 59:47–54.

_____ (1977b), Michelangelo's *Dying Slave*. *The Psychoanalytic Study of the Child*, 32:505–544. New Haven: Yale University Press.

Linscott, R. N., ed. (1963), *Complete Poems and Selected Letters of Michelangelo*, trans. C. Gilbert. New York: Random House.

Lubin, A. (1976), Mysticism and creativity. In: *Mysticism: Spiritual Quest or Psychic Disorder?* Group for the Advancement of Psychiatry, Report 9, pp. 787–798.

Oremland, J. (1978), Michelangelo's *Pietàs*. *The Psychoanalytic Study of the Child*, 33:563–591. New Haven: Yale University Press.

Peto, A. (1978), The Rondanini *Pietà*. Michelangelo's infantile neurosis. A. A. Brill Memorial Lecture.

Pollock, G. H. (1975), Mourning and memorialization through music. *This Annual*, 3:423–436. New York: International Universities Press.

_____ (1977), The mourning process and creative organizational change. *J. Amer. Psychoanal. Assn.*, 25:3–34.

Robbins, M. D. (1969), On the psychology of artistic creativity. *The Psychoanalytic Study of the Child*, 24:241–251. New York: International Universities Press.

Ross, J. B. (1974), The middle-class child in urban Italy, fourteenth to early sixteenth century. In: *The History of Childhood*, ed. L. de Mause. New York: Harper & Row, pp. 183–229.

Schapiro, M. (1956), Leonardo and Freud. *J. Hist. Ideas*, 17:147–178.

Shambaugh, B. (1961), A study of loss reactions in a seven-year-old. *The Psychoanalytic Study of the Child*, 16:510–522. New York: International Universities Press.

Steinberg, L. (1968), Michelangelo's Florentine *Pietà*: The missing leg. *Art. Bull.*, 50:343–359.

Sterba, R. & Sterba, E. (1956), The anxieties of Michelangelo Buonarroti. *Internat. J. Psycho-Anal.*, 37:325–330.

Symonds, J. A. (1892), *The Life of Michelangelo Buonarroti*. New York: Modern Library.

Vasari, G. (1568), *Lives of the Most Eminent Painters, Sculptors, and Architects*, ed. R. N. Linscott. New York: Modern Library, 1959.

Weissman, P. (1971), The artist and his objects. *Internat. J. Psycho-Anal.*, 52:401–406.

Wolfenstein, M. (1966), How is mourning possible? *The Psychoanalytic Study of the Child*, 21:93–123. New York: International Universities Press.

November, 1979

Index

Compiled by Glenn E. Miller.